British Justice and Turkish Leaders
Accused of War Crimes Against
Armenians in World War I

British Justice and Turkish Leaders Accused of War Crimes Against Armenians in World War I

REVISED SECOND EDITION

Walter C. Bandazian

Ibex Publishers,
Bethesda, Maryland

British Justice and Turkish Leaders Accused of War Crimes
Against Armenians in World War I
Revised Second Edition
by Walter C. Bandazian

Cover photograph by John D. Whiting shows the mayor of Jerusalem, Hussein Effendi el-Husseini, surrendering to the British on December 9, 1917. Courtesy of the Library of Congress. Map is detail from *The Daily Telegraph War Map of Egypt and the Near East*. Courtesy of the University of Wisconsin-Milwaukee Libraries.

Copyright © 2019 Walter C. Bandazian

All rights reserved. No part of this book may be reproduced or retransmitted in any manner whatsoever except in the form of a review, without permission from the publisher or author.

Manufactured in the United States of America

The paper used in this book meets the minimum requirements of the American National Standard for Information Services-Permanence of Paper for Printed Library Materials, ANSI Z39.48-1984

Ibex Publishers strives to create books which are complete and free of error. Please help us with future editions by reporting any errors or suggestions for improvement to the address below or:
corrections@ibexpub.com

Ibex Publishers, Inc.
Post Office Box 30087
Bethesda, Maryland 20824
Telephone: 301-718-8188
www.ibexpublishers.com

Library of Congress Cataloging-in-Publication Data

Bandazian, Walter C.
British justice and Turkish leaders accused of war crimes against
  Armenians in World War I / by Walter C. Bandazian.
Revised second edition. | Bethesda, Maryland : Ibex Publishers, Inc.,
  2019. | Includes bibliographical references.
LCCN 2018023302 | ISBN 9781588141842 (pbk. : alk. paper)
Armenian massacres, 1915-1923. | War crimes—Turkey—History.
  | War criminals—Turkey—History. | gIttihat ve Terakki Cemiyeti.
DS195.5 .B36 2019 | DDC 956.6/20154—dc23

The work is dedicated to
My Father and Mother
Garabed & Zartar (Dervishian) Bandazian

Acknowledgements

I wish to thank the late Patriarch of Jerusalem, Archbishop Yeghishe Derderian, who provided me access to the Turkish documents that were held at the patriarchate, especially the official gazette of the Ottoman Government, *Takvim-i Vekayi*. The archbishop also made available the staff who filmed all of the documents contained in *Takvim-i Vekayi*, relative to the genocide of the Armenian people in the Ottoman Empire. I wish to thank my dear friend, the late Harry Koundakjian, who was photo-Editor at the Associated Press in Beirut, and who expended many hours developing all the films of the official gazette.

Finally, I give many thanks to the late Rev. Krikor Guerguerian, an Armenian Catholic priest with whom I had the honor to work while I resided in Philadelphia. Rev. Guerguerian devoted his entire life to doing research on the Armenian genocide. He was the pioneer who made the importance of Turkish documents available to subsequent scholars, and it was he who made me aware of the Turkish documents contained in the patriarchate of Jerusalem. He used the pen name of KRIEGER. I am indebted to my friend Mr. Andrew Kevorkian, of Philadelphia, for his invaluable suggestions and emphasis on detail of the text.

CONTENTS

Foreword   vii
Map   x
Preface   3
Introduction   5
I. Allied Occupation of Constantinople and the Question of Turkish War Criminals   17
II. Arrest of Criminals   21
III. Deportation to Malta   25
IV. The Ottoman Courts Martial   29
V. Occupation of Constantinople and the Treaty of Sèvres   41
VI. The Final Solution of the Question of Turkish War Criminals (Phases 1)   45
VII. The Final Solution of the Question of Turkish War Criminals (Phases 2)   53
End Notes   59

DOCUMENTS

APPENDIX "A"
First List of Recommendations for Arrest, submitted to the Ottoman Government as of April 7, 1919   71

APPENDIX "B"
Conditions at the Seraskerat Prison, and the names of the detainees   79

APPENDIX "C"
Petition from prisoners on Malta   87

APPENDIX "D"
List of names of suspected Turkish criminals submitted by the British High Commission to the Turkish Government as of 12 February 1920   91

APPENDIX "E"
Suspects who have been accused of various crimes, arrested and incarcerated on Malta, as of 26 May 1920   101

APPENDIX "F"
War Office list of prisoners at Malta indicating those who should be retained and those recommended for repatriation   103

APPENDIX "G"
Opinion of the law officers of the Crown regarding the release or prosecution of the suspects held on Malta   113

APPENDIX "H"
Report of Committee Formed to Consider and Make Recommendations Regarding The Further Detention Or Immediate Release of The Turkish Prisoners Now At Malta 115

APPENDIX "I"
List of Prisoners 123

APPENDIX "J"
List of prisoners submitted to the British Embassy in Washington in order to enquire about evidence that the U.S. Government might have regarding the prisoners 373

APPENDIX "K"
Release of the last Turkish prisoners from Malta 379

Foreword

"Why did they do that"? Over the years, this question was asked by my father, Garabed V. Bandazian.

Garabed was born in 1907, in the town of Peri, Sanjak of Dersim, vilayet of Mamuret-ul-Aziz (Harpoot). He was the son of Vartan and Mariam Bandazian. Peri was the county seat – the Kaimakam resided there.

Garabed was orphaned as a result of the genocide in 1915. His father and male relatives were murdered as a consequence of the Ottoman government's official position. The Turks gathered many of the orphans and distributed them to Turkish families in the vicinity of their own locations – or near their places of birth. The orphans served as shepherds and did other menial tasks. Garabed, together with other orphans was sent to Pertak, about 20 miles south-west of Peri, within the same vilayet as their own villages.

Garabed was given to a Turkish family who were kindly toward him, but instructed him to never tell anyone that he was Armenian or those who had killed his family would come and kill him as well. His name was changed to Najeeb.

Garabed lived in Pertak for two years and in 1916 he was moved to the village of Saruk (Zaruk), about four miles south-west of Pertak, where he lived with another Turkish family. It was in Saruk that he learned many of the Turkish "mayas," such as Egin Havasi, and Harpoot Havasi. Of course his Turkish language ability became native, he did not remember any Armenian at all. It was interesting how he learned these Turkish songs.

During the harvesting season, the laborers would place Garabed on their shoulders while they swung their scythes, and would sing the songs that he learned very quickly. His voice was so good, that his Agha would give him a raw egg every morning to drink in order that his voice would be stronger. His singing of the Harpoot Havasi would bring tears to the eyes of the Turks. Sixty years later I would hear him quietly humming these same tunes.

In 1921, Garabed's older sister Tsaghig, who was taken by the Turks, somehow found him in the village of Saruk. She forced him to go with her to Kharpert (Harpoot), where the American missionaries had an orphanage. In the orphanage, Garabed felt very strange because he did not know Armenian and the food was inferior to the food in the home of his Turkish family. He ran off back to Saruk. His sister found him again, and this time Garabed stayed in the orphanage.

In 1922, hundreds of orphans were moved to the Near East Relief orphanages in Antelias, Lebanon. It was in Antelias that Garabed once again became an Armenian – learning the language, history and religion of his people. He did very well in track & field activities – winning many medals and ribbons. In addition, he became an expert swimmer – the Mediterranean Sea was his swimming pool: winning first prize in life-saving technique awarded by the YMCA. It was also at Antelias that he learned his profession as a custom tailor, which he later worked at in France and New York. He had great admiration for his teachers in Antelias, who were kind and had only the best interest toward the orphans.

Garabed left Lebanon in 1926, and lived in France until 1929, at which time he came to the United States.

Throughout the years, he never had a bad word relative to his Turkish "families." But from time to time, regarding the genocide, he would ask:

"WHY DID THEY DO THAT?"

A word about Zartar Dervishian, my mother.

Zartar was born in the town of Ureg (Urik) in 1912. Ureg is about eight miles SE of Pertak, and about nine miles NE of Kharpert. Her parents were Hovannes and Anna Dervishian. Hovannes was a lumberjack, transporting cut wood across the Peri River or the Murad (Euphrates R.).

Hovannes was on very good terms with the Begs of the region and in 1908, during the Hurriyet (Freedom) movement he was provided weapons by the Young Turk party (Ittihad) in case trouble started with the Kurds of the region. He was a Dashnagtsagan fedayee.

The situation between Armenians and Turks began to go bad as early as 1913, and in 1914 the Begs began to collect the weapons that had been provided to the Armenians. My grandfather refused to give up his weapons and told the Begs "When you collect the guns from the Kurds, then I will turnover my guns, not before." He was told that Kurds needed their weapons in order to protect the Armenians from predators. He again refused. In September, of 1914, Hovannes, while transporting wood across the Peri River, was ambushed and killed.

My grandmother, with six children, began the great trek to the east, toward the Caucasus. It took eight months to get to Alexandropol (present day Giumri). She buried three of her children on that trek, and arrived with three children – my mother, aunt and uncle.

After sometime in Giumri, my grandmother and her three children were moved to Yerevan, where the children were placed in an orphanage on Astafian Street (present day Abovian Street), and my grandmother did various tasks cleaning dwellings.

My mother Zartar and her siblings stayed in the orphanage from 1916 to 1921. It was during those years that my mother learned to read and write in Armenian, as well as learning the songs and dances of the Armenian people. She well remembered the dances that were taught by Tatul Altoonian. Of the greatest impression on her was the day that Armenia declared independence on May 28, 1918, when the Armenian soldiers carried the orphans on their shoulders during the street celebrations and parades. When the government changed in 1921, my grandmother and her children left for the United States, where my grandmother had relatives, and resided in Philadelphia, where Zartar and her siblings attended the public school system, and where Zartar added the name of Rose, and became Zartar Rose Dervishian. She was graduated from the Kensington High School for Girls.

Zartar was a sixty year member of the Armenian Relief Society.

It was in Philadelphia that Zartar met Garabed Bandazian, and the couple eloped in 1931.

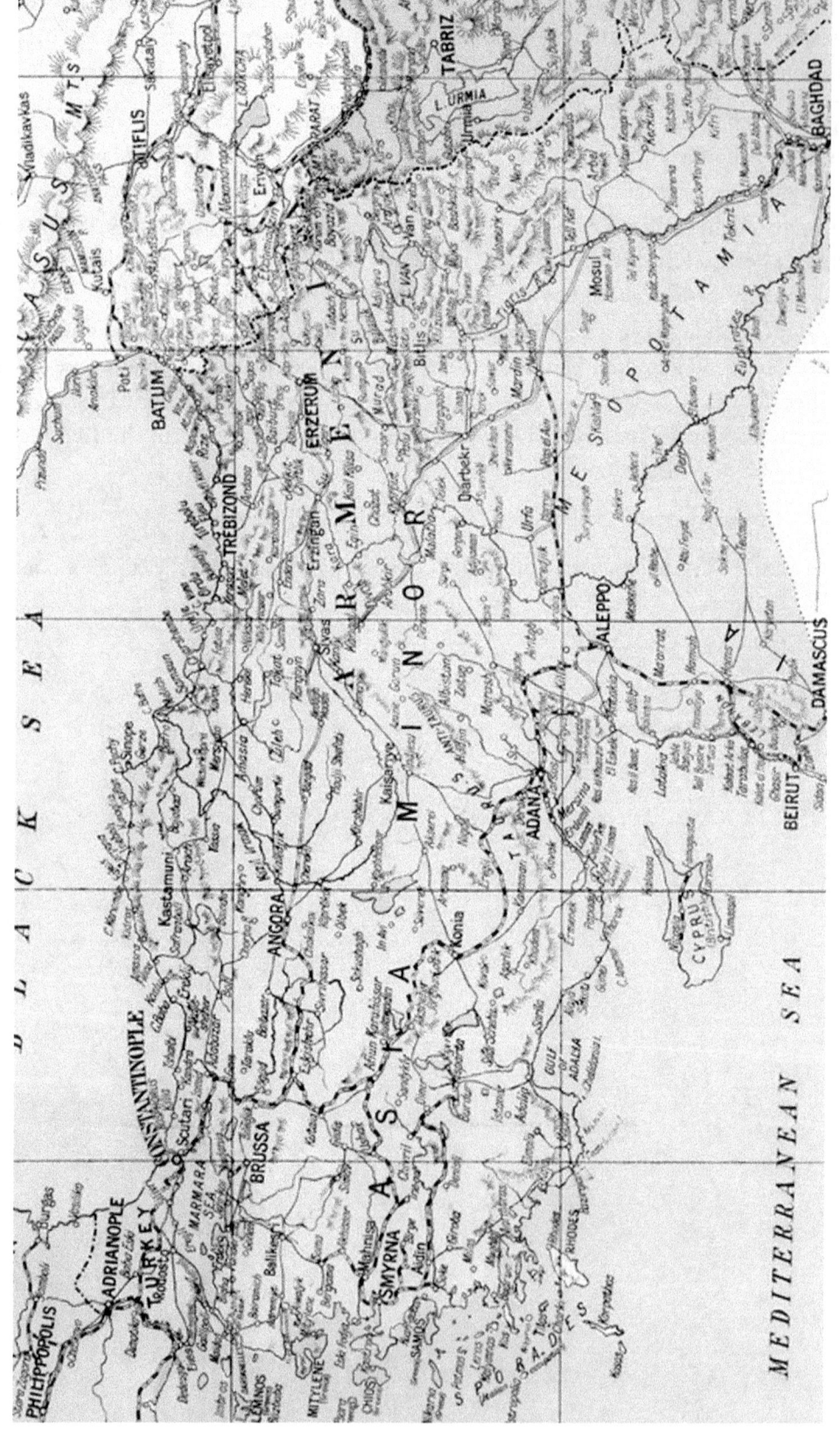

[May 23, 1915 press release by His Majesty's Government]

H. M. Government, in common with the Governments of France and Russia, make the following public declaration:

For about the last month KURDS and the Turkish population of ARMENIA have been engaged in massacring Armenians with the connivance and often the help of the Ottoman Authorities. Such massacres took place about the middle of April, at ERZEROUM, DERTCHAN, EGIN, BITLIS, SASSOUN, MOUSH, ZEITUN, and in all CILICIA.

Inhabitants of about 100 villages near Van were all assassinated. In the town itself the ARMENIANS' quarter is besieged by KURDS. At the same time the Ottoman Government at CONSTANTINOPLE is raging against the inoffensive Armenian population.

In face of these fresh crimes committed by TURKEY the Allied Governments announce publicly to the Sublime Porte that they will hold all the members of the OTTOMAN Government, as well as such of their agents as are implicated, personally responsible for such massacres.[1]

See: FO 371/2488/63095, May 23, 1915.

Preface

This short study traces some of the developments which led to the arrest, detention, and finally, the release of those Young Turks and their henchmen accused of committing war crimes during and after the First World War against the Christian population of Asiatic Turkey. The primary focus of the study includes the role played by the British in the Near East in addressing the Armenian Genocide. At the time, British authorities were in occupation of certain areas formerly belonging to the Ottoman Empire.

While it is true that the Ottoman Government in 1915 had executed plans to exterminate the non-Turkish elements of the Empire by destroying Armenians, Assyrians, Greeks and Arabs, their principle target had been the extermination of the Armenian people.

This paper will not dwell on the causes of the genocide of Ottoman Armenians, but will draw the readers' attention to the fact that the prosecution of Turkish war criminals was of primary concern to the newly established Ottoman Government in Constantinople after the Armistice of Mudros was signed. The Ottoman authorities, in 1919, were the ones who initiated courts-martial proceedings against members and former members of the Ittihat ve Terakki Cemiyeti (Committee of Union and Progress), also called the Young Turks. They were able to prove that not only were the Young Turks responsible for plunging the Ottoman Empire into the war, but that the Ittihat ve Terakki was responsible for conceiving, planning, and executing the extermination of the Armenian people.

This study dwells on the first international attempt to bring war criminals to trial, even before the Nuremberg trials of 1946–49. It also reflects on what position major countries took regarding the whole question of war crimes. It shows that initially there was a genuine interest to bring to justice those persons accused of perpetrating genocide against the Armenian people, but that immediate national interests were more important than broader notions of justice and morality. This study serves as an introduction and it is hoped that more detailed works will be undertaken on the issues raised.

Our sources have been derived from the United Kingdom National Archives in Kew (London), which contain literally thousands of documents related to Armenians. In addition, we have also used newspapers published during the period in question – especially those from Constantinople. Finally, our primary Turkish source has been the *Takvim-i Vekayi*, which was the official gazette of the Ottoman Government and published much information related to the courts -martial proceedings.

Introduction

The first international attempt to try war criminals took place after World War I, when, on January 25, 1919, the Preliminary Peace Conference at Paris established and created a Commission of Fifteen to "investigate and report on violations of international law that could be charged against Germany and her allies."[2]

The Commission was to be composed of fifteen members, two each from the United States, British Empire, France, Italy, and Japan; and five members of one each from Belgium, Greece, Poland, Romania, and Serbia.

The duties of the Commission were to enquire and report on the following points:

1. The responsibility of the authors of the war.
2. The facts as to breaches of the laws and customs of war committed by the forces of the German Empire and their Allies, on land, on sea, and in the air during the war.
3. The degree of responsibility for those offences attaching to particular members of the enemy forces, including members of the General Staffs, and other individuals, however highly placed.
4. The constitution and procedure of a tribunal appropriate for the trial of these offences.
5. Any other matters cognate or ancillary to the above which may arise in the course of the enquiry, and which the Commission finds it useful and relevant to take into consideration.[3]

The Chairman of the Commission was Mr. Robert Lansing who was also the representative for the United States on the Commission, in addition to Major James Brown Scott, Technical Delegate of the U.S. to the Peace Conference at Paris. The Vice-Chairman at the Commission was to be either Sir Gordon Hewart or Sir Ernest Pollock and the representative for Italy, Mr. [Vittorio] Scialoja.

Three Sub-Commissions[4] were appointed by the Commission.

Sub-Commission I – on Criminal Acts – was to collect evidence necessary to establish culpable conduct which brought about the war, "and took place in the course of hostilities."

Sub-Commission II – Responsibility for the War – was to evaluate, on the basis of what facts were established by the Criminal Acts Sub-Commission, whether "prosecutions could be instituted," and, if so, to prepare reports on individuals whom it considered guilty, and who were to be brought before a Court.

Sub-Commission III – Responsibility for the Violation of the Laws and Customs of War – was to determine, on the basis of the facts established by the Sub-Commission on Criminal Acts, whether prosecution could be instituted and, if the Sub-Commission decided that prosecutions could be undertaken, " . . . to prepare a report indicating the individual or individuals who were, in its opinion, guilty," and to recommend the court " . . . before which prosecutions should proceed."[5]

Report Presented to the Preliminary Peace Conference by the Commission on the Responsibility of the Authors of the War and on Enforcement of Penalties. The *Report* submitted to the Preliminary Peace Conference on March 29, 1919, contained five chapters pertaining to the relevant questions in the frame of reference of the Commissions' undertaking. Chapter I,[6] "Responsibility of the Authors of the War" concluded with the following points:

1. The war was premeditated by the Central Powers together with their Allies, Turkey and Bulgaria, and was the result of acts deliberately committed in order to make it unavoidable.
2. Germany, in agreement with Austria-Hungary, deliberately worked to defeat all the many conciliatory proposals made by the Entente Powers and their repeated efforts to avoid war.[7]

In Chapter II,[8] on "Violations of the Laws and Customs of War" the Commission considered a large number of documents submitted by the British Commission, the French Commission, the Belgian Government, the Memorandum of the Greek Delegation, the documents submitted by the Italian Government, the Memorandum of the Serbian Delegation, the Inter-Allied Commission on the violations of the Hague Conventions and of international law by the Bulgarians in occupied Serbia, the documents of the Polish Delegation, and the Romanian and Armenian Memoranda ". . . supplied abundant evidences of outrages of every description committed on land, at sea, and in the air, against the laws and customs of war and of the laws of humanity."[9]

The Commission severely castigated and condemned Germany and her allies for violating the rights of combatants and civilians.

> ... Not even prisoners, or wounded, or women, or children have been respected by belligerents who deliberately sought to strike terror into every heart for the purpose of repressing all resistance. Murders and massacres, tortures, shields formed of living human beings, collective penalties, the arrest and execution of hostages, . . . constitute the most striking list of crimes that has ever been drawn up to the eternal shame of those who committed them ...[10]

The Commission suggested that, because of the intense gravity of the crimes described, a special Commission be formed "to collect and classify information" under the following headings:[11]

1. Murders and massacres; systematic terrorism.
2. Putting hostages to death.
3. Torture of civilians.
4. Deliberate starvation of civilians.
5. Rape.

6. Abduction of girls and women for the purpose of prostitution.
7. Deportation of civilians.
8. Internment of civilians under inhuman conditions.
9. Forced labor of civilians in connection with the military operations of the enemy.
10. Usurpation of sovereignty during military occupation.
11. Compulsory enlistment of soldiers among the inhabitants of occupied territory.
12. Attempt to denationalise the inhabitants of occupied territory.
13. Pillage.
14. Confiscation of property.
15. Exaction of illegitimate or of exorbitant contributions and requisitions.
16. Debasement of the currency, and issue of spurious currency.
17. Imposition of collective penalties.
18. Wanton devastation and destruction of property.
19. Deliberate bombardment of undefended places.
20. Wanton destruction of religious, charitable, educational, and historic buildings and monuments.
21. Destruction of merchant ships and passenger vessels without warning and without provision for the safety of passengers or crew.
22. Destruction of fishing boats and of relief ships.
23. Deliberate bombardment of hospitals.
24. Attack on and destruction of hospital ships.
25. Breach of other rules relating to the Red Cross.
26. Use of deleterious and asphyxiating gases.
27. Use of exploding or expanding bullets, and other inhuman appliances.
28. Directions to give no quarter.
29. Ill-treatment of wounded and prisoners of war.
30. Employment of prisoners of war on unauthorised works.
31. Misuse of flags of truce.
32. Poisoning of wells.

The Commission made it clear that the aforementioned offences and the particulars given in Annex I were not exhaustive.[12]

The conclusions of Chapter II were the following:

1. The war was carried on by the Central Empires together with their allies, Turkey and Bulgaria, by barbarous or illegitimate methods in violation of the established laws and customs of war and the elementary laws of humanity.
2. A Commission should be created for the purpose of collecting and classifying systematically all the information already had or to be obtained, in order to prepare as complete a list of facts as possible concerning the violation of the laws and customs of war committed by the forces of the

German Empire and its Allies, on land, on sea and in the air, in the course of the present war.[13]

The *Report,* in this connection, contained an annex spelling out some of the particulars relating to the offences committed in the Near East. Specifically, it described, for example, under Number 1, "Murders and Massacres," the massacres of the Greeks in Smyrna, Aivali, Vourla, Adalia, Kirkilesse, Visa, Kessani, Adrianople;[14] and Armenians, "More than 200 000 victims assassinated, burned alive, or drowned in the lake of Van, the Euphrates or the Black Sea."[15]

Under Category 6, "Abduction of Girls" etc. the *Report* stated that a great number of Greek and Armenian women, girls and children were distributed "among Turkish houses."[16] Bulgarians and Turks were accused of rape against Greek and Serbian women.[17] Under Category 7, "Deportation of Civilians," Germans were accused of deporting French; Germans and Bulgarians of deporting Greeks in Eastern Macedonia; 400,000 Greeks deported by Turks to Greece; 500,000 Greeks deported into the interior of Asia Minor, where more than two thirds succumbed;[18] more than a million Armenians deported from their homes in Asia Minor by Turkish authorities and sent into Mesopotamia and Syria where hundreds of thousands perished.[19] In Category 29 – Ill-Treatment of Prisoners – Germans were accused of offences in Belgium, and against British prisoners;[20] Turkish offences against British prisoners during and after the march from Kut-al-Amara to Ras-al-Ain, by way of Baghdad and Mosul, and later while prisoners detained in Asia Minor.[21]

Chapter III[22] of the report related the decision of the Commission relative to point three of its investigative mandate – Personal Responsibility. The Commission held that regardless of the rank of the individual accused, even the Heads of State were not immune from responsibility, if that responsibility were established, ". . . before a properly constituted tribunal. . . ." The Commission was attempting to bring to trial the ex-Kaiser, "in view of the grave charges which may be preferred against. . . ." him. This view was pursued because the Commission believed that not to bring charges against the Kaiser would seriously prejudice the bringing to trial offenders who would find refuge behind the assertion that they were merely following "the superior orders of a Sovereign." To remove this contingency, the ex-Kaiser would have to be brought to trial[23] The conclusion, therefore, was:

> All persons belonging to enemy countries, however high their position may have been, without distinction of rank, including Chiefs of States, who have been guilty of offences against the laws and customs of war or the laws of humanity, are liable to criminal prosecution.[24]

The constitution of a tribunal was spelled out in Chapter IV of the Commission's report.[25] In this section, the Commission arrived at two classes of culpability. First, "Acts which Provoked the World War and Accompanied Its Inception"; and second, "Violations of the Laws and Customs of War and the Laws of Humanity".

In the first, the Commission considered acts not strictly war crimes, but acts which provoked the war. It also voiced apprehension regarding the subsequent successful attempts to place the blame on any one Power, because of the time any tribunal would need to properly undertake the investigation. Therefore, the Commission, after castigating those responsible for violating the neutrality of Belgium, drew the following conclusions:

1. The acts which brought about the war should not be charged against their authors or made the subject of proceedings before a tribunal.

2. On the special head of the breaches of the neutrality of Luxemburg and Belgium, the gravity of these outrages upon the principles of the law of nations and upon international good faith is such that they should be made the subject of a formal condemnation by the Conference. (Paris Peace Conference).

3. On the whole case, including both the acts which brought about the war and those which accompanied its inception, particularly the violation of the neutrality of Belgium and Luxemburg, it would be right for the Peace Conference, in a matter so unprecedented, to adopt special measures and even to create a special organ in order to deal as they deserve with the authors of such acts.

4. It is desirable that for the future penal sanctions should be provided for such grave outrages against the elementary principles of international law.[26]

In the second category of this Chapter, that is, "Violations of the Laws and Customs of War and of the Laws of Humanity" the Commission reported that every belligerent had the "power and authority" to try individuals alleged to be guilty of crimes as enumerated in Chapter II. Each belligerent had the power to set up tribunals – military or civil, for trial of such cases, and each court was to utilize its own procedure, and thereby reduce the delay and complications that would develop if all of the accused were to be brought before a "single tribunal." However, there were certain charges that could only be prosecuted by a High Tribunal, and these charges fell into four categories.

a. Trials of those persons accused of committing outrages against civilians and soldiers of allied nations; i.e. prisoner of war camps, and forced labor.

b. Persons of authority whose orders were executed on one or more battle fronts.

c. All authorities, military or civil, of the enemy countries, regardless of position – including "heads of States" who ordered, or who had the knowledge and power to intervene, but abstained from intervening, and who did not prevent or "put an end to" violations of the laws or customs of war.

d. To bring to trial such persons belonging to enemy countries, if it is advisable to bring them before a High Tribunal rather than another court.

Pursuant to these points, the Commission submitted the following plan: The High Tribunal would be composed of five countries of three persons from each: United States, the British Empire, France, Italy, Japan; and one representative from each of the following countries: Belgium, Greece, Poland, Portugal, Romania, Serbia and Czechoslovakia. The members were to be selected from national courts or tribunals – military or civil – from each respective country. The Tribunal would have the right to appoint experts to assist in the cases, and the law to be applied by the Tribunal would be " . . . the principles of the law of nations as they result from the usages established among civilised peoples, from the laws of humanity and from the dictates of public conscience."[27] The Tribunal would have the power to sentence the individual on the basis of the offence. A Prosecuting Commission of five members appointed by the United States, Britain, France, Italy and Japan was to select the cases for trial and direct and conduct prosecutions. Any person scheduled to be brought before the High Tribunal was not to be tried in the national court of any government. Finally, no trial or sentence by a court of any enemy country would bar the re-trial of the individual by the Tribunal, or a national court "belonging to one of the Allied or Associated States."

The conclusions of the Commission regarding the High Tribunal and the points under consideration in Chapter IV were the following:

The Commission has consequently the honour to recommend:–

1. That a High Tribunal be constituted as set out above.

2. That it shall be provided by the Treaty of Peace:–
   (a) That the enemy Governments shall, notwithstanding that Peace may have been declared, recognise the jurisdiction of the National Tribunals and the High Tribunal, that all enemy persons alleged to have been guilty of offences against the laws and customs of war and the laws of humanity shall be excluded from any amnesty to which the belligerents may agree, and that the Governments of such persons shall undertake their surrender to be tried.
   (b) That the enemy Governments shall undertake to deliver up and give in such manner as may be determined thereby:–
      (i) The names of all persons in command or charge of or in any way exercising authority in or over all civilian internment camps, branch camps, working camps and 'commandos' and other places where prisoners were confined in any of their dominions or in territory at any time occupied by them, with respect to which such information is required, and all orders and instructions or copies of orders or instructions and reports in their possession or under their control relating to the administration and discipline of all such places in respect of which the supply of such documents as aforesaid shall be demanded;

(ii) All orders, instructions, copies of orders and instructions, General Staff plans of campaign, proceedings in Naval or Military Courts and Courts of Enquiry, reports and other documents in their possession or under their control which relate to acts or operations, whether in their dominions or in territory at any time occupied by them, which shall be alleged to have been done or carried out in breach of the laws and customs of war and the laws of humanity;

(iii) Such information as will indicate the persons who committed or were responsible for such acts or operations;

(iv) All logs, charts, reports and other documents relating to operations by submarines;

(v) All orders issued to submarines, with details or scope of operations by these vessels;

(vi) Such reports and other documents as may be demanded relating to operations alleged to have been conducted by enemy ships and their crews during the war contrary to the laws and customs of war and the laws of humanity.

3. That each Allied and Associated Government adopt such legislation as may be necessary to support the jurisdiction of the International Court, and to assure the carrying out of its sentences.

4. That the five States represented on the Prosecuting Commission shall jointly approach Neutral Governments with a view to obtaining the surrender for trial of persons within their territory who are charged by such States with violations of the laws and customs of war and the laws of humanity.[28]

Two countries on the Commission were unable to accede to the conclusions arrived at and were not party to the decision of it. These were Japan and the United States. In Annex II of the report, the American members stated the reasons why the United States could not be part of the High Tribunal nor participate in its activities.[29] Robert Lansing and James Brown Scott made the following points:

First, the Americans took the position that there were two classes of responsibilities, legal and moral, and that legal offences could be adjudicated by appropriate tribunals, but moral offences " . . . however iniquitous and infamous and however terrible in their results, were beyond the reach of judicial procedure, and subject only to moral sanctions..." Lansing and Scott felt that the Commission had exceeded its competence when it also considered offences of the laws or the principles of humanity. The duty of the Commission, they said, was to determine what laws and customs of war were violated; that the question of humanity varies with individuals and should have been excluded from consideration. The Americans agreed with the Commission in so far as placing blame on those responsible for the origins of the war but little else.

They disagreed with the idea that Chiefs of States could be tried for crimes against humanity, since there was no known municipal or international law for which a precedent had been set; that the head of State was responsible only to the "political authority of his country" and not to any foreign power. To accede to the demands of a foreign power would deny the conception of sovereignty they said. The American Representatives believed that the procedure spelled out by the Commission subjecting "Chiefs of States to a degree of responsibility hitherto unknown to municipal or international law . . ." could not be considered valid; the chief executive was subject only to the organic law of his country. Further, the Americans argued that the head of State had to be actually performing his duties if he were to be subject to the tribunals of his own country; that if the head of State had resigned or abdicated, the rules did not apply. Moreover, punishment had to be prescribed by the law in force when the act was committed, "not punishment created after the commission of the act . . ."

Regarding the question of establishing a "special organ" in order to deal with the authors who were responsible for violating the neutrality of Belgium and Luxemburg, the American representatives concluded that, since there was no law making this action a crime with a penalty, it had to be considered a moral, not a legal crime, and that no judicial tribunal be created for that purpose. They were in agreement with the other members of the Commission that Germany and Austria should be condemned for undertaking such action—but nothing more severe.

The Americans came into total disagreement with the rest of the Commission on the question of the second part of Chapter IV, that is, "Violations of the Laws and Customs of War and of Laws of Humanity," and the establishing of a High Tribunal. Opposition was voiced on the aspect of a mixed-commission which would bring charges

> (a) Against all authorities, civil or military, belonging to enemy countries, however high their position may have been, without distinction of rank, including the heads of States, who ordered, or, with knowledge thereof and with power to intervene, abstained from preventing or taking measures to prevent, putting an end to or repressing, violations of the laws or customs of war (it being understood that no such abstention should constitute a defence for the actual perpetrators).[30]

Lansing and Scott argued that a person who committed or ordered others to commit an act constituting a crime was one thing; but entirely different from punishing "... a person who failed to prevent, to put an end to, or to repress violations of the laws and customs of war..." In the first case the individual "acts or orders others to act" thereby committing a positive offence. In the second, the individual was to be punished "...for the acts of others without proof being given that he knew of the commission of the acts in question or that, knowing them, he could have prevented their commission..."[31] The individual who was to be punished, they said "...should have knowledge of the commission of the acts of a criminal nature and that he should have possessed the power as well as the authority to prevent, to put an end to, or repress them. Neither knowledge of commission nor ability to prevent is alone sufficient. The duty or obligation to act is essential. They must exist in conjunction, and a standard of liability which does not include them all is to be rejected. . ."[32]

Further, the Americans did not consent to the Tribunal as recommended by the Commission, because the law that was to be used was not clear, in that liability was made to depend on violations of the laws, as well as violations of the laws and customs of war. In addition, the American representatives disagreed with the Commission on the question of bringing heads of States before a Tribunal, on the basis that, when the "alleged offences" were made, the Heads of States were not subject to the jurisdiction of the tribunal to be formed.

Moreover, while the Americans agreed that war by its very nature was inhuman, acts consistent with the laws and customs of war were also inhuman, but were not subject to punishment by a "court of justice." A judicial tribunal, they said, deals only with existing law "...leaving to another forum infractions of the moral law and actions contrary to the laws and principles of humanity..." Indeed, they were of the opinion that an act could not be a crime "unless it were made so by law" and that an individual "...could not be punished unless the law prescribed the penalty to be inflicted...."[33] In support of this position they cited a case decided upon by the U.S. Supreme Court: *United States v. Hudson* (7 Cranch 32), 1812: "...the legislative authority of the Union must first declare the court that shall have jurisdiction of the offence..." The American representatives knew of no statute, they said, that would make violations of the laws and customs of war or the laws and principles of humanity "an international crime" with a fixed punishment to it, or a court declaring jurisdiction over such violations.

They proposed that, since various members of the Allied and Associated Powers had defined certain acts violating the customs of war as crimes, and had established national tribunals to punish certain offenders, that these tribunals be used to bring to trial those persons suspected of having committed crimes. If, however, in the event the crime affected the nationals of more than one country, a tribunal made up from members of the tribunals of the countries affected be used for the purpose of the trials. Such tribunals, they believed, would have been legally formed. However, it is not clear why Lansing and Scott assumed that a procedure to be used by a mixed-tribunal would be automatically agreeable and satisfactory to the different nationals sitting on them, since there was no single uniform code which was to be implemented.

Finally, they took the position ". . . that a country could not take part in the trial and punishment of a violation of the laws and customs of war committed by Germany and her Allies before the particular country had become a party to the war against Germany and her Allies; . . ." Therefore " . . . the United States could not institute a military tribunal within its own jurisdiction to pass upon violations of the laws and customs of war, unless such violations were committed upon American persons or American property. . ." and consequently, ". . . the United States could not properly take part in the trial and punishment of persons accused of violations of the laws and customs of war committed by the military or civil authorities of Bulgaria or Turkey."[34]

Notwithstanding the reservations of the United States and Japan,[35] the report was submitted to the Preliminary Peace Conference and unanimously adopted.[36]

The report of the Commission became the working guidelines for the Peace Conference to use and put into effect. When the Treaty of Versailles was signed on June 28, 1919, certain articles contained within the Treaty acceded to pursue the recommendations made by the Commission. Part VII, "Penalties," included Articles 227 to 230, which spelled out which penalties were to be placed against Germany regarding war criminals.[37]

Article 227 provided for the arraignment of the former German Emperor, Wilhelm II not because of war crimes, but ". . . for a supreme offence against international morality and the sanctity of treaties."[38] But Wilhelm II had abdicated on November 9, 1918, and had fled to the Netherlands, and the Netherlands Government refused to extradite him despite the requests for his extradition made by the Allied and Associated Powers.[39] Therefore, the clauses of Article 227, were never fulfilled. The ex-Emperor remained in the Netherlands until his death on June 4, 1941.

Under Article 228, the German Government recognized ". . . the right of the Allied and Associated Powers to bring before military tribunals persons accused of having committed acts in violation of the laws and customs of war . . ." While Germany eventually signed the Treaty, she signed it after strenuously objecting to clauses 227-230. The German Government objected to the proposed extradition of Wilhelm II on the basis that Germany was not to be represented on the Tribunal, nor in determining what procedure must be used. In addition, they said, none of the participating states adhere to any law which ". . . threaten with punishment the violation of the moral law between nations or the breaking of penal treaties . . ." As far as Article 228 was concerned, Germany could not turn over to the Allies for prosecution any German citizens because such action would be contrary to Article 9 of the German code, which "forbids the surrender of Germans to foreign Governments." The German Government, under threat of more stringent action by the Allied and Associated Powers, did finally sign the Treaty. The important aspect of this attitude of Germany is that when, in 1919, the Turkish Government demanded the extradition of fugitive Turks who had fled Turkey before and after the Armistice of October 30, 1918, the German Government refused to extradite them even though it was aware of the presence in Germany of these Turkish nationals.[40]

Article 230, obligated the German Government to ". . . furnish all documents and information of every kind, . . ."

On February 3, 1920, the German Peace Delegation received a list of over 900 names of individuals "whose responsibility appears to be most seriously involved," the list being drawn up by the British, French, Italian, Belgian, Polish, Romanian and Serb-Croat-Slovene Governments. These individuals were to be extradited from Germany and any documents pertaining to them in possession of the German Government were also to be forwarded to the Mixed Arbitral Tribunal.[41]

The Head of the German Delegation, von Lersner, informed the President of the Peace Conference that Germany could not comply with extradition of Germans ". . . whatever the attitude adopted by the accused and whatever their names."[42] He said that he had already informed the representatives of the Allied and Associated

Governments "... ten times in writing and thirteen times orally, the reasons which make it impossible to comply with such a claim ..." Consequently, von Lersner resigned and left Paris. The list containing the more than 900 names was then submitted to the German Chancellor on February 7, 1920. On February 13, 1920, the German Delegation proposed to the Supreme Allied Council, that the German Government would hold proceedings against German nationals in the Supreme Court at Leipzig, "consistent with the execution of Article 228." The Allied Council consented and, on May 7, 1920, the Inter-Allied Mixed Commission submitted a revised list of 45 names to the German Government for prosecution.

The German war crime trials began on May 23, 1921, more than two years after the Commission had submitted its report. Of the six individuals brought to trial who were on the British lists, "five were convicted and given short sentences." Of the French and Belgian lists, six persons were brought to trial, and "one was convicted of shooting prisoners of war and sentenced to two years' imprisonment." Further, the proceedings were hampered by "... difficulties in bringing the accused to court and in securing evidence."[43] Two of the sentenced individuals escaped from detention. On January 15, 1922, a Commission of Allied jurists investigated the Leipzig trials and were unanimous in reporting that it was useless to continue the trials, because some who were acquitted should have been condemned, and that sentences meted out were not adequate. They recommended that the accused be handed over to the Allied Governments for trial.[44] The recommendation was not put into effect, and the prosecution of German war criminals came to a close."

Chapter I

Allied Occupation of Constantinople and the Question of Turkish War Criminals

I.

On October 30, 1918, an Armistice was signed aboard the British ship H.M.S. *Agamemnon,* off Mudros, bringing open combat to a close among the forces of the Ottoman Empire and the Allied Powers. Not long after, the Allies—British, French and Italian—created a military administration of the city of Constantinople. The city was partitioned and allied forces took up garrison duty in their respective zones. In addition, each of the Allies appointed a High Commissioner who was to be the administrative official representing his country. The United States also appointed a High Commissioner. Later, British token forces were stationed at Batum (which was the terminus pipeline for Baku oil), Samsun, the Dardanelles, and parts of the Anatolian railway. The British also occupied northern Syria and extended to Aintab in Asia Minor. The British had about 400,000 military personnel in the Middle East.

In April 1919, the Italians occupied Adalia, in South-West Asia Minor. The interior of Turkey, including the six Armenian provinces of Van, Bitlis, Mush, Erzerum, Trabizond and Mamuret-ul-Aziz were never occupied by Allied military forces. This situation remained basically the same until the final withdrawal of Allied military contingents from Turkey in 1923.

2.

After the Allies had positioned their garrison forces in Constantinople in 1918, it became apparent to the British High Commissioner, Admiral Calthorpe, that, aside from the relative security of Constantinople, the interior of Asia Minor remained in a state of anarchy and was beyond the Ottoman Government's or Allies' preparedness to bring the country under civil control. The only way the situation could have been rectified was if the Allies occupied all of Asia Minor and disarmed the returning Turkish troops. The Allies had every legal right to do so according to Article 24 of the Armistice.[46] Calthorpe repeatedly, in telegram 14 of 2 January, 1919, and telegram 158 of 23 January, 1919, informed the Foreign Office of infractions of the armistice[47] by Turkish forces operating in the Trans-Caucasus, who were committing outrages against the Armenian population.[48] The new Ottoman Government under Sultan Mehmet VI (which replaced the Cabinet of the Committee of Union and Progress on October 8, 1918) while giving "every evidence of goodwill, it is both useless and undignified" said Calthorpe, "to continue to make protests . . . Treatment of Armenians continues as outrageous as ever and orders of the Cabinet are not obeyed and thus we meet with incessant breaches of the Armistice . . ."[49]

Calthorpe suggested to the War Office that the Turkish Government should arrest offenders of the Armistice and that British Commanders take action locally. The War Office, in turn, stipulated that Military Courts should be set up by the General Officer Commanding and that "Turkish offenders be punished or detained until their case can be dealt with."[50]

In the early part of the Armistice, there was no real attempt made by the British, French or Italians to apprehend the perpetrators responsible for the genocide of the Armenian people. After five years of war, the Allies were not willing to fulfil the points made in their joint declaration of May 23, 1915, regarding the punishment of the Turkish officials responsible for the massacres. Further mutual rivalry and jealousy among the Allies discounted any cooperation and coordination in apprehending certain individuals, though the British military did, from time to time, arrest certain persons accused of committing outrages against British prisoners of war. This anomalous situation of distrust prevailed throughout the entire duration of Allied occupation of Constantinople. The problems encountered at the Paris Peace Conference embittered the relations of the Allies, to the detriment of realising the professed goals of justice regarding the Ottoman Empire.[51]

The Foreign Office on February 5, 1919, instructed Calthorpe to inform the Turkish Government to immediately "hand over to you or nearest Allied commander such Turkish officers and Officials as you or the Commanders concerned consider should be surrendered for the following reasons:[52]

1. Failure to comply with Armistice terms.
2. Impeding execution of Armistice terms.
3. Insolence to British Commanders and Officers.
4. Ill-treatment of prisoners.
5. Outrages to Armenians or other subject races both in Trans-Caucasia and in Turkey.
6. Participation in looting, destruction of property, etc.
7. Any other breaches of the laws and customs of war.

The Foreign Office told Calthorpe that under no conditions would the British Government give its consent for the trial and punishment by the Turkish authorities of Turks accused of the aforementioned seven points in parts of the Ottoman Empire "which are outside Allied occupation . . ."[53] but rather, that offenders arrested by the Turkish Government found in areas outside Allied occupation, be turned over to the British to be sent to detention camps on Malta and "there to await trial and punishment in such manner as the Allies may subsequently decide . . ."[54] The procedure for the trials would be discussed at Paris. The Foreign Office telegram of February 5, 1919, listing the seven categories under which Turkish offenders were to be arrested by the Turkish Government and turned over to the British authorities for incarceration, was not adhered to. The reason for this, according to various communications, was that the Turkish Government had already initiated courts martial proceedings against Turkish offenders, the first court sitting on February 5, 1919, in Constantinople, and the first case tried was regarding atrocities committed in Yozgat. The High Commissioner was of the opinion that the Sultan's Government was doing its best, and undue pressure would not be necessary as long as the British supported the Sultan, and this would give the Sultan confidence to pursue the courts martial. The High Commissioner believed that the Sultan was sincere in apprehending and bringing to trial former members of the Committee of Union and Progress.[55] Yet, the High Commissioner did not have official representation at the courts martial proceedings. On March 11, 1919, the High Commissioner informed the Foreign Office that[56] it would be content with the Turkish Government making the arrests rather than their surrendering the suspects to the British for incarceration, "as long as those arrested are kept in secure detention." The Foreign Office approved this procedure in Telegram 24 of 11 May, 1919.

Chapter II

Arrest of Criminals

1.

As already indicated, there was no coordinated effort among the Allies to systematically apprehend suspected Turkish criminals. The French General Officer Commanding, Franchet d'Esperet, informed Calthorpe that, in Franchet's opinion, in the non-occupied areas of the Ottoman Empire, the apprehension and trial of accused offenders fell to the Turkish Authorities, not to the Allies.[57] This reaction came forth after Calthorpe had made available to his French colleagues the Foreign Office orders concerning the seven categories under which Turkish offenders were to be arrested. It would appear that the French wanted to make it clear that they would object to any allied forces moving into the unoccupied areas of the Ottoman Empire. French officials on February 12, 1919, without the knowledge of the British High Commission, submitted their own lists of wanted Turkish officials to the Grand Vezir, indicating the names of former Cabinet members and "other persons responsible for criminal activities during the war, in order that they should be brought to justice . . ."[58] They were:

Said Halim Pasha	Ex-Grand Vezir
Hairi Effendi	Ex-Sheikh-al-Islam
Javid Bey	Ex-Minister of Finance
Ibrahim Bey	Ex-Minister of Justice
Shukri Bey	Ex-Minister of Public Instruction
(Ahmet) Nessimi Bey	Ex-Minister of Foreign Affairs
Halil Bey	Ex-Minister of Justice and President of the Chamber
Topal Rifaat	Ex-President of the Senate
Ali Munif	Ex-Governor of Lebanon
Hodja Ali Ghalib	Ex-Deputy
Ömer Nadji	Leading member of the Committee of Union and Progress
Yunus Nadi	Journalist (Editor of *Cumhuriyet* during period of the First Republic)

2.

As of April 3, 1919, the High Commission had demanded from the Turkish Government the arrest and surrender of those persons guilty of brutality to prisoners of war, and two deputies of Diyarbekir implicated in the massacre of Armenians—Zulfi Bey and Feizi Bey, who were subsequently arrested. The British did not assume the responsibility of directly apprehending those Turks accused of having committed crimes against Armenians or others. Rather, they did the following:

1. Suggested names of those who should be arrested to the Turkish Government;
2. Disclaimed all responsibility of guaranteeing evidence;[59]
3. Suspended demand, arrest and surrender of various classes of criminals "except those persons guilty of ill-treatment to prisoners of war . . .";
4. Assisted the Turkish Government with information.

The procedure of arrests was carried out by employing different methods. Certain Turkish criminals were arrested by:

1. The Turkish authorities who had begun arresting certain persons as early as November, 1918.
2. Formal demands made by the British High Commission to the Turkish authorities, (those accused of cruelty to P.O.W.s).
3. On the verbal suggestion of the High Commission.
4. On the demand by British Military authorities.
5. Arrests made by the British Military.
6. On the formal demand of the French High Commissioner.

But the British High Commission "refrained in general from appearing to urge officially that arrests should be made . . ."[60] On January 9, 1919, the High Commission had asked the Ottoman Government to arrest the following individuals: Talaat Pasha, Dr. Nazim, Enver Pasha, Bedri Bey, Dr. Beha-ed-Din-Shakir, Jemal Pasha, and Azmi Bey. However, these men had already fled the Ottoman Empire and were situated in various countries in Europe. Unfortunately, they were not extradited even though the Turkish Minister for Foreign Affairs Damad Ferid, had officially requested that the German Government extradite "all principal authors" of the war in the East, namely—Talaat, Enver, and Jemal Pashas.[61] But the German Government did not comply with this request.

On April 7 and 9, 1919, the High Commission's office submitted lists to the Foreign Office with the names of those accused which the High Commission had recommended be arrested by the Ottoman Government: these were recommendations and not formal demands.[62]

The primary sources of the names of those Turks accused of direct or indirect complicity in the massacres came from the following:

1. Turkish sources.
2. Bureau d'information Arménienne.

3. Armenians from the provinces who came to the High Commission with their testimony.
4. The Armenian Patriarchate.
5. British Intelligence Service.

The Armenian-Greek section of the High Commission had two card indexes, one contained 600-700 names of those persons implicated in atrocities, and another which contained the names of places where atrocities were committed.[63]

It should be kept in mind, however, that the British did not assume responsibility for any follow-up regarding the actual arrest of people on the list, the trial of such individuals, or the outcome of any trials that might have taken place. Even though the High Commission was aware that the Ottoman Government had initiated courts martial proceedings against suspected criminals, the High Commission did not have representation at the trials, notwithstanding the fact that the trials were open to the public. There were at the trials, however, reporters from the Armenian, Greek, and French press and the High Commission made some attempt to ascertain what was actually happening from these sources. In fact, the High Commission was of the opinion that most of the evidence was such that it could not be "placed before a court." However, the High Commission believed that a number of cases could be successful if witnesses and documents in the possession of the Turkish Government were made available in court.[64]

In this connection, there was no concerted effort or cooperation between the French, British or Italians. Neither knew what information pertaining to the Armenians the other might have. To make matters worse, there was also apparent inter-service rivalry among the British naval and military forces.[65]

In almost every instance, the High Commission reiterated the impossibility of gathering *legal* evidence ". . . until the Mandatory Power has established law, order, and security throughout the country . . ."[66] The lack of merit of this statement becomes obvious when one considers that the interior of Asia Minor was in a state of chaos and anarchy, and had been so since the Armistice was signed. However, the High Commission disregarded the fact that the Ottoman Government was compiling evidence, arresting suspects, and bringing them to trial, even with the disorder within the country. In addition, the High Commissioner was of the opinion that to punish all Turkish persons guilty of Armenian atrocities would necessitate the wholesale execution of Turks, and he therefore suggested that what should be done in the form of punishment was to dismember the Turkish Empire and bring to trial high Turkish officials "whose fate will serve as an example."[67] In anticipation of the Treaty between the Ottoman Empire and the Allies, the High Commission continued to compile testimony given by those who had survived the genocide and prepared dossiers on Turks accused of atrocities.

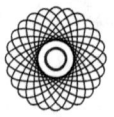

Chapter III

Deportation to Malta

1.

Since November, 1918, the Ottoman authorities had been making arrests and confining detainees in the Seraskerat prison in Constantinople. There, these persons would wait to be tried by Turkish courts - martial. The first session of the courts- martial regarding Armenian massacres convened on February 5, 1919, and took up the question of massacres at Yozgat.

In May, 1919, the Council of Four, at Paris, concerned about the massacre of Greek inhabitants who were in Asia Minor by Turkish Nationalist forces, suggested that Greek military forces land in Turkey-in-Asia, at Smyrna,[68] in the vilayet of Aidin to prevent such activity. This was accomplished on May 14-15, 1919.

Not long after the Greek landing at Smyrna, the newspapers in Constantinople, on the morning of May 22, 1919, reported that 41 persons who were detained in the court martial prison, had been released by the Ottoman Government. The British authorities became aware of this development only after it had been reported in the local press.[69] Therefore, on May 28, 1919, Admiral Calthorpe appropriated H.M.S. *Princess ENA*, and deported from the Seraskerat prison 12 ex-Ministers of high importance to Mudros; 41 ex-Ministers, politicians and ex-Valis to Malta; and 14 officers also to Malta, accused of committing offences against British POWs. Of the group of 41 deported to Malta, half were selected because of their direct or indirect complicity in Armenian massacres, and the others for precautionary measures.[70] The deportees designated for Malta were selected by Canon Whitehouse, who was attached to the High Commission and worked on the massacre problem.[71] The British put into effect the deportation scheme which had been on the books since February, 1919.

It should be kept in mind that the British demanded from the Ottoman Government some of their incarcerated prisoners. The Ottoman authorities were in no position to refuse nor did they refuse to comply with the deportation orders.

The French authorities, much to their consternation, were informed of the deportation of prisoners after the fact. They did not object to the deportation but to the fact that they were not kept informed of such developments or decisions.

Calthorpe, who had been in Smyrna when the prisoners were released from the courts martial, submitted a four page apologia to the Foreign Office explaining that the Turkish authorities had been informed, prior to the release, that the British would not countenance the release of prisoners. He continued that even though some of the prisoners ". . . were guilty of the most heinous crimes . . .,"[72] the British authorities in Constantinople had contemplated such action taking place ". . . when the decisions of the Supreme Council, extremely adverse to Turkey, were published, and this act of course coincided with the news of the occupation of Smyrna . . ."[73] Therefore, he said, French and British soldiers, under the orders of the British General-in-Command, were placed as guards over the prison. He related the difficulty of providing adequate custody over an ancient rambling prison whose ". . . inmates are unknown either by sight or by language to their new guardians . . ."[74] (i.e. British and French troops).

The prisoners who were released, he reminded the Foreign Office, "were very prominent members of the C.U.P. ..." and stringent measures were necessary to prevent their escape, which was important to the Turkish Government, who were "entirely in favour of the Allies . . ." Prevention of escape would also discourage, he said, active members of the C.U.P. still in the provinces and Constantinople.

The explanation given by Admiral Calthorpe leaves much to be desired. First, when Allied guards were placed at the prison, they could also have appointed Turkish speaking personnel alongside.

Second, the guards could have been properly instructed as to who should or should not leave the prison. If what Calthorpe said was in fact true, that the prisoners were very important persons, definite orders should have been given to the British and French Officers-of-the Day and, since the British General-in-Command was the senior officer in charge, it was incumbent upon him to issue such orders.

Third, Calthorpe admitted that such an occurrence was already contemplated by his office after the Allied decisions were published and could have taken more stringent measures to prevent the release of said prisoners.

Fourth, Calthorpe asserted that the Turkish Courts-Martial proceedings were dilatory and half-hearted, and might result in the release of the prisoners. Why were not Allied military and political personnel present at the proceedings, accompanied by interpreters? The High Commission attempted to put the onus of the incident on Admiral Webb, who was in charge while Admiral Calthorpe was in Smyrna, and on the British General-in-Command. However, in a report submitted by the General Officer Commanding, Army of the Black Sea, in June 1919, the absurd conditions at the Seraskerat prison are clearly enumerated.[75] This report describes the conditions at the prison *after* [italics mine] the release of the 41 prisoners in May, and one wonders about the security measures before Calthorpe took his "immediate" action. In addition, the High Commission did not know for sure, just how many or precisely who the people incarcerated in the Seraskerat prison were. This is demonstrated by the lists purporting to show who the C.U.P. prisoners in the Seraskerat prison were, submitted by the G.O.C. Army of the Black Sea. The names on the lists submitted by Saïd Bey, Commandant de la Ville, with 20 names, differs from the list submitted by the prison authorities, who were asked for the same information.[76] The third list which supposedly includes those arrested under martial law is also inaccurate because of the clear duplication of names. The High Commission was not aware of this duplication, it would appear. In September 1919, Admiral Calthorpe was replaced by Admiral de Robeck.

Throughout 1919 and 1920, prisoners were periodically deported to Malta, but no procedural action was spelled out in Paris as to what was to be done with them other than detaining them. On Malta, the prisoners had a great amount of leisure time and many wrote protesting letters to the High Commission to relay to the Foreign Office.[77] Ali Munif, ex-Minister of Public Works, while admitting that massacres took place in 1915, claimed that he had nothing to do with them and wanted to know under what charges he was being held.[78] On April 17, 1920, Ejzaji Mehmet, Malta No. 2790, charged with massacring Christian Ottoman subjects in the Sanjak of Erzinjan, in April, May and June 1915, wrote that he was very concerned as to the safety of the 500,000 rubles (Nicola and Kerenski) and 300 Turkish pounds the British confiscated from him at the time of his arrest. (These monies were contained in safe-keeping under seal in the High Commission, the High Commission reported). Ejzaji also hoped that his release would take place as soon as possible. It is not clear whether these monies were returned to him, but it almost appears, by the wording of the communication that Ejzaji was attempting a bribe. A communication from the deportees in Malta to the British Commander-in-Chief, Malta, dated May 12, 1921, contains a protest regarding their incarceration and is signed with multiple signatures of Malta prison members.[79] The communication cites the injustice of their imprisonment which, they said, was contrary to international law.

Throughout 1919-1921, about 120 prisoners were detained in Malta, with periodic decreases due to release and escape.

The removal from Constantinople of the detainees awaiting trial in Turkish Courts, deprived the Turkish authorities from prosecuting the many persons against whom the authorities were building cases. Nevertheless, persons continued to be tried in Turkish Courts.[80]

There does not seem to be a really logical explanation for the British to transfer the prisoners to Malta. With the existing Allied forces in Constantinople, it would seem that, had the security at the Seraskerat prison been seriously attempted, very few, if any prisoners would have been able to escape. Subsequently, when the Turkish prisoners were sent to Malta, just as many if not more escaped from the island than at the Seraskerat prison in Constantinople.

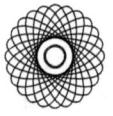

Chapter IV

The Ottoman Courts Martial

1.

Sultan Mehmet Vahid-ed-Din, a younger brother of Abdul Hamid II, became Sultan in July 1918. In October 1918, the Ittihat ve Terakki (Union and Progress) Cabinet resigned, with the principal characters fleeing Turkey. The Sultan began an attempt to discredit the former regime and to wipe out the remnants of this movement.[81]

By Imperial Penal Code, on November 23, 1918, a Commission of Enquiry was formed to investigate the activities of the Ittihat ve Terakki during the years 1914-1918. This Commission was presided over by Mazhar Bey, ex-Vali (Governor) of Ankara. It was the intention of the Turkish Government to bring to justice those accused of complicity in the Armenian Massacres. Many righteous men voiced their opinions to this effect in Parliament.

For example, Ahmet Riza Bey, in the parliamentary session of November 25, 1918, made the following statement:

> Considering that the Supreme Court formed will judge only the responsible individuals who demanded Turkish participation in the war, and the errors that were committed during the War, (the Supreme Court) will also judge other matters unprecedented and beyond imagination, crimes [which] have been committed by the two [Turkish] Cabinets against Arab, Armenian and Greek citizens. I forcefully urge that without any time being lost, the criminals be brought to justice...[82]

The Ottoman Government put into effect the arrest of persons who participated in the massacres as early as November, 1918. Individuals were arrested and detained in various locations throughout Asia Minor as well as in the prisons of Constantinople. On December 9, 1918, the Ministry of Justice classified those responsible for the Armenian massacres into four categories:

1. Major criminals would be tried before the Supreme Court.

2. The trial of functionaries who cooperated with the major criminals would be tried before civil courts; the Turkish State Council demanding that those persons in this group be tried by law applicable to government officials.

3. Common citizens were to be tried before lower courts.

4. The procedure for trying functionaries and common citizens was to be discussed between the State Council and the Ministry of Justice.[83]

On December 14, 1918, the Council of Ministers established that the extraordinary courts could try criminals, but the courts could not bring to trial all criminals according to Article 88 of the Ottoman Constitution.[84] It was therefore decided to zone the Ottoman Empire into ten regions and have courts martial proceedings in the zones where the crimes were committed.[85] Each region would have a President of the Court, an Attorney General, and Judges of Instruction.[86] These regions were in addition to the court martial proceedings in Constantinople. The ten regions were:

1. Ankara and Kastamuni provinces and the district of Bolu (Mustakil Sanjak) [independent-detached].
2. Province of Trebizond and the district of Samsun.
3. Provinces of Brusa and Adrianopl, and the district of Chatalja.
4. Province of Aydin, the district of Chanakkale, and the district of Carassi (Mustakil Sanjak).
5. Province of Konia, district of Eski Shehir, Karahisar, Kutahia and Antalia.
6. The Province of Sivas and the districts of Caeserea and Yozgat.
7. The Provinces of Diyarbekir and Mamuret-ul-Aziz.
8. The Provinces of Erzerum, Van and Bitlis.
9. The Province of Adana and the district of Marash.
10. Districts of Urfa, Aintab and Zor.

By January, 1919, the Attorneys General and judges of instruction had been selected for four of the 10 regions. Adana-Marash: Marash: Attorney General, Ismail Bey, Judge of Instruction, Aposlaki Effendi; Aydin-Dardanelles-Carassi: Attorney General, Mustafa Remzi Bey, Judge of Instruction, Aram Ipekian; Urfa-Zor-Aintab: Attorney General, Izzet Bey, Judge of Instruction, Kevork Effendi.[88]

The Ottoman Government assumed the responsibility of gathering evidence and preparing the cases against those implicated in the massacres. The Commission of Enquiry was authorized to collect all the evidence from the Valis throughout the Empire. The Commission instructed the Valis to submit to Constantinople all communications that were sent by the Young Turk regime to the provinces pertaining to the Armenians for the years 1914-1918. Many Valis complied, but others stated that they did not possess any such communications.[89] In addition, the Commission of Enquiry interrogated the statesmen and military commanders who served under the last two Cabinets of Said Halim and Talaat Pasha.

On December 21, 1918, Sultan Mehmet VI dissolved Parliament because it was learned after investigation that many of the Senators and Deputies were found to have been implicated in the Armenian massacres.[90] The Ministry of Justice ordered that all who were implicated be placed on special lists and, when new elections took place, these men would not be eligible to hold office. Others, however, were not satisfied with merely placing these men on lists. One member of Parliament said "This legislative Assembly [1914-1918] permitted, during the years, to be committed an unbelievable series of massacres, plunder, thefts, and illegalities that history has ever known . . ."[91] Others enjoined with "There are and prosecuted in justice . . ."[92] And during the last session of Parliament, on December 21, the Foreign Minister, Mustafa Reshad Pasha, stated, "A pallid light is extended upon the atrocities committed against the Armenians, atrocities which aroused the indignation of humanity; our land has been given back to us transformed into a gigantic slaughterhouse . . ."[93] Halide Edib, commenting on the atrocities said, "More civilized peoples should not be committed to the mercy of the Turks, who have proved that they are incapable of constituting a civilized government . . ."[94]

Further evidence regarding the massacres was also being gathered by the British military authorities in Aintab. The Turkish Ministry of Foreign Affairs sent a note to the British High Commissioner, Calthorpe, complaining that Major Mills, together with Mr. Murrill, Director of the American School in that city, on February 4, 1919, had demanded from the Mutasarrif all telegrams and correspondence exchanged between the vilayet and the Ministry of the Interior for the years 1914-1918.[95] Major Mills took the documents from the archive in Aintab and gave the Mutasarrif a receipt. This action was approved by Admiral Calthorpe. Presumably, these documents were forwarded to the British Foreign Office.

2.

In addition to compiling evidence within the Empire, the Ottoman authorities as early as November 12, 1918, instructed their legation in Switzerland to demand that the Swiss authorities extradite Talaat, Enver, and Jemal Pashas, as well as Dr. Nazim, Bedri Bey, Azmi Bey and Dr. Beha-ed-Din Shakir, in the event these men managed to enter Switzerland. Most of them had already taken refuge in Germany[96] and it was estimated that there were more than 200 members of the C.U.P. in Germany.[97] The Ottoman Ministry of War had addressed a protest to the German Government in which it demanded the extradition of former Turkish officials. The German Government promised to place all Committee of Union and Progress members under "provisional arrest with the exception of Enver and Talaat." However, nothing was done. The Germans denied that Enver and Talaat "were instigators of massacres" and regarding the large sums of money they brought with them, they claimed that these were to be used for "political purposes, and are not stolen property."[98] The British military authorities in Germany and Switzerland knew, as early as December 1918, the whereabouts of Talaat, Jemal and Enver, and that these three were hiding in Berlin.[99] The Foreign Office chose not to take action against these three before or after the signing of the Treaty of Versailles. (*See Special Note on pp. 34-35*) This behavior on the part of the British was quite peculiar, in view of the decision, which was approved by the British in the report submitted to the Peace Conference in March 1919, to prosecute those persons who were guilty of committing war crimes and crimes against humanity.

The Turkish Government, on its own initiative and later on the suggestion of the Allies, arrested hundreds of former officials and incarcerated them in various prisons including the Bekir Agha prison in Constantinople. Hundreds more were arrested and detained in prisons in the interior, awaiting trial. In addition to Constantinople, the accused were to be tried in the locale where the crimes were committed. However, by July 1919, the situation in the interior was rapidly deteriorating, in that opposition to the central government was being organized by the Committee of Union and Progress and Mustafa Kemal who was organizing the returning Turkish soldiery.[100]

By July 1919, in was announced that the court-martial at Constantinople was to bring to trial persons involved in deportations and massacres of Angora, Gerasoon, Sivas, Ada-Bazaar, Biledjik, Bitlis, Ismidt, Mamuret-ul-Aziz, Amassia, Der-ez-Zor, Kir Shehir, Diyarbekir, Caesarea, Konia, Changri, Adrianople, Karahissar, Adana, Tchatalja, Dardanelles, Bafra, Marash, Akhissar, Constantinople, and Kutahia. Some of the persons involved were Bedri Bey, former Chief of Police; Reshad Bey, former Chief of the Political Section of Police; and Shehat Bey, former Commandant of the Place–Constantinople.[101] By April 1920, the Commission of Enquiry had 110 dossiers yet to be examined, and the office of the Court Martial had more than 100 dossiers of individuals who were to be brought to trial.[102]

3.

On December 9, 1918, a court-martial was constituted to try *in absentia* Enver Pasha, Jemal Pasha and Talaat Pasha.[103] The verdict of the court, given on July 5, 1919, condemned to death, *in absentia*, Talaat, Jemal, Enver and Dr. Nazim; and condemned to 15 years hard labour (later commuted to 15 years exile) the former Sheikh-ul Islam, Musa Kiazim; to 15 years hard labour the former Minister of Finance, Djavid Bey.[104] The death penalty was decided after the Turkish Court Martial proved that these men were responsible for criminal acts which included massacres at Trebizond, Yozgat, and Boghazlian.[105] In addition, they were guilty of undermining and meddling in the affairs of the Central Government prior to the coup of 1913. This particular court martial did not dwell specifically on deportations and massacres.

An Extraordinary Court was formed for the purpose of bringing to trial those persons implicated in deportation and massacre.[106] Initially, the President of this court was General Mahmud Hairet Pasha, who was well respected. Military members of the court were Ali Nadir Pasha (Ret.), and Mustafa Pasha (Kurd), commander of the 27th Division. Civil members were Shevket Bey, Artin Mostijian, and Nihad Bey, who was Assistant Attorney General; Mose Zeki, Misak Makarian, Nazif Bey, and Abdul Hamid Bey. All the civil members were also members of various existing courts situated in Pera and Constantinople.

On February 5, 1919, the first case to be tried involved the massacres which had taken place at Yozgat.[107] Indicted was Kemal Bey, former Vali of Boghazlian and former Mutasarrif of Yozgat. The courts martial were open to the public and members of the press were present. The attorney for Kemal Bey was Saad-ed-Din, who, in the first session of the proceedings asserted that Kemal was a minor official who was merely carrying out orders received from his superiors, and that the Ministers and Governors-General should be brought to trial before Kemal.[108]

The Attorney General, Sami Bey, agreed that all officials were subject to superior orders, but that it was incumbent on the individual to ascertain whether the orders are in accordance with justice and law. On this basis, he said, there were officials who were opposed to such orders and had refused to carry them out.[109] Superior orders were not a defence. Saad-ed-Din remarked that the order to exile the Armenians resulted from the decision made by the Council of Ministers, ". . . a decision that had been approved by Imperial Penal Code . . ." The evidence proved, however, that the decision to carry out the extermination of the Armenian people was communicated to the provincial governors from the Central Government. Those who refused to carry out the orders were replaced. For example, Mazhar Bey, of Ankara, was replaced by Atif Bey; and Jemal Bey of Yozgat was replaced by Kemal Bey of Boghazlian.[110] The members of the Central Committee of the Committee of Union and Progress ". . . during the deportations had given instructions to the Governors General of the provinces . . . when certain members of the Government [provincial governors] did not show an inclination to serve their aims [Central Government], particularly Jemal Bey, Mutasarrif of Yozgat, Reshid Pasha, Vali of Kastamuni, and Mazhar Bey, Vali of Ankara, they were immediately removed from their positions." The Vali of Erzerum, Tahsin Bey, gave details during his interrogation which confirmed these facts.[111]

The Attorney General confronted Kemal with evidence and produced before the court the letters written by Kemal while he was Mutasarrif of Yozgat. The two letters contained instructions to be delivered to Bakirdji Zade Mahmud, Abdullah Effendi, and Mehmet Effendi in the village of Battal. At a designated time, the letters were to be read by the three aforementioned persons. One letter was to Shukri Chavoush, Commander of the Gendarmerie, who was ordered to carry out the instructions he would subsequently receive from the three persons. The second letter was signed by Vehbi Bey, Chief Accountant. Vehbi Bey's letter instructed the three to take possession of all that the women and young girls had with them during the deportation, and to deliver these possessions to the town. The Court Martial commented that, "The effects of these women and girls were already in the city, and consequently, when the order was given to take their possessions, this simply meant that they [the officials] were to take their possessions after having them killed. It could not be explained otherwise."[112]

Vehib Pasha, Commander of the Third Army, had given a long report in testimony, and the Court Martial more than once referred to this document. In it, Vehib Pasha elaborated and established that governors were responsible for putting into effect the deportation orders. Further, he asserted that the plan had been ordered and organized in the first instance, ". . . by the Delegates of the Union and Progress, and its offices."[113]

The military was also implicated in these developments, attested to by the Commander of the Fifth Army in Ankara (1915) Halil Rejai.[114] He told the Court: "I received a ciphered telegram from Colonel Shahab-ed-Din, acting commander of the 15th Division in Caesarea. In this telegram he said that on the same day 300 Armenians had been exterminated in Boghazlian." The Attorney General asked why Colonel Shahab Bey had communicated to Halil Rejai the information regarding the 300 exterminated Armenians. Halil Rejai answered that this was in conformance with the orders from the Commander in Chief (Enver Pasha). The President of the court asked Rejai whether there was a special order concerning the Armenians, to which Rejai replied that there was a special order. At this point, the secretary to the court read the telegram pertaining to the Armenians.[115]

The court also brought to trial Colonel Shahab-ed-Din and read several of the telegrams he had sent to Halil Rejai. The telegrams confirmed that the Armenians had been massacred and gave the number of persons killed as 1,500, 3,160 and so on.[116]

During the Yozgat trial, the President of the Court asked Kemal Bey, "Had you received the order to pick up and bury the corpses scattered in the streets and fields?" Kemal andswered "Yes, I received such an order, but this order was transmitted to the Vali."[117]

Kemal Bey, on the basis of the existing evidence, was found guilty and condemned to death for the part he played in the Armenian Massacres. He was hanged on April 10, 1919.[118]

As these trials proceeded, other courts martial would commence as soon as the prosecutors had prepared their cases. For example, the trial of Trabizond began on March 27, 1919, so that several proceedings were in session simultaneously.

SPECIAL NOTE: The Ottoman Government, it must be stated, did attempt to prosecute those persons guilty of effecting a blight against the honor of the Empire—namely the members of the Union and Progress Party. But, in order to do this, it must be remembered that the action it was taking was most unpopular, and would require the support of the Allied Powers if its endeavors were to be realized. This support, both moral and physical, was never forthcoming.

Moreover, in Constantinople and the Interior, there were still many former members of the C.U.P., who were actively doing all they could to undermine the actions of the Central Government. It was incumbent on the Allied Powers in Turkey to assist the Central Government with all the means in their power. But rather than do this, the Allies were at loggerheads deciding which of them was to reap the profits of the war.

Nothing can more poignantly demonstrate the volte face of the British than the remark made by David Lloyd George, during a meeting of the Council of Four at Paris, on 21 May, 1919, when he, concerned about the reaction of Britain's Muslims in India, Egypt and Sudan regarding the partition of Turkey, said, "as far as he knew, the Turk never had perpetrated any very serious atrocities in Anatolia, even if he had never governed well..." It must be assumed that this was also the view of the British Cabinet. See *P.P.C. 1919,* Vol. V, p. 758.

The Ottoman Government, feverishly attempting to destroy the power of the C.U.P., was thwarted by British inaction.

The British knew that Jemal, Talaat and Enver were in Berlin in 1919 and in 1920. This cannot be disputed because of reports sent to the Foreign Office by various British officials in Berlin alluding to the three. See, for example, F.O. 371/5173/4064, of 30 April, 1920. Lord Kilmarnock received information from Baron Eckhardstein regarding Jemal Pasha from a "high official [in the] German Secret Police." The German Secret Police knew where Jemal was hiding as well as his plan to travel to Azerbaijan and to incite "Mohamedans against the Entente Powers, after securing funds from Moscow." The "whole plan is being worked in conjunction with [Victor] Köpp and many influential Germans..." though not the German Government, it was said.

On 24 February, 1920 and 25 February, 1920, Major Ivor Hedley, DAAG, British Military Mission, Berlin, had meetings with Enver Pasha. See F.O. 371/5211/1311. In fact, Hedley had, as of 25 February, 1920, six interviews with Enver. The reports were sent by Hedley to Major General Neill Malcolm, Chief of British Military Mission, Berlin, who forwarded them to the Director of Military Intelligence, War Office, and thence to the Foreign Office. According to Kilmarnock, the question of Enver Pasha was raised in the German Cabinet meeting of April, 1920. Certain ministers were concerned that the integrity of the German Government was at stake. The Chancellor denied that he had knowledge of such activities. "A proposal to arrest Enver seems not to have been accepted." (See F.O. 371/5173/2119, 22 April, 1920).

The Foreign Office instructed Lord Kilmarnock "to suspend action on this matter..." and that the question of asking for Enver's surrender as a war criminal was to be referred to the Ambassador's Conference. *Ibid.*

The presence of Talaat in Berlin was also known to the British, for he was seen as early as February 1920. Hedley knew of Talaat's whereabouts from several sources, one of which was the German General, Hoffmann, who spoke to Talaat in the Unter den Linden, and was surprised that he had not been "hanged long ago in Constantinople." (See F.O. 371/5211/1311, p. 33).

Lord D'Abernon [Edgar Vincent], who was in Berlin, sent Curzon a dispatch dated 5 December, 1920, enclosing a report of a conversation between Talaat and a private friend of Talaat's. D'Abernon did not mention who this friend was, but some of the points of the conversation are worth noting. (See F.O. 371/5173/15552, 5 December, 1920).

Talaat stated that the efforts of the Ottoman Government to come to an understanding before the war with Great Britain were in vain, owing to the opposition of Russia, because "Russia's interest in the Turkish Empire were more immediate and more vital from the point of view of the integrity and sovereignty of the country than of any other European Power. As far back as 1908, he had endeavored to pacify British opinion by proposing a solution of the Armenian Question." This was to be done by Great Britain nominating an inspector, who would be furnished with extraordinary powers. Talaat said that he had visited Great Britain and the British Government acquiesced but withdrew the commitment because of the protests of the Russian Government. As far as the situation in 1920 was concerned, Talaat said that the "Treaty of Sèvres was driving the Turkish nationalists into the arms of the Bolshevists . . ." Enver had gone to Moscow and had obtained support for Mustafa Kemal['s] [action] in Armenia. Some two hundred thousand rifles and two and a half million pounds had been delivered and promises of more had been made, . . ." The purpose was to have Enver organize the Muslims from Turkistan to Asia Minor and incite them against Great Britain.

Talaat also said that in Berlin there was a "semblance of an independent Turkish Government . . . and that Enver Chekkeb Arslan was the Minister of Foreign Affairs. They lived under assumed names in order not to embarrass the German Government. Talaat had been to Italy and Switzerland and had a Swiss passport, using the name Monsieur Dupont. Talaat also made it clear that Great Britain could benefit from a reconciliation with the Turkish nationalists. Mesopotamia, Turkistan and the Caucasus could be easily subdued. The oil could be exploited by the British, because Turkey was not an industrial country and did not have a need for oil. He also said that amnesty should be granted to the leaders and political prisoners in Malta, and some Turkish influence be permitted north of the line Alexadretta–Mosul. If Turkey secured some financial help, a settlement in favor of Great Britain was possible. Finally, he said the struggle of Europe against Bolshevism would be enhanced by the support of the Mohammedan republics bordering Russia, "which were a natural barrier against Bolshevism or any other form of Russian penetration . . ." He could count on the support of 20 million Muslims. Talaat was not a fool, it is extremely probable that he knew such information would reach the ears of the British. These comments by Talaat in December 1920, were also similar to the ones made by Enver as early as February 1920, when Enver told Major Hedley the same story regarding the Muslims. At that time, Enver told Hedley, Great Britain should accede to his proposition, namely:

* Turkey to remain in Europe;

* Maintain considerable amount of Asiatic possessions;

* Independence of Caucasia and Turkistan;

* Great Britain recognizes the independence of Afghanistan;

* Egyptian independence extended to the Sudan and an Anglo-Egyptian treaty to be signed;

* Arabia should be granted self-determination, and Smyrna and Thrace to be settled in Turkey's favor;

If these changes came to pass, Enver would abandon the Bolsheviks and come on the side of Great Britain. It appears that all Enver had proposed, were coming to pass. It is also interesting that Enver was killed in 1922, fighting the Bolsheviks. See F.O. 371/5211/1311, pp. 39-40.

4.

While the military and civil authorities were implicated in direct or indirect involvement in the massacre of Armenians, a specific organization had been formed for the purpose of exterminating the deportees. This was proved by the Turkish courts - martial.

In July 1914, immediately after mobilization, Talaat, Enver and Jemal began to put into effect their secret projects: they organized the Teshkilât Mahsussa (Special Organization) which was composed of criminals released from prisons who would form the irregular bands *(chetes)* with very special orders and instructions. During the early stage of mobilization, it was generally believed by many Turks that these bands would participate in the war. However, the courts -martial proved otherwise: ". . . But evidence is clear from the proof and documents concerning the bands that these aforementioned bands were formed for the purpose of massacring and exterminating the convoys of deportees."[119]

The Minister of Justice (1914), Piri Zade Ibrahim Bey, established a special office in the Ministry of Justice for the purpose of organizing groups of released criminals and designated medical doctors who were charged to examine the physical and mental capacities of these criminals.[120] Dr. Beha-ed-Din Shakir, later sentenced to death in absentia by Turkish courts, was the President of the Teshkilât Mahsussa. The court continued, "The members and leaders of the Union and Progress Party had prepared in the Center [Constantinople] as well as in the provinces a Special Organization. It was through this Special Organization that they executed the plan to massacre the people, pillage the property, burn buildings and corpses, destroy villages, dishonor women whom they tortured and tormented."[121]

During the Trebizond trial, the Police Commissioner of Trebizond, Nuri Bey, delivered to the President of the Court Martial an order signed by Jemal Azmi Bey, former Vali of Trebizond, in which it was noted that in 1915, the Armenians of Trebizond had been given five days to prepare for deportation.[122] Nuri testified that "the representative of the Union [and Progress] took counsel together with the Vali; they put into effect atrocities by the use of gangs *[chetes]* and the deportees were massacred between Trebizond and Gümüsh-Hane."[123] The court found Jemal Azmi, former Vali of Trebizond, guilty because he issued secret orders and took measures to carry out these orders. Nayil Bey, Executive Secretary of the Committee of Union and Progress in Trebizond, was found guilty because he collaborated in these secret orders and helped Jemal Azmi. The court stated:

> Apparently they had to deport [Armenians] following the issue of secret orders, but, in order to slaughter the Armenians and exterminate them, they had gangs organized, composed of cruel and recidivist criminals who were sent with the caravans of Armenian deportees, and were accompanied by gendarmes who were their [the criminals'] accomplices, and who ostensibly were to protect the caravans [but] helped the criminals carry out their business of extermination . . .

... The guilt of the Vali Jemal Azmi, the Responsible Secretary Nayil, and Mehmet Ali Effendi, was established in accordance with the 45th Article of the Imperial Penal Code ...

... The convicted persons, Jemal Azmi and Nayil, are sentenced ... in accordance with the provisions of the Article [170] ... Jemal Azmi and Nayil are sentenced to death, deprived of civil rights, and their properties shall be seized."[124]

5.

The Turkish Government had intended to bring to trial individuals responsible for committing various crimes in accordance with the existing penal codes, and trials were to have taken place in the locale where certain crimes had been committed. But because law and order were virtually non-existent in the Interior, and, after May 1919, opposition to the Central Government was open and blatant, trials were carried out in Constantinople. But even before the Smyrna landing by the Greeks, certain zealous prosecutors were being removed from their posts and replaced by more sympathetic prosecutors. For example, as early as January 1919, the President of the Court at Constantinople, Mahmud Hairet Pasha, was replaced.[125] He, on many occasions, prodded the Commission of Enquiry to carry out the instructions which would bring the accused to trial more expeditiously.

The various trials were open to the public and the press. However, it does not appear that the British authorities had representatives at the trials, but acquired their information through the press and from Armenian or Greek members attached to the High Commission. The High Commissioner had a clip-out service which sent to the Foreign Office the reports of the trials as cited in the local press.

As the trials progressed, many proceedings proved to be flawed, but others benefited by honest and brave officers, who carried out their duties in a professional manner. However, the British Authorities in Constantinople, ever pompous, labelled the courts martial proceedings as farcical and deleterious. This position was taken in spite of the evidence, testimony and verdicts passed down by the courts regarding the guilty defendants. How the British came to this conclusion after the Turkish Government tried, convicted and hanged former participants and officials of the Ittihat is open to question. No-one denies that the trials, in some instances, had glaring shortcomings, but to condemn all the trials as farcical was baseless.

The major leaders of the Ittihat ve Terakki were tried in absentia and condemned to death. As the various trials proceeded, other officials, and in no small numbers, were also condemned to death. Even more testimony and evidence could have been compiled had not the British Authorities whisked away some of the most important prisoners to Malta, depriving the Turkish courts of bringing these men to trial. Could it be that the Turkish courts were doing too good a job? The Ottoman Commission of Enquiry had prepared hundreds of dossiers in preparation for trial; but with many of these men sent to Malta, public hearings against them could not be made, and, consequently, evidence could not be published in the official gazette of the Ottoman Government—*Takvim-i Vekayi*.

The *Takvim-i Vekayi* published the events which took place at the courts - martial proceedings, including the activities of the Committee of Union and Progress. The courts-martial proved and the results were recorded in the *Takvim-i Vekayi* that the Young Turk Government planned and executed the premeditated extermination of the Armenian people of the Ottoman Empire. The courts - martial proceedings terminated on May 21, 1921. *

*See for a cogent discussion of the results of the courts-martial proceedings the following. Vahakn N. Dadrian's, *The History of the Armenian Genocide: Ethnic Conflict from the Balkans to the Caucasus (Providence & Oxford: Berghahn Books, 1995); also, Dadrian's 4th revised edition, 1997; Dadrian's Warrant for Genocide, (New Brunswick, New Jersey: Transaction Publishers, 1999). See also, Taner Akcam, Young Turk's Crime Against Humanity: The Armenian Genocide and Ethnic Cleansing in the Ottoman Empire, (Princeton,NJ, Princeton University Press, 2012).*

See also, Raymond Kevorkian, The Armenian Genocide: A Complete History, (New York, I.B. Tauris, 2011).

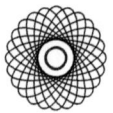

Chapter V

Occupation of Constantinople and the Treaty of Sèvres

1.

By 1920, the situation in Asia Minor was as chaotic as before the armistice was signed. In fact, it was more so because of the organization and activity of Mustafa Kemal and the reorganization of the Turkish military forces. Even though the Ottoman Government made attempts to quell the nationalists, its attempts failed because there was very little support forthcoming from the occupying powers, and such actions proved very unpopular with the general populace. There were in fact two Turkish Governments, one at Angora [Ankara] and one at Constantinople; and the one at Constantinople was permeated by pro-Kemalists leaving the Sultan's government with the status of a puppet organization.

The British, using this situation as an excuse, and with the support of France and Italy, occupied all of Constantinople on March 16, 1920. The occupation included the physical take-over of the various governmental ministries as well. This included the Ministry of Posts and Telegraph in which were deposited voluminous telegraphs and communications from the period 1914 onward. However, because the British were unable to translate the various communications which were written in Ottoman Turkish, they employed local Armenians and Greeks who were conversant with the language. The British authorities confiscated boxes of these telegrams which were to be translated, and some of these documents were removed from the Ministry. In some cases, some of the documents turned up in the Western World.

The British High Commissioner, Admiral de Robeck, continued to recommend to the Ottoman Government lists of persons who were to be arrested for having committed various crimes as enumerated above.[126] Many of the names included those who were suspected of complicity in the Armenian atrocities. On February 18, 1920, de Robeck sent a communication to the Foreign Office which explained that the Turkish courts martial sentenced to death in absentia, Dr. Beha-ed-Din Shakir, who was at that time domiciled in Germany.[127] De Robeck said "Behaeddin Shakir Bey was a member of the small secret committee known as the Teshkilat Mahsoussi *[Teshkilat-i-Mahsusa]* or Special Organization, formed by the Central Committee of Union and Progress to organize the extermination of the Armenian race." Dr. Beha-ed-Din Shakir, was not merely a member of this organization, but was in fact President of the *Teshkilat-i Mahsusa,* Second Branch.[128]

On May 26, and June 15, 1920, de Robeck submitted to the Foreign Office the names of persons arrested and sent to Malta.[129] Throughout 1920, the British would send to Malta certain persons who were allegedly involved in the massacres. They by no means sent all of those who were arrested; for the Ottoman authorities were also incarcerating suspects in prisons in Constantinople. De Robeck did not believe that all the suspects could be prosecuted, and in March, 1920, the War Office had suggested that some of the detainees should be repatriated and some held over for trial.[130]

2.

It should be noted that, the Turkish prisoners sent to Malta, in some cases, were not charged with specific crimes, but were to await trial at such time as the Peace Conference came to a decision as to what the procedure was going to be. The Treaty of Versailles was signed on June 28, 1919, and contained within it penalty clauses pertaining to war crimes. The same method was to be applied to Turkish war criminals, with the pertinent clauses to be contained in the treaty between the Ottoman Empire and the Allied Powers. However, the procrastination and inaction by President Wilson prevented a treaty from coming into existence until almost two years after the war had ended. In those two years the entire posture of the Allies vis-à-vis Turkey had changed because of jealousy and rivalry among the victors, to the extent that neither France, Italy, Great Britain, nor the United States trusted each other enough to work in concert in order to expedite a treaty. The United States, of course, while not a party to the Treaty of Sèvres, was primarily responsible for the Treaty of Sèvres not being drawn up soon after the war ended. When the Treaty of Sèvres finally was signed on August 10, 1920, there was no way its clauses could be implemented without the use of force –and the Allies had no intention of employing force.[131]

In addition, the Ottoman Government had, in those two years, lost confidence in what the Allies could do for Turkey, and subsequently, the government at Constantinople came to an agreement with the "government" at Ankara. With the major nations clamoring to get back to "normalcy," it was futile to assume that any country would be willing to commit troops in order to put into effect the Treaty of Sèvres.

Part VII of the Treaty pertaining to "Penalties," contained Articles 226 – 230.[132] First, in Article 226, the Turkish Government was to recognize "the right of the Allied Powers to bring before military tribunals persons accused of having committed acts in violation of the laws and customs of war . . . ." This provision would apply notwithstanding any "proceedings or prosecution before a tribunal in Turkey or in the territory of her Allies." The Turkish Government was to turn over to any of the Allied Powers who so requested, "all persons accused of having committed an act in violation of the laws and customs of war, . . ." whether or not they had been tried by Turkish courts martial.

Article 228, provided for the Turkish Government "to furnish all documents and information of every kind, the production of which may be considered necessary to ensure the full knowledge of the incriminating acts . . ." In Article 230, the Turkish Government was to hand over to the Allied Powers persons considered "responsible for the massacres committed during the continuance of the state of war on territory which formed part of the Turkish Empire on August 1, 1914."

"The Allied Powers reserve to themselves the right to designate the tribunal which shall try the persons so accused, and the Turkish Government undertakes to recognize such tribunal." These clauses pertaining to penalties are almost identical to the Penalties section in the Treaty of Versailles, relative to the question of German war crime trials. The primary difference is, however, that in the Versailles Treaty the Allied Military Tribunal was first to extradite the accused Germans and Austrians, whereas, in the Turkish situation the accused were already incarcerated in Malta by the British, and in Constantinople by the Turkish Government. What remained to be done in the Turkish case was to implement the clauses contained in the Treaty of Sèvres which, of course, was never done.

For all intents and purposes, the Treaty of Sèvres was a dead letter even before it was signed by the Allied Powers and the Ottoman Government.[133]

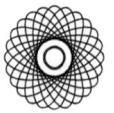

Chapter VI

The Final Solution of the Question of Turkish War Criminals: Phase I

1.

The repatriation of Turkish prisoners of war from Malta was considered by the Supreme Council as early as December 31, 1919.[134] Certain individuals were in fact released as early as January 2, 1920, February 1920, and May 1920.[135] Some of the prisoners released in 1920, were accused of direct or indirect complicity of massacres and atrocities. The Army Council, War Office, had under consideration the question of releasing more prisoners from Malta because of the ". . . cost of their maintenance while interned." With this view in mind, the Army Council submitted to the Cabinet a list of prisoners which was to be revised by the Attorney General, in order to release those prisoners against whom definite proceedings were not going to take place. What criteria were to be used by the War Office in order to determine who was to be released is not clear. But it is known that as early as April 19, 1920, the Foreign Office had already determined that certain prisoners would be released and informed the War Office accordingly. There does not seem to be any indication that the High Commissioner was kept informed about what decisions were being made by the Foreign Office or the War Office until late in the game. On May 15, 1920, the War Office instructed the Commander in Chief, Malta, to release certain prisoners.

On August 4, 1920, the Law Officers of the Crown submitted their opinion to the War Office regarding the question of prisoners on Malta, in the form of a *Memorandum*.[136] The report directed its comments to the prisoners who had been sent to Malta by the High Commissioner.

The report stated that the prisoners fell into three classes:
1. Political offenders.
2. Persons accused of deportations, pillage and massacres.
3. Persons accused of ill-treatment of Prisoners of War; and some who had been detained without and reason given.

The Law Officers said that they were having difficulty because many Turks had the same or similar names, and that the third class was the only one that came within their purview because they had no knowledge of the individuals contained in the other classes.[137] They also said that "the only person they could clearly identify was Major Mazloum Edit Bey; that Djellal Bey, 2676; Tewfik Mehmet, 2679; Tewfik Ahmed, 2680; Djemal Effendi Abdul, 2694; and Hakki Bey Ibrahim, 2710, may be identical with persons with similar names."[138] They felt that with the existing evidence, the aforementioned persons were ". . . the only ones whose detention on the ground of ill-treatment of prisoners of war seems desirable . . ..." But, they asserted, in view of the fact that the High Commissioner had had these men arrested, his office should be consulted before any of these men on the list be released. The memorandum was signed by Gordon Hewart and Ernest M. Pollock. The action of the Law Officers of the Crown is most perplexing; for it was Sir Ernest M. Pollock who was the British representative on the Commission charged by the Peace Conference with defining war crimes and crimes against humanity. The absurdity of their not being able to identify individuals raises doubts as to the seriousness of their undertaking, or, for that matter, one can question the degree of sincerity of the British Government in actually wanting to bring the accused to justice.

Further, it should be remembered that this report was submitted on August 4, 1920, six days before the Treaty of Sèvres was actually signed. If none of the accused were identifiable as criminals and had no cases prepared against them, then against whom were the "Penalty" clauses in the Treaty of Sèvres to be applied? Instead of preparing and gathering evidence, the British were preparing to release the prisoners. In addition, by incarcerating the prisoners on Malta, the British deprived the Ottoman officials from bringing to trial all those safely stowed away on Malta. Why was it that the Ottoman authorities could compile evidence, and the British, who had physically occupied Constantinople, could not? The truth is that the High Commissioner's Office did in fact have a great amount of incriminating evidence, but the Law Officers were, it would appear, reluctant to use any of it.

On the basis of the report of the Law Officers, the Army Council requested that the High Commissioner ". . . state the names of those Turkish prisoners now at Malta who he considers can be released at once, with the exception of those specially referred to in the enclosed [Law Officer's Report] memorandum."[139]

2.

Between September and November, 1920, Admiral de Robeck was replaced by Sir Horace Rumbold as High Commissioner. The removal of one High Commissioner after another was bound to lead to confusion in handling the question of prisoners.

Sir Horace, acceding to the suggestion made by the Army Council, formed what was officially known as the *Committee Formed to Consider and Make Recommendations Regarding the Further Detention or Immediate Release of the Turkish Prisoners Now at Malta.*[140] The results of the activities of the Committee were contained in the report made by the Committee.[141]

The members of the Committee were Jan M. Smith, Military Attaché; R.W. Graves; Lt. Commander F.H. Ruxton; and A.K. Helm.

The duties of the Committee were:

1. To separate G.O.C.'s Malta prisoners from those of the High Commissioners.

2. Taking the latter only, to separate those only deported on the ground (a) of political expediency from those (b) to be prosecuted under the terms of the Treaty of Sèvres.
3. As regards (a) to consider whether any of these could, in view of the *changed circumstances,* be allowed out now either to return to Constantinople or to proceed to some place in Europe until the coming into force of the Treaty; and, as regards (b) to decide whether there is sufficient evidence against each person to justify his further detention or whether it would be preferable to release him now under either of the above conditions.[142]

The *Report* said that, although the Foreign Office instructed the High Commissioner that the dossier of each prisoner, "whether military or a High Commissioner one, should be examined and recommendations made." This procedure, in fact, was not implemented because "this was found to be impracticable as the Military Authorities had been unable to associate themselves with the work of the Committee . . ."[143] The Committee examined only the papers relative to the prisoners who were arrested on the recommendation of the High Commissioner.

The Committee distributed the prisoners into three classes:

1. Those prisoners who should be brought to trial under the provisions of the Treaty of Sèvres.[144] The Committee felt that, in their opinion, there was a prime facie case against the deportees, derived from their own knowledge of the case; from statements made by reliable sources; and on the basis of information derived from the Armenian Patriarchate . . .." In addition, they said, it was their belief that the High Commission had no *locus standi* ". . . in the matter of prosecution, no legal evidence exists, nor, with few exceptions, can witnesses be expected to come forward under the conditions which have prevailed and still prevail in Turkey."[145]
2. The second category pertained to those persons who should be released after the Treaty of Sèvres was ratified by at least four of the signatory powers, but who should be detained until then.[146]
3. The third category included those prisoners who could be released immediately, but the Committee suggested that they be retained " . . . with a view of possible exchange for British prisoners in the hands of Nationalists [Kemalists] . . .." These persons fell into two groups.
   (a) Those who could be released but not permitted to return to Turkey until ratification of the Treaty of Sèvres by four signatories;[147]
   (b) Those who were to be released with no objection if they returned to Turkey.[148]

As far as the prisoners pertaining to the Military Authorities were concerned, the G.O.C., in his letter to the High Commissioner on July 29, 1920, (3211 "I" 785), divided the military deportees into two categories:

1. Those persons against whom, under section 208 of the Treaty, there was military objection;[149] and those against whom, under section 208 of the Treaty, "there is no military objection."[150]

2. The Committee concluded that in this last section on military prisoners, some were important from a political as well as a military point of view, " . . . whose release the Nationalists would be most likely to demand in exchange for the British prisoners in Anatolia. . . ."[151]

The Committee recommended that the G.O.C. in Constantinople had to give the final decision in the question of exchange, and "that the Military Authorities be immediately consulted regarding the possibility of the early return to Turkey or the necessity for the further detention at Malta of some of the deportees."[152]

It should be noted that in "H1," the group to be held over for trial, all were accused of massacres and atrocities, of whom 56 were finally designated for trial. The dossiers of each in précis form, were submitted to the Law Officers of the Crown for their opinion regarding the probability of convicting them. (See Appendix "G" "H1"—52 dossiers).

In "H2," Mehmed Kibar Effendi; Zia Gök Alp, 2759; and Ali Bey, were released, leaving a total of 12. All these, including the three released were accused of atrocities. (See Appendix "G" "H2"). In "H3," all four were accused of atrocities. (See Appendix "G" "H3"). In "H5," all were accused of atrocities. Suleiman Nazif was first placed on the list of those against whom there was no military objection; then placed on the list of those to be brought up for trial and, finally, placed on the list of those to be released and against whom there was no objection to return to Turkey.

3.

By 1921, it was quite obvious that the Greek thrusts into Asia Minor were becoming unsuccessful and, without Allied support, the Greeks could not continue to maintain hostilities against the Kemalist forces who were receiving munitions and money from the Bolsheviks and had already come to agreements with the French and Italians.[153]

Unofficial negotiations between Turkey and the Allies had been going on for some time, and British Military Intelligence was aware of these negotiations.[154]

When the French signed the Armistice of May 22, 1920, stopping hostilities with the Turkish Nationalists in Cilicia, there had already been three attempts by the French to come to terms with the Nationalists. The fourth attempt resulted in the Armistice being signed.[155] Georges Picot, Admiral Lebon, Cardinal Dubois, and General Gouraud were participants in these negotiations.[156]

The Italians sent a mission to Ankara from Adalia in June, 1920, whose chief was Lt. Colonel Fago, protégé of Count Sforza, who "appears" to have offered the Nationalists moral support, as well as captured Austrian war material and a loan of £T3,000,000, in return for cereals and mining concessions to be given to the Italians.[157]

4.

Because it was obvious that the Allies were not about to implement the Treaty of Sèvres, another meeting was held in London in March, 1921, in order to "modify" the Treaty of Sèvres. On March 16, 1921, an agreement was signed by Bekir Sami (Sami Bekir) representing the Turkish Nationalist Government at Ankara, and Mr. Robert Vansittart, representing Great Britain. The Turkish Delegation made its way from Turkey to Rome, and "according to Press reports the Italian Government did everything to facilitate their journey, including the provision of a destroyer for the voyage from Rhodes to Brindisi."[158] From Rome, the Delegation went to Paris and then to London. The Turkish group was composed of six Delegates, five Technical Delegates, and five Secretaries.[159]

However, the Foreign Office received a dispatch from the High Commissioner in Constantinople on March 3, 1921, to the effect that three members of the Turkish Delegation were definitely implicated in deportation and massacres.[160] They were Nedjate Bey, a C.U.P. official in 1915, in Ankara, "and principal organizer of persecution in that Vilayet,"[161] Sirri Bey, identified as Hussein Sirri, who "was Governor of Malatia from September, 1915, to October, 1916, and responsible for the massacre of Armenian deportees between Malatia and the Euphrates,"[162] and Zekai Bey, who was Governor of Caesarea from May, 1915 to May 1917 and responsible for carrying out massacres "with peculiar zeal."[163] Yet, neither the British nor the Allies took any action regarding these men.

The conference itself was called by Lloyd George and included Great Britain, Italy, France, Greece, and the two Turkish Governments – Constantinople and Ankara. An impasse was reached when the Greeks refused to accept the Turkish demands to return Smyrna to Turkey, and the Turks refused to submit to Greek claims to Thrace. The Turkish Nationalists would not accept the independent Armenian state, ". . . nor the financial and economic terms of Sèvres. Instead the Greeks opened a new offensive in Asia Minor and the Nationalists signed a treaty with the Bolsheviks...."[164]

The document signed by Vansittart and Bekir Sami was entitled *Agreement for the Immediate Release of Prisoners*.[165] It was composed of three articles with three annexes. Article 1 pertained to the immediate release of "all British prisoners of war and other British nationals or members of the British forces held in Turkey against their will . . . who were to be conveyed to Constantinople...."

Article 2, pertained to "The repatriation of Turkish prisoners of war and interned civilians now in the hands of the British authorities . . . ." This was not to include, however, those prisoners whom the British intended to bring to trial " . . . for alleged offences in violation of the laws and customs of war, or for massacres committed during the continuance of the state of war in territory which formed part of the Turkish Empire on August 14, 1914 . . . ." The Article stipulated that certain individuals not be permitted to go to Constantinople upon release, until a state of peace was declared. The British would have the authority to arrest anyone violating this condition.

Article 3, of the Agreement stated that execution of Articles 1 and 2 were to proceed as quickly as possible.

Annex 1, listed the number of members of the British forces held by the Turkish forces. This included 22 men of whom 11 were British, 5 Sepoys, 2 Ghurkas, and 4 interpreters, two of whom were Armenian: Guiragossian, 766; and Kudodoian, 930. From this list, it would appear that the British Government was aware of only 22 men being held by the Turkish nationalists. The contents of this clause did assert that, even if the names of other British forces personnel were not given, this would not affect their release.

Annex 2, listed those Turkish "persons whom His Majesty's Government are prepared to release under Article 2." This included 64 persons many of whom were accused of committing atrocities and massacres.[166] Aside from these 64 persons who were to be released, there were 54 others who were supposedly to be brought up for trial.

5.

Simultaneously with the London discussions the High Commissioner in Constantinople, Sir Horace Rumbold, submitted a list of 59 persons who were to be brought up for trial to the Foreign Office.[167] Of these 59 prisoners, two had escaped, and one had been released, leaving a total of 56 persons.[168] Jevdet Bey (Tahir Jevdet Bey), 2690, escaped on December 6, 1920; Adjente Mustafa, 2796, escaped on December 6, 1920; and Safet Osman Bey, 2813, was released in error between December 31, 1920, and January 11, 1921.

On March 16, 1921, Rumbold submitted to the Foreign Office 56 dossiers in précis form of those individuals whose prosecution he recommended.[169] He did, however, ask the Foreign Office to bear in mind, when receiving the information, the following points:[170]

1. "That none of the Allied, Associated and Neutral Powers have been asked to supply any information.
2. Since the Treaty of Sèvres had not come into force, no "sort of pressure" could be placed on the Turkish Government, "and no official documents are available."
3. Since there was no public security in Anatolia and no transportation being available from the Interior to Constantinople, "very few witnesses have come forward." Few male Armenian witnesses of the massacres had survived and among them in Constantinople there were few educated refugees. Of the witnesses who had come forward, they did so "under the promise of secrecy," fearing for the lives of any surviving relatives who might still have been in Anatolia. Of those witnesses, many had gone to America and could no longer be traced.
4. Under these conditions, the Prosecution would place "itself under grave disadvantages" until "security of life and property exists in Turkey."
5. The Armenian Patriarchate had, up to the present, (1921) been the main source of information.

In the pursuance of "gathering" evidence, the Foreign Office on March 31, 1921, sent a communication to the British Ambassador to the United States, Sir A. Geddes, and instructed him to ascertain if the U.S. Government was in possession of any evidence "that would be of value for purposes of prosecution."[171] On June 1, 1921, Sir Geddes sent a telegram to the Foreign Office and reported that, while the State Department possessed ". . . a large number of documents concerning Armenian deportations and massacres, these refer rather to the events connected with perpetration of crimes than to persons implicated . . . ."[172] The State Department would place these documents at the disposal of the British Embassy, " . . . on the understanding that the source of the information will not be divulged." Sir Geddes also stated that he was doubtful whether the documents would prove useful as evidence in prosecuting Turks. On June 16, 1921, the Foreign Office again submitted a list to Sir Geddes, and asked him if the U.S. Government had any evidence that could be used against the named persons. However, instead of the 56 names, the Foreign Office submitted a list of 45 names.[173] Subsequently, a member of the British Embassy in Washington visited the State Department and was permitted to see a selection of reports from American Consuls regarding the Armenian atrocities. There were several hundred documents. However, the British Embassy reported to the Foreign Office " . . . that there was nothing therein which could be used as evidence against the Turks who are being detained for trial at Malta ...."[174] The reports, while furnishing full accounts of the atrocities, mentioned only two Turkish officials – Sabit Bey (2686) and Suleiman Faik Pasha (2807).[175] Further, the State Department expressed the wish, that no information supplied by them was to be used in a court of law.[176] The Ambassador stated that there was no point in further enquiries being addressed to the U.S. Government.[177]

6.

Pursuant to carrying out the agreement with the Turkish Nationalists, the British released a total of 40 prisoners from Malta between March 24 and April 30, 1921.[178] These forty persons were part of the original 64 scheduled for release agreed to in London on March 16. It was at first mutually agreed to by the British and Nationalist Turks that the Turkish prisoners would be released from Malta and sent to Rome. The British conveyed 33 prisoners to Taranto, on H.M.S. *Crysanthemum* and H.M.S. *Hibiscus*. The prisoners arrived in Taranto on May 1, 1921, much to the surprise of the Italian Governor of Taranto.[179] After four days of trying to sort out the botched up affair, the situation was finally solved with the arrival of a telegram from the British Embassy in Rome, stating that the disposal of the Turkish prisoners was entirely the matter of the Turkish representative and in no way concerned the British.[180] Leaving the prisoners with the Italian authorities, the British Officers withdrew from Taranto. Six Turkish prisoners had been previously released, but up to the end of May, no British prisoners had been released. But by July 5, 1921, nine British prisoners had reached Constantinople.[181] Initially, the British had suggested that, for every British prisoner released by the Turks, the British would release three Turkish prisoners. This system never materialized. On June 11, the Turkish Minister of Foreign Affairs, Izzet Pasha, of the Constantinople Government, suggested to the High Commissioner, on behalf of the Nationalist Government at Ankara, that an all for all exchange of prisoners take place, and that those accused of crimes be brought to trial at Ankara, the same way German prisoners were being tried in Germany.[182] On April 23, 1921, the British authorities added seven more names to the list of British prisoners held by the Turks, bringing a total of 31 British prisoners held by the Nationalist forces. However, of the nine prisoners released by the Nationalists, only five were considered by the British authorities to be technically British. Therefore, according to the calculations of the British authorities, the Nationalists were still holding 24 British prisoners, for whom there was a great concern shown by the G.O.C., the High Commission, and the Cabinet. On June 25, 1921, the Government at Ankara sent a message to the British High Commissioner, repudiating Bekir Sami's agreement, and stated that the Ankara Government was ". . . ready to surrender all British prisoners for the surrender of all Turkish prisoners and detained persons."[183]

Chapter VII

The Final Solution of the Question of Turkish War Criminals: Phase II

1.

On May 31, 1921, the Foreign Office submitted to the Attorney General's Office a request for an opinion on what the probability of success of prosecuting the Turks held at Malta would be. On July 29, 1921, Mr. R. W. Woods, of H.M. Procurator General's Department, submitted an answer to the Foreign Office's request.[184] Woods made a distinction between those Turkish prisoners accused of direct or indirect complicity in the massacring of native Christians, and those Turks accused on charges of cruelty to British Prisoners of War.

Woods felt that there would be more difficulty in securing proof in the former cases than the latter. The Procurator General's Office referred to the report submitted by the High Commissioner of 16 March 1921[185] enumerating the difficulties of acquiring evidence against the accused. Woods expressed his opinion that "inherent difficulties" would face the prosecution if the Military tribunals before which the prisoners would be arraigned were required to produce evidence which would be " . . . admissible before an English Court of Justice . . . ."[186] He also stated, erroneously, that no statements had been taken from witnesses who could " . . . depose to the truth of the charges made against the prisoners . . . ." As far as witnesses were concerned, he thought it uncertain whether any witnesses could be found, especially "in a country so remote and inaccessible as Armenia, . . ." after such a long lapse in time. If the charges made were true, he said, it was probable that the majority of witnesses were dead or "irretrievably dispersed." In this connection, he said that the Law Officers were not informed whether the Armenian Government was willing or even in a position to "assist in providing evidence; nor was it certain how far the Turkish Government could be relied on to assist by producing their archives."[187] Therefore, without the assistance of these two Governments, it seemed improbable that the charges made against some of the accused would be capable of "legal proof in a court of Law."[188] The Cabinet had not, as of July 29, 1921, authorized the Law Officers to proceed and collect evidence against the accused.[189] Thus, said Woods, " . . . No steps have, therefore, at present been taken to collect the evidence against them."[190] He concluded by stating that, of the 56 dossiers of the accused, if the facts could be established by admissible evidence, some of the prisoners would probably be convicted. But, until more "precise" information were available " . . . the Attorney General does not feel that he is in a position to express any opinion at the prospects of success in any of the cases submitted for his consideration."[191]

Attached to this document was another document submitted by the Foreign Office to the High Commissioner in Constantinople, dated August 10, 1921, No. 851.[192] The following observations and comments were made. Regarding the French, the Foreign Office believed that the general attitude of France vis-à-vis Turkey made it useless to ask the French to produce any evidence.[193] As far as the Treaty of Sèvres was concerned, it was improbable that France or Italy " . . . would agree to participate in constituting the court provided for in Article 230 of the Treaty of Sèvres."[194] Therefore, the British saw little prospect of enforcing Article 230, and, in consequence of these difficulties, the British Government could not release any Turkish prisoners (they had already released over 40) until the British prisoners held in Anatolia were released.[195] The British Government, then, in the general settlement with Turkey "must contemplate including . . . the release of the 43 Turks who remain at Malta on charges of cruelty to native Christians."[196] As far as the Turkish Government was concerned, the Foreign Office felt that it was futile to expect the Turkish Government to add any evidence, even though a considerable amount of incriminating evidence was collected by the Turkish Government during the period of the Courts-Martial.[197]

On August 20, 1921, Lt. General C. H. Harington, C. in C. Allied Forces of Occupation (Turkey) sent to the War Office a telegram[198] (no. 881) pertaining to the question of British prisoners held by Nationalists. General Harington, concerned about the plight of the British prisoners held by the Nationalists, expressed that in a few days, he would obtain " . . . reliable information as to the real feeling at Ankara regarding our prisoners." He stated that, the Nationalists held 24 British prisoners who were suffering at the hands of the Turks, and the British held 24 Turkish prisoners, plus 51 who were to be brought up for trial. Of the 51 internees, Harington felt that many would not be brought to trial because " . . . there is not sufficient evidence and never can be . . . ."[199] He continued, " . . . More than half are suspected of being connected with massacres of Christian Ottoman subjects but this we shall never be able to prove. Those arrested for serious crimes for which we have evidence, such as ill-treating British and Indian prisoners of war, are another matter and should be tried but there may be some of these against whom evidence is insufficient. . . ."[200] Harington was of the opinion that of the 51 internees only about 20 could be brought to justice, leaving 31 against whom there was insufficient evidence. He suggested a head per head exchange of 24 prisoners and if the Kemalists did not agree, he and the High Commissioner examine the cases of all 51 internees and be allowed to barter with those not likely to be convicted.[201] The Army Council agreed entirely with General Harington's proposal and submitted a report of Harington's proposition to Lord Curzon on August 26, with the recommendation that he also concur in their view.[202]

On August 30, 1921, Horace Rumbold submitted a report to the Foreign Office[203] in answer to the Foreign Office communication of August 10, 1921 (E 8745). Rumbold requested that Judge Sir Lindsey-Smith, Major Sims Marshall, Legal Adviser to General Harington, and Mr. Ball of the High Commission, discuss the question of continued detention at Malta of Turkish detainees accused of cruelty towards native Christians.

Judge Lindsey-Smith wrote[204] his opinion of the situation on August 24, 1921 and submitted it to the High Commissioner. It must be stated, however, that Lindsey-Smith seemed merely to parrot the Foreign Office observations of August 10, rather than evince an opinion based on thorough knowledge of the subject. Lindsey-Smith stated that ". . . It does not appear from the files what, if any, evidence the British authorities have, . . ." He relied on the opinion of the Attorney General dispatch of 29 July, 1921 (E 8745),[205] that sufficient evidence to convict the prisoners in a Court of Law was not available, and, therefore he accepted that as conclusive.[206] It appeared to him that " . . . an abortive trial would do more harm than good . . ." because it would give the prisoners an opportunity to claim that they were wrongfully detained: "The only alternative is therefore to retain them as hostages only and release them against the British prisoners . . . ." If a reason was needed to justify not proceeding with the trials, Lindsey-Smith submitted that even though " . . . incriminating evidence was collected by the Turkish Government, it is idle to expect to get it . . . ."[207] He did say that the Turkish Government could be asked to supply the evidence and if they refused, a ground for deciding not to go on with the prosecution would present itself ". . . for it must be remembered they were the original accusers and made the original arrests."[208]

In addition, he felt that a lapse of five years "(the massacres were I think in 1916)" would make it " . . . impossible to conduct a trial which would be fair either to the accusers or the accused and that fact alone seems a good ground for dropping the prosecution."[209] His remarks, he said, did not apply to the eight prisoners accused of cruelty to prisoners.[210]

The High Commissioner's dispatch, in which Lindsey-Smith's opinion was contained, also included remarks made by the High Commissioner regarding the prisoners. Rumbold concurred with the report of Lindsey-Smith that all the Malta prisoners should be made available for exchange except the eight mentioned above, and four others accused of atrocities against Christians;[211] these four should be held, he said, unless the British were ready to drop the penalty clause of the Treaty of Sèvres. If the four were to be tried, the trial should begin without delay, otherwise the four should be released. However, he continued, Major Sims Marshall felt that the four could not be tried until the Treaty of Sèvres was ratified.[212] Of the eight accused of cruelty to British prisoners, trials could begin at once. Further, Rumbold said that the Ankara Authorities were almost certain to suggest an all for all exchange; in view of no evidence coming forth from the U.S. Government, " . . . we cannot anticipate any useful result from bringing those Turks to trial. And failing to produce proper evidence which would satisfy an English Court of Law, it would be a technical injustice to further detain the Turks in question. . . ." Finally, in order to save face in this matter, Rumbold considered that all the Turks except the 12 mentioned should be made available for exchange and, even contemplate the release of the four should the Ankara Government make that a condition for the release of British prisoners.[213] But, he said, " . . . we should, however, insist in any event on the retention of the eight Turks accused of cruelty to British prisoners of war."[214] In a communication[215] attached to Rumbold's report, General Harington agreed with the High Commissioner's views.

On September 6, 1921, 16 Turkish prisoners escaped from their confinement on Malta.[216] These men were technically prisoners but were given the designation of being on parole; that is, they had privileges of movement on the island not ordinarily given to regular prisoners. In such an instance, a prisoner gives his word of honour that, given certain "country club" privileges, he will not attempt to escape. British naval intelligence on September 27 reported that the escape was organized by Basri Bey and Rifky Bey at Rome.[217] A sailing boat was chartered with Basri Bey on board. The boat lay for eight hours in Malta harbour, presumably undetected. The escapees were transported to Messina (Sicily) and then went to Rome, where they were given passports to leave Italy.[218] Of the 16 escapees, 10 went to Germany and six to Anatolia. All 16 were accused of atrocities and scheduled to be brought up for trial.[219] The interesting point is that of the four prisoners accused of cruelty to native Christians, contemplated by the High Commissioner to be brought up for trial, three escaped with this group of 16. They were: 2719, Ahmed Muammer Bey; 2733, Memduh Bey; and 2774, Hassan Tahsin Bey. This situation, then, left nine prisoners who were liable for trial.

By mid-September, 1921, the Kemalist forces had already thwarted the Greek offensive and had, in fact, pushed the Greeks back. It would have been futile for the British at this juncture to attempt to bring to justice those Turks accused of various crimes. It could have been done only with the active participation of British military forces. This contingency of course was not about to take place.

On September 14, 1921, General Harington informed the War Office that the Ankara Government was favorably disposed to agree to an all for all exchange of all British prisoners for all Turkish prisoners.[220] On September 16, 1921, the War Office submitted its recommendation to the Secretary of State for Foreign Affairs, the Marquess Curzon, for his consideration.[221] The communication reiterated the development regarding the question of the 12 Turkish prisoners who were to be brought up for trial, and noted that three had already escaped, leaving one in custody, plus the eight others accused of cruelty to prisoners. The report said that the Army Council, after carefully considering the question of the eight internees, came to the conclusion that ". . . no military object would be gained by pursuing further charges against them. The Council fully admit that these individuals deserve punishment, and that such punishment might act as a deterrent to others, if similar circumstances should arise in [the] future; but they are advised that the collection of eye witnesses may prove no easy matter, owing to the lapse of time since the offences were committed, and that it is by no means sure that a conviction would result in every case, which would ensure the award of an exemplary sentence."[222] The Council, however, was gravely concerned regarding the health of the British prisoners in Anatolia. The Council believed that, if these prisoners remained in Anatolia, under great hardship and privation over another winter, they could be sure that several would die in captivity. The Army Council considered "... that it is vastly more important to save the lives of these British subjects than to bind ourselves by the strict letter of the law as regards the Turkish prisoners in Malta."[223] The Council, therefore, was prepared to reverse its claim to bring the eight Turkish prisoners to trial and hoped that Curzon would concur with this point of view and withdraw the charges against the eight. In addition, the Army Council hoped that the Foreign Secretary would exercise magnanimity in the case of prisoner No. 2800, Mustafa Abdel Halik, so that General Harington would have a free hand to initiate an all for all exchange.[224]

On September 19, 1921, the Foreign Office sent a telegram to the High Commissioner authorizing him to negotiate as he had proposed; and that the War Office was ready to forego the trial of the eight Turks, if release of all British prisoners could be secured before winter.[225]

On September 27, 1921, the Foreign Office sent a telegram[226] to Rumbold in Constantinople, to the effect that the Foreign Office and the Attorney General concurred in the proposal put forth by the War Office. The eight Turkish prisoners would be "... released unconditionally, claim to bring them to trial, whether by Turkish or other courts, being entirely waived . . . ."[227] The difficulty of collecting witnesses long after the offences would not ensure conviction. The "... gravity of the charges, the possible deterrent effect of trial and probability that release may lead to withdrawal of part or all Penalty Clauses of Treaty of Sèvres were fully realised but held to be outweighed by necessity of obtaining release of our prisoners before the winter." This being the case, the way was now open for an all for all exchange. In pursuance of this decision, on October 25, 1921, all 59 of the remaining Turkish prisoners were placed aboard H.M.S. *Chrysanthemum* and R.F.A. *Montenol* and transported to Constantinople. Seventeen high ranking officers were placed on H.M.S. *Chrysanthemum* because it had better accommodations; and 42 prisoners of lesser rank were placed on the *Montenol*. The British naval authorities included on the *Montenol* six Maltese servants who were to look after the comfort of the Turks.[228]

Almost all these men were accused of having committed the most heinous crimes yet recorded in modern history. The Allied Powers cast aside justice and honor, and replaced them with expediency and dishonor. From the Allied point of view, the question of Turkish war criminals ceased to exist.

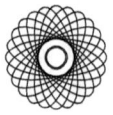

ENDNOTES

1. See FO 371/2488/63095, May 23, 1915.
2. Gerhard von Glahn, *Law Among Nations: An Introduction to Public International Law*. 2nd ed., London: The Macmillan Company, 1970, p. 699, *passim;* and Pamphlet No. 32, Division of International Law, *Report Presented to the Preliminary Peace Conference by the Commission on the Responsibility of the Authors of the War and on Enforcement of Penalties,* Introduction by James Brown Scott, 1919, p. 1, *passim,* contained in *American Journal of International Law,* No. 14, (1920), Supplement, pp. 95-154.
3. Pamphlet No. 32, p. 1.
4. *Ibid,* pp. 2 and 3.
5. *Ibid,* p. 3. Robert Lansing was selected as Chairman of Sub-Commission III.
6. *Ibid,* p. 4.
7. *Ibid,* p. 11 See also Fritz Fischer.
8. Pamphlet No. 32, p. 16.
9. *Ibid.*
10. *Ibid,* p. 17.
11. *Ibid,* pp. 17-19.
12. Not shown, but contained in the report.
13. *Ibid,* p. 19.
14. *Ibid,* p. 30.
15. *Ibid.*
16. *Ibid,* p. 34. While this paper will deal with offences committed in the Near East, (Asia Minor), Bulgarian authorities were also accused of offences committed against Greeks and Serbs in Macedonia.
17. *Ibid,* p. 35.
18. *Ibid.*
19. *Ibid.*
20. *Ibid,* p. 55.
21. *Ibid.*
22. *Ibid,* p. 19.
23. *Ibid.*
24. *Ibid.*
25. *Ibid.*
26. *Ibid.* p. 23.
27. *Ibid.* p. 24. This statement is taken from the Preamble to the Hague Conventions of 1899 and 1907.
28. *Ibid,* pp. 58-79.
29. *Supra,* p. 8.
30. *Ibid,* p. 24.
31. *Ibid,* p. 72.
32. *Ibid.*
33. *Ibid,* p. 74.
34. *Ibid.* p. 76. In view of the position taken by the U.S., it would appear that, while the U.S. outwardly bemoaned the destruction of the educational institutions established by American missionaries throughout Turkey, and the loss of American lives in Turkey, these aspects did not in any way alter the continued U.S. position of non-involvement in the Near East. The

posture taken by the American representatives on the Commission expressed the official sentiments of the U.S. Government.

35 The reasons given by the Japanese Government for their inability to go along with the Commission's decisions are contained in the report in Annex III, pp. 79-80.

36 For the German reaction to the Commission's report see *Papers Relating to the Foreign Relations of the United States, The Paris Peace Conference, 1919.* (Washington D.C.: Government Printing Office, 1947), Vol. VI pp. 781-794 and also pp. 874-876. Hereafter cited as P.P.C.

37 *P.P.C. 1919* Vol. XIII, pp. 371-380. The entire text of the Treaty of Versailles is contained in this volume, as well as other treaties. For the German reaction to the clauses of the Treaty of Versailles before it was signed on June 28, 1919, see *Foreign Relations P.P.C.* 1919, Vol. VI, specifically pp. 874-876.

38 This referred to the treaties guaranteeing the neutrality of Belgium and Luxemburg, April 19, 1839, and May 11, 1867 respectively.

39 *Foreign Relations P.P.C. 1919,* XIII pp. 374-375.
The Netherlands Government replied on June 7, 1919, that the Government of the Netherlands "must reserve to itself the free expenses of its sovereignty." And, on January 23, 1920, the Netherlands Government assisted that "If in the future there was instituted by the League of Nations an international jurisdiction competent to judge, in case of a war, acts that are qualified crimes and submitted to sanction by a prior statute, the Netherlands would properly associate itself with this regime."

40 The Turkish Government of Sultan Vehad-ed-Din wanted Talaat, Enver and Jemal Pashas, as well as Dr. Nazim and Dr. Beha-ed-Din Shakir, in order to bring them to justice before Turkish Courts-Martial. Subsequently these individuals were sentenced to death *in absentia* by the Turkish courts, since no extradition took place. It should also be noted that the British authorities in Berlin in 1920 were also aware of the whereabouts of these men and even had discussions with Enver Pasha.

41 The Treaty of Versailles provided for the establishing of a mixed Arbitral Tribunal for the arraignment and trial of suspected criminals. See "Treaty of Versailles" Part X, Section VI, Article 304, in *Foreign Affairs, P.P.C. 1919* Vol. XIII pp. 624-626.

42 *Ibid.* p. 377.

43 *Ibid.* p. 379.

44 *Ibid.*

45 See Glahn p. 700 for references regarding this subject. See also GEORGE SCHWARZENBERGER, *International Law and Totalitarian Lawlessness,* (London: Jonathan Cape, 1943).

46 Article 24 of the *Armistice (Mudros): The Ottoman Empire and the Allied Powers, 30 October, 1918* stated: "In case of disorder in the six Armenian vilayets, the Allies reserve to themselves the right to occupy any part of them." See Great Britain *Parliamentary Papers,* 1919, Cmd 53, pp. 25-27.

47 War Office to General Officer Commanding Constantinople F.O. 371/4173/74483, January 25, 1919.

48 F.O. 371/4173/73364, January 25, 1919.

49 *Ibid.*

50 W.O. to G.O.C. F.O. 371/4173/74483, January 25, 1919.
British military courts were set up in Syria, Mesopotamia and in Trans-Caucasia. The Foreign Office made it clear that it would be necessary to have "representatives of Allied Powers on such court . . ." since the British were "responsible that Armistice terms are enforced . . ." in Asia. See F.O. 371/4173/73364, January 25, 1919. Obviously, the British were opposed to

having French or Italian personnel present in the Caucasus, especially since the final outcome of what was to happen to Baku oil was yet to be determined. See Thomas A. Bryson "An American Mandate for Armenia: A Link in British Near Eastern Policy," *The Armenian Review*, Vol. XXI, (Summer, 1968), pp. 23-41.

51 See Laurence Evans, *United States Policy and the Partition of Turkey, 1914-1924*. Baltimore: The Johns Hopkins Press, 1965, especially Chapter IV. See also Michael Paillares, *Le Kemalisme Devant, Les Alliés*, Constantinople and Paris, 1922. Paillares was editor of the newspaper *Bosphore* (Constantinople).

52 F.O. 371/4173/75079, February 8, 1919.

53 *Ibid*. The Turkish Government was preparing ten zones in which Courts-Martial proceedings were to take place. More about this will be said below.

54 *Ibid*.

55 Cited in F.O. 371/4174/118377, August 1, 1919.

56 *Ibid*.

57 F.O. 371/4173/42787, March 5, 1919.

58 *Ibid*.

59 F.O. 371/4174/118377, August 1, 1919, p. 2.

60 *Ibid*.

61 F.O. 371/4173/98910, July 10, 1919. The Imperial Ottoman Government did attempt to extradite those it considered responsible for the war in the East, in order to bring these men to trial before courts-martial. After the Treaty of Versailles was signed, Damad Ferid made an official request from the German Government. The Germans agreed to extradite all individuals who had fled from Turkey *except*, Talaat, Enver and Jemal. The Ottoman Delegation to the Peace Conference sent a note to Mr. Clemenceau explaining the situation, and requested that he demand that the German authorities comply with the obligation imposed upon them by Articles 228 and 229 of the Treaty of Versailles. Further, the Ottoman authorities requested that the "German Government furnish the names of the banks in which these criminals have deposited considerable sums . . ." *Ibid*. The German Government did not comply. Subsequently, on July 5, 1919, the Turkish Courts-Martial, trying C.U.P. criminals, sentenced to death *in absentia*, Talaat Pasha, Enver Pasha, Jemal Pasha and Dr. Nazim, for their parts in the Armenian genocide and in being responsible for undermining the Ottoman Government during the tenure of the C.U.P. More about this in a later section.

62 Appendix "A" F.O. 371/4173/62442, 7 April, 1919.

63 *Ibid*. p. 8.

64 *Ibid*. The High Commission was of the opinion that the Turkish Courts-Martial proceedings were deleterious and, it would appear, the High Commission placed no credibility on the procedure or results of these proceedings; the High Commission was awaiting the formalization of the treaty between the Allied and Associated Powers and the Ottoman Empire in which would be spelled out the procedure for trials—similar to the German treaty. There is little doubt that this behavior undermined the morale of those Turkish officials who had, without Allied prodding, undertaken the initiative to bring to trial those persons suspected of committing various crimes. The German Government lacked such courage.

65 See F.O. 371/5090/5357, 9 May 1920.

66 F.O. 371/4173/62442, p. 11.

67 F.O. 371/4173/5335, 3 April, 1919.

68 See *P.P.C. 1919*, Vol. V, pp. 484, 467, 570-571, 717. In early May, the Italians had already landed troops on the South-Western coast of Turkey—Scala Nuova, in addition to Adalia. This operation was carried out by the Italians without the consent of the Council of "Three," since Orlando had returned to Italy and was not present in Paris. The Italians employed the

article of the Armistice under which the Allies could land forces if the breaches of the Armistice were executed. This action by the Italians was frowned upon by Wilson, Lloyd George and Clemenceau. It could very well be that in order to thwart Italian ambitions, the Allies were willing to pit the Greeks against the Italians, since both Greeks and Italians had been promised Smyrna and the Dodecanese islands. In addition, neither French nor British troops in large numbers were landed at Smyrna. As it turned out, the Greeks became the sacrificial lamb, for it became apparent, subsequently, that neither the French nor the British were prepared to thwart Turkish Nationalist action. While the French and British distrusted each other and each opposed the other's influence in Asia, both were doubly opposed to the Italian ambitions in Asia Minor.

69 F.O. 371/4174/88761, 30 May 1919.
70 F.O. 371/4174/118377, p. 5, 1 August 1919.
71 When relations between the Turkish Republic and Great Britain were normalized, Canon Whitehouse became Chaplain of the British Embassy.
72 F.O. 371/4174/88761, 30 May 1919.
73 *Ibid.*
74 *Ibid.* p. 3.
75 In a communication from the G.O.C. Army of the Black Sea to High Commission on 28 June, 1919, the report described the laxity regarding security in the Seraskerat prison.
  * Prisoners could mix freely with each other.
  * Prisoners had visitors all day long.
  * Visitors were not subject to inspection.
  * Women were allowed in all times during the day.
  * Turkish guards mixed freely with the prisoners.
  See F.O. 371/4174/105794, July 6 1919.
76 Appendix "B" F.O. 371/4174/105794, July 6 1919.
77 From Ali Djenany, ex-Deputy of Aintab; Edjzadji Mehmet, Erzingan; Ali Munif.
78 F.O. 371/5091/14130, 19 October, 1920.
79 Appendix "C" F.O. 371/6503/6728, June 11, 1921.
80 In August, 1919, Halil Pasha, uncle of Enver Pasha, and Küçük Talaat Bey, escaped from the military prison in Constantinople. This occurred even though Allied guards were stationed at the prison. Again, in August, 1919, Nuri Pasha, Enver's half brother, escaped from confinement in Batum. The British were responsible for the guarding of prisoners at Batum. See F.O. 371/4174/117662, 18 August, 1919.
81 B. Lewis, *The Emergence of Modern Turkey,* London: Oxford University Press, 1961, p. 240.
82 *Takvimi-i Vekayi* official gazette of the Ottoman Government.
83 *Takvim-i Vekayi.*
84 Article 88: The various categories of tribunals, their competency, functions and the compensation/fees of the judges are to be settled by law.
85 See *Le Spectateur d'Orient,* (Constantinople), July 12, 1919.
86 *Azadamart* (Constantinople), December 16, 1918. See also *Jamanag,* November 24, 1918, for the discussions of the Council of Ministers.
87 The January 7, 1919 issue of *Jagadamard,* reported that "Besides Constantinople, it has been decided to establish Courts Martial in Adana, Edirney, Yozgad, Brussa, Samson, Aintab, Ankara, Smyrna, Bandarma, and Rodosto. These Courts are charged with investigating the cases of those responsible for the deportation and massacres of Armenians."
88 *La Renaissance,* January 13, 1919.
89 It was a common occurrence for Valis to send such communications.
90 *La Renaissance,* December 22, 1918, No. 13; and May 1, No. 128; and May 4, No. 131.

[91] *La Renaissance*, December 24, 1918, No. 15.

[92] *La Renaissance*, December 27, 1918, No. 17.

[93] *La Renaissance*, December 22, 1918, No. 13.

[94] *Yeni Gun* as cited in *La Renaissance*, December 22, 1918, No. 13.

[95] See F.O. 371/4174/102551, 27 June, 1919.

[96] F.O. 371/3411/189162, 12 November, 1918.

[97] F.O. 371/3411/202004, 7 December, 1918.

[98] See F.O. 371/3411/206293, 13 December, 1918.

[99] See F.O. 371/3411/210622, 18 December, 1918.

[100] It would appear that, during this early period (1919-1920) the former members of the C.U.P. and the so-called Kemalist Nationalists, were working together. It should also be remembered that many former members of the C.U.P. were active members in the "Nationalist" movement. In addition, Lenin had come to an understanding with Enver Pasha – to aid the Turks – as early as 1919.

[101] *Nor Gyank*, 19 July (Sat.), 1919; and *Le Spectateur d'Orient*, 18 July 1919 (Fri.).

[102] *La Renaissance* 8 April 1920, No. 416.

[103] *La Renaissance* 10 December 1918, No. 2, Tuesday.

[104] See F.O. 371/4174/118392, 7 July 1919.

Djavid Bey subsequently worked for Mustafa Kemal, and was hanged by Kemal's order in the 1920s, accused of working against the State. For the verdict regarding Talaat, Jemal and Enver, see *Takvim-i Vekayi*, No. 3543, 8 May 1919, pp. 15-31.

[105] See *Takvim-i Vekayi*, No. 3604, 5 July 1919 pp. 217-220. See also F.O. 371/4174/118392, 7 July 1919.

[106] *La Renaissance*, 23 December 1918, No. 14.

[107] See *Takvimi-i Vekayi*, No. 3604, 5 July 1919, pp. 217-220. *Takvim-i Vekayi*, No. 3617, 7 August 1919, pp. 1-2. The *Takvim-i Vekayi* was the official gazette of the Turkish Government.

[108] See *La Renaissance*, 6 February 1919, No. 58; and *Jamanag*, 6 February 1919.

[109] *La Renaissance*, 6 February 1919, No. 58.

[110] See *Terjumani Hakikat*, 5 August 1920. This issue of the journal contains within it the statement "all these [massacres by order of the Turkish Government] are confirmed by the documents and decisive reports which can be found in the records of the Courts- Martial. . ."

[111] See *Takvim-i Vekayi*, No. 3571, 26 May 1919, pp. 127-140.

[112] See *La Renaissance*, 25 March 1919, No. 97.

[113] See *Takvim-i Vekayi*, No. 3604, (Vehib Pasha's written report of 5 December 1918 in reply to Mazhar Bey's order. Mazhar Bey was President of the Commission of Inquiry. He was also ex-Vali of Ankara.

[114] See *Takvim-i Vekayi*, No. 3617, 7 August 1919, pp. 1-2. Most of the telegrams exchanged between various officers were read at the courts martial proceedings. "Sentence of Yozgat."

[115] See *La Renaissance*, 19 February 1919.

[116] See *La Renaissance*, 20 February 1919.

[117] See *La Renaissance*, 7 March 1919, No. 82.

[118] See F.O. 371/4173/61185, 17 April 1919. See *Takvim-i Vekayi*, No. 3617, Session of 8 April 1919, "Sentence of Yozgat," 7 August 1919. For a full translation of the sentence and verdict, see Haigazn K. Kazarian, "A Turkish Military Court Tries the Principal Genocidists of the District of Yozgat," *The Armenian Review*, XXV, (Summer, 1972), pp. 34-39.

[119] See *Takvim-i Vekayi* No. 3604, 5 July 1919, session of 27 April 1919, Indictments.

[120] *Sabah,* as cited in *La Renaissance,* 19 January 1919, No. 40. Initially, the doctors were unaware of the purpose of this recruitment, but many reported that the men they had examined were mentally unfit for military or civil duty. Doctors gave examinations to prisoners incarcerated in prisons throughout the provinces.

[121] See *Takvim-i Vekayi* No. 3571, 26 May 1919, pp. 127-140.

[122] See *Trabzonda Meshveret,* June 13, 1915.

[123] See *La Renaissance,* March 27, 1919, No. 99, the first session of the Trebizond trial.

[124] See *Takvim-i Vekayi,* No. 3616, August 6, 1919. "Sentence of Trebizond," pp. 1-3. See *La Renaissance,* January 29, 1919.

[126] See Appendix "D," F.O. 371/5080/1346, 12 February 1920 and F.O. 371/5089/5746, May 16, 1920.

[127] F.O. 371/5090/949, 18 February, 1920.

[128] There were in fact two branches of this organization. One was formed for the purpose of disseminating propaganda in Muslim countries and to generally fan the flames of hatred against the British and French. For an explanation of the activities of this branch, see Philip H. Stoddard, "The Ottoman Government and the Arabs, 1911 to 1918: A Preliminary Study of the *Teshkilat-i Mahsusa*" (Unpublished Ph.D. dissertation, Princeton University, 1963) The other branch, as we have stated before, was for the sole purpose of exterminating the Armenian people.

[129] See F.O. 371/5089/6630, and 7334, Appendix "E," 26 May,1920; and 15 June, 1920.

[130] See Appendix "E," F.O. 371/5089/2293, 11 March 1920.

[131] *Major Peace Treaties of Modern History, 1648-1967.* Introduction by A. Toynbee, Ed. by Fred L. Israel, Vol. III, New York Chelsea House Publishers and McGraw-Hill Book Company, 1967, pp. 2134-2135.

[132] *Ibid.* See Articles 226–230, pp. 2134-2135, Penalty clauses of the Treaty of Sèvres.

[133] Though the Treaty of Sèvres was not ratified by the Allied Powers, certain clauses within it pertaining to minorities were included in the subsequent Treaty of Lausanne, signed on July 24, 1923, which is still a valid, internationally recognized instrument. See, for example, articles 37 – 44 in *Major Peace Treaties of Modern History, 1648-1967* Introduction by A. Toynbee, Ed. by Fred L. Israel, vol. IV, New York Chelsea House Publishers and McGraw-Hill Book Company, 1967, pp. 2316 – 2319.

[134] See 165036/ME/16, 1920.

[135] Major Eshref Bey was released by the British authorities from Malta on January 2, 1920, by order of the War Office. See F.O. 371/5089/37, 11 February, 1920. Eshref was reportedly released in error and was again placed on a list for arrest, circulated by the High Commissioner: "a most dangerous criminal propagandist." See F.O. 371/5090/1346, 12 February, 1920.

[136] See F.O. 371/5090/10431, 25 August, 1920. Appendix "G."

[137] *Ibid.*

[138] *Ibid.*

[139] *Ibid.* That the Army Council would consider releasing those prisoners suspected of inflicting cruelties on British prisoners of war is deplorable. Since this was the attitude of the Army Council regarding their own people, it is certainly vain to hope that the British authorities would place any importance as bringing to justice those persons responsible for the Armenian massacres.

For a description of what the British P.O.W.s went through during their captivity, see Ronald Millar, *Kut: The Death of an Army,* London: Secker and Warburg, 1969; and especially Russel Braddon, *The Siege,* London: Jonathan Cape, 1969, Chaps. 21-28.

[140] F.O. 371/5091/15116, November 24, 1920. Appendix "H."

[141] *Ibid.*

[142] *Ibid.*

[143] *Ibid.* Why the Military authorities were unable to work with the Committee is not clear. But, if the general ineptness of the British Command in the Middle East theatre of operations from the very beginning of that campaign is any indication, one need not look far for an answer. It is common knowledge, from Gallipoli on, that inter-service rivalry was rampant in the British forces, and the Command and General Staff conducted the campaign in the Near East as though the year was 1840, rather than the second decade of the twentieth century. It is likely that the Military did not appreciate being subordinate to a High Commissioner who was part of the naval branch or, subsequently, to a civilian.

[144] F.O. 371/5091/15116, p. 2. H_1 Appendix "A."

[145] *Ibid.*

[146] *Ibid.* Appendix H_2 Appendix "B."

[147] *Ibid.* Appendix H_3 Appendix "C."

[148] *Ibid.* Appendix H_4 Appendix "D."

[149] *Ibid.* Appendix H_5 Appendix "E."

[150] *Ibid.* Appendix H_6 Appendix "F."

[151] *Ibid.* p. 3.

[152] *Ibid.*

[153] Unofficial negotiations between Turkey and the Allies had been going on for some time; and British Military Intelligence was aware of these negotiations. See F.O. 371/5165/1428, July 13, 1920.

[154] British intelligence stated that a report from Ahmed Riza Bey, in Paris, to the Turkish Government dated January 1, 1920, in which Ahmed Riza is reported to have said that Millirand considered the return of Adana to Turkey possible "but . . . certain points regarding concessions to be made to France still remain to be discussed." Ahmed Riza had received this information from M. Petit of the French Foreign Ministry. British intelligence also reported that Ahmed Riza had seen the Italian Counselor " . . . with a view to settling the question of the Diarbekir-Caesarea-Birejik Railway Line . . . and that the Counselor had promised the support of Italy on the question of Smyrna, in return for concessions to be granted to that country [Italy] in the islands and in the province of Konia." See F.O. 371/5165/1428, July 13, 1920.

[155] A separate peace treaty was signed between the Kemalist Government and France on October 20, 1921, "ending a state of war between the two countries."

[156] See F.O. 371/5052/7993, July 8, 1920. In this report, while it is noted that the accuracy of the information being "purely derived from conversations with the Nationalist Cabinet," it can be seen in hindsight that the points mentioned in the Armistice were instrumental in influencing the French to cease hostilities against the Nationalists. As far as Cilicia was concerned, French business concerns were to have preferential treatment in the cotton enterprises; all patents and concessions in Cilicia were to be awarded to the French; no action against the Nationalist movement was to be taken by the French; and "the political aims of the Nationalist Government was to receive the unofficial support of France."

[157] See F.O. 371/4886/1985, July 13, 1920; F.O. 371/5167/5072, April 30, 1920, and Evans pp. 353-356.

[158] See F.O. 371/6466/2495, 21 February, 1921.

[159] *Ibid.*

[160] F.O. 371/6466/2846, 3 March, 1921.

[161] *Ibid.*

[162] *Ibid.*

[163] See Appendix "D": (B-129).

[164] Evans, pp. 349-350.

[165] F.O. 371/6500/3375, 17 March, 1921.

[166] In addition, the Nationalists asked the British to release the following six men: Jemal Bey, 2694; Mummer Bey, 2719; Sabit Bey, 2686; Shukri Bey, 2738; and Murad Bey, 2804. Aside from Jemal Bey, 2694, the other five were accused of direct or indirect complicity in massacres and atrocities, and were to be brought up for trial. The Foreign Office communicated with the High Commissioner in Constantinople in order to determine whether these men could be released.

[167] F.O. 371/6500/3552, 12 March, 1921.

[168] *Ibid.*

[169] See F.O. 371/6500/3557, 16 March, 1921. Of the 56 dossiers available, all are shown in this study. See Appendix "I."

[170] *Ibid.*

[171] F.O. 371/6500/3552, March 31, 1921.

[172] F.O. 371/6503/6311, June 1, 1921, No. 374.

[173] See Appendix "J."

[174] F.O. 371/6504/8519, July 13, 1921, No. 722.

[175] *Ibid.*

[176] *Ibid.*

[177] *Ibid.* It should be noted that the U.S. did not wish to become involved in any activity regarding the trials, especially in the Near East, since the U.S. was not and had not been engaged in a state of war against the Ottoman Empire.

[178] F.O. 371/6506/10117, September 1, 1921.

[179] See F.O. 371/6503/6187, May 30, 1921.

[180] *Ibid.*

[181] F.O. 371/6504/10117, September 1, 1921.

[182] *Ibid*

[183] *Ibid*

[184] See F.O. 371/6504/8745, July 29, 1921.

[185] F.O. 371/6500/3557, March 16, 1921.

[186] F.O. 371/6504/8745, July 29, 1921.

[187] *Ibid.*

[188] *Ibid.*

[189] *Ibid.*

[190] *Ibid.*

[191] *Ibid.*

192 *Ibid.*

193 *Ibid.* Article 230 referred to the Penalty Clause.

194 *Ibid.*

195 *Ibid.*

196 *Ibid.*

197 *Ibid.*

198 See F.O. 371/6504/9724, August 8, 1921, p. 256.

199 *Ibid.*

200 *Ibid.*

201 *Ibid.*

202 *Ibid.*

203 See F.O. 371/6504/10023, August 30, 1921.

204 *Ibid.* pp. 271-272.

205 *Supra.*

206 F.O. 371/6504/10023, August 30, 1921, p. 271.

207 *Ibid.*

208 *Ibid.*

209 *Ibid.*

210 The eight charged with cruelty to prisoners were Lt. Colonel Tewfik Mehmet (Mehmet Tewfik Bey), 2679; Colonel Tewfik Ahmed, 2680; Capt. Jemal Abdul Effendi, 2694; Colonel Jevad Ahmed Bey, 2700; Major Ibrahim Hakki Bey, 2710; Capt. Tahir Bey, 2745; Major Arif Mohammad Bey, 2767.

211 These included Ahmet Muammer Bey, 2719; Memduh Bey, 2733; Hasan Tahsin Bey, 2774; and Mustafa Abdul Halik, 2800.

212 While the Treaty was accepted by the Constantinople Government, the British were in fact dealing with the Nationalists at Ankara, who, it is clear, had already rejected the Treaty of Sèvres.

213 F.O. 371/6504/10023, August 30, 1921, p. 270.

214 *Ibid.*

215 *Ibid.* p. 273. No.A.F. 98/"L," August, 1921, Harington to Rumbold.

216 F.O. 371/6504/10319, September 8, 1921.

217 *Ibid.*

218 *Ibid.*

219 The escapees were: Sabit Bey, 2686; Nevzad Bey, 2696; Bedri Bey, 2701; Madjid Bey, 2704; Muammer Bey, 2719; Ghani Bey, 2723; Ahmet Bey, 2724; Memduh Bey, 2733; Faik Bey, 2737; Shukri Bey, 2738; Feizi Bey, 2743; Gen. Mahmud Kiamil, 2758; Tahsin Bey, 2774; Suleiman Nedjami Bey, 2812.

220 F.O. 371/6504/10411, September 16, 1921.

221 *Ibid.*

222 *Ibid.*

223 *Ibid.* p. 307.

224 *Ibid.* p. 308.

225 *Ibid.* Tel. No. 525, September 19, 1921.

[226] F.O. 371/6504/10662, September 27, 1921.
[227] *Ibid.*
[228] See F.O. 371/6505/12511, November 12, 1921. Appendix "K."

DOCUMENTS

APPENDIX "A"[*]

First List of Recommendations for Arrest, submitted to the Ottoman Government as of April 7, 1919.

British High Commission
Constantinople
7th April 1919.

First List of Recommendations for Arrest

Abdul Kader Pasha
President of U.&P. at Mardin, accused of organising massacres. Dr. Faradjalian, Armenian Catholic at Aleppo, witnesses that he saw him send the whole of the antiquities of the Armenian church to a German agent, Mme. Koch, at Aleppo.

Ahmed Agaoglou or Ahmed Agayeff
Encouraged and defended massacres in his German-subventioned paper, *Terjuman-i-Hakikat*. Bad recent record in Caucasus massacres. (Now under police surveillance).

Ahmed Nessimi Bey
Responsible for massacres as a member of the Cabinet and Central U.&P. Committee, 1915.

Ali Munif Bey
Governor General of Lebanon, organised starvation of population. Under-secretary of State for the Interior under Talaat during the massacres period.

Ali Nazmi
Public Prosecutor at Ankara, member of U.&P. organised massacre at Kirshehir. Evidence of eye-witnesses, Aram Fosbikian and Agop Terzie.

Dr. Mehmed Assaf
Now in Adana vilayat, travelling Government Doctor. Evidence of Sisak Nalbandian and Azniv Sayatian, that he organised Moush massacres. Accused of murder of Dr. Nerses Chahbaglian.

Atif Bey
Vali of Ankara during massacres.

Bedri Bey
Ex-Mutessarif of Mardin during massacres in 1915. Now believed in Constantinople, 13 Kapali Furnu, Eski Zaptie, Stamboul.

Major Burhaneddin
Ex-O.C. Kirshehir, now in Beshiktash. Aram Fosbikian and Agop Terzie, eye witnesses, state that he was in charge of groups of Armenians sent to the slaughter-place.

---

[*] F.O. 371/4173/62442, 7 April, 1919.

Kaimakam Kadri (Hafiz Nedjibzade)
Accused of burning children and drowning deportees at Palou. Now Mutessarif at Moush. Was Kaimakam at Palou during massacres.

Djevdet Bey
Ex-Vali of Van etc. Now in Smyrna, Pen-Marik on Quay. Much American evidence about him for massacres. Brother-in-law to Enver.

Feizi Bey
M.P. for Diarbekir. Accused of massacres and attempts to break Armistice. Now under arrest.

Ghani Bey
Now at 11 rue Anadol, Appartment Sarandi No. I Pera. Assisted Muammer in organising massacres at Sivas. U.&P. representative there. Accusation on authority of B.I.A. supported by personal evidence of Mr. Ohannes Cantar.

Hadji Ilias
M.P. at Moush. Now at Beshiktash, Orta Bagtche, Tchingflakli Bostan 134. Sisak Nalbandian and Azniv Sayatian, the latter of who escaped from his harem, accuse him of responsibility for massacres.

Dr. Hadji Mehmet Effendi
M.P. for Harpoot. American missionary, Mr. Riggs, accuses him of playing with Sabit the principal role in the massacres there.

Halid Bey (son of Hadji Tahir Pasha)
M.P. for Erzinjan. Believed at Constantinople; accused of "noyades" [drowning] of children (B.I.A.), hanging six men at Tortan and looting church. (Authority, Armenian Patricarchate).

Halil Bey
President of Council of State in 1915, must therefore share responsibility for massacres. Now under arrest.

Hilmi Bey
Ex-Mutessarif at Kirshehir, responsible for massacres. Evidenceof Aram Fosbikian and Agop Terzie, eye witnesses.

Ibrahim Bey
Ex-Minister of Justice 1915, shares responsibility for massacres.

Ihsan Bey
President of Samsoun Court Martial 1916/17. Stylianos Papadopoulos and George Maurides give sworn evidence that he hanged 200 Greek peasants.

Ismail Djamboulat
Ex-M.P. for Constantinople and Prefect of Police during massacres. Now in prison.

Ismail Hakki
Vali of Adana during massacres during period 1915/16.

Appendix "A"

Kairi Bey
As Sheik-ul-Islam during 1915, shares responsibility for massacres.

Professor Kiazim Bey
Now Director of Sultanie school at Smyrna. Evidence of complicity in the Kirshehir massacres (Aram Fosbikian and Agop Terzie).

Midhat Shukri Bey
Secretary-General of U.&P. during massacres and therefore must share responsibility.

Muammer Bey
Ex-Vali for Sivas. Responsible for massacres there. Now under arrest.

Mustafa Sheriff Bey
Ex-Minister of Commerce 1915/16, and must share responsibility.

Oghuz Djemal Bey
Leading U.&P. man, responsible for massacres, extortion and Tchangiri. Evidence of Mr. Garabedian secretary of Armenian Patriarchate, eye-witness.

Rafet or Rifat Pasha
Ex-Military Governor of Samsoun; sworn evidence of Stylianos Papadopoulos and Yorghios Mayrides that he burnt 178 villages and deported whole of Greek population.

Sabit Bey
Vali of Harpoot, now under arrest. American missionary, Mr. Riggs, accuses him of complete responsibility for massacres.

Said Halim Pasha
Ex-Grand Vizier, now under arrest. A Grand Vizier in 1915/17 must share responsibility for massacres.

Shukri Bey
Ex-Minister for Education in 1915. Must share responsibility for massacres.

Tahsin Bey
Vali of Erzeroum during massacres.

Zekaria Bey
Kaimakam of Rodosto during deportations and rewarded to vilayet of Adrianople; bad record.

Zeki or Salih Zeki Bey
Ex-Mutessarif of Der-Zor, promoted to be mektoubdji at Constantinople. Now in Scutari. Evidence of Dr. Faradjalian that he personally superintended massacres at Rakkie from start to finish: evidence of Kevork through Mr. Ryan that he played the leading role in the events at Caesarea: corroboration of B.I.A.

Zulfi Bey
Ex-Deputy of Diarbekir, accused of massacres and attempts to break Armistice. Under arrest.

Faik
Kaimakam of Merzifoun, app. Scoure No. 3, Nishantash.

Mahmoud Kiamil
Commander of the gendarmerie at Meraifoun. Now in Constantinople.

Dr. Suleiman Nouman

Feizi
Formerly Deputy of Diarbekir.

Eulfi
Formerly Deputy of Diarbekir.

Veli Nedjdet
Formerly at Diarbekir, at present employed in the Directorate of the Refugee Committee.

Bedri
Formerly Secretary of the Vilayet Diarbekir, and later Governor of Mardin. Now living in No.13, near Kapali Fouroun, Eski-Zaptie, Stamboul.

Atif
Formerly Governor of the Vilayets Ankara and Castamouni.

Tahsin
Formerly Governor of Syria.

Ali Numif
Formerly under Secretary of State for the Interior.

Nail
Head of the C.U.P. at Trebizond.

Ahmed Aghaieff
Now living at Cadikeuy.

Mahmoud Nedim
Formerly Deputy of Ourfa.

Sheikh Savfet
Formerly Deputy of Ourfa.

Halet
Formerly Deputy of Erzindjian.

Salih Zeki
Formerly Kaimakam of Develi.

Zekeria
Formerly Governor of the Vilayet Adrianople.

Rechad
Formerly head of the political department of the Directorate General of the Police.

Mahir
Formerly Commander of gendarmerie at Merzifoun. To be found in Constantinople, although disappeared from his residence at Arnaoutkeuy.

Kiremitdjizade Hadi

Merchant. Has shown great activity at merzifoun. Now living at App. Gelerini No.11, Nishantash.

Tevfik

Formerly President of Court Martial at Caesarea. Gendarmerie Officer.

Zekiai

Formerly Head of the C.U.P. organization at Kirshehir. Now in Constantinople. Some days ago he was delivered to the Police station of Emin Eunu, by two Armenians who accused him of having murdered their parents. After a while the Officer of the Police station has left him free.

Serey Bey

Mutessarif of Amassia. Formerly at Kharput and connected with massacres there. Has been distributing arms at Amassia.

LIST OF OFFICIALS IMPRISONED IN COURT MARTIAL PRISON

Name	Position	Date of arrest
1. Hilmi Bey Bin Mehmed	Governor of Kirk-Kilisse	January 5
2. Mehmed Tevfik bin Osman	Commdr. Gendarm. Tchoroum	January 6
3. Niazi Bey Bin Zekaria	Merchant in Trebizond	January 6
4. Mehmet Ali Bin Hadji Ahmed	Custom Officer of Trebizond	January 6
5. Agent Bey Bin Moustafa	Merchant	January 6
6. Mehmed Kemal Bin Arif	Governor of Bogazlian (Kaza)	January 7
7. Izzet Eff. Bin Chevket	Secretary of Court of Appeal of Ankara	January 13
8. Ali Eff. Bin Ismail	Ass. Police Commissaire Ankara	January 13
9. Ibrahim Nessib Bey Bin Faik	Second Class Police Commissaire at Ankara	January 13
10. Harum Bey Bin Halil	Lieutenant	January 13
11. Sabit Bey Bin Moustafa Vehbi	Former Vali of Sivas	January 14
12. Mehmed Memdouh Bin Tayar	Former Vali of Mosoul	January 18
13. Madjid Bey Bin Nedjib	Inspector of Department of Accounts	January 21
14. Ahmed Mouammer Bey Bin Mehmed Sami	Former Vali of Sivas	January 21
15. Riza Bay Bin Ali	Member of Central Committee of C.U.P.	January 23
16. Hassan Effendi	Policeman at Eskishehir	January 26
17. Captain Djemal Effendi	Comm. Nouhafiz Buluk	January 27
18. Ali Osman Bin Ali Osman	Former Vali of Broussa	January 30
19. Feyaz Ali Bin Loutfi	Evkef Memourou of Yozgat	February 2
20. Ibrahim Bey Bin Sadreddin	Inspector of C.U.P. Broussa	February 6
21. Muhendis Midhat Alias Mihran Yazidjian	Merchant in Caesarea	February 9
22. Captain Hevzad EffendiMilitary	Governor of Mosoul	February 18
23. Tchakir Redjeb Bin Ahmed	Ashik Pasha quarter of Kirshehir	February 20
24. Mazloum Bey	Cdr. Of Garrison of Afion-Kara Hissar	February 20
25. Nouri Eff. Bin Eumer	Police Officer, Yozgat	February 20
26. Abdulhadi Eff. Alias Carabed	Appartements Galerina Pangalti C'ple	February 24
27. Mehmed Eff. Bin Ibrahim	Tchanak Mahalle, Yozgat	February 26
28. Shukri Eff. Bin Suleyman	Tchanak Mahalle, Yozgat	February 26
29. Abdullah Eff. Bin Tevfik	Eski Pazar Mahalle, Yozgat	February 26
30. Dervish Eff. Bin Ali	Nohourdlou Zuber Mahalle, Yozgat	February 26
31. Corporal Ismail Bin Moustafa Daghtanli Zade		February 26
32. Osman Talaat Bey Bin Ali	Director of School of Gendarmerie	February 28
33. Noury Bey Bin Mehmed	Director of the Vilayet of Trebizond	February 28
34. Dr. Ali Saib Bey	Former Sanitary Inspector Trebizond Vilayet	March 3
35. Selaheddin Effendi	Merchant	March 12
36. Stamat Veledi Sotiry		March 13
37. Rahmi BeyFormer	Governor of Smyrna	February 17
38. Riza Hamid Bey	Former Deputy of Broussa	February 17
39. Ahmed Bey Bin Ibrahim	Former Governor of Sivas	February 17
40. Hussein Djahid Bey Bin Ali Riza	Former Deputy of Constantinople	February 17
41. Tevfik Hadi Bey Bin Moustafa	Former Director of the Police	February 17
42. Hussain Kadri Bey Bin Ahmed	Former Deputy of Carassi	February 17
43. Ibrahim Bedreddin Bey	Former Vali of Diarbekir	February 17

Appendix "A"

44.	Ruchdi Bey Bin Hadji Hussein	Physician	February 17
45.	Agiah Bey Bin Ahmed Noury	Lt. Col. In retreat	January 31
46.	Ismail Djanbolat Bey	Former Minister of Interior	February 17
47.	Hussein Tossoun Bey	Former Deputy of Erzeroum	February 17
48.	Dervish Mehmed Bin Hadji Ahmed	Official of the Privy List	February 17
49.	Ali Shouhouri Effendi	Governor of the Bagtchedjik Nahie (former)	March 10
50.	Ahmed Vahbi Eff. Bin Houloussi	Former Governor of the Nahie Derbend	March 10
51.	Ahmed Tchaoush Bin Moustafa		March 10
52.	Vehib Pasha	Comm. of Group of Ott. 5th Army Corps	March 10
53.	Selaheddin Bin Tahir	Former Director of Military flour mill "Tahnie"	February 17
54.	Seifeddin Bey Bin Riza	Former Director of Intell. Dept.	January 19
55.	Selaheddin Bey Bin Mehmed Ali	Control Officer of the War Off.	February 17
56.	Moustafa Salim Bey Bin Ismail	Prof. at Ottoman Engineering School, C'ple,	February 17
57.	Suleyman Nouman Pasha	Former Sanitary Inspector of Troops	January 19
58.	Zia Geuk Alp Bey	Former Deputy of Argani-Maden	February 17
59.	Suleyman Soudi EffendiFormer	Deputy of Lazistan	February 17
60.	Hadji Adil Bey	Former President of the Ottoman Senate	February 17
61.	Mahmoud Kiamil Pasha	Former Commander of the 5th Army	February 21
62.	Ferid Bey Bin Djemil Eff.	Clerk in the C.U.P. offices Cons/ple	February 17
63.	Kemal Bey	Former Minister of revictualling	February 17
64.	Ahmed Djevad Bey, Col.	Former Military Governor of C'ople	January 29
65.	Carasso Effendi	Former Deputy of Constantinople	February 17
66.	Mehmed Rifaat Bey	First Lieutenant	February 9
67.	Midhat Shukry Bey	Former Deputy of Bourdour	February 17
68.	Izzet Bey Bin Emin, Major	Surgeon of Tokat Hospitals	February 17
69.	Veli Nedjdet Bey Bin Hassan		February 17
70.	Habib Bey	Merchant and former Deputy of Bolou	March 16
71.	Izzet Bey	Director of "Ekmekdji Shirket"	March 16
72.	Sabandjali Hakki Bey	Merchant	March 16
73.	Hassan Fehmi Bin Hadji Hassan	Former Deputy of Synope	March 16
74.	Nafi Bey Bin Mehmed	Bank of Salonica, Galata, Merchant	March 16
75.	Abdulkerim Effendi	Former Police Merkez-Memour	March 16
76.	Djaberzade Hilmi Bey	Former Deputy of Ankara	March 16
77.	Selah Djimdjoz Bey	Former Deputy of Constantinople	March 16
78.	Fazil Bey	Former Deputy of Changiri	March 16
79.	Ali Munif Bey	Former Minister of Public Works	March 16
80.	Moustafa Rechid Bey	Former Mutessarif of Bolou	March 16
81.	Said Halim Pasha	Former Grand Vizir	March 16
82.	Rifaat Bey	Former President of the Ottoman Senate	March 16
83.	Ibrahim Bey	President of the Council of State	March 16
84.	Fethi Bey	Former Minister of Interior and Deputy of Constantinople	March 16
85.	Halil Bey	Former Minister of Justice	March 16
86.	Ismail Mishkat Bey	Secretary of the Senate	March 16
87.	Shukri Bey	Former Minister of Public Instr.	March 16
88.	Kiazim Bey, Major	Comm. of the Garrison of Yozgat and Malgara	March 17
89.	Sherif Bey	Comm. of the Garrison of Ankara	March 17
90.	Abdulkadir Bey	Assist. President of Sanitary Corps of 6th Army	March 17
91.	Youssouf Zia Bey	Inspector of Prisoners' Camps	March 17
92.	Moussa Kiazim Effendi	Former Sheich-ul-Islam	March 17
93.	Kemal Bey, Major G.S.	Member of the Court Martial	March 18

94.	Mehmed Tevkif Bey Bin Youssouf	Lt. Col. In retreat	March 18
95.	Moustafa Abdulhalik Bey	Former Governor of Broussa	March 18
96.	Ahmed Agaieff Bey	Former Deputy of Kara-Hissar	March 20
97.	Nessimi Bey	Former Minister of Foreign Affairs	March 20
98.	Major Hazim Bey		March 20
99.	Osman Nafiz Bey	Colonel in retreat	March 20
100.	Ihsan Bin Namik Ibrahim	Representative of the Perrier Bank in C'ple	March 20
101.	Fazil Bey Bin Mehmed Ali	Merchant	March 20
102.	Ihsan Bey	Adjutant of the Minister of the Marine	March 21
103.	Galib Bey	Former Deputy of Carassi	March 22
104.	Halil Fahri Bey	Former Inspector of Public Security	March 23
105.	Ismail Hakki Bey	Tenant of AKIET YOURDOU at Chekirgui (Broussa)	March 24
106.	Faik Bey		February 17
107.	Ahmed Tevfik Bey, Colonel		February 19

APPENDIX "B"*

Conditions at the Seraskerat Prison, and the names of the detainees.

FROM: The General Officer Commanding-in-Chief, Army of the Black Sea, Constantinople.

TO: His Excellency, The British High Commissioner, Constantinople.

> General Headquarters,
> Constantinople.
> 28th June 1919.

Your Excellency,

    I have the honor to acknowledge the receipt of your letter No.R.1632 dated the 8th instant and in reply to state that the arrangements which at present exist at SERASKERAT prison are not considered sufficiently adequate to ensure the proper supervision of safeguard of the persons confined therein, owing to the laxity and lack of system of control prevailing there. The following points have been noted:

a) All prisoners, of whom there are 112, are allowed to walk about the prison and mix freely together during the day.

b) Visiting hours for friends are supposed to be between 12:00-14:00 hours daily, but these hours are not kept to, and individuals may be seen going and coming from the prison throughout the day.

c) Except for a casual glance at their passes, individuals are not subject to any inspection on entering the prison, and large packets are often to be seen being carried in by individuals, stated to be food, but might be anything.

d) Women are allowed in all times during the day, and are never inspected.

e) Turkish soldiers who are detailed to look after the prisoners mix freely with them, moving in and out of the prison at will, and if susceptible to bribery it would be very easy for them to aid a prisoner's escape.

    Attached are two copies of the list of all prisoners at present confined in SERASKERAT Prison. Of these the list marked "A" supplied by SAID BEY, Commandant de la Ville, showing the members of the C.U.P. or Young Turk party under arrest differs from the list marked "B" supplied by the Prison Authorities, who were asked

---

* F.O. 371/4174/105794, July 6 1919.

for the same information. It is to be noted that in neither case is CARASSO shown to belong to the C.U.P. or Young Turk Party.

It is presumed that the persons in the attached lists are the men referred to in the copy telegram from the Foreign Office (No.9609 dated 5th June) accompanying your letter.

        I have the honour to be,
        Your Excellency's obedient Servant,

        (signed) for

        General,
        Commanding-in-Chief,
        THE ARMY OF THE BLACK SEA.

A
List of members of Party of Union & Progress now under arrest, supplied by SAID BEY, Commandant de la Ville.

1.	Secretary of the "Reform Party"	Hussein Selaheddin Bey
2.	Member of Central Committee of C.U.Party	Telaat Bey
3.	Representative of U.P.P. at Eskishehir	Dr. Bessim Zihdi Bey
4.	Inspector of U.P.P. at Erzindjian	Abdul Gahani Bey
5.	Secretary of U.P.P. at Gyumush Souyou	Mehmet Djemal Bey
6.	Representative of U.P.P. at Mirgun	Djevet Bey
7.	Secretary of U.P.P. at Manisa	Avni Bey
8.	President of "Reform Party"	Hussein Hussni Pasha
9.	Ex-Director of Intelligence Branch	Seiffreddin Bey
10.	Director of Bakers' Union	Izzett Effendi
11.	Ex-Mutessarif of Bolu	Mustafa Rachad bey
12.	Ex-Vali of Hudavendikiar	Mustafa Abdul Halik Bey
13.	Lt. Col.	Aziz Bey
14.	Ex-Chief Accountant of Yozgat	Vehdi Bey
15.	Representative of U.P.P. at ADA BAZAR	Hamid Bey
16.	Ex-Commandant de la Place	Shehaheddin Bey
17.	Ex-secretary of U.P.P. at Makrikeuy	Hassan Fahmi Bey
18.	G.O.C. 6th Army	Khalil Pasha
19.	Member of Central Committee of U.P.P.	Hussein Zade Ali Bey
20.	Municipal Sanitary Officer at Ghemlik.	Zia Bey

B
List provided by Prison Authorities of members of C.U.P. party under arrest.

Name	Prison Number	Remarks
1. Dervish Mehmet Bey	57	
2. Hussein Salaheddin Bey	62	(1)
3. Izzet Bey	82	(10)
4. Pres. of Senate Riffat Bey	93	In hospital Gyumush Souyou
5. Mousa Kiazim Effendi	104	
6. Osman Nazif Bey	112	
7. Khalil Fahri Bey	119	
8. Lt. Col. Aziz Bey	125	(13)
9. Hussein Remzi Bey	129	
10. Mehmet Nazif Bey	130	
11. Hussein Nejati Effendi	131	
12. Ahmed Ali Bey	133	
13. Hussein Djevdet Bey	137	
14. Mehmet Telaat Bey	141	
15. Abdul Kadir Effendi	142	
16. Dr. Bessim Zihtu	148	(3)

17. Ali Effendi	149		
18. Ahmed Rifki Bey	151		
19. Avni Bey	156	(7)	
20. Elias Sami Bey	158		In asylum at Timar Hane Scutari
21. Hamid Bey	159	(15)	
22. Midhat Bey	167		
23. Yunus Vasfi Effendi	188		
24. Mehmet Djemal Effendi	189	(5)	
25. Mehmet Shukru Effendi	253		
26. Mehmed Kiamil Effendi	254		
27. Emin Bey	274		
28. Chalib Bey	310		
29. Hashim Bey	318		
30. Zia Bey	319	(20)	
31. Mehmet Nouri Bey	320		
32. Djevdet Bey	326	(6)	
33. Mahmoud Effendi	327		
34. Hussni Pasha	328	(8)	
35. Hussein Ali Bey	330		
36. Nihat Bey	335		
TOTAL	36		

Note: Number in brackets refers to List A.

Appendix "B"

The following have been arrested under Martial Law and are imprisoned at SERASKERAT Prison.*

1. Izzet Effendi — Secretary of the Ankara Court of Appeal 13-1-19 charged with deportations.
2. Ali Effendi — sous commissionaire de police Ankara, 13-1-19 charged with deportations.
3. Lieut. Haroun Eff. — 13-1-19 deportations.
4. Hassan Effendi — Policeman at Eski Sheir. 26-1-19 deportations.
5. Feyz Asli Bey — in charge of the Evkaf at Yozgad, 2-2-19 deportations.
6. Chakir Rejeb — from Kir Sheir, 20-2-19 (at present in Haidar Pasha Hospital) deportations.
7. Mehmed Effendi — native of Bostepe from Yozgad, 26-2-19 deportations.
8. Shukri Effendi — from Yozgad, 26-2-19 do.
9. Tewfik Zade Abdullah Eff. — from Eski Bazar district, 26-2-19 do.
10. Dervish Effendi — son of Jian Yozgad, 26-2-19 do.
11. Daghistanli Zade Corporal Ismail 26-2-19 do.
12. Dr. Ali Saib Bey — Ex-Director of medical dept. in Trebizond 3-3-19 deportations.
13. Staff Lt. Col. Agiah Bey — 13-1-19 deportations.
14. Dervish Mehmed Bey — working in the Imperial Treasury 17-2-19 charged with disturbing internal security.
15. Ali Shuori Eff. — Ex-Mudir of the Bagoodjik Nahie 10-3-19 deportations.
16. Vehiji Effendi — Ex-Mudir of the Derbend Nahie 10-3-19 deportations.
17. Ahmed Chaouch — 10-3-19 do.
18. Vehib Pasha Ex. — G.O.C. 3rd Army, 10-3-19 do.
19. Hussein Selheddin Bey — Responsible secretary at Pera of the Reform (Tejedud) Party, 17-2-19 disturbing internal security.
20. Lt. Col. Seiffeddin — Ex-Chief of the Intelligence Department charged with betrayal of confidence 10-1-19.
21. Emmanuel Carasso Effendi — Ex-Deputy of Constantinople charged with hoarding (accaparement) 17-2-19.
22. Izzet Effendi — director of Bakers' Union Society 16-3-19 charged with hoarding (accarpement).
23. Sabanjali Hakki Bey — tradesman 16-3-19 charged with hoarding (accarpement).
24. Mustafa Reshad — 16-3-19 Ex-Mutessarif of Boli charged with exiling.
25. Refaat Bey — Ex-president of Senate (at present in Gumush Souyou Hospital) 13-3-19, disturbing internal security.
26. Mussa Kazin Effendi — Ex-Sheik-ul-Islam 17-3-19 disturbing internal security.
27. Mustafa Abdul Halik Bey — Ex-Vali of Brussa 19-3-19 charged with murder.
28. Retired Col. Osman Nafiz Bey Charged with disturbing internal security 20-3-19.
29. Ihean Namik Bey — representative in Constantinople of Perrier Bank 20-3-19 charged with hoarding (accarpement).
30. Fazil Bey — tradesman 20-3-19 charged with hoarding (accarpement).
31. Halil Fahri Bey — Ex-inspector of Public Security charged with disturbing internal security 20-3-19.
32. Lt. Col. Aziz Bey — do. 26-3-19.
33. Hussein Remzi Bey — from the Custom House Stamboul do. 27-3-19.
34. Mehmed Nazif Bey — Merchant do. 27-3-19.

---

* Item numbers 27-50 are repeated in the following list with minor variations in spelling as 51-77

35. Hussein Nejatti Eff. — Coffee house owner. Do. 27-3-19.
36. Ahmed Ali Eff. — From Export Custom House. Do. 27-3-19.
37. Vehbi Bey — accounted at Yozgad, deportations and massacres.
38. Talaat Bey — member of the Central Committee of U.P.P. 30-3-19. disturbing internal security.
39. Abdul Kadir — teacher at Konia, 30-3-19, deportations.
40. Doctor Bessim Zuhdi Bey — representative of U.P. at Eski Shehir 31-3-19 disturbing internal security.
41. Ali Effendi — farmer at Adrianople do. 31-3-19.
42. Ahmed Rifki Eff. — Ex-Major of Adrianople do. 31-3-19.
43. Abdulgani Bey — Inspector of U.P.P. at Erzindjian 1-4-19. betrayal of confidence.
44. Avni Bey — responsible secretary of U.P.P. at Manisa 1-4-19. disturbing internal security.
45. Elias Sami Bey — Ex-Deputy of Mush (at present in Haidar Pasha Hospital) 2-4-19. disturbing internal security.
46. Hamid Bey — U.P. representative at Ada Bazar. 2-4-19 deportations.
47. Essad Bey — asst. director of Public Security Directorate 2-4-19 murder.
48. Bekir Effendi tanner — at Ankara 3-4-19 deportations.
49. Mehmet Hidayet Eff. — policeman 7-4-19 do.
50. Mushtak Bey — Ex-Mutessarif of Ertougral 8-4-19 disturbing internal security.
51. Shehabeddin Bey — Ex-Commandant de la Place, oppression 8-4-19.
52. Yunus Vasfi Eff. — Director of the medical department of Konia 8-4-19 disturbing internal security.
53. Mehmed Djemal Bey — responsible secretary of U.P.P. at Konia 8-4-19 disturbing internal security.
54. Fazil Bey — tradesman 20-3-19, charged with hoarding (accarpement).
55. Halil Fahri Bey — Ex-inspector of Public Security, charged with disturbing internal security.
56. Lt. Col. Aziz Bey — do 26-3-19.
57. Hussein Remzi Bey — from the Custom House, Stamboul do 27-3-19.
58. Mohmed Hazif Bey — Merchant, do 27-3-19.
59. Hussein Nejatti Eff. — Coffee house owner do. 27-3-19.
60. Ahmed Ali Eff. From — Export Custom House do 27-3-19.
61. Vebbi Bey — accountant at Yozgad, deportations and massacres.
62. Talaat Bey — member of the Central Committee of U.P.O. 30-3-19. disturbing internal security.
63. Abdul Kadir teacher — at Konia, 30-3-19, deportations.
64. Doctor Bessim Zuhdi Bey — representative of U.P. at Eski Shehir 31-3-19 disturbing internal security.
65. Ali Effendi — farmer at Adrianople do. 31-3-19.
66. Ahmed Rifki Eff. — Ex-Major of Adrianople do. 31-3-19.
67. Abdulgani Bey — Inspector of U.P.P. at Erzindjian 1-4-19. betrayal of confidence.
68. Avni Bey — responsible secretary of U.P.P. at Manisa 1-4-19. disturbing internal security.
69. Elias Sami Bey — Ex-Deputy of Mush (at present in Haidar Pasha Hospital) 2-4-19. disturbing internal security.
70. Hamid Bey — U.P. representative at Ada Bazar. 2-4-19 deportations.
71. Essad Bey — asst. director of Public Security Directorate 2-4-19 murder.
72. Bekir Effendi — tanner at Ankara 3-4-19 deportations.
73. Mehmet Hidayet Eff. — policeman 7-4-19 do.
74. Mushtak Bey — Ex-Mutessarif of Ertougral 8-4-19 disturbing internal security.

Appendix "B"

75.	Shehabeddin Bey	Ex-Commandant de la Place, oppression 8-4-19.
76.	Yunus Vasfi Eff.	Director of the medical department of Konia 8-4-19 disturbing internal security.
77.	Mehmed Djemal Bey	responsible secretary of U.P.P. at Konia 8-4-19 disturbing internal security.
78.	Captain Ferid Eff.	of Mosul 4-5-19, betrayal of confidence.
79.	Djemal Ougous Bey	3-4-19, Murder (at present in hospital).
80.	Ibrahim Fehmi Eff.	Mudir of Jihanbekli Nahie, deportations.
81.	Mehmed Kiamil Eff.	Major of Ak Shehir 8-4-19, disturbing internal security.
82.	Emin Bey	Controller of Revenue and Expenditure in the Vilayet of ADRIANOPLE 7-5-19, do.
83.	Hassan Fehmmi Eff.	Ex-responsible secretary of U.P.P. Macrikeuy deportations 15-5-19.
84.	Ghalib Bey	Chief Controller of the Regie at Ismid 17-5-19 disturbing internal security.
85.	Djeydet Bey	representative of U.P.P. at Emirghian. Do.
86.	Circassian Limping Suleiman	8-4-19 (in hospital) deportations (no.185).
87.	Hashim Bey	Ex-Minister of Posts and Telegraphs disturbing internal security.
88.	Baki Bey	of Sapanji, son of Mehmet, merchant 16-4-19 hoarding (accarpement).
89.	Doctor Midhat Bey	3-4-19, disturbing internal security.
90.	Zia Bey	Municipal doctor at Gemlik 4-6-19 do. 111 treatment of Ps of W.
91.	Major Kiazim Bey	O.C. Yozgad P. of W camp 17-3-19 (at present in hospital).
92.	Colonel Yussuf Zia Bey	inspector of P.of W. camp (in hospital) 17-3-19, do.
93.	Major Abdul Baki Bey	President of P.W. Committee 26-3-19 (in hospital) do.
94.	Captain Tahir Eff.	O.C. Ankara construction Coy. 30-3-19 do.
95.	Retired Captain Hilmi Eff.	2-4-19 do.
96.	Lt. Gen Halil Pasha	Ex. G.O.C. 6th Army 7-4-19, betrayal of confidence.
97.	Surgeon Col. Hilmi Bey	Ex-Chief Medical Officer at Haidar pasha Hospital charged with ill-treatment of P. of W. 8-4-19.
98.	Surgeon Major Fuad Kiamil Bey	Ex-acting Chief Medical Officer Haidar Pasha Hospital 9-4-19 charged with ill-treatment of P.of W.
99.	Field Cashier Izzet Effendi	10-4-19 do.
100.	Mehmed Nouri Bey	Ex-Deputy of Dersim 4-6-19, murder and pillage.
101.	Djevdet Bey	9-6-19 disturbing internal security.
102.	Reserve Officer Mahmoud Effendi	9-6-19 do.
103.	Hussein Hussni Pasha	Senator President of the Reform (Tejedul) Party 10-6-19, arrested without stated cause.
104.	Hussein Zade, Aly Bey	12-6-19 do
105.	Hassan Effendi Tradesman	29-5-19 deportations.
106.	Keur Riza	7-6-19 fooding accarpement and pillage.
107.	Binbashi Zade Ali Effendi	18-6-19 do.
108.	Policeman Nouri Effendi	20-2-19 deportations.
109.	Hadji Abbas Eff.	of Yozgad 9-6-19 do.
110.	Hadji Youdsouf Effendi	of Yozgad 19-6-19 do.
111.	Nihad Bey	Director of Ada BAZAR factory 19-6-19 hoarding accarpement.
112.	Commissaire de Police Ibrahim Effendi	13-1-19 deportations.

Note:- This list is correct to 22/6/19. The dates given against each name refer to the date of arrest.

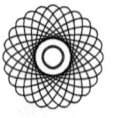

APPENDIX "C"[*]

Petition from prisoners on Malta.

Polverista,
May 12, 1921

To His Excellency,
The Governor and Commander in Chief,
Malta.

Your Excellency,

When the British invaded Constantinople after the Armistice, they were approached by two classes of people. One of them was composed of a limited number of Turks who wanted to use the British as an instrument for exterminating political rivals and obtaining power. The second class consisted of Armenians and Greeks of suspicious character who wanted to sell their services to the invaders in capacities of spies, secret agents, and interpreters.

Both of these classes had the common interest of eliminating the enlightened and patriotic members of the Turkish nation.

They were prompted by personal interests, racial hatred, political rivalry, and business competition.

As a result of their intrigues, and denunciations, the British were induced to disregard every principle and notion of international law. They seized us, partly two years ago, partly after the occupation of Constantinople on March 16, 1920, from our homes, from the Parliament, from Government offices, business places and streets, and deported us to Malta.

It is a plain fact that the British authorities have no sort of competence to deprive us of our personal liberty; the British courts have no justification over us; and the British Attorney General has no authority to bring charges against us. Therefore, we could not be considered under arrest in accordance with British laws.

We can not be considered war prisoners, as we have been arrested and deported after the Armistice, on the other hand, the international law does not give any justification to consider us as hostages.

If the British Government has been keeping a certain number of patriotic Turks away from their families and their country, in order to secure a dominating position in the

---

[*] F.O. 371/6503/6728, June 11, 1921.

Near East, the time and the events have proved this scheme to be based on wrong premises.

As a result a part of us have already been completely released.

The British Government can hardly think of realising any special purpose by keeping fifty-one Turks in this sort of detention. The release of some of us cannot do away with the injustice committed in our regard. Besides, the fact that some of those in exactly the same positions and situations are released and some are being further detained, proved in a very clear way, that there is no logic in the whole thing and that the British authorities are simply not inclined to assume the moral courage of liquidating at once the whole unjust situation which they have finally recognised as such by releasing some of us.

Your Excellency is representing in Malta a great nation reputed to be very respectful of personal liberty. You certainly have, at least, some responsibility in connection with our being arbitrarily deprived of our personal liberty. We entreat Your Excellency to go through our acts. You will be surprised to find out that those released and those not released belong in many cases to the same categories. After this you will understand that all of us are merely victims of heartless denunciators.

We all have families. While we are suffering here since two years of an unjustified and illegal imprisonment, our children have lost the source of their livelihood and the possibility of getting an education. Some members of our families have succumbed to the unusual privations they became exposed to.

We entreat Your Excellency to bring the present to the knowledge of the competent authorities and to be instrumental in securing our immediate release, and in saving us and our families from further suffering.

With this hope, we are, etc.,

(Sgd.)

Ali Jhsan, 2667, General
Adil, 2819, Lieut. Colonel
Atif, 2811, Dentist
Ilias Sami, M.P. 2810
Tahsin, 2774, ex-Governor, General of Syria, M.P.
Feizi M.P., 2743
Sabit, 2686, ex-Governor General of Sivas
Memdouh, 2733, ex-Governor General of Moussoul
Moustafa Abdoul Halik, 2800, ex-Governor General of Aleppo
M. Reshad, 2798, ex-Governor of Sinop
Hilmi, 2712, ex-Governor of Kir-Shehir
Basri, 2801, Lieut. Colonel
Rifat, 2706, Merchant
Rehfet, 2792, Major General
Shukri, 2738, former Civil Inspector
Mouri, 2816, former M.P.
Dr. Fazil Berki, 2698, former M.P.

Mehmed, 2790, Druggist
Teofik, 2680, Colonel
Madjid, 2704, official of the Court of Accounts
Dr. Faik, 2737, former Vice Governor of Merzepan
Gani, 2723, merchant
Mazlum, 2707, Major
Ibrahim Hakki, 2710, Major
Mourad, 2804, former Vice Director General of Police
Dr. Suleiman Nouman, 2732, Major General
Suleiman Faik, 2807, Major General
Djevad, 2700, Colonel
Hilmi Abdoul Kadir, 2789, Major
Veli Nedjet, 2687, ex-Inspector of migration
Nevzad, 2697, Captain
Ali Nazmi, 2808, former Attorney General of Kir-Shehir
Burhaniddin, 2814, Major
Nazim, 2809, Major
Kiamil, 2795, journalist
Mehmed Ali, 2817, former Director of Customs in Trebizond
Djemel Oghous, 2818, merchant
Rifat Salim, 2815, former Director of Police of Sivas
Tahir, 2745, Captain
Bedri, 2701, former Governor General of Diarbekir
Hadji Ahmed, 2790, Merchant,
Djemal, 2693, Captain
Tevfik, 2679, Lieut. Colonel
Rushdi, 2820, Military Secretary

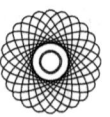

APPENDIX "D"*

List of names of suspected Turkish criminals submitted by the British High Commission to the Turkish Government as of 12 February 1920.

> British High Commission,
> Constantinople.
> 12th February, 1920.

a) Cruelty to British prisoners, marked A.
b) Cruelty to native Christians, marked B.
c) Breach of Armistice, marked C.

LIST A
10th February 1920

List of Turks whose surrender it is recommended should be demanded on account of cruelty to British prisoners of war or for breach of Armistice.

Foreign Office telegram No:- 58 of 23rd January 1920.

All those listed below have been Scheduled for Prosecution.

1.	Abdul Sebuni or Abdul Ghani	Commanding Mosul Camp
2.	Ahmed Hilmi Bey or Mehmed Hilmi Bey	Commanding a working camp in the Ankara group
3.	Bedri Bey	Commanding Nisibin Working Camp
4.	Djemal Effendi	Commanding Daridja Camp, near Constantinople
5.	Fuad, Captain	In command of last column of Prisoners of War on march from Mosul to Rasl-el-Ain about May 1916.
6.	Ibrahim Hakki Bey	Commanding Mosul Camp
7.	Kemal Bey	Colonel. Acting Head of the Prisoner of War Department of the War Office.
8.	Lufti Bey	Commanding a Work Camp in the Ankara group (No:-3 Camp. 7th Railway Regiment)

---

* F.O. 371/5080/1346, 12 February 1920.

9.	Muhamad Bey	Commanding a Working Camp (?Kulbala) in the Ankara group.
10.	Nazim Effendi	Commanding Manak Camp. Ankara group.
11.	Nuri Bey	Commanding Diarbieza Camp.
12.	Suleiman	Corporal. Commanding a Working Camp in the Ankara group.
13.	Osman Bey (Ali Osman Bey)	Lieut. Colonel. Commanding a Working Camp in the Ankara group.
14.	Raghib Effendi or Refik Effendi	Commanding Telhadi (or Tel-el-Helif) Working Camp in July 1918.
15.	Saadeddin Efffendi	Commanding a Working Camp in the Ankara Group.
16.	Salih Bey	Commanding Nisibin Camp in June 1918.
17.	Suleiman Bey	Naval Officer Commanding Afion Kara Hissar Camp.
18.	Yussuf	Staff. Officer. Commanding escort to Prisoners of War between Kut and Ras-el-Ain.

LIST B

10th February 1920

List of Turks whose surrender it is recommended should be demanded on account of cruelty to native Christians or for other reasons, as required by Foreign Office telegram no. 58 of 23rd January 1920.

The names in this list are those accused of cruelty to native Christians. The abbreviations "atrs" stands for atrocities, that is, participation direct or indirect in wholesale massacre.

1.	Abdul Kadir	Kaimakam of Ghumush Khana, Trebizond vilayet. Doldaban atrs. 1915.
2.	Abdul Kadir	President Committee of Union & Progress, Mardin, Diarbekir Vilayet. Mardin atrs. 1915-1916.
3.	Adjente Mustapha (Kerzade Mustafa)	Agent of the Seiri Sefain S.S. Company at Trebizond in 1915. Now merchant in Stamboul, domicile in Pera. Trebizond atrs.
4.	Aghia Bey	Lieut. Colonel. Commandant at Mamure. Arrested by Turkish Authorities on 31 Jan. 1919 for massacres in Taurus district.
5.	Ahmed Bey	Mutesarrif of Aintab, 1915. Atrs. in the Aintab sanjak.

Appendix "D"

6.	Ali	known as Ali Pasha, brother of Mehmet, Kaimakam of Adiaman, Harput vilayet. Atrs. between Malatia and River Euphrates.
7.	Ali Bey	Son of Major Hussein Hakki Bey of Karamursal in sanjak of Ismid. Karamursal atrs.
8.	Ali Chaoush	late a Gendarme, now a clother in the Telal Bazar, Malatia. Hassan Chelibi atrs.
9.	Ali Ghalib	Secretary of Mutessarif of Ismid, Bagchejik atrs.
10.	Ali Nazim	Public Prosecutor, Ankara. Kirshehir atrs.
11.	Ali Sahib Bey	Doctor. Chairman of Sanitary Board at Trebizond. Scientific murderer.
12.	Ali Shuhuri	Mudir of Bagchejik, Ismid. Bagchejik atrs.
13.	Arpaje Zade Hadji Muhammad	Mayor of Malatia 1919. Atrs. in Malatia district.
14.	Assaf (Mehmed Assaf)	Doctor, travelling Medical Officer in Adana vilayet. Mush atrs.
15.	Atif Bey, Dentist	Makrikeuy. Deportations, extortions, sacrilege in Istambul vilayet.
16.	Atif Bey	Acting Vali of Ankara in 1915, afterwards Vali of Kastamuni. Ankara atrs.
17.	Atta Zade Hakki	Delegate (or Secretary) of the C.U.P. at Diarbekir. Now in Diarbekir Atrs.
18.	Aziz Bey	Directeur de la Surete Generale.
19.	Batal Oghlu	Rich farmer and notable of Hassan Chelebi in the sanjak of Malatia. Hassan Chelebi massacres.
20.	Bedri Bey	Mutessarif of mardin, previously Mektoubji of Diarbekir. Diarbekir, Mardin atrs., also in Syria.
21.	Behaeddin Bey	Colonel. Chief of Staff of the Yildirim Army. Atrs. in Tarsus district.
22.	Behidj Bey	Colonel. In 1920 2nd Chief of Staff at the War Office; late director of Personnel at the War Office. Aghajli mines atrs.
23.	Burhaneddin	Major, commanding a Militia Battalion. Kirshehir -Ankara vilayet atrs.
24.	Djellaledin Bey	Police Commissioner in Brussa, 1915. Brussa atrs. in June & July 1915.
25.	Djemal Oghuz Bey	Commission agent and C.U.P. delegate at Tchangiri. Tchangiri atrs.
26.	Djemil	C.U.P. delegate at Boghazlian, Ankara vilayet, in 1915. Karakotch massacres.

27.	Eckhardt, Franz	Perverted German missionary. Urfa atrs. (Sublime Porte reported him killed at Midia, but report considered doubtful).
28.	Edhem Bey (Badjanak Zade Edhem)	Of Sivas and now there. Sivas atrs.
29.	Edib Bey	Kaimakam of Sungurlu in the Sanjak of Chorum in vilayet of Ankara, in 1915. Kamishlik (Yozgad) massacres.
30.	Emin Bey	(Bafrali Emin Bey) lawyer of Samsun.
31.	Emin Bey	Major. Officer Commanding troops at Merzifun in May, June, 1915. Merzifun atrs.
32.	Emir Pasha Zade Haimd Beyand	Notable of Sivas; now Mudir of Yeni Khan. Atrs. in Sivas Koch Kissar massacre.
33.	Faik Bey	Gendarmerie officer, Trebizond in June 1915; Doldaban (Ghumush Khana) atrs.
34.	Fakhri Bey	Mudir of Beuyeuk Yenikeuy in the Kaza of Orkan Gazi in the vilayet of Brussa. Atrs.
35.	Feyaz Ali Bey	Director of Evkaf; Yoazgad, Kella atrs.
36.	Ghavranizade Memduh or Memduh Kevranlizade	Commissioner of Police, Diarbekir. Diarbekir & Mardin atrs.
37.	Hadji Ali Hafiz Zade Eumer	President of the National Defence, Trebizond. August 1919. Trebizond atrs.
38.	Hadji Ali Hafiz Zade Eumer	Brother of above. Trebizond atrs.
39.	Hadji Bedr Agha	Chief of Reshan Kurds (Harput vilayet) Erzerum atrs., and between Malatia and River Euphrates.
40.	Hadji Ghalib Agha	Chief of bands. Notable of the village of Hekim Han in the Kaza of Agha. Hassan Chelibi (Malatia) atrs.
41.	Hadji Yerjes Zade Keur Yussuf	Notable of Diarbekir and now there. Atrs.
42.	Hadji Kaya	Chief notable of Izoghlu on the road Harput to Malatia. Atrs. in vilayet of Mamuret-ul-Aziz.
43.	Hadji Mehmet Effendi	Deputy for Harput. Atrs.
44.	Hadji Reshid Kamil oghlu Hadji Mustafa	Urfa atrs.
45.	Hafiz Nedjeb Zade Kadri	Native of Diarbekir and now living there. Kaimakam of Palu (1912-1916) in Diarbekir Vilayet. Mutasserif of Mush in Bitlis vilayet. Palu and Mardin atrs.
46.	Haidar Bey	Vali of Bitlis. Mussul. Van. Now deputy for Van. Atrs. in Zeitun, Marash, Mosul, and Bitlis.
47.	Halet Bey	Known as Saghirzade, deputy for Erzingan. Atrs. in sanjak of Erzingan.

48.	Halil Pasha	General. Atrs. In Bitlis, Mush, Urumia.
49.	Halil Bey	Major. Superintendent of Aghajli coalmine near Kiathane. atrs.
50.	Hamitli Riza Bey	Now deputy for Kirshehir. Atrs. in Ankara vilayet, Denek Maaden, Geul Bashi.
51.	Harun Effendi	Lieut. of Gendarmerie. Diarbekir Villayet. Mardin atrs. Arrested by Turkish authorities on 13.1.19 and escaped from prison.
52.	Hashim Bey oglu Mahammad Bey	Of Malatia. Harput and Dersim, atrs.
53.	Hassan Effendi	Prison Director, Mezre (Harput). Murder of Mgr. Etienne Israelian and many others near Arghana Maden in July 1915.
54.	Hassan Effendi	Notable of the village of Hekim Han. Kaza of Argha, Sanjak of Malatia. An army Reserve Officer. Hassan Chelebi massacres.
55.	Hassan Fuad Effendi	Captain Medical Corps. Mossul atrs.
56.	Hilmi Bey	Public Works, road engineer. Mossul atrs.
57.	Hilmi Bey (Serfitcheli Hilmi)	Mutasserif of Sairt, lately of Menteshe. Now living in Ankara. Sairt atrs.
58.	Hodja Ilias	Deputy for Mush. Atrs.
59.	Hurshid Bey	Major of Gendarmerie. Zeitun atrs. Kilis atrs.
60.	Hussein Effendi	Son of Batal Oghlu. Rich farmer and notable of the village of Hassan Chelebi, in the Kaza of Argha in the sanjak of Malatia. Hassan Chelebi massacres.
61.	Hussein Effendi	Known as Salik Begzade Hussein, or as Hussein Husni; mayor of Merzifun. Atrs.
62.	Hussein Hussri	Native of Harput; Chief of Police at Harput in 1915. Diarbekir and Harput atrs.
63.	Ibrahim Tchete bashi (Deli Ibrahim)	Director of Central Prison Stamboul. Bardizag, Ismid, Adabazar atrs.
64.	Ihsan Bey	President of Court-Martial, Samsun 1916-1917 Baffra and Samsun atrs.
65.	Ismail Hakki	Inspector General of Armenian refugees Aleppo 1916. Der Zor atrs.
66.	Ismail Hakki	Colonel-Major on General Staff. Adana and Marash atrs.
67.	Khulussi	Lieutenant. Gendarmerie Commandant at Boghazlian, Ankara vilayet, Karahotch and Yozgad atrs.
68.	Kiremitdji Zade Hadi	Now of Pera. Merzifun atrs.
69.	Koniali Ibrahim	Delegate of the C.U.P. at Brussa. Atrs.
70.	Kratovali Hadji Hatib Mustafa	An examining Magistrate. Daday, Kemakh, and Erzingan atrs.
71.	Kurd Zenal Agha	Massacrer in chief in district South of Malatia.

72.	Mahir Bey	Gendarmerie Commandant, Merzifun, June 1915. Merzifun atrs.
73.	Mehmet Bey	Son of Hakim (or Hashim) Bey, Deputy for Malatia. Harput and Malatia atrs.
74.	Mehmet Bey	Of Karabiga, Ismid, capturing and enslaving Serbian P.O.W. after the Armistice.
75.	Mehmet Bey	Kaimakam of Adiaman, Harput vilayet. Atrs. between Malatia and River Euphrates.
76.	Mehmetje	Chief of the Political (Armenian) Section of the Secret Police 1909-1918, Brussa June 1915, Ismid and Yalova atrs.
77.	Mehmet Ali Bey	Director of Custom House Trebizond 1915. Trebizond drownings.
78.	Mehmet Nuri	Known as Babosh Mustafa; deputy for Dersim and for Harput. Harput atrs.
79.	Memduh Bey	Chief of Police at Diarbekir, later at Mardin, Mardin atrs. Kara-Keupreu atrs. etc.
80.	Merdjimet Ahmed Bey	Bilejik (Brussa vilayet) atrs.
81.	Muhurdarzade Assim	Erzerum atrs.
82.	Murad Bey	Assis. Director General of Police. Constantinople atrs.
83.	Mussa Kiazim Effendi	Sheik-ul-Islam
84.	Mustafa Abdul Halik	Vali of Bitlis. Aleppo atrs.
85.	Nail Bey	Delegate of the C.U.P. at Trebizond. Trebizond atrs.
86.	Nazif Bey	Commanding Gendarmerie in Kaza of Sungurlu, sanjak of Chorum, Vilayet of Ankara in 1915. Kamishlik (Yozgad) atrs.
87.	Nazim Bey	President of Samsun Court Martial. Samsun hangings.
88.	Nazim Nazmi Bey	Known as Erzerumli Nazmi. Commandant of Gendarmerie. Atrs. in Bitlis and Mossul vilayets.
89.	Nedjati Bey	Delegate of the C.U.P. at Ankara. Yozgad and Ankara atrs.
90.	neshid Bey	Mudir of Hassan Chelibi (Harput vilayet) atrs.
91.	Niazi Bey	Merchant of Trebizond. Trebizond drownings and Ordu atrs.
92.	Nuri Bey	Major of Gendarmerie, Caesarea. Samsun atrs.
93.	Nuri Pasha	General. Baku atrs. in Sept. 1918.
94.	Nusret Bey	In 1915 Kaimakam of Bailurt, now Mutassarif of Urfa. Bailurt atrs.
95.	Omar	Commanding gendarmerie Der Zor. Raka atrs.
96.	Osman Bey	C.U.P. Samsun. Baffra atrs.
97.	Osman Bey (Ali Osman)	Vali of Brussa atrs. 1915.
98.	Pirinjdjizade Sidki	Of Diarbekir. Notable and sometime Mayor of Diarbekir. Atrs.
99.	Redjayi Nuzhet	Mudir of Sabanja, Kaimakam of Adabazar, (Ismid): atrs.

Appendix "D"

100.	Reshid Bey (Kurd Reshid)	(Mushler Mehmet Reshid Bey) Mutassaraf of Malatia in 1915. atrs.
101.	Rifaat Pasha	General. Samsun and Baffra atrs.
102.	Rifaat Bey	Chief of Police. Sivas. atrs.
103.	Riza Bey	Merchant of Orkhan Ghazi in Brussa vilayet. Beuyuk Yenikeuy atrs.
104.	Salik (Direkdji Zade Salih)	Notable of Diarbekir. Son of Ali Hoto of Diarbekir. Diarbekir atrs.
105.	Salih Bey	Police Commissioner Merzifun in 1915 atrs.
106.	Sami Bey. (Ghiridli Sami)	Police Commissioner at Caesaria later at Adrianople, Caesarea atrs.
107.	Sefulla Bey	Deputy for Erzerum. Atrs.
108.	Shefik Bey	Mutassarif of Mardin. Atrs.
109.	Shehab, Major	Vice President of Caesarea Court-Marital. Atrs.
110.	Shemseddin	Hodja of Ankara. Well known influential, rich notable. Atrs.
111.	Sherif Bey. (Mufti Zade Sherif)	Son of Mufti of Diarbekir. Atrs.
112.	Shevki	Son of Yahsin Effendi. of Diarbekir. Commandant of Battalion of Militia. Diarbekir atrs.
113.	Shukri Bey	Of the Regie at Yozgad. Atrs.
114.	Simco (Ismail)	Agha of Ketur. Shenakh atrs.
115.	Sirri Bey. (Suleiman Sirri Bey)	Mutassarif of Malatia and of Amassia in 1915. Now deputy for Ismid. Malatia and Amassia atrs.
116.	Suleiman Nedjmi Bey	Samsun atrs.
117.	Tahir	Merchant of Bey Shehir in Konia vilayet. Bitlis atrs.
118.	Tahsin Bey	Vali of Van, Erzerum, Syria, Smyrna. Now deputy for Smyrna, Erzerum atrs.
119.	Talaat Bey	Known as Kutchuk Talaat. Inspector of Gendarmerie. Member of central C.U.P.
120.	Tcherkess Rushdi	Major of Gendarmerie. Diarbekir atrs.
121.	Topal Osman Feridun	Now Mayor of Kerasun; Trebizond atrs., Kerasun atrs.
122.	Vehbi Effendi	Mudir of Kavak, Sivas vilayet. Guluch Ala atrs.
123.	Vehib Mehmet Pasha	General. Erzerum and Batum atrs.
124.	Veli Bey	Notable and rich farmer of the village of Hassan Chelebi, in the sanjak of Malatia and now there. Massacres of Hassan Chelebi.
125.	Yahia Agha	Kehaja of the Makanas (Chief lightermen). Trebizond drownings.
126.	Yunus Nadi	Editor of "Yeni Gun" Constantinople now Deputy for Smyrna. Inciting to suppress Christian population.

127.	Yussuf Zia Effendi	Major. Last Commandant de Place, Urmia. 1918. Urmia atrs.
128.	Zeki Bey. (Sali Zeki)	Kaimakam of Everek; of Develi. Der Zor, Everek, Rakkie atrs.
129.	Zekiai Bey	Mutassarif of Caesarea; of Talas, Eskishehir and Caesarea, atrs.
130.	Zihni Bey	Kaiamakam of Argha in the sanjak of Malatia; also Recruiting Officer for the district. Massacres of Hassan Chelebi in his Kaza May 1915 to January 1916.
131.	Adavlli Oghlu Mehmet	Militia officer. Kurt Dere (Yozgat) atrs. 1915.
132.	Adnan Bey, Doctor	Deputy for Constantinople ex-Secretary-General of the Red Crescent Society. Notorious C.U.P. leader and now Nationalist. (On 24.3.20 the H.C. requested G.O.C.-in-C., A.B.S., to effect his arrest).
133.	Ali Djenani Bey	Deupty for Aintab. Ainatb atrs. 1915.
134.	Babosh Mustafa	Deputy for Harput. Itchme (Harput) atrs. 1915.
135.	Basri Bey	Chief of Staff to Halil Pasha, XVIth Army Corps, 1915-1918. Later Chief of 1st Section (Military Movements) at War Office. Mossul atrs.
136.	Bessim Zahdi Bey	C.U.P. delegate at Afion Kara Hissar. Arrested by the Turkish Government on 31.3.19 and released end of 1919. Afion Kara Hissar atrs.
137.	Eshref Kushjibashi Zade	Was released in error from Malta as an ordinary prisoner of war on 2.1.20. A most dangerous and criminal propagandist.
138.	Fevzi	Now Kaimakam of Makri (sanjak of Mughla). Gross impudence to Commander of H.M.S. Asphodel on 3.12.19.
139.	Hadji Ahmet	Of Keldik. C.U.P. delegate at Sivas. Sivas atrs.
140.	Hassan Fehmi	Commissioner of Police at Afion Kara Hissar, 1915. Kara Hissar atrs.
141.	Mehmet Kiamil	Journalist & informer. Mossul atrs. 1917 & 1918.
142.	Mustafa Bey, Doctor	Medical officer to the Municipality of Afion Kara Hissar and in charge of the Civil Hospital 1915-1917. Afion Hissar atrs.
143.	Nazim Bey	Native of Resne. C.U.P. delegate at Harput in 1915. Was condemned in contumaciam to 15 years imprisonment by Turkish tribunal whilst at the same time he was freely living in Constantinople. Harput atrs.
144.	Reshad Bey	In 1915 Head of the Political Section of the Police in Constantinople. Subsequently Mutessarif of Aidin, Kangri, Bolu. Arrested by Turkish Government on 16.3.19 and released on Oct. 1919. Deportations from Constantinople & subsequent atrs.
145.	Shevket Bey	Mutessarif of Afion Kara Hissar in 1915. Kara Hissar atrs.

146.	Suleiman Faik Pasha	G.O.C. XIth Army Corps; ad interim Vali of Harput, end of 1915. Harput atrs. committed after they had officially ceased.
147.	Zekele Neshat	Recidivist murderer. Released from Trebizond prison in 1915 to become chief executioner of the noyades [drownings] of that place, summer of 1915.

LIST C

10th February 1920

SCHEDULE of names of Turks, not previously submitted, to be included in list required by the Foreign Office, on account of breach of Armistice terms or for other military reasons.

1.	"Kutchuk" Djemal Pasha and Djevad Pasha	For general obstruction and disobedience to orders and given under terms of Armistice.
2.	Mustapha Kemal Pasha	For giving instructions that certain Kurds were to be incited to act against the British.
3.	Haidar Bey	For carrying out the above instructions given by Mustapha Kemal, from which the murder of British Officers resulted.
4.	Kiazim Karabekir	For obstruction of terms of the Armistice in refusing to surrender armament surplus to that quantity allowed by orders issued in accordance with the terms of the Armistice.
5.	Ali Fuad Pasha	For carrying out troop-movements in contravention of orders issued under the terms of the Armistice.
6.	Chefki Pasha	For obstruction of the terms of the Armistice during the withdrawal of the IX Ottoman Army from Trans-Caucasia, notably the destruction of the Wireless Station at Kars.
7.	Khalid Bey	For contravention of the terms of the Armistice in maintaining communication with the Kars Shura after IX Army had withdrawn into Turkish Territory, and sending assistance in men, etc., to the Kars Shura.
8.	Omar Loutfi Bey	For moving regular Ottoman troops in contravention of orders issued under the terms of the Armistice.

APPENDIX "E"[*]

Suspects who have been accused of various crimes, arrested and incarcerated on Malta, as of 26 May 1920.

British High Commission,
Constantinople,
26th May 1920.

My Lord,

In continuation of my despatch No. 402/R.2886 of the 25th March 1920, I have the honour to inform Your Lordship that the following arrests have been made by the Military Authorities, and that all those listed below have been transferred to Malta for safe detention:-

AS NATIONALIST UNDESIRABLES:
1. Major-General Ali Said Pasha.
2. Islam Ali, servant to Ali Said Pasha, accompanied that Officer to Malta.
3. Ebrizia Zade Velid Bey, Journalist.
4. Djelal Nuri Bey.
5. Suleiman Nazif Bey. Ex-Vali.
6. Ahmed Emin Bey, Journalist.
7. Ali Seid Bey, Senator.
8. Kel Ali Bey, Deputy.
9. Evis Avni Aka Kutus.

FOR MILITARY REASONS:
10. Mehmet Muammer Bey, Director of the Political Section of the Police in Constantinople.

FOR MASSACRE OF CHRISTIAN OTTOMAN SUBJECTS:
11. Brig-General Refet Pasha, Samsoun.
12. Mehmet Kiamil, Journalist. Mossul.
13. Adjente Mustafa, Merchant. Trebizonde.
14. Brig-General Mursel Pasha, Baku.
15. Eyub, Private, servant to Mursel Pasha, accompanied that officer to Malta.
16. Ejzaji Mehmet, Merchant, Erzinjan.
17. Colonel Hilmi Abdul Kadir, Mossul.

In addition to the above, the following have been transferred from Egypt to Malta:
18. Major Mehmet Arif Bey, for outrages on British prisoners of war.
19. Yussuf Tsawish ibn Nuri Bitlissi, for massacre of Christian Ottoman subjects.
20. Mehmet Kiamil, Journalist and informer, Mossul.

---

[*] F.O. 371/5089/2293, 11 March 1920.

21. Abdus Selami Pasha, Surgeon-General (Retired List).
22. Adjente Mustafa, Merchant, Trebizond.
23. Hadji Ahmet, of Kildik, C.U.P. Delegate, Sivas.
24. Mustafa Reshad Bey, Director of the Political Section of the Prefecture de Police, Constantinople.
25. Mustafa Abdul Halik, Vali of Bitlis.
26. Basri Bey, Lieutenant-Colonel, Mossul.

AS NATIONALIST UNDESIRABLES:
27. Ubedullah Bey.

3. The arrest of Nos. 1 to 5 was reported in my telegram No. 295 of 27th March; of Nos. 6 and 11 in my telegram No. 523 of 30th April.

>I have the honor to be,
>My Lord,
>Your Lordship's obedient Servant,
>
>Admiral de Robeck
>HIGH COMMISSIONER

APPENDIX "F"[*]

War Office list of prisoners at Malta indicating those who should be retained and those recommended for repatriation.

British High Commission,
Constantinople,
11th March 1920.

My Lord,

With reference to Your Lordship's despatch No. 170564/ME/44 of 20th January, 1920, I have the honour to forward the undermentioned lists as requested by the War Office, under date 2nd January, viz.,:-

List A., being a list of individuals who should be retained in custody on general repatriation; with annexes A1 and A2.

List B., being a list of individuals who may be released on general repatriation.

2. List A contains 67 names of whom 2 are now in custody at Chanak, one believed to be in Egypt, and 64 are interned at Malta. List B contains 32 names.

3. I would invite Your Lordship's attention to the fact that in the list of recommendations for release (List B), I have inserted the names of only 5 individuals (Nos. 2685, 2688, 2693, 2729, & 2730) of those Turks originally deported on my authority. The remainder of those originally deported on my authority (i.e., the 52 names marked "A/T" in List A), I strongly recommend should be retained in custody, not because **all** could be prosecuted for participation direct or indirect in atrocities, but because the return of any of them would be most inexpedient until after the Treaty of Peace is in force.

I have the honour to be,
My Lord,
Your Lordship's most obedient Servant,

Admiral de Robeck
HIGH COMMISSIONER

---

[*] F.O. 371/5089/2293, 11 March 1920.

LIST A
being a list of individuals who should be retained in custody on general repatriation (F.O. despatch No:-170564/ME/44 of 20th January 1920).

1. List A, in conjunction with List B, together contain all the names given in War Office List, sent under cover of above quoted despatch.
2. Column 'a' of list gives the Malta Number. Column 'b' "P/W" signifies that the individual is detained under the authority of the General Officer Commanding-in-Chief, Army of the Black Sea, for outrages on British Prisoners of War. "A/T" signifies that the individual is detained for direct or indirect participation in outrages on subject Christians. "K" signifies that he was deported from Kars as a political undesirable. Column 'c' gives the name of the individual. Column 'd' contains High Commissioner's or General Officer Commanding-in-Chief remarks.
3. With reference to the second paragraph of the War Office letter of January 2nd 1920, the names in this list of persons scheduled for prosecution have been underlined to facilitate easy reference.

Appendix "F" 105

A	B	C	D
2666	P/W	Georges Nicoloff	Arrested by order of G.O.C. in C.A.B.S. Sent to Malta on authority of W.O. 7408 P.W. dated 17.3.19. On 2.3.19. the W.O. by cable No:-5726. P.W. ordered that this man's case would be dealt with by the Peace Conference. There are allegations that he ill-treated British P.O.W. and the French Authorities also made allegations against him. Copy of their dossier is attached (Annex [?])
2667	A/T	Ali Ihsan Pasha	Detained under point 5 of F.O. telegram No:-233 of 5.2.19. "Outrages to Armenians or other "subject races both in Turkey and in Trans Caucasia".
2675	A/T	Hussein Djahid Bey. Deputy for Constantinople.	Ditto.
2676	P/W	Djelal Bey. Colonel.	"Commandant Psamatia Camp. This is an adverse report signed by Captain Vedi S.M.O. of the Turkish Army against this man and a copy is attached. There is at present no further reliable evidence against him but he should not be released yet." Copy of report marked A.2.
2679	P/W	Mehmet Tevfik Bey. Lt. Col. Commandant at Kastamuni.	"Although not yet scheduled for prosecution his conduct is severely commented upon in Committees of Inquiry into offences against Laws of War at page 54."
2680	P/W	Ahmet Tevfik Bey.	"Scheduled for prosecution by the Committee of Enquiry into offences against laws of war."
2682	A/T	Tevfik Hadi Bey.	As for No:-2667.
2684	A/T	Yussuf Riza Bey.	Ditto.
2686	A/T	Sabit Bey.	Ditto.

2687	A/T	Veli Nedjet Bey.	Ditto.
2689	A/T	Fethi Bey.	Ditto.
2690	A/T	Tahir Djevdet Bey.	Ditto.
2691	A/T	Rahmi Bey.	Ditto.
2692	A/T	Ismail Djambolat.	Ditto.
2694	P/W	**Djemal Bey. Capt.**	As for No:-2680.
2696	A/T	Nevzade Bey.	As for No:-2667.
2697	A/T	Mumtaz Bey.	Ditto.
2698	A/T	**Fazil Berki Bey.**	As for No:-2667.
2700	**P/W**	**Ahmed Djevad.**	As for No:-2680.
2701	A/T	Ibrahim Bedriddin.	As for No:-2667.
2702	A/T	Atif Bey.	Ditto.
2703	A/T	Ferid Bey.	Ditto.
2704	A/T	Madjid Bey.	Ditto.
2705	A/T	Hussein Kadri.	Ditto.
2706	A/T	Hodja Rifaat.	Ditto.
2707	**P/W**	**MazlumBey.**	As for No:-2680.
2708	P/W	Haidar Ahmed Bey Major.	"Commandant at Konia. Alleged he was guilty of outrages against caste of Indians – Sikhs. Responsibility for flogging of Indian Officers and other ranks."

Appendix "F"

2709	P/W	Sami Bey. Col.	"Commandant. Changri. The Committee of Inquiry into offences against the Laws of War devote a page of their report to this camp but do not mention Sami Bey. He should be retained.
2710	P/W	Ibrahim Hakki Bey. Major.	"Assistant Commandant Ras-el-Ain. The Committee have scheduled a man of this name as Commandant, Mosul, for prosecution and it may be this man. He should be detained on that ground."
2712	A/T	Hilmi Bey.	As for Number:-2667.
2718	A/T	Zekeria Zihni Bey.	Ditto.
2719	A/T	Ahmed Muammer Bey.	Ditto.
2723	A/T	Ghani Bey.	Ditto.
2724	A/T	Ahmed Bey.	Ditto.
2728	A/T	Selah Djimdjoz Bey.	Ditto.
2732	**P/W**	**Suleiman Numan Pasha.**	As for No:-2680.
2733	A/T	Memduh Bey.	As for No:-2667.
2734	A/T	Hairi Effendi.	Ditto.
2735	A/T	Ibrahim Sahib Bey.	Ditto.
2736	A/T	Ahmed Nessimi Bey.	As for No:-2667.
2737	A/T	Faik Bey.	Ditto.
2738	A/T	Shukri Bey.	Ditto.

2739	A/T	Hadji Ahmed Pasha.	Ditto.
2740	A/T	Hamid Riza Bey.	Ditto.
2741	**P/W**	**Jakob Gallus**	As for No:-2680.
2742	A/T	Zulfi Bey.	As for No:-2667.
2743	A/T	Arif Feizi Bey.	Ditto.
2745	**P/W**	Tahir Bey.	As for No:-2680.
2752	A/T	Fahreddin Pasha.	As for No:-2667.
2754	A/T	Halim Abbas Pasha.	Ditto.
2755	A/T	Said Halim Pasha.	Ditto.
2756	A/T	Midhat Shukri Bey.	Ditto.
2757	A/T	Hadji Adil Bey.	Ditto.
2758	A/T	Mahmud Kiamil Pasha.	Ditto.
2759	A/T	Zia Geuk Alp.	Ditto.
2760	A/T	Halil Bey.	Ditto.
2761	A/T	Mustafa Kemail Bey.	Ditto.
2762	A/T	Ali Munif Bey.	Ditto.
2763	A/T	Ahmed Shukri Bey.	Ditto.

Appendix "F"

2764	A/T	Ahmed Agayeff.	Ditto.
2765	A/T	Hussein Tussum Bey.	Ditto.
2767	**P/W**	**Muhammad Arif.**	Interned, Malta on 28.1.20. Deported from Egypt. Identity doubtful. May be the same as the Major Arif Bey who is scheduled for prosecution.
2768	A/T	Yussuf Tsawish.	Interned Malta 28.1.20. Deported from Egypt. As for No:-2667.
2770	A/T	Mursel Pasha.	Interned Malta. Deported from Chanak on 28.2.20. As for No:- 2667.
2790	A/T	Ejzaji Mehmet.	Detained at Chanak. As for No:-2667.
2789	A/T	Hilmi Abdul. Colonel.	As for Number 2667.
	P/W	Clauss. Snr.	Believed to be interned in Egypt. As for number 2680.

LIST B

being a list of individuals who may be released on general repatriation.
(F.O. despatch No:-170564/ME/44 of 20th January 1920).

1.   List B, in conjunction with List A, together contain all the names given in War Office List, sent under cover of above quoted despatch.

2.   Column 'A' of list gives the Malta Number. Column 'B' "P/W" signifies that the individual is detained under the authority of the General Officer Commanding-in-Chief, Army of the Black Sea, for outrages on British Prisoners of War. "A/T" signifies that the individual is detained for direct or indirect participation in outrages on subject Christians. "K" signifies that he was deported from Kars as a political undesirable. Column 'C' gives the name of the individual. Column 'D' contains High Commissioner's or General Officer Commanding-in-Chief' remarks.

A	B	C	D
2668		Ibrahim Ahmed, Corporal.	Batman to General Ali Ihsan Pasha. No charge against him.
2671	P/W	A.L. Rosenburg.	Released on 4/2/20, on authority of G.O.C. in C., A.B.S.
2675	P/W	Hazim Mehmet Bey, Major Commandant at Samara.	Evidence appears insufficient to obtain conviction.
2681	P/W	Omar Bey, Major.	Released 2.1.20 on authority of G.O.C. in C., A.B.S.
2685	A/T	Habib Bey. Deputy for Boli.	Grounds for further detention appear to be insufficient.
2688	A/T	Hassan Fehmi, Deputy for Sinope.	Grounds for further detention appear to be insufficient.
2693	A/T	Midhat Bey, Secty. C.U.P., Boli.	Grounds for further detention appear to be insufficient.
2699	P/W	Halil Bey, Doctor – Captain.	As for No:-2678.
2711	A/T	Assim Bey.	Released 22.2.20.
2713	K	Aziz Jehangirov.	As for No. 2685.
2714	K	Pabel Djamtschow.	Release has been arranged for.

Appendix "F"

2715	K	Hassan Khan Dschanghiow.	As for No. 2685.
2716	K	Mehmet Bey Ali Zade.	Ditto.
2717	K	Ibrahim Bey Dschanghiow.	Ditto.
2720	K	Musa Bey Salahkowa.	Ditto.
2721	K	Yussuf Yussufoff.	Ditto.
2722	K	Tauchitgin Mamlejeff.	Ditto.
2725	K	Radjinski Matroi.	Ditto.
2726	K	Stefan Vifiades.	Release has been arranged for.
2727	K	Muchlis Bey Mamadow.	As for No. 2685.
2729	A/T	Mehmed Sabri Bey, Deputy for Saruhan.	Ditto.
2730	A/T	Suleiman Sudi Bey, Deputy for Lazistan.	Ditto.
2744	P/W	Michael Saraf Oghlu.	As for No. 2678.
2746	P/W	Izzet Basri Bey.	Ditto.
2747	P/W	Mehmet Hilmi Bey.	Released 4.2.20.
2748		Abdulla Murgan, Sergeant.	In attendance on General Fakhri Pasha. No charge.
2749		Mohamed Abed, Private.	Ditto.
2750		Moustafa Sidki, Corporal.	Released 22.2.20.
2751		Cheoket Zia Bey, Lieutenant.	Ditto.
	P/W	H. W. F. Meinhoff. Dr.	Not scheduled for prosecution. Evidence appears insufficient to obtain conviction.
	P/W	H. P. Hanneman Dr.	Ditto.
	P/W	F. A. Finger	Ditto.
			N.B. These three Germans were interned in Malta and neither the General Officer Commanding-in-Chief, Army of the Black Sea nor the High Commissioner has been advised of their release.

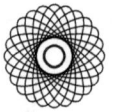

APPENDIX "G"[*]

Opinion of the law officers of the Crown regarding the release or prosecution of the suspects held on Malta.

WAR OFFICE
LONDON S.W.1
August 1920.

Sir,

With reference to your letter No. E. 7334/37/44 dated July 1st and previous correspondence relative to the arrest and deportation to Malta of certain undesirable Turkish subjects by the High Commissioner at Constantinople, I am commanded by the Army Council to forward for the information of Earl Curzon of Kedleston, the enclosed copy of a memorandum by the Law Officers of the Crown on this matter together with a nominal roll of the Turkish Political Prisoners in question.

I am to acquaint you that the Council have had under consideration the question of release of these individuals on account of the cost of their maintenance while interned, and with this in view they submitted a list of the Prisoners to the Cabinet for revision by the Attorney General, in order that those prisoners against whom it is not proposed to take any definite proceedings might be released.

The Council desire me to refer Lord Curzon to the enclosed memorandum by the Law Officers of the Crown and to request that the High Commissioner at Constantinople may be asked, in view of the fact that it is not considered desirable to release any of these prisoners without reference to him, to state the names of those Turkish prisoners now at Malta who he considers can be released at once, with the exception of those specially referred to in the enclosed memorandum.

With regard to the enclosed nominal roll I am to inform you that it includes those prisoners of war referred to in your letter No. E. 3194/37/44 dated 19th April 1920, and whose release has been ordered in a letter addressed to the Governor and Commander-in-Chief, Malta, dated 15th May 1920.

The Under-Secretary of State,
Foreign Office,
S.W.1.

---

[*] F.O. 371/5090/10431, 25 August, 1920.

Memorandum by the Law Officers of the Crown

The list of Turkish subjects who have been sent to Malta on the instructions of H.M. High Commissioner at Constantinople and are there detained falls roughly into three classes –
1. Political offenders.
2. Persons accused of Deportations, Pillage and Massacres.
3. Persons accused of ill-treatment of Prisoners of War.

There are also some, the reason for whose detention is not stated.

The third class is the only one which comes within our purview, and we have no knowledge as to the individuals contained in the other classes.

The identification of those charged with the ill-treatment of Prisoners of War is a matter of some difficulty, owing to the fact that many Turks bear the same or a similar name, the spelling whereof varies considerably. The only person on this list who appears to be quite clearly identifiable with an individual whose prosecution has already been recommended by the Committee which has enquired into allegations of breaches of the Laws of War is 2707 Major Mazloum Bey Edib. The case of this Officer appears to be a particularly bad one. In addition, it is possible that 2676 Djellal Bey, 2679 Tewfik Mehmet, 2680 Tawfik Ahmed, 2694 Djemal Effendi Ebdul and 2710 Hakky Bey Ibrahim may be identical with persons of similar names, whose prosecution has been recommended, but this can not on the information contained in this list be established with any certainty.

So far as concerns the material that has been before us, the above are the only persons whose detention on the ground of ill-treatment of Prisoners of War seems desirable, but we would observe that the arrests have all been made on the instructions of the High Commissioner at Constantinople. He no doubt acted on evidence which came into his hands and reference to him would appear to be desirable before any definite action is taken for the release of any of these men.

(Signed) Gordon Hewart.
Ernest M. Pollock.

4th August 1920.

APPENDIX "H"[*]

Report of Committee Formed to Consider and Make Recommendations Regarding The Further Detention Or Immediate Release of The Turkish Prisoners Now At Malta.

British High Commission,
CONSTANTINOPLE
24th November 1920.

IMMEDIATE

My Lord,

With reference to my telegram No. 1225 of the 20th instant, on the subject of the Turkish prisoners now interned at Malta, I have the honour to enclose herein, for Your Lordship's information,

Enclosures.

copies of the Report of the Committee which I had formed to enquire into and to make recommendations regarding future disposal of these deportees.

2. In accordance with the last paragraph of the Committee's Report, I am consulting the General Officer Commanding-in-Chief, Army of the Black Sea regarding the possibility of the exchange, if the opportunity presents itself, of some of the prisoners who have been interned at the instance of the military authorities against the British prisoners now in the hands of the Nationalists.

I have the honour to be,
My Lord,
With the highest respect,
Your Lordship's most obedient humble Servant,

HORACE RUMBOLD
HIGH COMMISSIONER

---

[*] F.O. 371/5091/15116, November 24, 1920.

The Right Honourable,

The Earl Curzon of Kedleston, K.C., P.G.,

Etc. etc. etc.

MEMBERS – LT. Col. I. M. SMITH, D.S.O.

R. W. GRAVES Esq., C.MG., O.B.E.

Mr. RUXTON

Mr. HELM (Secy.)

The duties of the Committee were:

1. To separate G.O.C.-C's Malta prisoners from those of the High Commissioner.

2. Taking the latter only, to separate those only deported on ground (a) of political expediency from those (b) to be prosecuted under the terms of the Treaty of Sèvres.

3. As regards (a) to consider whether any of these could, in view of the changed circumstances, be allowed out now either to return to Constantinople or to proceed to some place in Europe until the coming into force of the Treaty; and, as regards (b) to decide whether there is sufficient evidence against each person to justify his further detention or whether it would be preferable to release him now under either of the above conditions.

Although instructions had been received from the Foreign Office that the dossier of each prisoner, whether a 'military' or a 'High Commission' one, should be examined and recommendations made, this was found to be impracticable as the Military Authorities had been unable to associate themselves with the work of the Committee. The latter were therefore compelled to confine themselves to an examination of the cases of the High Commissioner's prisoners, and their recommendations in respect of them come under three distinct heads:

A. Persons who should continue to be imprisoned and in due course be brought up for trial in accordance with the provisions of the Treaty of Sèvres (Appendix A)

By the expression 'brought up for trial' the Committee mean that, in their opinion, there appears to be a prime facie case against the deportees, derived (a) from their own knowledge of the case, or (b) from statements made by reliable informants, or (c) from information supplied by the Armenian Patriarchate. The High Commission having no locus standi in the matter of prosecution, no legal evidence exists, nor, with few exceptions, can witnesses be expected to come forward under the conditions which have prevailed, and still prevail, in Turkey.

B. Persons who should be released on the ratification of the Treaty by at least four of the Signatory Powers, but whose detention until then is desirable (Appendix B.)

C. Persons who may be released now, except in so far as it may be considered desirable to retain them with a view to a possible exchange for British prisoners in the hands of the Nationalists. These persons fall into two distinct classes viz:

> 1) Those who may be released now but who should not be allowed to return to Turkey pending the ratification of the Treaty by at least four of the Signatory Powers (Appendix C)
>
> 2) Those who may be released now and to whose return to Turkey there is no objection. (Appendix D)
>
> In his letter to the High Commissioner of 29th July 1920. (3211'I' 785) G.O.C.-in-C divided the 'military' deportees into two categories viz:
> (a) Those to whose eventual repatriation under Section 208 of the Treaty there is **no** military objection. (Appendix E.)
> (b) Those to whose eventual repatriation under Section 208 of the Treaty there **is** military objection (Appendix F.)

Several of these are, however, as important from the political as from the military point of view and are among those deportees whose release the Nationalists would be most likely to demand in exchange for the British prisoners in Anatolia. The question of their exchange, is therefore, one in which the G.O.C.-in-C. must give the final decision and the Committee recommend that the Military Authorities be immediately consulted regarding the possibility of the early return to Turkey of the necessity for the further detention at Malta of some of the deportees.

British High Commission,	(Signed)	IAN M. SMITH
CONSTANTINOPLE.		Mil. Attaché
23rd November 1920	"	R. W. GRAVES
	"	F. H. RUXTON
	"	A. K. HEIM
		(Secy.)

APPENDIX H₁
APPENDIX A

High Commissioner's deportees who should continue to be imprisoned and in due course be brought up for trial.

2667	Ali Ihsan Pasha
2686	Sabit Bey
2687	Veli Nedjet Bey
2690	Djevdet Bey
2692	Ismail Djambolat
2696	Nevzade Bey
2698	Fazil Berki Bey
2701	Ibrahim Bedreddin Bey
2704	Madjid Bey
2706	Hodja Rifaat Effendi
2712	Hilmi Bey
2718	Zekeria Zihni Bey
2719	Ahmed Muammer Bey
2723	Ghani Bey
2724	Ahmed Bey
2732	Suleiman Nouman Pasha
2733	Memduh Bey
2735	Ibrahim Pirizade Sahib Bey
2736	Ahmed Nessimi Bey
2737	Faik Bey
2738	Shukri Bey
2743	Atif Feize Bey
2752	Fakhri Pasha
2754	Abbas Halim Pasha
2755	Said Halim Pasha
2756	Midhat Shukri Bey
2758	Mahmud Kiamil Pasha
2760	Halil Bey
2761	Mustafa Kemal Bey
2762	Ali Munif Bey
2763	Ahmed Shukri Bey
2764	Ahmed Agayeff
2768	Yussuf Chawish Ibn Nuri Bitlissi
2774	Tahsin Bey
2789	Hilmi Abdul Kadir
2790	Ejzaji Mehmet
2792	Refet Pasha
2795	Mehmed Kiamil
2796	Adjente Mustafa

2798	Mustafa Reshad
2799	Hadji Ahmed of Kildik
2800	Mustafa Abdul Halik
2801	Basri Bey
2804	Murad Bey
2805	Ali Djenani Bey
2806	Akdaghli oglou Mehmet
2807	Suleiman Faik Pasha
2808	Ali Nazmi
2809	Nazim Bey
2810	Hodja Ilias Sami Bey
2811	Atif Bey
2812	Suleiman Nedjmi
2813	Safet Osman Bey*
2814	Burhaneddin Hakki Bey
2815	Mehmet Rifaat Bey
2816	Mehmet Nuri Bey
2817	Mehmet Ali Bey
2818	Djemal Oghuz Bey
2819	Adil Hadji Ahmet

* This man will be brought back from Malta for further identification; a doubt in the matter has lately arisen.

APPENDIX H₂
APPENDIX B

High Commissioner's deportees who should be released on the Treaty coming into force but whose detention until then is desirable.

2682	Tewfik Hadi Bey *	
2684	Yussuf Riza Bey *	
2691	Rahmi Bey	
2697	Mumtaz Bey	
2702	Atif Bey	
2703	Ferid Bey	
2740	Hamid Riza Bey *	
2742	Zulfi Bey *	
2759	Zia Geuk Alp **	
2782	General Ali Said Pasha with his servant	
2786	Islam Ali who is serving voluntarily	
2794	Ali Seyid	
2797	Abdul Selami Pasha	
....	Ali Bey **	Arrested in the Crimea
....	Mahmud Kibar Effendi **	and interned at Chanak.

* Unless further information is forthcoming.
** Available for exchange if desired unless further information is forthcoming.

APPENDIX H₃
APPENDIX C

High Commissioner's Deportees who may be released now but who should not be allowed to return to Turkey pending the coming into force of the Treaty.

2675 Hussein Djahid Bey
2705 Hussein Kadri Bey
2757 Hadji Adil Bey
2765 Hussein Tossoun Bey

APPENDIX H₄
APPENDIX D

High Commissioner's Deportees who may be released now and to whose return to Turkey there is no objection.

2689 Fethi Bey
2728 Selah Djimjaz

2738 Hairi Effendi (Being released now)
2739 Hadji Ahmet Pasha
2770 General Mursel Pasha, with his servant
2769 Eyub, Pte. Who is serving voluntarily
2784 Suluman Nazif (see E2156 & E2721)

See also 3 persons in list B marked ** (see E2156).

APPENDIX H₅
APPENDIX E

General Officer Commanding-in-Chief's Deportees to whose eventual repatriation there is no military objection.

2679 Mehmed Tewfik Bey
2708 Haidar Ahmed Bey
2709 Sami Bey, Colonel
2710 Ibrahim Hakki Bey, Major
2783 Velid Bey
2784 Suleiman Nazif Bey (transferred to list A – see E1306/21)
2785 Djelal Nouri Bey
2787 Ahmed Emin Bey
2788 Mehmed Muhammer
2791 Evis Avni Aka Kudus
2803 Shukri Pasha

APPENDIX H₆
APPENDIX F

General Officer Commanding-in-Chief's Deportees to whose return there is military objection.

2680 Ahmed Tewfik Bey
2693 Midhat Bey
2694 Djemal Bey
2700 Ahmed Djevad Bey
2707 Mazlum Bey
2713 Aziz Jehangirov
2715 Hassan Khan Jehangirov
2716 Muhamed Bey, Ali Bekov (or Ali zade)
2717 Ibrahim Bey Jehangirov (or Karsli)
2720 Mussa Bey Slahkova
2721 Yussuf Yussupov
2722 Dan Uddin Ha or Tauchitgan Mamlijeff
2725 M.T. Rachinski, Matroi

2727   Muklis Mainedov
2730   Suleiman Sudi Bey
2731   Ubedullah Bey
2745   Tahir Bey
2767   Arif Bey, Muhammed
2772   Djemal Pasha, General
2773   Djevad Pasha, General
2775   Essad Pasha
2776   Hussein Reouf Bey
2777   Shevket Bey, Colonel
2778   Vassif Bey, Colonel
2779   Mehmed Sherif Bey
2780   Faik Bey
2781   Numan Ousta
2793   Kel Ali Bey

APPENDIX "I"[*]

No. 277/1983/24

British High Commission,
Constantinople
16th March, 1921

My Lord,

With reference to Your Lordship's despatch No. 153 dated the 16th of February, and in continuation of my despatch No. 268 dated 12th of March, I have the honour to forward herewith a precis of information concerning each one of the 56 internees whose names appear in Appendix "A" to my despatch No. 1552/W.3667, dated the 24th of November, 1920. This appendix contains 59 names, but tw.o (2690 Djevdet Bey and 2796 Adjente Mustafa) have escaped and one (2813 Safet Osman Bey) has been released in error since the list was despatched. Thus there remain 56 persons whose prosecution I have recommended.

2. When reviewing the information contained in the annexed precis, I would ask Your Lordship to bear in mind the following considerations:

(a) that none of the Allied, Associated and Neutral Powers have been asked to supply any information. The American Government, in particular, is doubtless in possession of a large amount of documentary information, compiled at the time of the massacres were taking place.

(b) as the Treaty has not yet come into force no sort of pressure could be brought to bear on the Turkish Government or officials. Consequently no Turkish official documents are available.

(c) as there has been no public security in Anatolia and no possibility of travelling to Constantinople very few witnesses have come forward. Of the male Armenian eye-witnesses to the massacres few indeed survive and among them there are practically no men of any education who are refugees in Constantinople. Those witnesses who have come forward have almost all done so under the promise of secrecy, fearing as they do not only for themselves but chiefly for the safety of their relatives who may still survive in Anatolia.

---

[*] Report from British High Commissioner Horace Rumbold (Constantinople) to Lord Curzon, dated 16 March, 1921 in F.O. 371/6500-6501.

Again of those witnesses who have come forward during the last two years, some have gone to America and many could now no longer be traced.

3. Under these circumstances the Prosecution will find itself under grave disadvantages, until such time as real security for life and property exists in Turkey.

4. Up to the present the Armenian Patriarchate has been the principal channel through which information had been obtained.

>I have the honour to be, My Lord,
>With the highest respect,
>Your Lordship's most obedient,
>humble Servant
>
>[Horace Rumbold]
>HIGH COMMISSIONER

Schedule

The dossiers are arranged in the order of the Malta Numbers.

The List given below corresponds to the one given in Appendix A to High Commissioner's despatch No. 1552/W.3667, dated 24 November 1920, under the heading: "High Commissioner's deportees who should continue to be imprisoned and in due course be brought up for trial."

Malta No., Name of Internee, Scene of Alleged Crimes

2667	ALI IHSAN PASHA	Mossul, Van, Persia.
2686	SABIT BEY	Mamuret-ul-Aziz.
2687	VELI NEDJET BEY	Diarbekir.
[2690]	DJEVDET BEY	Escaped 6.12.20.
2692	ISMAIL DJAMBOLAT BEY	Central Police Administration.
2696	NEVZADE BEY	Mossul.
2698	FAZIL BERKI BEY	Sivas.
2701	IBRAHIM BEDRI BEY	Diarbekir.
2704	MADJID BEY	Erzingan.
2706	HODJA RIFAAT EFFENDI	Ismid.
2712	HILMI BEY	Kirshehir, Angora.
2718	ZEKERIA ZIHNI BEY	Adrianople.
2719	AHMET MUAMMER BEY	Sivas.
2723	GANI BEY	Sivas.
2724	AHMET BEY	Aintab, Aleppo.
2732	SULEIMAN NUMAN PASHA	War Office (Army Medical Services).
2733	MEMDUH BEY	Erzinjan, Bitlis, Mossul.
2735	IBRAHIM PIRIZADE SAIB BEY	Ministry of Justice.
2736	AHMED NESSIMI BEY	The Cabinet 1915.
2737	FAIK BEY	Merzivan, Sivas.
2738	SHUKRI BEY	Aleppo.
2743	ATIF FEZI BEY	Diarbekir.
2752	FAKHRI PASHA	Urfa, Aleppo.
2754	ABBAS HALIM PASHA	The Cabinet 1915.
2755	SAID HALIM PASHA	Grand Vizierate.
2756	MIDHAT SHUKRI BEY	The Cabinet and Central CUP, 1915.
2758	MAHMUD KIAMIL PASHA	Erzerum.
2760	HALIL BEY	The Cabinet, 1915.
2761	MUSTAFA KEMAL BEY	The Cabinet and Central CUP, 1915.
2762	ALI MUNIF BEY	Ministry of the Interior. Lebanon.
2763	AHMED SHUKRI BEY	The Cabinet, 1915.
2764	AHMED AGAYEFF	Constantinople; Baku.
2768	YUSSUF TSAWISH IBN NURI	Mardin; Diyarbekir.
2774	TAHSIN BEY	Erzerum.

2789	HILMI ABDUL KADIR BEY	Mossul. Persia.
2790	EJZAJI MEHMET	Erzinjan.
2792	REFET PASHA	Samsun.
2795	MEHMET KIAMIL	Mossul.
[2796]	ADJENTE MUSTAFA	Escaped 6. 12. 20.
2798	MUSTAFA RESHAD	Central Police Administration.
2799	HADJI AHMED of Kildik	Sivas.
2800	MUSTAF ABDUL HALIK	Bitlis - Aleppo.
2801	BASRI BEY	Mossul.
2804	MURAD BEY	Central Police Administration.
2805	ALI DJENANI BEY	Aintab; Aleppo.
2806	AK DAGHLI OGLU MEHMET	Yozgad; Angora.
2807	SULEIMAN FAIK PASHA	Mamuret-ul-Aziz.
2808	ALI NAZMI BEY	Kirshehir; Angora.
2809	NAZIM BEY	Samsun.
2810	HODJA ILIAS SAMI BEY	Mush; Bitlis.
2811	ATIF BEY	Constantinople.
2812	SULEIMAN NEDJMI BEY	Samsun.
[2813	SAFET OSMAN BEY	Released in error.]
2814	BURHANEDDIN HAKKI BEY	Kirshehir; Angora.
2815	MEHMET RIFAAT BEY	Sivas.
2816	MEHMET NURI BEY	Mamuret-ul-Aziz
2817	MEHMET ALI BEY	Trebizond.
2818	DJEMAL OGHUZ BEY	Changri; Kastamuni.
2819	ADIL HADJI AHMET	Erzerum.

ALI IHSAN PASHA

Malta No. 2667

Interned 29.3.19

Appointments. General ALI IHSAN Pasha, after the fall of Bagdad commanded the 13th Corps with headquarters at Sulimanie. The 13th and 18th Army Corps formed the VIth Army under Halil Pasha, headquarters at Mossul. At the beginning of 1918 he was commanding the 4th Army Corps of the IIIrd Army.

At the time of his arrest he was commanding the VIth Army.

Lists. On none.

Arrest. R. 1447

1. F.O. Telegram 244 of 7.2.19 to High Commissioner. "You should demand from Turkish Government immediate recall of ALI IHSAN Pasha, Commander of 6th Turkish Army, who is defying Allied Military Authorities at Jerablus. He should be replaced by a senior and reliable Turkish officer as was done in the case of Fakhri Pasha at Medina."

Above communicated to Minister for Foreign Affairs by letter of 10.2.19.

Turkish Government issued necessary orders on 10.2.19.

2. Telegram of 19.2.10 from Egyptian Expeditionary Force to High Commissioner informs that IHSAN should arrive Konia on 23.2.19. in charge of a British escort which has been instructed to conduct him to Constantinople and hand him over to you, (i.e. the High Commissioner). "Please make arrangements for forward journey from Konia and for his disposal as you consider necessary at Constantinople."

3. On 24.2.19 High Commissioner asks General Officer Commanding-in-Chief to make arrangements to place ALI IHSAN in custody pending a decision as to his future disposal.

"General IHSAN's offence falls under Article 1 of Foreign Office telegram 233 of 5.2.19. I have requested General Allenby to forward documentary evidence on the subject."

4. On 8.3.19 High Commissioner requests General Officer Commanding-in-Chief to evacuate ALI IHSAN to Malta there to be interned until further instructions are received from His Majesty's Government.

(ALI IHSAN reached Malta on 29.3.19.)

5. **1st Petition.** On 10.3.19 General Officer Commanding-in-Chief passed to High Commissioner a letter from ALI IHSAN in which he says that he was arrested at Haidar Pasha and taken to a very bad prison in Galata. No reply given.

6. On 16.3.19 High Commissioner writes Egyptian Expeditionary Force that ALI IHSAN is in custody and will be sent to Malta. Offence under Article 1 of Foreign Office telegram 233. Also sending a copy of ALI IHSAN's complaint, (see para. 5). Copies of above to General Officer Commanding-in-Chief on 18.3.19. also to Mr. Balfour.

7. **2nd Petition.** On 11.4.19 ALI IHSAN from Malta petitions General Allenby. Later on 20.4.19 passes the petition to High Commissioner saying: "Beyond the attitude of obstruction which he took up in front of my Forces, I have nothing against him. I

therefore have no objection to his return to Turkey provided he is not reinstated." The above passes to G.O.C. on 14.5.19.

8. **M. 1642.** At a High Commissioners' meeting on 14.5.19: M. Defrance read accusations of massacre against ALI IHSAN in report from French Foreign Office. Mr. Defrance will send us a copy. This report is probably the one referred to below (para. 20) from French Consul at Tabriz.

9. **3rd Petition.** On 24.5.19. Assistant High Commissioner minutes: "I have an idea General Milne is hotly against his release". This minute made on receipt of a petition from ALI IHSAN through Governor Malta on 15.5.19, passed for information to General Officer Commanding-in-Chief on 28.5.19.

10. A memorandum dated 28.5.19. from list Lieut.-Colonel E.H. Keeling:

   (a) 'Intelligence' have General Allenby's reports about his obstruction in carrying out terms of the Armistice.

   (b) Also a report about his share in Armenian atrocities.

   (c) Quoting I.M.S. officers' reports of bad treatment of British Prisoners of War between Nisibin and Jezire on 28.10.18.

   (d) ALI IHSAN's bad treatment of Col. Keeling in January 1919 at Mardin. Opinion in Diarbekir, Mardin, Urfa, including the opinion of American Missionaries was that ALI IHSAN was actively fomenting anti-British and anti-Christian feeling.

11. On 5.6.19 at High Commissioners' Meeting "It is noted that ALI IHSAN is now at Malta. No action."

12. On 10.6.19 the High Commissioner minutes: - "I think if he is not whitewashed he had better stay where he is."

13. On 25.4.19 Foreign Office wire asking whether Turkish Government were at all concerned in the arrest and deportation, on 28.4.19. High Commissioner answer "No".

14. **4th Petition.** On 24.7.19 the Minister for Foreign Affairs petitions for his transfer as ALI IHSAN has not been able to acclimatise himself in Malta. No action.

15. **5th Petition.** On 10.12.19 letter from General Officer Commanding-in-Chief passing petition from wife to join him etc. On 19.12.19 High Commissioner asks Governor Malta to report as to ALI IHSAN's health.

15a. Governor of Malta on 5.1.20 reports him in good health; suffering from slight rheumatism.

16. Petition of 8.12.19 from ALI IHSAN to High Commissioner, duplicate to General Officer Commanding-in-Chief. Latter passed on for information.

16a. **R. 1447. Summary of correspondence, 1920 – 1921.** On 16.1.20 Assistant High Commissioner decided that ALI IHSAN should be considered a High Commissioner prisoner. Governor of Malta and General Officer Commanding-in-Chief informed on 18.1.20.

   7th Petition. R. 1447. Petition of 3.12.19, received 19.1.20.

   8th Petition. Petition of 6.2.20.

9th Petition. 133/24. Petition of 10.12.20, through Governor of Malta of 14.12.20, asking to be allowed to go to a sanatorium in Switzerland.

N.B. In High Commissioner's despatch to F.O. No. 1552/W.3667. dated 24.11.20, covering report of special committee, it was recommended that ALI IHSAN Pasha be detained at Malta until brought up for trial.

ACCUSATIONS

17. **R. 1447.** On 8.3.19 Colonel Cox, Teheran, wires re Armenian massacres: "In this connection ALI IHSAN should not be forgotten. If necessary I believe proof could be obtained that he not only instigated massacres but boasted of their performance."

Above telegram to General Officer Commanding-in-Chief on 14.3.19.

18. **5027.A.5.** On 12.3.19 Colonel Wilson sends from Bagdad a long report by Col. Agha Petros, Commander-in-Chief of the Assyrian Army in Urmia, on ALI IHSAN's atrocities on Assyrians of Urmia and other places. This report details fairly fully a number of outrages committed against Assyrians and Russians during the war; the murder of Mgr. Gontac (Sontag, French Lazarist) the papal delegate to Persia (on 31.7.18 in Urmia) together with 600 others (?Nestorians); massacre of 10,000 of people of Urmia between Khoy and Sain Kaket (Kala); massacre of Christians wounded in hospital on 19th May ? July 1918, including murder of Mr. John Nooshy, an American Journalist suffering from typhus; murder of a British Officer Captain Nickel, taken prisoner at Sain Kaleh (Kala) on 23.7.18.

Above could be testified by trustworthy Russian, American, and French witnesses (i.e. in March 1919). A note by Major Noel, dated 12.3.19, appended to the report by Col. Wilson challenges Col. Petros's report in his well known Kurdophile manner.

19. On 6.4.19 Military Attaché minutes that the Grand Vizier the Sultan and a host of others are continuously asking that ALI IHSAN should at least be told what crimes are alleged against him, implying that he is wrongfully detained. On 21.4.19 Military Attaché minutes:- "I gave Grand Vizier gist of the allegations (i.e. presumably Col. Petros') making it quite clear that they were allegations and were communicated to him personally and unofficially. I added, however, that these allegations, together with other information from independent sources, amply justified, in our opinion, the detention in custody of ALI IHSAN until the matter could be further elucidated. Grand Vizier agreed, and I do not think we shall hear any more about ALI IHSAN for the present.

20. On 27.5.19 Mr. Rohler communicated copy of a letter, dated Paris 28.4.19, from French Minister for Foreign Affairs to Monsieur Defrance covering copy of a report by French Consul at Tauris (Tabriz). Minister for Foreign Affairs instructs Mr. Defrance to have ALI IHSAN tried as the author of massacres in collaboration with other High Commissioners. The report dated Tauris 8.3.19 implicates ALI IHSAN in atrocities in North Persia in July 1919, also of the murder at Deliman of a French Lazarist. Mr. Rohler minutes that he is told that the writer of the report is a very reliable official.

21. On 28.1.19 Col. Keeling reports: "The influence of ALI IHSAN is paramount in all the districts I visited and is anti-Christian as well as anti-British. He organised the later massacre at Van . . ."

22. On 10.3.19 "Joghovourt" published an account of ALI IHSAN's activities by an officer who had served three years under his orders. The following is a translation. "This sad hero, during 1914/1915, was on the front of Caucasus as Commander of 51st Division. At that time Halil Bey (now Pasha), the uncle of Enver, was commanding the 52nd Division. ALI IHSAN together with Halil, murdered all Armenians attached to those two Divisions: doctors, apothecaries, officers and others.

ALI IHSAN was during 1916/17 on the Persian front. At Kirmanshah he edited in the Persian language the newspapers "Ahbar", and in Hamadan the "Taze Iran".

ALI IHSAN was the dictator of all the occupied countries in Persia. One day the newspaper "Taze Iran" was writing in regard to Armenians, "Oh Persian brothers, your Custom House, Gendarmerie, Treasury, Post and Telegraph and all Persia is in the hands of Armenians and she is the slave of these faithless men. Why and to what day are you waiting to get rid of this slavery and regain your independence? Destroy, then, your enemies."

In a pamphlet he wrote the following to excite the criminal feelings of the Moslem mob: "Until when the Moslems will tolerate the Christians? Since the day when Bishop Horen took the leadership of Armenian volunteers and gave up to have the usual wine during the Consecration in the Church, but instead of that wine, he violated a Moslem girl . . . ." ALI IHSAN used to sign "Mirdar of Turkish and Persian Armies and Chief of Union of Islam."

In the month of April 1918, after the battle of Dilman, he published an order addressed to the Army saying that even Armenian women, old men and children must not be spared.

When ALI IHSAN Pasha settled down at Mosul, as Commander of the VIth Army, together with the Commandant de Place Divas Bey (? Nevzade Bey), who used to cry out that he did not wish to see an Armenian's shop left open in Mosul, he collected all male deported Armenians from 14 to 70 and formed from them a working battalion. This battalion was to make a road called "Fouran Yolou"[Oven Road] which would lead to Caucasus. The officers of this working battalion received the following instructions.

1. If any soldier gets sick, do not send to hospitals. In consequence of this more than 70 Armenians died within two days, on the way from Mosul to Guver.

2. It is necessary to shoot those who try to escape or remain back. As the result of this instruction, all the officers were provided with Mauser rifles and were invited to fulfil their duty very strictly.

3. In case one of these soldiers tried to escape, orders were given to the officers to shoot down all his relatives.

On the front of Ravanduz, the Commander of the 22nd battalion, Hadji Ibrahim took prisoner nearly 200 Armenian volunteers from the group of Agha Bedros.

On the other hand the Armenians had 800 Turkish prisoners. The Armenians sent in a list of all these 800 prisoners to the Turkish Commander notifying that these prisoners had been handed over to the British Authorities, and at the end of the War all would be sent back.

Hadji Ibrahim did quite the contrary and all these 200 Armenian prisoners were divided between his soldiers and massacred.

The Turkish Commander-in-Chief, who was aware of the good conduct and treatment of Armenians towards the Turkish prisoners, called Hadji Ibrahim and reprimanded him. Hadji Ibrahim replied to the Commander-in-Chief very coldly "I was so much excited with patriotism that I did not know what I was doing". It was this assassin that ALI IHSAN promoted to the rank of Colonel.

We do not know whether these atrocities will constitute titles of honours to ALI IHSAN Pasha and we do not know also if the Cabinet of Ferid Pasha will try to save this assassin from the hand of Justice. We will see. In any case Justice would be blind and lame if ALI IHSAN should not be condemned after all these mischiefs done by him."

23. **5035/A/31.** On 14.4.19 "1" sent report by an Arab Christian, Tevfik Layegh, in which he mentions the massacre of Nestorians on ALI IHSAN's orders.

24. **'Renaissance' 14.6.19.** (for Mihran Boyadjian's evidence before Court-Martial on 3.5.19. See C.1.) 'Renaissance' of 14.6.19 contains an account of ALI IHSAN's atrocities in the region of Mosul in 1918. The account is signed M.B. The following more or less specific accusations are made:

   (a) Massacre of Armenian soldiers of Labour Battalion. If any escaped it was due to the intervention of Col. Leachman, British Political Officer, Mossul, on British occupation of that place.

   (b) Hanging without trial of the baker Serope, his sister and his partner.

   (c) Just previous to the Turkish evacuation of Mossul in October 1918, ALI IHSAN ordered the deportation and massacre at Zakho of one hundred Christian families.

25. **5033/A/8.** Intelligence report from Aleppo, dated 22.5.19.

"The following report has been received from an intelligent and reliable agent. (1) Re Captain Assir Bey, passport officer on railway; re George Tanti, Station master at Ras-ul-Ain; re Monsieur Ashe at Nissibin . . . "The indiscriminate sales of these German stores brought IHSAN Pasha untold wealth. When Ihsan Pasha was deported to Constantinople, he begged the British to allow him a whole special train on the payment of £10,000 in paper. In this train IHSAN Pasha took away with him most of the worst C.U.P. characters."

26. Letter and report, dated 27.1.20, from Mr. H. P. Packard, in charge of the American Hospital in Urumia from 1906 to 1920, written from Constantinople on his way to America. "I enclose a brief statement of outrages that resulted from the Turkish push, under ALI IHSAN Pasha, into North-West Persia. The worst single outrage, among military men, for which the Turks were responsible, was committed by one of ALI IHSAN's subalterns, Yosif Zia Effendi, bimbashi, the last Moslem Commandant of the Turks in Urmia. It would be hard to find a more cold-blooded murderer. He asked me for a list of wounded in our hospital and the dates of their admission. Later he sent doctors to investigate the scars and wounds of over 20 men. Eleven were selected as men who were most probably wounded by the Turks in the fighting about Urmia. He said that he must take these men, indicating that he intended to send them back to a base hospital. One evaded them by lying about his wounds; but ten were taken from the Hospital about September 19th 1918, (the records have all been lost). They went to the

gate of the Hospital yard, several on crutches, for 3 had amputated legs and others had bad wounds with bone disease and from the gate their crutches were returned with the word that they would not need them. Three days later I heard that a number of spies had been captured and executed. It took little investigation to prove that the alleged spies were the unfortunate cripples and that their execution was simply the mangling of defenceless and helpless cripples, dragged from a hospital.

There were many outrages committed in the Urmia region, but they do not bear so directly on the case of ALI IHSAN Pasha. It was the instruction and practice among the Turks to execute their Armenian or other Christian soldiers. We saw some of this in the first Turkish occupation of Urumia, January 4, to May 21 1915."

26a. On June 18 and 19, 1918 the Christian refugees who escaped from Khoy, reached Urumia, to the number of 1,200. These were listed by the American Relief Committee and given one distribution of relief before their flight to the South. Before they left Khoy their number was 3,300. 2,100 had disappeared, 287 selected young men killed by the outlaw Ismail Agha [Kurd] (Simco) and the rest massacred by Turks and Persians when the North-West of Persia was occupied by Turkish forces under ALI IHSAN Pasha. The above mentioned were all mountain Nestorians, men of Mar Shimun who escaped from Turkey during the second year of the war. 5,000 of these refugees were scattered in 31 villages of the Khoy region. Some 1,700 wandered off in the Caucasus and our relief lists showed 3,300 at the time of the arrival of the Turks in 1918. In addition to these Syrians or Assyrians who were killed in Khoy, some 700 Armenians residents of Khoy were also massacred at the same time, June 1918.

The Salmas Christians, residents and refugees [fleeing] from Turkey, also fled to Urumia in June 1918. No guard was placed to protect the flying [fleeing] Christians, and 5,000 or more were cut off by Kurds and Turks. On the arrival of a few escaped refugees, a few days later, we learned of the massacre of all these, save 200. Now 176 are still alive in Salmas, fed by American relief. Mr. Lhotellier, a French Lazarist priest, and several other priests were murdered at this time. We all believed that ALI IHSAN Pasha was responsible for these outrages, and Christians were everywhere fearful that his arrival would be a signal for massacres in Tabriz, Maragha and Urumia, as well as in Khoy and Salmas. Threats of it reached us. On July 30th and 31st 1918, the Christians fled from Urumia to the south. This included residents and refugees from Khoy and Salmas (Diliman) and mountaineers from Turkey and some 16,000 Van Armenians. As many as 75,000 started on that fateful flight. Many were old and feeble, or ill and unprepared, or unable to make any provision for the journey and remained. Perhaps 5,000 remained behind in Urumia. Nearly 1,000 were killed on that day, July 31st 1918, which was the day that the Turks entered the city, almost on the heels of the flying Christians. The Turks took over the American Mission Yards. One was used as headquarters for the Pan-Islamic propaganda and later a school. One was used as headquarters for the Commandant, the first Military Governor of the city of Urumia. He entered our City Mission Yard, where I was with my associate Dr. W.

P. Ellis, at about 11am, July 31st 1918. Persians must bear the responsibility for some of the crimes of that day for they were eager to commit outrages and did commit them when the presence of the Turks made it safe to do so with impunity.

The murder of the Director of the American Orphanage at 4.30 to 5.30 p.m. on July 31st, 1918, must be counted against the Turks, for it happened not less than 5 hours after they were in control of the city of Urumia. The Turks also are responsible for the murder of the older orphan boys and the refugees, Armenians and Syrians, who fled to the Orphanage, and Turks shared with the Persians in the looting of the place. The Turks deported 2,500 Syrians and Armenians from Urumia to Salmas in August and October and less than two hundred lived to return to Urumia in November.

The murder of Monseigneur Sontag, Superior of the French Lazarist Mission and Papal legate to the Shah, and the massacre of 620 persons in the French Mission at Urumia on July 31, 1918 was only a part of the murders, outrages and rapine that characterised the last drive of Turkish forces under ALI IHSAN Pasha into North-West Persia. Even if it is proved, as it may be, that Persians were responsible, it can easily be proved that they were those who shared in inviting the Turks into Persia and helped them in carrying out their diabolical schemes to cut off the Christians root and branch.

The attitude of Turks in Tabriz shows the sort of instruction and propaganda that was abroad among them. Some Persians saw Turks committing massacres close by a mosque and remonstrated with them. The Turks cursed the Persians and said, "There are no Moslems here. If there were, infidels would not be walking on your streets". After our deportation to Tabriz, October 8th 1918, we heard from many Syrians and Armenians, physicians, dentists and merchants of the terrible fear that they had of extermination, when they heard that ALI IHSAN would probably come to Tabriz. The 3,000 to 4,000 massacred in Khoy; the 5,000 massacred in Salmas and the 1,000 killed in and about Urumia must be credited chiefly to ALI IHSAN Pasha. Mojil-i-Sultaneh, the famous Persian madman, (captured by the British and proved by them to be worthy of death on any one of five counts, according to Col. Sanders of the British Intelligence Service, in the Caucasus but afterwards turned over to the Persian Government) had a part in the Turkish push in Persia. He with other outlaws, and a few Turks pushed after the Christians, who fled from Urumia to Hamadan, July 31st 1918. He telegraphed from Miaudnab to Tabriz "I have sent 'Giavours' to Gehanna."

To prove that ALI IHSAN was responsible for this and to show that it was his purpose to massacre the Christians after capturing them, as he hoped to do in Urumia, the testimony of Sabit Bey Effendi, head of the 6th mobile hospital with the fourth Colordou which came to Urumia, (would be useful). This important man told me that Salah-i-Din Bey, Commander of the 4th Colordou, was accused by ALI IHSAN Pasha of being responsible for permitting the escape of Christians to the South. For this reason Salah-i-Din Bey, en route from Urumia to Constantinople for a rest, was arrested in Tiflis.

K.2. Extract from a Patriarchate report of 26.2.21 on Suleiman Nazif, Vali of Mossul, up to December 1914:– "The names of the chief executive agents and helps of Suleiman Nazif are ALI IHSAN, Hussein Reouf Bey (a General Officer Commanding-in-Chief deportee), Ibrahim Fazi (on Foreign Office list, not yet arrested) etc.

The evidence against all these men will be found in the dossiers containing the secret correspondence between Central Headquarters (of the C.U.P.) and Suleiman Nazif.

SABIT BEY
(SAGHIR ZADE SABIT BEY, of KEMAKH)
Malta No. 2686

Interned 2.6.1919

Appointments. Mutessarif of the sanjak of Dersim (capital of the sanjak: Khozat) from 17.8.09 to 10.7.14. The deputy for Dersim, Mehmed Nuri (a Malta deportee) had him transferred as:- Vali of Mamouret-ul-Aziz. In February 1916 (? or 1917) he was transferred as: Vali of Erzerum, when in April 1918 he was transferred as: Vali of Sivas. From this last post he was "removed by the Council of Ministers upon an Administrative necessity recognised at the time".

N.B. As his appointment to Erzerum is said to have been dated 19.2.17 it is possible that he was without a post from February 1916 to February 1917.

He is known to have been on leave in Constantinople in the autumn of 1917.

He was nominated as Vali of Sivas by Izzet Pacha but only held that appointment for a few months.

Lists. On list III, that is his arrest was suggested by Mr. Ryan to the Grand Vizier on 27.3.19.

Arrest. He was arrested early in 1919 by the Turkish Government. He was amongst those surrendered to the British Military Authorities on 28.5.19, and deported to Malta.

Trial before Turkish Court-Martial. It is probable that SABIT BEY was brought up before the Court Martial.

Petitions. R. 2785. (a) Petition of 3.2.19 from wife. Enclosing ? copy of telegram from American Consul, Harput to Embassy, dated 25.2.17 asking that SABIT should not be transferred from Harput (to Erzerum) "in view of his courtesy towards Americans and others and our personal friendship." **5030/A/4.** (b) Petition from wife of 21.8.20 per Mr. Ryan.

ACCUSATIONS

5030/A/4. Report dated 4.3.19 by Dr. H. H. Riggs, American missionary at Harput. See Appendix A. On this report Admiral Webb minuted on 5.3.19 "both must be hanged, obviously." 'Both' referred to SABIT BEY and Hadji Mehmet Effendi, deputy for Harput, (on Foreign Office list, but not yet arrested).

5035/a/11.b. His name appears as 42nd on list of first hundred criminals supplied by the Armenian Patriarchate in December 1918.

C. 18. Alleged original orders from SABIT BEY to Assim Bey, Kaimakam of Harput, with reference to the deportations. **N.B.** These documents were handed in by the wife of Assim Bey (now released from Malta) and require verification.

C. 9 69. Statement by Hagop Megurian of Samsun giving an account of the Hassan Chelibi massacres, on the main road from Sivas to Malatia, in the Kaza of Argha, in the sanjak of Malatia, in the vilayet of Mamouret-ul-Aziz, at the time when Reshid Bey was Mutessarif of Malatia and SABIT BEY the Vali of the Province.

E. 18. Statement by Mehmet Namik Bey, Director of Police, Harput; see Appendix B.

H. 4. Important telegrams from or to SABIT BEY; see Appendix C. All these telegrams were communicated to the High Commission in translation. They are alleged to be translations of Turkish official telegrams.

G. XV. SABIT BEY is listed in the Patriarchate's detailed list of September 1920 with the note: "Guilty of the greatest cruelties."[*]

J. 32. The chief of the Techkilati Mahsousse, Behaddine Chakir to the Vali of Mamouret-ul-Aziz, SABIT BEY. Ciphered telegram No. 5 of 21st June 1331 [1915].

"For NAZIM BEY. Do you liquidate the Armenians who are deported from there? Do you destroy the dangerous persons whom you say you expatriate or banish; or do you deport them only? Please answer me clearly on this point, dear friend."

J. 24, 126, 162, 167, 174, 177, 177 bis, 176, 180, 181, 183, 184. French translations of alleged official Turkish telegrams to or from SABIT BEY, February 1915 to December 1915. See Appendix D.

N.B. All the above telegrams were communicated to High Commission in translation. They are alleged to be translations of Turkish official telegrams.

30/A/4

APPENDIX A

**ARMENIAN DEPORTATIONS FROM HARPOOT
THE ATTITUDE OF THE VALI**

The impression gained by the American residents of Harpoot during the deportations was that the extreme severity of the measures taken, and the absolute licence given to those who murdered and abused the Armenians, were due to the personality of the Vali, **SABIT BEY,** who, I learn, is now on trial in the Turkish courts.

The grounds on which the impression was based are somewhat as follows:

1. The Armenian men, who were massacred en masse, within the boundaries of the vilayet, were marched out bound and under heavy armed guard, and murdered within a few hours of their departure. The guards were gendarmes, sometimes aided by a few police. I have known of no evidence that the massacres were committed by any others than the guards themselves, and they were constantly under the orders of the Vali, who, at the time, seemed in autocratic control.

2. The abuse of women and children, and their neglect to the extent that they died by thousands, took place under our eyes. I have seen the brutality of police and Gendarmes in beating and otherwise abusing Armenian women, and never knew of any case of such abuse being rebuked or punished by the Vali. The detention camp where Armenian exiles stopped on their way south was within a few minutes' walk of the Vali's house, and the house, and the horrible conditions, the unbearable stench

---

[*] The note appears in French and has been translated into English –WCB.

and the ceaseless activity of the burying squad at that camp were matters of common observation for months, but the Vali took no steps to stop the continual loss of life that took place there, which, by inference, was known to be taking place all along the road through the province.

3. The number of survivors passing through Harpoot from the north was very great, but comparatively few were known to have passed on beyond the Vilayet. Two Americans, Consul L. A. Davis and Dr. H. H. Atkinson, went over the road along which these exiles passed on from Harpoot, and they both reported to me that within twenty miles of the Vali's headquarters they had seen dead bodies to an estimated number of ten thousand, unburied, and a large proportion of them being freshly murdered on the spot. Most of them were women and children, and bore marks of horrible mutilation. These facts were matters of common knowledge even before these witnesses made their investigations. There was at that time no uprising of any sort among the inhabitants of that region, and the conclusion was inevitable that the massacre of thousands of exiles, who had survived the journey from their distant homes into the Vilayet of Mamouret-ul-Aziz, was by the direct command of the man who was at that time supreme in that province, the Vali, SABIT BEY.

4. The attitude of SABIT BEY was further made evident to me by the way in which he made full promises of protection and safety for the exiles, and then acted exactly contrary to his promises. For example, a few days before the majority of the Armenian men of Harpoot were arrested and marched off under his guards to their death, SABIT BEY said to me, in response to an appeal made by the foreign residents of Harpoot, "I promise you (Sizi Te emin ederim) that no man will be sent away under arrest. All will be allowed to travel with their families." This was only one instance of a large number, where he displayed perfidy as well as cruelty.

APPENDIX B
STATEMENT OF MEHMED NAMIK BEY

Late Director of Police of Harput. (Introduced by Dr. Keshishian, now of 27 Rue Bilezik, Pancaldi; see Mehmet Nuri's dossier.)

13.9.20, signed original in E 18. SABIT BEY was born at Kemach and is now aged 38 years. He is son of an Eshraff of Kemach. His first appointment was an ad interim Mutessarif of Dersim. When the Minister of War, Nazim Pasha, was killed and the CUP came into power he became Mutessarif of Dersim, (from Feb. 1328 [1912] to May 1330 [1914]. He worked very hard in favour of CUP in that town and sent large sums of money to the Central Committee where his services were appreciated and he was promoted as Vali of Harput in June or July 1914. SABIT BEY remained there until August 1916. SABIT BEY was the soul of the Armenian deportations, together with Nazim Bey, CUP Delegate and Mehmed Nuri Bey, an influential member of the local CUP. SABIT BEY ordered me to collect arms and to round up the representatives of the Dashnaktzutioun. I found only 29 persons belonging to this Armenian Organisation and but a very few bombs. I brought this to the notice of SABIT BEY and urged him to punish these men only. SABIT BEY refused to listen replying that orders had come from the Central Government, signed by Behaeddin Shakir, that the whole Armenian population had to be deported and annihilated. As he was a true disciple of the CUP he carried out the orders to the letter. He deserves to be punished very severely.

(N.B. Mehmet Namik was dismissed from his post by SABIT BEY, apparently for not being sufficiently zealous.)

APPENDIX C
TRANSLATION OF COPIES OF TELEGRAMS FROM OR TO SABIT BEY, Vali of Mamuret-ul-Aziz; SULEIMAN FAIK PASHA, Vali ad Interim of Mamuret-ul-Aziz; TAHSIN BEY, Vali of Erzerum

N.B. Suleiman Faik Pasha (now at Malta) acted for the Vali, SABIT BEY, whilst the latter was touring his province during the deportation period.

1. **H 4.** Telegram No. 33, dated 16th ? 1915 from SULEIMAN FAIK Pasha to the Commander of the 3rd Army Corps at Torkum. The application of the measures decided upon having been left (for execution) to the Vilayet the Amele Taburu (Labour Battalion) was to have been sent to Diarbekir (from Harput). The Battalion reached Maden (Arghana Maden) without incident. After passing Maden and in the vicinity of Keban Bogaz (i.e. in the Vilayet of Diarbekir) Armenian Bands suddenly appeared on both sides and opened fire. This caused excitement among the men of the Labour Battalion mentioned above, all of whom broke from the column and ran to join the Armenian bands. (The escort) opened fire on those who were disobeying the order to stand. A great many of the men of the Labour Battalion, as well as men of the Armenian Bands were killed. Both the Commandant and the Provincial Government sent out reinforcements, but in view of the inaccessibility of the ground they were not able to make any prisoners. The rebels are being hunted down. During the fighting one soldier (of the Turkish escort) was killed, three rifles and one bayonet were rendered unserviceable. The detachment (escort) considered it useless to remain any longer and they have now returned.

    The above is from a report by the officer commanding the detachment (or escort).

2. **Nazim Bey, Delegate of the CUP at Harput. On F.O. List for arrest. Mehmet Nury Bey, deputy for Dersim (Vilayet of Mamuret-ul-Aziz). Now at Malta.** Telegram No. . . . . dated 25th July 1915, from SABIT BEY at Dersim (the sanjak north of Harput and in the same vilayet) to the Ministry of the Interior.

    With the exception of the centre Malatia, which will be cleared within the next few days, no Armenians are left in the vilayet (of Mamuret-ul-Aziz) and its dependencies (i.e. ? the sandjak of Erzingan in 1915).

    With a view to prevent the many abuses taking place through the deportation of the Armenians and seeing that a thorough overhaul was necessary, Suleiman Faik, Vali ad interim and Commander of the Army Corps, has today sent me the following copy of a telegram. I regret to say that I am convinced as to the truth of the whole question. I suggest that Inspector Nazim Bey should be recalled to Constantinople, that further measures against Nazim Bey and Deputy Mehmet Bey should be decided upon in Constantinople, and that the officials of the Vilayet, whose complicity is proved should be at once dismissed. I am ready to carry out whatever instructions are conveyed to me.

2.A. Copy (from SULEIMAN FAIK (? at Mezre) to SABIT BEY at Dersim).

    Nazim Bey Inspector of the Union and Progress considering the Armenian Deportations a great occasion to enrich himself has proceeded to several measures which later on became perfectly clear; and all this a little before your visiting Dersim.

Appendix "I"

Great sums of money were stolen and everything done in the name of the CUP reached a point which cannot be tolerated by anybody. Even the members of the Central Committee have recently resigned and only the afore-mentioned Nazim Bey, together with the Secretary General Shevki Bey, are still connected with it. One of those who played the greatest role in these affairs is Mehmed Bey, deputy of Dersim. The Inspector, profiting by his position, has stolen much money and other things, and now begins to threaten the Sirianis (?) [Assyrians]. Under these circumstances I hope that in future you will continue to enjoy the unparalleled and perfect public confidence in view of your noble attitude, and that being connected with the honourable Committee, I particularly express to you my special satisfaction. Signed SULEIMAN FAIK.

2.B. To Vali SABIT BEY at Dersim.

Nazim Bey, Inspector of the CUP, considering the Armenian deportations a great occasion for increasing his personal wealth has a little before your visit to Dersim, proceeded to several measures which became quite obvious later on. Thousands of pounds are being stolen. The evils done in the name of the CUP have become intolerable. Six members of the Central Committee have recently resigned. He, together with the Secretary General and the Defterdar only remain. One of those who played the greatest role in these affairs is the Deputy Mehmed Bey. The Inspector, profiting by his position has looted much money, goods and girls, and now begins to threaten the Sirianis (?). Goods excepted, the amount of money collected up to now in the name of the Committee amounts to more than 10,000 pounds. Under these circumstances we hope that in future too you will continue to enjoy the unparalleled and perfect general confidence because of your noble attitude, and we consider it our patriotic duty to express to you our special satisfaction. Please take from the telegraph office the copy of the telegram.

Signatures:
   MEHMED ALI Central Commander
   FERID Regimental Gendarmerie Commander
   FERID Maarif Mudiri
   RUCHDI Police Mudiri

N.B. Of the signatures, Mehmed Ali may be the Mehmed Ali Pasha who committed suicide on 11.3.19. Ferid Bey is the Provincial Director of Education who was arrested by the Turkish Authorities on 20.7.19 and released in January 1920. The other Ferid was a Major commanding the gendarmerie at Mezre, the headquarters for the Vilayet, noted as one of the principals in the Harput atrocities, Rushdi, the police Mudiri is not yet on Index.

3. Telegram No. . . . dated the 16th July 1915, from Tahsin Bey, Vali of Erzerum to SABIT BEY, Vali of Mamuret-ul-Aziz.
The details given by Your Excellency on the 13th July 1915 have made a great impression on me. The state of things described amounts to anarchy and it is

contrary to the wishes of the Government and of our Party. I have communicated to the Minister, Talaat Bey, your statements as well as all that I have seen and heard. The welfare of the country requires that everyone at all responsible should be at once withdrawn. Everywhere I am saying that whatever we did, we have **not** done it in order to fill with money the pockets of some persons. It is because we are after the salvation of the Government that we are deporting the Armenians to the south. This is the sole object. It is advisable that you too should write in this sense to the Ministry. Anyhow, please send the deported groups of Erzeroum via Malatia. It may be that they will be attacked at Eghin. Please send trustworthy officials to the District between Kamahk and Eghin. It is necessary that officials should know the object and intentions of the Government. The army advances with full success. I am going to inform you that 800 prisoners were taken.

N.B. Tahsin and Memduh both at Malta. The route taken by the Majority of the Erzerum deportees was via Erzingan (then a Sanjak dependent on Erzerum), down the valley of the Kara Su, past Kemakh and Egin, to Arabkir, Malatia and the South. Very large numbers were duly massacred between Kemakh and Egin (under instructions from Tahsin and his Mutessarif of Erzingan, Memduh Bey.)
The boundary between Erzingan and Mamuret-ul-Aziz is just north of Egin.

APPENDIX D
FRENCH TRANSLATION of TELEGRAMS to or from SABIT BEY*

J. 24 The Vali of Mamuret-ul-Aziz, SABIT, at Nabi, Mutessarif of Malatia. Ciphered telegram dated 2nd February, 1915.

"Where is the formation? Is it ready to be realised? I ask you earnestly to use all your efforts and activity to send within 30 days some police force to the main town of the vilayet".

J. 126 The Vali of Mamuret-ul-Aziz, SABIT, to the Minister of the Interior, Talaat. Ciphered telegram dated 28th July, 1915.

"The first convoy coming from Erzeroum has been received at Kourou Tehri by the interim Kaimakam of Egin, Abdulkader Effendi, who escorted it, safe and sound, with the Kaimakam of Kemakh up to Egin. Then Abdulkader Effendi has left the town with the convoy to escort it via Arabkir, up to Malatia. The Kaimakam of Kemakh has stayed at Egin. Measures have been taken to ensure the passage of the second and third convoys in the same conditions. I have also asked with insistence the Mutessarif of Malatia that on the arrival of the convoys in this town, they should be sent away under the protection of the Kaimakams and of reliable officers."

J. 162 The Vali of Mamuret-ul-Aziz, SABIT, to the Mutessarif of Malatia, Reshid. (Kurd Reshid was Mutessarif for a few months in 1915. He succeeded Nabi Bey and was himself replaced by Hussein Sirri Bey in September 1915. Both Reshid and Sirri Beys are on the F.O. List.) (Sirri Bey is a member of the Kemalist delegation to the London Conference).
Dated 21st August, 1915.

"I learn that in spite of repeated communications, one finds again on the roads too many dead bodies. I need not tell you all the inconvenience this presents and the Ministry of Interior has just repeated its orders as to the severe punishment of the civil servants who would show negligence. Once more I ask you earnestly to invest a sufficient number of police forces and of superior civil servants with the task of having buried with great care all the dead bodies which might be found within the limits of the Vilayet and with this view to send the above mentioned persons in all directions. Keep me informed. I am awaiting your answer."

J. 167 The Vali of Mamuret-ul-Aziz, SABIT, to the Mutessarif of Malatia, Reshid. Dated 10th September 1331 [1915].

"It comes to my knowledge that there still exists in the regions of Husnimanssour and of Behesni festering dead bodies. In my former and recent communications I have sufficiently stressed that it should not be allowed, as well as from the point of view of Government policy as from that of public hygiene, to let stand uncovered

---

* The original document appears in French and has been translated into English –WCB.

and festering these dead bodies. Please give formally the strictest instructions to Kaimakams of the said Kazas, so that they have buried all these dead bodies."

J. 174 The Vali of Mamuret-ul-Aziz, SABIT, to (?).
Ciphered telegram of the 21st September 1331 [1915].
"It comes to my knowledge that contrary to my repeated communications one still finds too large a number of dead bodies on the roads. It is vain to speak here of the many inconveniences that this state of affairs presents and the Ministry of Interior has just, once more, ordered to punish severely the civil servants who would show negligence in this matter. I repeat once more that you must send to all points of the Vilayet enough police forces under the orders of some well known civil servants with the mission to bury with care all the dead bodies which will be found. I await your answer with information on that subject."

J. 177 The Vali SABIT, to Erzindjan, at the Vilayet of Mamouret-ul-Aziz (i.e. Suleiman Faik Pasha, Vali ad interim)
Dated 21st October 1331 [1915]
"It comes back to my knowledge that there is still here and there a rather considerable number of Armenians, men and women coming from various places, and without support. As this situation is of a nature to prepare the ruin of the country, I ask you to call them together and send them under safe guard via Diarbekir and to inform me."

J. 177 bis The interim Vali d'El-Aziz SABIT, To Erzindjan.
Ciphered telegram dated 21st October 1331 [1915].
"A commission of enquiry had been set up with the view of discovering the Armenians of the country and those arrived from the exterior, who have stayed here in hiding and it has already sent a convoy recently. According to the orders of your Excellency it has been speeded up, still more, it's working and in a few days' time an end will have been put to this situation." (in Turkish: bou guibilerine arkassi alnadjak).

J. 178 The Mutessarif of Malatia (Hussein Sirri to the Vali (of El-Aziz) i.e. Suleiman Faik, Vali ad interim, or SABIT, the Vali).
From 3rd October 1331 [1915].
"I have the honour to inform your Excellency of what follows: 1,582 houses with a population of 3,341 men and 3,594 women were registered at Malatia. The Armenians of 1,550 houses, i.e. 3,246 men and 3,492 women have been sent away. The remaining part, 32 houses with 95 men and 102 women belong to the class of the "esnaf" and have been retained for this reason. Moreover 30 men and 60 women who had not left or who had escaped from the convoy are back in town and being prosecuted; lastly, about 600 men and 400 women including persons without support, and children, arrive from the exterior, are at the Orphanage or live with the inhabitants. There still exists 130 men and 185 women Catholic, 50 men and 80 women, Protestant, and 30 Latins of both sexes, who because of the delay of

deportation have been left here by the chief of the Police, in accordance with the special order. A convoy of more than 3,000 persons was sent a few days ago and another important convoy is on its way to Malatia coming from Hekim-Khan".

J. 180 The Mutessarif of Malatia to the Vali of El-Aziz (SABIT).
Dated 5th November 1331 [1915].
"From news received from the Kaimakams, there is no Armenian left at Bihesni or at Kiakhte. At Aktche-Dagh, there is no native Armenian and the women who have been brought there from other places have taken the Moslem religion and married. Also at Husnu Mansour there is no native Armenian left to be sent, 3 or 4 families of artisans have taken the Moslem religion. The formalities relative to these conversions are being terminated, similarly for children under age of both sexes in the protection of reliable persons, and for the young virgins who are engaged to be married. If other Armenians come along, besides these, the necessary measures will be taken."

J. 181 The Vali SABIT to Mutessarif of Malatia.
On the 12th November 1331 [1915].
"There is no objection to set free the prostitutes, preferably the Catholics and Protestants, so long as their number is not more than 15."

J. 183 The Minister of Interior, Talaat, to the Valis.
On the 19th December 1331 [1915].
"I am informed that in certain parts corpses have been found which are not buried. I ask you to give the most stringent orders so that these corpses or their debris which might be in your Vilayet be buried, and to suspend the civil servants of the Kazas on whose territories corpses may be found, giving their names".

J. 184 The Vali SABIT to Mutessarif of Malatia.
On the 25th December 1331 [1915].
"I have deciphered above a ciphered telegram from the Ministry of Interior. As soon as these sorts of corpses are found in the Kaza, the Kaimakams, the Mudirs and the 'commandants of gendarmerie' will be immediately suspended from their functions and sent to the tribunal. I am awaiting your answer."

VELI NEDJET BEY

Malta No. 2687

Interned 2.6.19

Appointments. Chief Clerk in the Secretariat of the Diarbekir Vilayet. Chief of Police, ad interim, replacing Hussein Effendi in May 1915.

Lists. On list I, i.e. he was suggested for arrest by Mr. Ryan to Grand Vizier Izzet Bey on 23.1.19.

Arrest. Arrested by the Turkish Government on 30.1.19 and among those surrendered to the British Military Authorities on 28.5.19. He was among those deported on 28.5.19. – under point 5 of F.O. telegram 233.

Petitions. W. 2178 Petition of 26.7.20 in which he describes himself as a clerk in the Diarbekir Provincial Secretariat (Mumeyiz). In December 1914 he was appointed Assistant Director of the section of the tribes at the office of Emigrants at Constantinople.

Arising out of this petition much correspondence of a general nature ensued. Sir H. Lamb and Captain Armstrong wished to refer the revising of all cases against deportees to Mr. H. Pears. For a long minute on the subject by Mr. Ruxton see Appendix A. Finally H.C. wrote to G.O.C.-in-C. suggesting a joint revision of all cases by legal experts. G.O.C. declined suggestion.

In November 1920 the High Commissioner appointed a special committee to revise the lists of Malta deportees. This committee drew up a report with appendices which were submitted to the F.O. under cover of despatch No. 1552/W 3667, dated 24th November 1920.

ACCUSATIONS

A. 20. Vague and unsigned statement: He was employed in the Direction Générale des Deportés. He is responsible for the massacres (in Diarbekir) and as an Inspector attached to the Secretariat of the Vilayet he took charge of the jewelry and monies of the deportees, without any sort of control being exercised. As a reward for his services the house of Tirpandjian, an Armenain notable was offered to him.

C. 19. Report by Mihran Boyadjian, late a 1st Class Inspector in the Eastern Vilayets, on Fezi Bey deputy for Diarbekir, dated 13.2.20.

In this report VELI NEDJET is mentioned as a member of the Teshkilat Mehsusse formed by Fezi Bey and Dr. Reshid, the Vali of Diarbekir in 1915. This special organisation began the work of massacring the Christian population of the Vilayet, some 120,000.

D. 29. In "Faits et Documents: Episodes des Massacres Arméniens de Diarbekir", published in 1920, VELI NEDJET is listed on page 15 as among those directly responsible for the massacres in the vilayet of Diarbekir.

H. 13. Report by Mihran Boyadjian on VELI NEDJET, dated 7.9.20. Appendix B.

H. 14. Patriarchate's report, dated 8.9.20, on VELI NEDJET. Said to be the son of a renegade Italian Dr. Bonelli known as Veli Baba. Before the War he was Clerk to the Diarbekir Criminal Court. He became chief of the Correspondence Bureau of the Vilayet. In 1915 the C.U.P. dismissed Dersimli Hussein Effendi the Chief of the Police, and put in VELI NEDJET in his stead; he was thus Acting Chief of Police during the three months in which the deportations took place. An associate of the notorious Vali Dr. Reshid it was he who planned and ordered the execution of the terrible atrocities that took place.

VELI NEDJET sent off the first convoy of Armenian notables from Diarbekir. This convoy numbered some six hundred (men). VELI NEDJET had them all slaughtered at about 2 hours' distance from the town with the exception of the Armenian prelate Tchigatian Vartabed. "After having kept that prelate under the obligation of seeing the Armenian butchered before his eyes, he had him brought back to the Prison and had him tortured in the most atrocious manner."

"The house of VELI NEDJET was situated behind the prison and the shrieks of the prelate, tortured in the hall at some yards of the house, were heard for hours by VELI NEDJET who expressed only his contentment."

"As a reward for the cruelty he had shown in the extermination of tens of thousands of Armenians of the town of Diarbekir, the C.U.P. granted him the permission to rob at his pleasure the banking house of Tirpandjian, the renowned Armenian Banker of Diarbekir. In the house of Tirpandjian, there was a stock of jewels of a value of more than two hundred thousand pounds, left there as a guarantee for loans of Armenians from different parts of the vilayets, who had been brought to the dire necessity of borrowing money to satisfy the greedy exactions of the Turkish functionaries during the period preceding the deportations. Full power was given to VELI NEDJET by the C.U.P. to become the owner of the house of Tirpindjian, the banking office situated in it, and all the wealth that was contained in it.

VELI NEDJET began to be considered as the legal owner of the succession of Tirpandjian and his family whom he had slaughtered and become a rich man in Diarbekir enjoying the esteem of his fellow citizens.

The witnesses against VELI NEDJET are:
1. Kevork Fikri, Armenian judge at the court of appeal of Diarbekir, who escaped deportation and saved his life by becoming a Moslem with his wife. He is presently in Constantinople.
2. Sheker Badj and her mother, an Armenian woman employed in the orphanage of Yedi-Koule.

3. Doctor Krikorian and his sister at Minassian's home Kadikeuy.
4. A valuable witness is also Houloussi Effendi presently First President at the court of first instance of Stamboul, who during the high deeds of VELI NEDJET was president of the Court of Appeal at Diarbekir. He would testify before the Allied Tribunal named by the League of Nations, although as it is the case with the majority of the honest Turks, he is not to be relied on, to formulate his accusations before a Turkish Tribunal.

APPENDIX A
Re Sir H. LAMB's minute of 11.8.20

W. 2178
26.7.20

1. (a) No one of the deportees was arrested on any evidence in the legal sense. In this particular case VELI NEDJET was arrested by the Turkish Government on 30.1.19 apparently at the request of High Commissioner made on 23.1.19. The Turkish charge against him, which was reported to the F.O., was "Massacre, pillage". He was amongst those prisoners taken over by the British Military Authorities from the Turks on 28.5.19. He was deported under the authority of point 5 of F.O. telegram 233 of 5.2.19.

    (b) Those who are being detained without any real justification have been recommended for release in accordance with Article 208 of the Conditions of Peace (draft list now in circulation). But all depends upon what is held to be real justification.

    (c) The whole case of these deportees is not satisfactory, due to the long delay in making peace and public insecurity over the whole massacre area. The deportees have been considered to be 'Prisoners of War and Interned Civilians who have not already been repatriated'. (Article 208 and 212).

    (d) If I am right in classing the deportees as Prisoners of War or Interned Civilians as referred to in Articles 208 and 212 then the fault for their having been interned for the past 15 months rests with their nationals, since the case of all ordinary prisoners of war whose nationals made war on us. Now it is time that judicial methods were taken up and these depend on the nature of the Court to be designated by the Allied Powers, the law to be enforced, the class of cases to be prosecuted and the nature and powers of the Prosecution itself. Owing to the inherent difficulties of the Prosecution, it appears to me that unless there is whole-hearted cooperation and will to act among the Allies, the trials will fall to the ground and the direct and indirect massacres of about one million Christians will get off unscathed. Rather than this should happen, it were better that the Allies had never made their declarations in the matter and had never followed up their declarations by the arrests and deportations that have been made.

    (e) With regard to the last paragraph, there are no dossiers in any legal sense. In many cases we have statements by Armenians of differing values in some cases, including that of VELI NEDJET, we have nothing but what is common report and an extract from a printed pamphlet. It is safe to say that very few "dossiers" as they now stand would not be marked "no case" by a practical lawyer.

    (f) In any case it is submitted that the matter should be dealt with as a whole and not piecemeal.

2. My own view as to the prosecution, stated briefly, would be:

    (a) For the Allies to appoint a judicial commission to travel over the principal massacre areas, armed with power to demand documentary evidence of the Turkish provincial administrations, and to draw up statements of evidence; or:-

(b) To leave it to the local Armenian and Greek authorities to carry on the prosecution under Allied control.
3. The present section of the High Commission, consisting of one officer with no authority, can only collect such information as is passed to it or which voluntarily finds its way here. The section now has recorded in easily available form a large mass of information concerning the 118 deportees and some 1,000 others, all alleged to have been guilty, directly or indirectly, in participation in massacres. Though none of this information is in itself of strict legal value, still no Prosecution could get to work without it.
4. As the officer responsible for making recommendations for arrest or surrender, since 1st July 1919, such recommendations have been made upon information which, in my opinion and under the circumstances amounted to a prima facie case against the person whose arrest or surrender was recommended.
5. At this point perhaps the difficulties in the way of obtaining information, not to mention statements of evidence might be emphasised. These might be summarised as follows:
(a) Impossibility of obtaining any Turkish official information, e.g. orders or instructions issued by the Central Government or the Provincial Administrations &c.
(b) The disinclination of the Allied Governments to take any part in the prosecution of massacres. The French must be in possession of information concerning the massacres in the countries they now occupy and the Americans must be in possession of a mass of invaluable material in the shape of the report of their Consular officers in 1915-1916.
(c) The apparent apathy of our authorities in the Middle East as evinced by their replies to the H.C.'s queries in the matter.
(d) The massacre of the great majority of the adult male Armenian population of Anatolia and of practically all the "intellectuals".
(e) The lack of public security and want of confidence as to the intentions of the Allies with regard to the massacres, evinced to me on several occasions and resulting in the great disinclination to come forward to give evidence.
(f) The release of prisoners from Malta which is at once reported in all the Armenian papers, also has a bad effect from this particular point of view.
6. On consideration of the above I venture to hope that the sending of the draft letter to G.O.C. may be delayed until the whole subject can be dealt with as a whole. In any case certain emendations as to facts contained in the draft letter would have to be made.

APPENDIX B
VELI NEDJET

VELI BEY was Chief Clerk of Secretary's office of Diarbekir. He was the Delegate of the C.U.P. at Diarbekir, who came to Constantinople in 1914 and participated in the Union and Progress Congress where was decided the Deportations of the Armenians.
HUSSEIN Effendi the Chief of Police, being a naïve man, was dismissed as superannuated, and was succeeded by VELI BEY as ad-interim in May 1915.
Then the deportations and horrible massacres began in Diarbekir. VELI BEY and FEYZI BEY and their accomplices organised the tchetes and killed, tortured, and massacred men, women and children in such a barbarous manner that humanity has never seen or heard.
TCHILGADIAN, the Armenian Bishop was terribly tortured and in the gaol situated behind the house of VELI BEY, they pulled out the nails, beard and eyes of the Bishop, and VELI BEY was hearing the howling of pain of the Bishop and was amused in his house.
The above statement made last Sunday by KEVORK FIKRI EFFENDI, the former public prosecutor of Diarbekir and his wife. They were both converted to Islam and remained in Diarbekir till the Armistice. They are the father and mother of Madame Aslanian (of Trebizond). They are fearing from Turks to come and give evidence. This evidence was given at presence of MOSTIDJIAN ARTIN Effendi member of the Court of Cassation.
7th September 1920.
(sgd) MIHRAN BOYADJIAN
Ex Inspecteur Civil de 1^{ière} Classe

N.B. Mons. BOYADJIAN has long been known as thoroughly reliable.

ISMAIL DJAMBOLAT BEY
Malta No. 2692
Interned 2.6.19
Appointments.
Director of the Intelligence Bureau of the Ministry of the Interior from December 1913 to April 1914.
Director of the Sûreté Générale from April 1914 to February 1915.
Vali of Constantinople and Prefect de la Ville from February 1915 to April 1916.
Under Secretary for State for Interior from April 1916 to October 1916.
Minister to Sweden from April 1917 to December 1917.
Minister of the Interior from July 1918 to October 1918 when he resigned.
Lists. On List III, i.e. Mr. Ryan suggested his arrest to Grand Vizier.
Arrest. Arrested by the Turkish Authorities on 30.1.19 and was among those surrendered to the British Military Authorities on 28.5.19.
Reasons for Deportation.
A. As reported to Foreign Office: - "Ex Minister de l'Intérieur (avoir troublé la sécurité publique)".
B. Minute by General Deedes: - "Deported both on account of his complicity in deportations etc. of Armenians and as a precautionary measure in War time".
C. Minute by Mr. Ryan on 22.7.19: - "He was selected for deportation on purely political grounds as a dangerous politician of ex-Ministerial rank. I am less in sympathy with him than with many, because of one murder he committed years ago when he shot a policeman sent to arrest him under Kiamil Pasha's regime".
Petitions.
1. **W/2592.** Petition from wife dated 21.7.19, enclosing documents in his favour.
2. **do.** Petition from him dated 8.11.20, through Malta on 13.11.20, asking to be allowed to join his wife in Italy. No action.
3. **do.** Petition from him dated 13.12.20, through Governor, Malta of 15.12.20 asking for answer to his petition of 13.11.20.
4. **W/1507/24.** Reminder from Governor, Malta of 31.2.21 re 2 and 3 above.

N.B. High Commissioner's special Committee recommended that ISMAIL DJAMBOLAT should continue to be detained at Malta and in due course be brought up for trial. This recommendation was sent to Foreign Office under cover of despatch No. 1552/W/3667, dated 24.11.20.

ACCUSATIONS.
G. II. In recent carefully prepared list of criminals ISMAIL DJAMBOLAT and HUSSEIN DJAHID are listed as Talaat's principal auxiliaries in the organisation at Constantinople of the massacres.
5014/6. It was at his house in Nishantash at 9.30 pm on 24.1.19 that the meeting was held to concert measures for the escape (successful) of the most notorious Dr. Reshid Bey, (who committed suicide on his re-arrest on 6.2.19).

G. II. In Patriarchate's detailed list of criminals of September 1920 ISMAIL DJAMBOLAT is duly listed under the general heading "Constantinople", i.e., directing agents.

H. 10. Patriarchate's report of 22.12.20 on Mustapha Reshed Bey and the Police Organisation mentions ISMAIL DJAMBOLAT as a member of the "Council of Terrorism" under Talaat Pasha at the beginning of the war. ISMAIL DJAMBOLAT was at that time Prefect of Constantinople and Director of the Sûreté Générale, i.e. Chief of the Gendarmerie and Police organisation for the whole of the Empire.

ISMAIL DJAMBOLAT is of Circassian origin. His Father was a Circassian Officer in the Turkish Army. Passing, in his early youth, through the Turkish preparatory pupils' training schools, for preparing officers for the Turkish army, he was finally sent to Kuleli, and after having finished his course there, to the military school of Harbié, where he graduated in 1899.

Before the Constitution he was at Salonika in the capacity of a gendarmerie captain.

He was an affiliate and an influential member of the C.U.P. secret Committee there. He was one of those who attempted to murder Col. Nazim, the Military Commandant of Salonika (the same Nazim who was the brother-in-law of Enver and who became after a Unionist).

As soon as the Constitution was proclaimed he was elected Deputy of Constantinople in the Turkish Parliament.

Of an adventurous character, unscrupulous and cruel in all his acts, he became one of the worst leaders of the C.U.P. Committee, being one of the promoters of the persecutions against the Bulgarian population of Macedonia, a political method which was the cause of the Balkan war.

Under the Ministry of Kiamil Pasha when the Itilaf [Liberal Party] was in power ISMAIL DJAMBOLAT was arrested and escaped by killing the policeman who was conveying him to prison. He ran away to Roumania and saved himself from punishment.

With the rise again of the Young Turk party, he came again into power and was nominated Governor of Constantinople.

Member of the Central Committee, he shares full not only responsibility incurred by the C.U.P. in deporting the Armenians, but he has a direct participation in the crimes committed by arresting Armenian notables in Constantinople and sending them to Tchangiri to be murdered, and in deporting thousands of Armenians of the poorer classes, who although born in the provinces, were in Constantinople earning a living.

An intimate friend of Bedri to whom he was related by matrimonial ties, he had a hand in all the robberies committed by the C.U.P., and his reputation was so bad that he was submitted to a diplomatic rebuke from the Swedish Government, when he was sent there as plenipotenitiary during the great war. He had the same mishap at the socialist congress held in Stockholm, where he had been sent with Nessim Mazliah to represent Turkey.

NEVZADE BEY, Captain
Malta No. 2696
Interned 2.6.19
Appointments. Commandant de Place at Mosul, June 1917 to . . .
Lists. On none.
Arrest. Arrested by the Turkish Government early in 1919. He was amongst those surrendered to the British Military Authorities, on 28.5.19 and deported.
Before Turkish Court Martial 'R' 10.4.19. According to the **Renaissance** of 10.4.19, NEVZADE Bey was placed on trial before the Turkish Court Martial on 8.4.18 [sic] on charges
1. Organising the massacre of deportees.
2. Organising the massacre of the Armenian Labour Corps.
3. Organising the murder of Bederkhan Zadé Abdul Rezak Bey, (a court official under Abdul Hamid).

Prosecutor: Réchad Bey: "Je réclame l'instruction immediate de son porcès."
His trial was never brought to a conclusion.
On 27.1.20 the trial of his fellow accused Captain Nur Bey (?) was adjourned for further evidence from Diarbekir.
On 19.3.20 'Renaissance' announced the acquittal of NEVZADE's assistants at Mossul, Captain Ferid Bey and Lieutenant Zekai Bey.
Petitions.
1315. D. Wife's petition to join husband of 9.9.19.
5035. A. 93. Wife's petition to join husband of 13.6.20.
N.B. High Commissioner's despatch No. 1552/W/3667 of 24.11.20, covering report of special committee, it was recommended that NEVZADE be brought up for trial.

ACCUSATIONS.
5035/48. Complicity with Memduh Bey, Vali of Mossul and Halil Pasha, Commanding VIth Army, in the deportation of 500 Armenians to Zoho (Mr. Rizzo's annexe A.)
5030. A. 21. Mentioned in a statement by a member of the Labour Battalion. Mossul May 1918.
G. XIX. Listed on Patriarchate's detailed list of September 1920.
K. 4. Patriarchate's report of 26.2.21 on 2789 Hilmi Abdul Kadir:
"In the latter half of 1915 when all that was left of the huge caravans of deportees began to crowd into Mossul, Lt. Colonel Basri Bey, NEVZADE and Vali (Reshid Bey) began to think of the means of exterminating these Armenians . . .
The case of Hilmi must be judged with that of NEVZADE for their misdeeds in the Vilayet of Mossul. Already in the trial of NEVZADE before the Court Martial the name of Hilmi was always being mentioned and this dossier of the Mossul trial, when consulted, will furnish evidence".

C. 1. French translation, signed by Mr. Mihran Boyadjian, late 1st Class Civil Inspector of the Vilayets of Bitlis and Mossul, of his evidence given before the Turkish Court Martial on 3.5.19. In his evidence Mr. Boyadjian states that on 11.3.17, after the fall of Bagdad, Halil Pasha and his staff and NEVZADE Bey arrived in Mossul. In June 1917,

NEVZADE having been made Commandant de la Place de Mossul, the sufferings of the Armenians became intolerable. NEVZADE confiscated all foodstuffs arriving in the town, so that within a few months five thousand Armenians died of starvation. On 17th September Memduh Bey (a deportee) arrived at Mossul as Vali of the Vilayet. He sent for and nominated as head of the Gendarmerie the notorious massacrer Nazem Nazmi, who, in conjunction with Halil Pasha, Memduh, NEVZADE and Halil's Chief of Staff Basri Bey (a deportee) did all they could to aggravate the already precarious situation of the Armenian deportees. They proceeded to enrol all Christian males between the ages of 10 and 70 in Labour Battalions for the construction of roads under conditions which meant the extermination of the workers, which as a matter of fact was the result. NEVZADE himself ordered all Armenian shops to be closed and imprisoned all the traders in the cellars under his house without giving them food and putting them to every form of torture. After letting them suffer for 8 or 10 days, he sent them away in small groups with instructions to the escort: do the necessary, which meant: Kill them away from the town. Thus the Armenian traders and artisans of Mossul city were mostly done away with. Further, NEVZADE sent his agents out to the villages where there were a number of Armenian deportees, and made them undergo the same fate.

The witness proceeds to describe the killing of one Artin of Adana on the written instructions of NEVZADE.

FAZIL BERKI BEY, Doctor

Malta No. 2698

Interned 2.6.19

Appointments. Deputy for Changri (Kastamuni).

Lists. On none.

Arrest. Arrested by the Turkish Government and amongst those surrendered to the British Military Authorities on May 28th 1919.

Petitions. None to date 4.3.21.

N.B. In H.C.'s despatch 1552/W/3667 of 24.11.20, covering report of special committee, it was recommended that FAZIL BERKI be brought to trial.

ACCUSATIONS.

5029/A/6. In this report from the Armenian Patriarchate, Dr. FAZIL BERKI is mentioned as an accomplice of Muammer, Vali of Sivas from 30.3.13 to 1.2.16.

G. XVI. In the Patriarchate detailed list of September 1920, Dr. FAZIL BERKI is listed second only to Dr. Behaeddin Shakir on the list of those responsible for the Sivas Massacres. The note appended against his name runs: Special Delegate (i.e. from C.U.P. headquarters in Stamboul) for the massacres in February 1915.

B. 53. Unsigned fiche, dated 18.8.19, in which he is denounced as an organiser of deportations in the Black Sea Coast Districts.

H. 8. Patriarchate's detailed accusation against Gani Bey, C.U.P. Secy., at Sivas.

Herein FAZIL BERKI is mentioned as a propagandist before the Commission of Enquiry presided by Nazim Pasha.

H. 12. Patriarchate's special report on FAZIL BERKI, dated 22.12.20:-

FAZIL BERKI was born at Dadai, about (1882-1884), a village near the town of Castamouni. His parents were of a very humble condition, being poor villagers. They sent him to the Idadié preparatory school in Castamouni, and as he was among the promising pupils, he was sent later to Constantinople as a boarder to the school of Medicine, from where he graduated a year before the Constitution in 1907.

The Medical School of Constantinople was a great centre of propaganda for the Young Turkish somewhat hazy ideals, which evolved later on in unionist pan-touranistic ideals and FAZIL had become during his stay there an enthusiastic Young Turk neophyte.

He had also added to his name of FAZIL the nickname of BERKI (brightness). At the proclamation of the Constitution, when there was no more danger but on the contrary profit in being a Unionist, Dr. FAZIL devoted himself, body and soul, to the Unionist work.

Clever and eloquent, he showed his capacities in the propaganda line, first at Kadikeuy, where he made a sensation in Unionist gatherings as a speaker.

Patronised by Behaedine Shakir and Dr. Nazim, (two of the Principal Eight), he soon became an influential member of the C.U.P. and was trusted with missions of importance.

He was thus, in the and of August 1908, sent to organise the C.U.P. in the Vilayet of Castamouni. The two chiefs of the Young Turk Party in Castamouni, who had come forward at the proclamation of the Constitution, were two honest men:

Hodja Sidki, surnamed Guiavour Hodja, for his sympathy towards Christians, and who is dead actually and Husni Bey, actually Kalem Mahsousé Mudiri at the Ministry of Public Instructions.

Of course the C.U.P. organisation and the orientations which these two men were beginning to establish, in the Vilayet, was not of the kind to satisfy the Central Committee of the Union and Progress, and FAZIL BERKI had the mission to make them stand aside.

For two months he travelled in the Vilayet of Castamouni making attractive propaganda by means of conferences and by his leading articles in the official paper of the Vilayet, and the "ILGAZ", and Unionist paper published in Castamouni.

He organised the C.U.P. clubs in Castamouni, Bolou and Tchanguiri. The town of Tchanguiri was considered reactionary and devoted to Sultan Hamid and for this reason FAZIL BERKI took a special care to organise the C.U.P. there, in accordance with the desires of the Central Committee.

A certain Atta Effendi, (an imam) was placed at the head of the C.U.P. club there and seven members among the most rabid and unscrupulous of the small clique of the Unionist in the town there elected to form the administrative council of the C.U.P. club there.

These seven members were:–

Palandji Zadé Hadji Shakir

Gurun Keuylu Hassan

Defterdan Hakki

Ali Effendi

Abdullah Effendi

Hadji Effendi Zadé, Hadji Ismail

Tefedji Zadé Djémal

(Tefedji Zadé Djémal going always to and from Tchanguiri to Castamouni, was also elected member of the Central Club of Castamouni and acted as a "liaison" member between the Unionists of the two towns.)

As proof that the choice made by FAZIL BERKI was altogether in accordance with the secret aims of the C.U.P. it must be noted here that at the deportation time all these members under the guidance of Djemal Oghuz, who had become in 1914 the responsible secretary of the C.U.P. at Tchanguiri, became leading members of the

Endjumen (the secret council to execute the deportations) and organised the Teshkilat Mahsousé and the Emlak Metrouké [abandoned properties] to murder and plunder the Armenians.

The first stay of FAZIL BERKI in Tchanguiri was not more than 6 or 7 days but he had left the guidance of the C.U.P. in good hands and thanks to the exertions of his nominees, about three hundred affiliates were found; the functionaries shadowed or changed and the way of the C.U.P. on Tchanguiri established.

FAZIL BERKI did the same work in Bolou and Castamouni and hereafter from time to time he was going to make short inspecting tours in the Vilayet and keep and eye on the development of the C.U.P. affairs there.

On his return to the capital he was given another mission of trust, the one of developing the Donama Djemieti. He became the organiser of its propaganda and its most influential member and his success in that line was the cause that he was trusted also with the extension of the Mudafai Milli (Society for the National Defence) another by-production of the C.U.P.

FAZIKL BERKI made regularly tours in Anatolia for collecting funds and of course the Vilayet of Castamouni was the region where he was most successful.

From 1909 to 1914 his activities are specially devoted to the progress of the Donama Djemieti and Mudafai Milli.

He seemed to have reached the maximum of success in the money collecting line, at Castamouni and Diarbekir, in his tour during the period 1912-1913.

At the great war when the C.U.P. and its rabid members thought that the time had come for the realization of their ultimate aims of wiping out all non-Turk and non-Moslem elements from the Empire. FAZIL BERKI was given the mission of going to Anatolia for an anti-Christian propaganda tour, assisting and completing thus the work of Behaedine Shakir and Dr. Nazim.

In March 1915 he passed through Konia with Hodja Ilias who was going with the same mission to Moush.

The two worthies separated at Oulou Kishla. FAZIL BERKI going for his part to Sivas, where he conferred with Mouammer, the Vali, and Gali the responsible delegate of the C.U.P. After the conference at the Sivas C.U.P. Club, he stated openly the work of propaganda against the Armenians, by making a speech against them in the chief mosques, where he expounded at length that the Armenians were the natural foes of the Turks and ought to be annihilated.

In proof of it there is a declaration of Mehmed Rifaat Police Commissary of Sivas at that period to the Commission of Inquiry set up after the Armistice.

After having strengthened the anti-Armenian movement in Sivas FAZIL left for Erzeroum.

On his return to Constantinople, after having accomplished his mission to the entire satisfaction of the C.U.P., he was some months later, when the deputy of Tchanguiri Kherderlekdji Zadé Sabri died, elected deputy of Tchanguiri.

Then he went there and in his short stay conferred with Shemal Oghuz and decided with him and the other worthies of the C.U.P. there all the arrangements for the deportations, plunder and slaughter of the Armenians.

Intelligent, energetic, eloquent, unscrupulous, rabid pan-islamist and pan-touranist, FAZIL BERKI is a personality of mark among of the C.U.P. members and very dangerous.

Spending lavishly enormous sums of money, he has a share in all the robberies made under the pretence of collecting funds for the Donama Djemieti or the Mudafai Milli [National Defense Committee] and knows much about the secret channels which drained the greatest part of the spoils of the Armenians realised by the Emlaki Metrouké.

BEDRI BEY (IBRAHIM BEDRI BEY)
Malta No. 2701
Interned 2.6.19
Appointments.
Kaimakam of Balia, 18.5.13 to 2.9.14.
Mektubji of the Vilayet of Basra
Mektubji of the Vilayet of Mossul   2.9.14 to 12.9.15
Mektubji of the Vilayet of Diarbekir
Mutessarif of Mardin, (Vilayet of Diarbekir), 12.9.15 to 11.12.16
Vali of Diarbekir, 24.1.17 to 22.1.18 (?22.11.18?) when he was dismissed "on account of a necessity which was recognised".
Lists.
A. On List III i.e. his name was suggested for arrest by Mr. Ryan to the Grand Vizier on 27.3.19.
B. 5030/A/1. Foreign Office despatch of 7.3.19; Sublime Porte to be urged to arrest in connection with Diarbekir atrocities.
Arrest. He was arrested by the Turkish Government in January, 1919, for being implicated in the massacres, (see Turkish list in 5035/A/67).
He was amongst those surrendered to the British Military Authorities on 28.5.19, and deported to Malta.
Petitions. None to date, 4.3.21.
N.B. In High Commissioner's despatch No. 1552/W/3667 of 24.11.20 covering report of special Committee, it was recommended that Ibrahim Bedri Bey should be brought up for trial.

ACCUSATIONS.
5035/A/31. Account of Mardin atrocities by two Arab Christians; BEDRI collaborated with Memduh Bey. q.v.
Episodes des massacres arméniens de Diarbekir. p. 12. BEDRI collaborated with Vali Dr. Reshid Bey, committed suicide when faced with arrest.
p. 33 BEDRI was sent from Diarbekir to Mardin by Dr. Reshid for the purpose of exterminating the Armenians.
H. 2 page 6. Extract from statement made at British High Commission by Shefik Bey, late a Kaimakam of several Kazas in the Eastern Vilayets: - "The massacres in the desert region (Ras-ul-Ain and Der Zor) were organised by Zeki Bey, Kerim Refi and Ibrahim Bedreddin, the Mektubji of Diarbekir. They met together in 1916 at the Nahie of Hassidje [Hasake, Syria], a convenient meeting place for all three, and concerted measures. Bedreddin was for causing the Christians to starve in the desert . . . I know Bedreddin well as he is my fellow compatriot of Bolu. He was known to Talaat who had verified the 'good work' he had accomplished in the matter of the Greek deportations from Bigha after the Balkan war."
G. XII. In Patriarchate's detailed list of criminals of September 1920, Bedri Bey is duly listed.

MADJID BEY

Malta No. 2704

Interned 2.6.19

Profession. Employed in the audit at Erzingan in 1915 and became Chief of the Civil Transport.

Delegate of the C.U.P. at Erzingan.

Later Secretary of the Senate.

Lists. On none.

Arrest. Arrested by the Turkish Authorities early in 1919 and surrendered to the British Military Authorities on 23.5.19 and deported.

Charge as reported to the Foreign Office: "avoir trouble la sécurité publique."

There is no record of his having appeared before the Turkish Court Martial and there have been no petitions from him or on his behalf. (4.3.21)

N.B. In High Commissioner's despatch No. 1552/W/3667, of 24.11.20, covering report of special committee, it was recommended that MADJID Bey should be brought up for trial.

ACCUSATIONS

H. 5. 22.8.19. Mr Ryan minutes: "If I remember rightly he did a trip in the Interior, Erzeroum way, at the time when the massacres were proceeding. You will find a good deal about him in some of the earlier proceedings of the Turkish Court Martial."

H. 5. 15.3.20. Statement by Mihran Boyadjian, ex-Inspector Civil de 1^{ière} classe in the Eastern Vilayets. (Informant well known to us).

MADJID was the delegate of the C.U.P. at Erzingan. He is about 35 years old. He was the chief organiser of Tchetes and consequently of the massacres. He was always dressed in Tchete uniform. I consider him the most cruel of all the Erzingan massacrers. There are many witnesses to the atrocities committed by MADJID and his companions: the Mutessarif Memduh Bey, the Deputy Halet Bey, and Ejzaji Mehmed at Samara Deressi, five miles from Erzingan. In 1914 it was decided to send Inspectors from the Audit Office to the Vilayets. MADJID was sent to Erzingan. At the beginning of 1915 he was sent for special work as Chairman of the local Mudafai Milli (National Defence Committee).

N.B. During the deportations the Inspectors of Finances in the Vilayets wrote reports for Talaat on how things were going. These important reports have not yet been destroyed and could be had through MADJID Bey's friend in the Audit Office.

5027/A/14. 9. 6. 19. Report from 'Intelligence' Tiflis, dated May 1919 giving information as to the Erzingan atrocities supplied by Kourkin Kellerian.

Six men are said to have formed the Committee which planned and carried out the massacres of Armenians at Erzingan:

Memduh, the Mutessarif (Malta).
Ejzadji Mehmet, C.U.P. (Malta).
Halet Bey, Deputy (on F.O. List).
Madjid Bey of Constantinople, Chief of Civil Transport and member of local C.U.P. (Malta).
Ismail Hakke of Tokat, in Sivas Vilayet, Commandant of Gendarmerie at Erzingan (Indexed).
Wahad Din Bey of Constantinople, a doctor of Medicine.

5035/A/19. 14. 3. 19. In an Intelligence report by Captain Hoyland, dated 14.3.19 MADJID Bey is mentioned amongst those who participated in the massacres in the Sanjak of Erzingan.

5027/A/33. Further long account of Erzingan massacres by Kellerian, dated 2.9.20, MADJID Bey being mentioned among the chief organisers of the Kemakh gorge atrocities.

C. 22. Intelligence report, dated Tiflis 25.5.19. Evidence of Ardashess Lepian, merchant of Erzingan, then of Batum. Mentions Memduh and MADJID as members of the directing Committee engaged in planning the great massacres that occurred in the Sanjak of Erzingan.

The above corroborated by Hinganoush Bogossian of Erzingan.

5027/A/12. Signed statement by A.H. Lebian, dated 6.8.19. Ejzadji Mehmet, being the leader of the C.U.P. organised a special Committee composed of Halet Bey, MADJID Bey and Mehmet Bey to carry out the massacres.

G. XI. In Patriarchate's detailed list of criminals of September 1920, MADJID Bey, Secretary of the Mutessarifate of Erzingan, is duly listed.

HODJA RIFAAT EFFENDI
Malta No. 2706
Interned 2.6.19
Appointments.
C.U.P. Delegate at Ismidt.
Lists. On none.
Arrest. Arrested by the Turkish Government and among those handed over to the British Military Authorities on 28th May 1919, - Offence as reported to the Foreign Office: - "Représantant du Comité Union et Progres, (Pillage)."
Turkish Court Martial. His case was apparently before the Turkish Court Martial for on 3.3.20, "Renaissaince" reported that the Public prosecutor had asked for his acquittal.
Petitions. W. 2178. Petition of 30-6-20.
N.B. High Commissioner's despatch No. 1552/W/3667 of 24.11.20, covering report of special committee, recommended that he should be brought up for trial.
ACCUSATIONS.
G. IV. In the Patriarchate's list of criminals dated September 1920, under the heading of Ismidt, HODJA RIFAAT's name stands first. The note appended runs: HODJA RIFAAT and Ibrahim, Director of Prisons of Constantinople, were sent in 1915 to Ismidt as special envoys of the C.U.P. for the purpose of carrying out the deportations. They committed fearful atrocities and returned ladened with riches.

5035. Lt. Slade in his report dated 28.3.19 recommend the removal and exile of Hadji Ali, Moukhir Bey, Veysi Bey, Djemal Bakkal, RIFAAT HODJA – all powerful C.U.P. men of Ismidt.

5035.3.

(a) A letter which appeared in the Armenian paper **Vertchine Lour** of 26.12.18, by an Armenian employed in the Ministry of the Interior in defence of Midhat Bey (q.v.)

(b) On 12.4.19 Captain Silley, Control Officer, Ismidt, reported the arrest of HODJA RIFAAT by the Turkish Authorities.

(c) In Capt. Campbell's (N. Intell. Off. (Ismidt)) report of 28.2.19, HODJA RIFAAT is described as "a fanatical Turk". "He was formerly a poor man but by unscrupulous work, as in the case of Veissi Bey, he has gained much. He is a most active member of the local organisation and carried on persistent propaganda in favour of the C.U.P. and the Germans as well as against the Allies". Further, "considered a danger to the peace of the district . . ."

(d) In May 1919 the Armenian Patriarch, acting on information supplied to him by Ipranossian, a converted Armenian and partner of HODJA RIFAAT, apparently had petitioned the High Commissioner for release of RIFAAT from Turkish custody. To this action of the Patriarch's the Armenian Bishop of Ismidt strongly protested on 8.6.19.

HILMI BEY

Malta No. 2712

Interned 2.6.19

Appointments. Mutessarif of Kirshehir, Angora Vilayet.

do. Kirk Kilisse, Adrianople Vilayet.

Deputy for Manteshe (Aidin Vilayet 1920).

Lists. On List III. I.e. Mr. Ryan suggested his name for arrest to Grand Vizier on 27.3.19.

Arrest. Arrested by the Turkish Government and surrendered to the British Military Authorities on 28.5.19.

Offence. Offence as reported to Foreign Office: - Massacre et deportation arméniens de Trebizond.

Petitions. 870/24. of 14.1.21, through Governor, Malta of 18.1.21.

N.B. In High Commissioner's despatch 1552/W/3667 of 24.11.20 covering report of Special Committee, it was recommended that HILMI BEY be detained and brought up for trial.

ACCUSATIONS.

C. 14. Notes on Deputies, from a reliable source and dated 20.2.20. Received through Mr. Ryan.

Elected Deputy for Menteshe (Aidin Vilayet) though at the time he was detained in Malta. He is a Civil Inspector. He was arrested for participation in the deportations.

G. 14. In Patriarchate's list of September 1920, HILMI Bey is listed under the heading: - "Guilty officials of Kirshehir".

E. 9. Signed statement by two eye-witnesses of Kirshehir, primarily against Ali Nazmi, wherein the Mutessarif HILMI is mentioned as the senior Civil official responsible for the atrocities.

5032/2. Memorandum by Aram Fosbikian and Hagop Terzie both of Kirshehir, describing the massacres of Kir Shehir (Geul Hissar), when HILMI Bey was Mutessarif, in July and August 1915.

5031/A/7. Further report by Aram Fosbikian, describing the atrocities of Kirshehir and mentioning HILMI Bey as the Chief organiser and executant. This report was sent to Military Attaché by G.S. "I", on 7.3.19.

5035/A/94. Signed statement by Hoosep Haladjian of Nemli Zade No. 42, Kadikeui, against Ali Nazmi but also implicating HILMI Bey the Mutessarif.

ZEKERIA ZIHNI BEY

Malta No. 2718

Interned 2.6.19

Appointments. Mutessarif of Sinope, before the War.

Mutessarif of Rodosto, 1914 to 15.10.15.

Vali of Adrianople, 15.10.15 to 12.12.18.

Lists. On List II, i.e. arrest was suggested by Mr. Ryan to the Grand Vizier in February 1919.

Arrest. Arrested by the Turkish Government on 30.1.19 and among those surrendered to the British Military Authorities on 28.5.19.

Petitions. None to date, 1.12.20.

N.B. In H. C. despatch No. 1552/W/3667, dated 24.11.20. (Committee's report), it is recommended that he should be detained at Malta and brought up for trial.

ACCUSATIONS

5035/A/11b. In Patriarchate's list (Part 1) of January 1919, he is listed: "... un monster, organisateur de la deportation des arméniens du Vilayet."

(N.B. No massacres actually took place within the Vilayet.)

Report No. 00599, dated 12.3.20:- ZEKERIA ZIHNI Bey was Mutessarif of Rodosto in 1914 and succeeded Haji Adil Bey as Vali of Adrianople owing, it is understood, to the disinclination of the latter to occupy that post whilst the deportations of Armenians were taking place. Haji Adil Bey however arranged the whole matter and left it to ZEKERIA ZIHNI Bey to carry out, which he did. Confiscation of Armenian property and sale of Armenian goods also took place under the regime of ZEKERIA Bey at Adrianople. He remained as Vali until January or February 1919 when he was removed on the representations of the British Military Representative, Adrianople.

Note. Full details of this man's doings at Adrianople can be obtained from Père Arslan, now acting as religious head of the Armenian community in Adrianople.

G. III. Patriarchate's detailed list of September 1920. Listed with the mention: 'he caused the Armenians to be deported who had previously been authorised to remain.'

Patriarchate's special report of 2.12.20 is as follows:- ZEKERIA ZIHNI Bey is of Circassian origin. He graduated in Constantinople from the Mulkié school, and was director of a preparatory school until the Constitution. Being secretly affiliated to the C.U.P. he was, after the Constitution promoted Director of Public Instruction in Salonika, succeeding Ahmed Shukri. Shortly after he was nominated Mutessarif in one of th Sandjaks of Mossovo.

Most unscrupulous and cruel, he was one of the functionaries who were nominated after the Balkan War to Administrative posts in the European Province of Adrianople, with the secret mission of suppressing the Christian element.

ZEKERIA ZIHNI Bey was thus Mutessarif of Rodosto and during the war he deported the Armenians of Rodosto most ruthlessly and took an active part in the plundering of their property. His capacities in that line were fully appreciated by the C.U.P. and Haji Adil Bey and thus he was nominated Vali of Adrianople with the mission of deporting the Armenian population of that town; a mission which he accomplished with the same relentless cruelty as in Rodosto.

MUAMMER BEY

Malta No. 2719

Interned 2.6.19

Appointments. Vali of Sivas: 30.3.13 to 1.2.16

Vali of Konia: 8.2.16 to 19.10.16, when "he was removed, in consequence of an administrative necessity, by the Council of Ministers."

Lists. On List III, i.e. his arrest was suggested by Mr. Ryan to the Grand Vizier on 27.3.19.

Arrest. MUAMMER BEY was arrested by the Turkish Government in December 1918 ('Renaissance' of 13.12.18). He was among those handed over to the British Military Authorities on 28.5.19, and deported.

Petitions. None to date (1.12.20.)

ACCUSATIONS.

C. 11. Detailed account of events in Merzifun, Sivas Vilayet, from April 1915 onwards, by Mr[s]. Aroussiag Y. Iskian, of Merzifun, now of 8 Anderlich Street, Pancaldi.

In May 1915 the Vali MUAMMER himself visited Merzifun. (See Appendix A).

C. 10. Statement by Mrs. Captanian of Samsun, now of the American Red Cross Home, Rue Selamsiz, Scutari describing her deportation through Sivas vilayet and the massacres at Tunus, between Sivas and Tokat, in Sivas Vilayet. (See Appendix B).

G. XVI. Listed in Patriarchate's detailed list of September 1920, with the mention: "Il se rendit avant les massacres à Erzerum et participa aux deliberations des Valis des provinces arméniennes. C'est dans ce Conseil tenu sous la présidence de Mahmud Kiamil Pasha, que fut arête le plan de l'éxtermination de l'élément arménien."

5031. A.11.b. Patriarchate's List, Part I.

"Vali de Sivas, un des plus renommés par ses crimes atroces, l'éxterminateur de la population Arménienne de Sivas, Samsun, Ammasia, Tokat, etc."

5029. A.12. Statement compiled by "the surviving Armenians of Sivas", dated 29.4.19.

Crimes. Eviction of all the Armenians in the city and province of Sivas, also the murder of 2,000 soldiers of the Labour Battalions, 1915-1917. "The slaughter of 2,000 . . . was officially proven by the execution of one Keure Nur, Yuzbashi of Gendarmes in Sou-Schehry, in accordance with the sentence of the Court Martial there, as the person who had carried out the order of the Vali, MUAMMER BEY. The Vali himself went scot free."

5029. A.6. A history of the Sivas massacres and of the murder of Bishop Odabashian on 31.12.14, compiled by the Patriarchate. Many names of Turks mentioned, all working under the orders of AHMED MUAMMER BEY, who was appointed Vali of Sivas on 13.4.13.

5029. A.7. A "Note for Canon Whitehouse", March 1919, "I have had a call today from Reverend G. White, President of Anatolia College, Merzifun. Dr. White was present throughout the whole of the deportations. He wished especially to draw our attention to the four following principal leaders and executors of the massacres and deportations. (MUAMMER BEY, Faik Bey, Mashir Bey, Hussein Effendi, Sabit Bey Zadé).

MUAMMER BEY, Governor of Sivas Vilayet. He is an absolutely heartless villain, and was responsible for the deportation of over 100,000 Armenians from the Vilayet. Dr. White gave me a number of instances of the cruelty of this man and recommended very strongly that he should be hanged for his misdeeds."

NOTE. "Please do not let Dr. White's name appear in connection with this evidence, as he has returned to Merzifun and he does not want his position there prejudiced."

'Renaissance' 30.1.19. Amassia atrocities, 16,000 persons.

5020/125. Destruction of church at Konia in 1917, when MUAMMER was Vali. Also of ancient Christian sculptures.

H. 8. Patriarchate's accusation of Gani Bey, C.U.P. Secretary at Sivas. Many mentions of the Vali MUAMMER especially in connection with the massacre by Nuri of the men of the Amele Tabouri assembled at Chifai Medresse.

H. 12. Patriarchate's report of 22.12.20 on Fazil Berki Bey deputy for Changri. In this report Fazil Berki is reported as going on an anti-Christian propaganda mission in the spring of 1915. He began by conferring with the Vali MUAMMER and Gani Bey, responsible C.U.P. Secretary, then started openly his mission against the Armenians in the vilayet, preaching in the mosques.

J. 4 et Sq. Series of telegrams to and from MUAMMER relating to the murder of Bishop Odabashian of Erzindjan, late of Brusa.

J. 188 et sq. Long series of telegrams between the Mutessarif and the Kaimakam referring to the detail of the deportations, transmitting instructions from the Ministry of the Interior, etc. Names of senders and addresses are not given, but this series appear chiefly to emanate from the office of the Mutessarif of Sivas and the Vali (i.e. MUAMMER BEY) is also Mutessarif of the home sanjak. The telegrams are dated in the summer of 1915; they are of considerable general interest.

N.B. All these telegrams were communicated to the High Commission in French translation. They are alleged to be translations of Turkish official telegrams.

APPPENDIX A

MERZIFUN AND ANGORA

Address: 8 Anderlich Str. Pangalti. Pera.

STATEMENT IN ENGLISH MADE BY MADAME AROUSSIAG Y. ISKIAN, WIFE OF YERVANT ISKIAN, ANTIQUE DEALER OF ANGORA, DAUGHTER OF THE LATE BOGHOS TORIKIAN, MERCHANT OF MERZIFUN, MASSACRED NEAR AMASIA ON 12TH JUNE 1915, AND SISTER OF MRS. CAPTANIAN.

C. 11. I was born in Merzifun. I had been living there since 1912 with my children who were being educated at the American College. Dr. White was Principal and Miss Charlotte Willard in charge of the girls' department; Dr. Mardin was in charge of the hospital. In May 1915 there were the first signs of something about to happen. MUAMMER was Vali of the Province. **Sirri** Bey was Mutessarif of Amassia and Faik Bey, now at Malta, was Kaimakam of the Kaza of Merzifun. **Mahir** Bey was in command of the troops and Major **Emin** Bey was his second in command. A lawyer, **Ahmed Effendi**, was also in close touch with this ruling gang. Fear began to fall on the Armenian population in Merzifun in May; it was felt or known that the Government was about to take measures against us. There was no question of a Turkish popular rising against us; the whole thing was done by Government order. The Turkish population remained gladly callous throughout. The deportations and massacres that ensued were carried out by the Government only through its officials, though of course very many Turkish men volunteered for the official job of butchering the Christians. In the country the Turkish peasants, men and women, took an active part in massacring and torturing, but always with official sanction. Throughout the massacre period, there was never any excitement among the Turkish populace; all was cold blooded murder by official order or at any rate with official sanction.

One night in April, police and gendarmes arrested some 50 of the Armenian intellectuals and took them to prison. They were subjected to torture and after some days sent to Sivas by night to prison. They have all disappeared. MUAMMER caused them to disappear. In May 1915 the Vali, MUAMMER, visited Merzifun. Just after he left 70 more young intellectuals were imprisoned and tortured. One of these is still alive and can give evidence; his name is Mr. Manuk Adjderian, Rue Anderlich, apartment house; near G.H.Q.

On June 12th (N.S.) the Government took away all the Armenian men of the town. My father was taken by night in his nightgown to gaol and placed underground. It was on a Friday night. Monday morning he was no longer in the barracks – then used as a prison. He had been made to disappear. Every night for a long time batches of men were taken out by night in different directions and massacred within a few hours of the town. They were always taken out to the place of massacre by gendarmes and police in uniform.

Mahir Bey gave me his signed permit to remain in Merzifun. It cost me Lt. 500 gold in jewels etc. given to **Faik, Mahir**, and **Emin** through the lawyer, to save my husband. Emin Bey once showed me a packet full of telegrams from MUAMMER and said that they in Merzifun were not properly carrying out the orders of the Vali; i.e. they were too lenient. Emin Bey gave permission for my husband and brother to go to Angora.

9. 2. 20. Since last speaking I have found out further details from Armenian friends from Merzifun who escaped massacre because they were rich, became converted to Islam and were friends of the Commandant, **Mahir** Bey.

My father was sent off on Sunday night together with about 200 others all roped together under an escort of gendarmes and police. Major **Emin** Bey, commanding the military was present at the departure of the convoy. The convoy took the road to Amassia. Near Amassia an escort from Amassia took over the convoy. In a valley near the fountain of Kaimakam Puna, they were all murdered by gendarmes and tchetes.

Sirri Bey, the Mutessarif of Amassia detained the Merzifun convoy some little time in Amassia so that the news should not be known at once in Merzifun. Before returning them he made them swear to keep the secret. The Police Commissaire of Merzifun at the time was **Salih** Bey.

After this first wholesale massacre the batches of those to be butchered were no longer directed torwards Amassia but were butchered close to Merzifun in a valley called Teunek on the road to Chorum, under the direct supervision of **Faik** and **Mahir**.

All men from boys to old men were massacred except those who could bribe sufficiently.

Mahir has himself boasted of his part in the massacre to one of my friends though he disclaims responsibility for the first massacre near Amassia. **Mahir** was a fanatice pan-Turanian. No one can tell where **Mahir** is now to be found.

APPENDIX B

Samsun deportations, massacres of Tunus & Hassan Chelebi.

MRS. PAILADZU CAPTANIAN, WIDOW OF ARAKEL CAPTANIAN, OF SAMSUN, AT PRESENT RESIDING AT THE AMERICAN SCHOOL, American Red Cross House, Selamiz Str. Scutari, **MAKES THE FOLLOWING STATEMENT IN ENGLISH AT THE HIGH COMMISSION ON JANUARY 15th, 22nd and FEB. 2nd 1920.**

I am the daughter of the late Boghos Torikian, merchant at Merzifun. I married in 1908 and lived chiefly in Samsun. About June 20th 1915 in pursuance of orders received from Constantinople and transmitted to the Armenian population by posters we were ordered to be deported. Medjimi Bey was then Vali of Samsun. I left my two boys in charge of the Greek Metropolitan. My husband and I travelled 15 days together on the road to Tokat via Amassia. Arrived at **Tunus**, 2 hours from Chiflik in the Vilayet of Sivas the escort separated all the men and locked them up in a stable, about 300 all pressed together. I was permitted to say goodbye to my husband through a window. Not one of those 300 is today alive. We the women were pushed on the road to Malatia – avoiding

Sivas. The next day we heard all had been killed. MUAMMER was Vali of Sivas and the order came through him; the actual butchers I do not know. The escort and chief of escort were continually changing.

22.1.20. One day's march from Tunus we were all stopped by the escort and robbed of all our jewels, valuables and money. This was done systematically, it took a day and a night. Many women saved some gold liras by swallowing them. I gave up my gold jewels and a gold lira, all the rest I possessed, 9 liras I saved in my horse's nose bag. We were one month on the road from Samsun to Malatia, avoiding Sivas. It is impossible to say how many Armenians left Samsun and how many arrived at Malatia for the numbers, altogether apart from murders and deaths from hunger etc. were continually varying.

We passed Kangal (S.S.E. of Sivas) and arrived at **Hassan Chelebi**, on the main road was Sivas to Malatia, a small village in the Harput vilayet. Here the men were again separated from the women, locked up and later led out of the village and massacred. I was in the village at the time and saw the men led out of the village towards a deep valley. They were escorted by gendarmes and followed by the Turks of the village, all armed with swords, knives and sticks. This was in the early afternoon. Before nightfall the Turkish butchers returned carrying the clothes of the slaughtered Armenian men. I estimate their number as over 400 chiefly from Amassia. Some of the Samsun lads who were not murdered at Tunus were murdered here.

One Samsun boy, named Hagop Megurian, escaped at the last moment as he was a druggist and they wanted one. He is here now and can give evidence. This murder was in July. The actual murderers, I have found out from later enquiries were: Ali Shaoush of Malatia, Neshet (Neshid) Bey, Mudir of Hassan Chelebi, the Tchete Reis (Brigand leader) Hadji Ghislib agha of Hekim Khan, and Batal of Hassan Chelebi.

A week later I reached Malatia. We did not go into the town itself. Here those who still had horses were deprived of them. By leaving my group at night and sheltering with a newly arrived one I managed to remain in the open near Malatia for some days. From later enquiries I have found that the Mutessarif of Malatia at the time was Reshid Bey. Reshid was relieved by Sirri Bey in Nov. 1915. Sirri also is a massacrer and now a deputy in the Turkish Parliament. At last I left Malatia and went on southwards; it took us say 6 weeks to reach the river (100 kils). We were sent up and down mountains, never on a road. The escort were trying to kill us by hunger and fatigue. All this rough country was full of corpses – the stench was terrible. Of the group with which I left Malatia certainly more than half perished before reaching the Euphrates at Murad. During this part of the journey the caravan was in charge of the two Kurd brothers, Zenal Bey and Hadji Bedir Agha commissioned by the Mutessarif of Malatia.

I have spoken to both of these men. Zenal took by force one of my pupils for his own use, I twice met Hadji Bedir agha, once in company with a German.

The crossing of the Euphrates was a terrible performance, in the barges the boatmen set upon us, beat us and robbed us again, nearing the bank they threw us into the water and many were drowned. We got to the other side wet, nearly naked and no food whatsoever. However, shortly after, our escort was relieved by gendarmes from Aleppo who treated us well. We were taken to Serudj (West of Urfa). Here for the first time in some three months since leaving Samsun I received a loaf of bread from the Government.

Serudj was a dispersal centre. I managed to board a train and got to Aleppo. There I became a servant in a Turkish household and remained three months.

GANI BEY
Malta No. 2723
Interned 2.6.19

Profession. Secretary (? or under-Secretary) of the C.U.P. at Sivas in 1915.

Lists. On List III, i.e. Mr. Ryan suggested his arrest to the Grand Vizier on 27.3.19.

Arrest. The date of his arrest by the Turkish Authorities is not known. He was amongst those surrendered to the British Military Authorities on 28.5.19.

Petition. W. 2178. Petition of 22.6.20. sent direct to High Commissioner. In this petition he states that:

(a) He is the victim of mistaken identity;

(b) This mistake caused his arrest in Sivas where he was exclusively occupied with commercial pursuits.

(c) That his innocence was established by the findings of a Mixed Commission that sat in Sivas, which Commission published a lengthy report. (Nothing is known of this Commission or of its report.)

(d) That (c) can be confirmed by Miss Graffam who knows him well.

Petition of 9.10.20 from wife (sent direct to High Commissioner.)

Wife's address:- Shefiks Hanum, chez Salim Bey; Ouzounjou Ova No. 71 Quartier Roum Ali; Beshiktash.

In this petition, with photograph of GANI BEY attached, the wife states that: -

He was C.U.P. under-Secretary at Sivas

That he was destituted of his functions "avant deux ans" for helping Armenians.

That Vehib Pasha caused him much trouble.

That when arrested he was mistaken for another Gani, who had been C.U.P. Secretary at Adrianople.

The photograph is certified to by Miss Graffam at Sivas as follows:

"This is to certify that the accompanying photograph is a likeness of GANI BEY a native of Erzerum, who was for four years Secretary of the Sivas Branch of the Union and Progress Party.

"At the time of the Armenian deportations he was absent from the city and so far as I know had personally nothing to do with these events.

"His wife is the bearer of this letter and is on her way to Constantinople to establish the identity of her husband, about which there seems to be a complication, there being another Gani Bey who has been represented to certain authorities as this one."

"MARY L. GRAFFAM

"Director Sivas Unit."

ACCUSATIONS.

5029/A/7. Detailed statement of the Sivas atrocities by Mr. Karageuzian, a member of the B.I.A., dated January 1919. In this account occurs the name of GANI BEY as well as those of Dr. Fazil Berki Bey (at Malta), the deputy for Sivas, Rassim Bey, Colonel Agassi Ali, as accomplices of the notorious Muammer Bey, Vali of Sivas (now at Malta).

G. XVI. In the latest carefully compiled B.I.A. List of principal massacrers, the name of GANI BEY of Erzerum appears as 'Sécrétaire' Responsable of the C.U.P. at Sivas, whilst that of Shekerli oglou Ismail appears as President of the local club.

'Renaissance' of 20.12.18. quoting 'Joghovourt' names GANI BEY perpetual secretary of C.U.P. as having been present directing massacres at a farm close to the School of Arts some 3 hours from Sivas where the Armenian men were put to death, June 1915.

Mr. Ryan's List of 27.3.19. "Assisted Muammer in organising massacres at Sivas. Union and Progress representative there." Accusations of authority of the Bureau d'Information Arménien supported by personal evidence of Mr. Ohannes Cantar.

'Renaissance'. GANI BEY reported as having appeared before the "Commission d'Enquête de la Court Martiale."

R. 8. Copy in W. 2178. Detailed statement, dated 3.11.20 from Armenian Patriarchate. The statement is a complete indictment of GANI BEY. Also a letter dated 30.10.20, under cover of above from the Union Senekerimian de Sivas, No. 6. Commando Han, Stambul, protesting against any possibility of release of GANI BEY.

R. 8. The following witnesses, sent by the Union Senekerimian, made statements on 30.11.20.

H. 8. (A) Signed statement by Kricor Habechian of Comando Han No. 6. Stambul states that GANI BEY, known as Erzerumli GANI, was the Secretary of the local C.U.P. Club at Sivas from 1914 to the end of 1916. Together with Vali Muammer Bey and Colonel Pertev Bey, Adjoint du Commandant du $10^{\text{ième}}$, Corps d'Armée, GANI BEY was a leader in the deportations from Sivas.

Before the deportations began, i.e. end of June 1915, GANI BEY went to Constantinople, as did all other Club Secretaries, in order to receive the instructions of the Central C.U.P. with regard to the carrying out of the deportations. He was absent about one month.

It was Gani BEY's custom to accompany out of town the groups of deportees, 80 to 100 at a time. At the time I was in a Labour Battalion, 1st Birindji, at a place called Yon Youcouch, 3 hours distant from the town of Sivas, and have seen GANI BEY himself shoot down two Armenian men from one group of deportees, who were unable to walk any further.

GANI BEY sometimes dressed as a Tchete, sometimes as an Army officer, but in Sivas itself he never wore uniform.

H. 8. (B) Signed statement by Kapriel Missakian of Yarem Han, Mahmoud Pacha, Stamboul.

GANI was the C.U.P. responsible Secretary at Sivas from 1914 to 1918. Before the deportations took place he went from Sivas to Constantinople; on his return to Sivas the deportations of men, women and children began.

When working as a carpenter at Moumoune Tchiflik, two hours west of Sivas, I saw pass on one occasion a group of male Armenian deportees, tied together in fours, escorted by gendarmes. In this group I recognised Mardiros Kaprielian, dragoman of the Vilayet; Vahan Vartanian, druggist, Hovannes Paladian, Dikran Apelian, clerk in the employ of the Oriental Carpet Manufacturers, Sivas; and Manouk Beylerian, owner of the hotel Afion. Shortly after the convoy had passed the farm I saw GANI BEY, the Vali Muammer, both dressed as tchetes, and Colonel Pertev Bey in military uniform in a carriage, going in the same direction as the convoy. None of the Armenians whom I saw pass under escort have since been heard of.

(C) Signed statement by Yervant Aghinian of Cherif Pacha Han 50, Stambul.

GANI BEY was the C.U.P. responsible Secretary at Sivas from 1914 till 1918. Together with Geundji Riza, GANI visited all the Armenian villages, arrested all the males, and deported part of them towards Kotch Hissar and Sivas and had them massacred on the way. (He was with the last witness at Noumoune Tchiflik and corroborates Missakian's statement as to the events witnessed there.)

(D) Statement by Vahan Mermirian of Mahmoud Pacha, Yarem Han 5.

GANI BEY was the principal instigator of the deportations and massacres in Sivas; he was the responsible secretary of the C.U.P. from 1914 till 1918.

About the time of the Armistice, he was arrested by the Turkish Government. GANI BEY was a partner in the Turkish firm of Kardastar Chirketi which was formed out of the properties of deported Armenians.

(The witness was also present at Noumoune Farm and corroborates Missakian's statement.)

H. 8. (E) Signed statement by Madame Lousaper Boghossian of Ralli Han No. 31, Sirkedji, c/o Yervant Tchamlian.

"I am a native of Sivas and married to an Armenian doctor who was serving in the Turkish Army at Erzerum during the War. GANI BEY was a friend of our house and often visited us. Before the wholesale deportations he imprisoned twelve notables of the town and after five weeks' detention in the prison (March 15th 1915 to the end of April) he sent them away with gendarmes to murder them.

The same day we, a number of women, went to see Muammer, GANI, or Pertev to ask their clemency for these twelve men, but they were not in town and they told us that all three were away that day.

I being the wife of an Army doctor was allowed to remain in Sivas after the deportations. I have seen with my own eyes all the details of the Armenian deportations (June, July, August). GANI personally superintended the deportations with the help of gendarmes.

When in September 1, with my two children and mother-in-law, we were ordered to leave Sivas, GANI came to our house with his wife and asked me to give up our house with the furniture which we did at once.

When we were at Saghir Dere (four or five hours distant from Sivas) on our way to exile, GANI came towards us in Tchete dress, accompanied by Gendarmes and took away my husband's orderly, an Armenian young man, a soldier, and shot him before our eyes.

Then GANI shot my mother-in-law, we were left all alone. He took all the money and valuable things that my mother-in-law had, then he left us on our way onwards and returned to Sivas.

After the Armistice I returned to Sivas where GANI's family was living in our house with all our furniture in it. Much of our furniture and clothing had been sold to different Turks of the town in whose houses I have recognised our property."

H. 12. In Patriarchate's report of 22.12.20 on Fazil Berki Bey, deputy for Changri, GANI BEY and Vali Muammer are mentioned as conferring with Fazil Berki in the Spring of 1915 at Sivas when the latter was on an anti-Christian propaganda mission.

AHMET BEY (Native of Brussa)
Malta No. 2724
Interned 2.6.19

Appointments. Assistant Vali of Bagdad, Dec. 1914 to March 1915.
Mutessarif of Aintab. August 1915 to May 1916.
Police Mudiri, Constantinople. 1916 to 1918.
Vali of Sivas. April 1918 to October 1918.

Lists. On none.

Arrests. Arrested by the Turkish Government and among those handed over to the British Military Authorities on 28.5.19 and deported.

Petitions. 1734/24. Wife's petition of 18.2.21 to go to Malta.

ACCUSATIONS.

R. 2714. This pack contains several series of captured telegrams which have been deciphered. Originals probably found in Aleppo, etc. on occupation by British troops. Many of these telegrams are from or to this AHMET when he was Mutessarif of Aintab in 1915 and 1916. Those from him are particularly harsh and venomous. The most important are:

Series I.	7.9.15 urging that a proportion of female Armenian deportees be sent for use in his sanjak.
	6.9.15 urging further deportations.
Series II.	7.9.15; 6.9.15; 15.3.16.
Series III.	Nothing remarkable.

5035/A/83. A short letter of 18.3.20 from Dr. Peet in answer to our enquiry: "his record seems to be rather an unsavoury one."

5035/A/2. A List from the American Commissioner, dated Consple. 24.2.19. headed: "Main authors of the Deportations of Armenian Aintab (about 25,000), Vilayet of Aleppo; of these about three fourths have perished."

"AHMET BEY ... active, relentless, Chauvin Ittihadji."

Naim's Memoirs p. 56. Telegram between him and Mustapha Abdul Halik, Vali of Aleppo.

Cipher-telegram sent from the Government of Aleppo to the Government of Aintab – (AHMET BEY, 29.8.15 – We hear that there are Armenians from Sivas and Kharput in your vicinity. Do not give them any opportunity of settling there, and, by the methods you are acquainted with, which have already been communicated to you, do what is necessary and report the result.

(S) Governor-General
MUSTAFA ABDULHALIK

From the Government of Aintab. To the Government of Aleppo. An answer to the cipher telegram of Jan. 11th 1916.

Jan. 18th 1916. – It has been ascertained that there are about 500 people from the said provinces in the vicinity of Roum Kale, which is under our jurisdiction. The Kaimakam of Roum Kale reports that most of them are women and children, and that, in accordance with the methods with which the Turkish officials were acquainted, communicated to them earlier, these women and children have been sent under Kurdish [guards], with the understanding that they are never to return.

"Governor AHMET"

E. 14. AHMET BEY succeeded Bedri Bey as Director-General of Police at Constantinople. His successor was Azmi Bey. Murad Bey (deportee) served under all three as Assistant Director.

G. XVIII. Listed on Patriarchate's list of criminals of September 1920; with a note: as a reward for the way in which he carried out the massacres of Aintab he was nominated Chief of Police at Constantinople.

SULEIMAN NUMAN PASHA

Malta No. 2732

Interned 2.6.19

Appointments. General. Director of the Army Medical Services. Member of the Central C.U.P.

Lists. On List I. i.e. Mr. Ryan suggested his arrest to the Grand Vizier on 23.1.19.

Arrests. Arrested by the Turkish Government on 30.1.19. **"Renaissance"** "pour avoir deliver un rapport medical au fuyard Ismail Hakki". ("R" of 1.2.19).

The Turkish List on 5035/A/67 gives the reason for his arrest as: - "Complicity in massacres". He was amongst those surrendered to the British Military Authorities on 28.5.19 and deported.

Charge as reported to F.O. The charge as reported to the Foreign Office in June 1919 was: - "Inspécteur des services sanitaires de campagne (avoir empoisonné)".

General Deedes minuted that he was deported by us under point 5 of Foreign Office telegram 233 of February 1919.

Petitions. None to date 4.3.21.

G.O.C.-in-C. prisoner. SULEIMAN NUMAN PASHA is, firstly, a G.O.C.-in-C. prisoner and, secondly, a H.C. prisoner. He was scheduled for prosecution in connection with the segregation of Prisoners of War at Tash Kishla Barrack Hospital in the spring of 1915. F.O. despatches of 19.8.19 in R/2178 and 153 of 16.2.21 in 1983/24. For further details as to his outrages on British Prisoners-of-War, see War Office Confidential report, pages (I) 2, and (V) 31 in Part II; R/1315 D.

In G.O.C-in-C.'s letter 3211 "I" of 29.7.20, in W/2178, G.O.C. informed H.C. that he had military objections to the return of SULEIMAN NUMAN PASHA.

N.B. In H.C.'s despatch to Foreign Office No. 1552/W/3667 of 24.11.20, covering report of special committee, the name of SULEIMAN NUMAN PASHA is included under Appendix A, i.e. "H.C.'s deportees who should continue to be imprisoned and in due course be brought to trial". This recommendation was made in the event of his not being brought to trial by the G.O.C.-in-C., A.B.S.

ACCUSATIONS.

(Apart from those which may be brought against him by the G.O.C.-in-C., A.B.S.)

G. II. In the Patriarchate's detailed list of criminals of September 1920, under the General heading of High Military Officers who participated in atrocities on Armenians, the name of SULEIMAN NUMAN PASHA is duly listed, with the note:- Director of the Army Sanitation; responsible for the murder of the Armenian Military Medical officers.

Patriarchate's biographical notice on SULEIMAN NUMAN PASHA, dated 26.10.20 is as follows:-

"SULEIMAN NUMAN belongs to the clan of Salonika renegade Jews known under the name of "Deunmes".

"His father, Numan Agha, was an overseer of road building attached to the staff of the Public Works Ministry."

"Suleiman Numan graduated from the Medical Faculty of Constantinople in 1891."

"He was sent by the Turkish Government to Berlin to terminate his studies, with a group of other students."

"As it was the custom then, among the Turkish students who were sent to Europe under the auspices of the Sultan Abdul Hamid, he used to spy upon his comrades and send detailed reports (Journal) on their true or unfounded participation in constitutional plots against the Turkish autocratic regime, to the Sultan Abdul Hamid."

"His spying was particularly harmful to a certain Hikmet Bey. Suleiman Numan thus succeeded in bringing himself under the notice of Sultan Abdul Hamid and in winning his approbation. On his return from Berlin he was provided with the necessary funds to open a well furnished clinic and was in the same time appointed professor to the Medical School.

At the time of the Constitution he became an enthusiastic C.U.P. member and, behaving prudently, he managed to wipe out his past and win the confidence of the C.U.P.

At the outbreak of the Great War, his German-ophily was the cause of his being called at the head of the Health Department.

This nomination had the most awful consequences, through his incapacity and cruel nature, for the Army was kept under dreadful Sanitary conditions.

Suleiman Numan is also responsible for the huge percentage of deaths among the Prisoners-of-war, due to exhaustion and unhealthy surroundings.

The enquiry of Mustapha Pasha of the Commission of Inquest brought also to light that Suleiman Numan had even ordered to his sanitary staff the murder, by poisoning, of the sick among the populations of the regions of Erzeroum, Sivas, Erzingan, under the pretext that it was the only means of safeguarding the healthy part of the population against epidemics and starvation.

Suleiman Numan, member of the C.U.P. Central Committee was entirely in accordance with his C.U.P. fellow members in the question of the Armenian deportations and massacres. The Patriarchate knows him to be responsible for the murder of the Armenian physicians enrolled in the army.

As head of the Military Health Department, their nomination to the different Army Corps was his prerogative.

Suleiman Numan used to send them to the places where the hatred against the Armenians was the most active in 1915–1916, condemning them thus to a certain death. He never made any enquiry about the numerous murders in the provinces of his Armenian subordinates.

MEMDUH BEY

Malta No. 2733

Interned 2.6.19.

Appointments. Mutessarif of Erzinjan [39.44N – 39.29E] 9.11.14 to 6.9.15.

Vali of Bitlis 6.9.15 to 8.2.16.

Vali of Bagdad ? for 3 days.

Vali of Mossul 10.10.17 to 8.11.18.

(N.B. In no case can reliance be placed on the exact dates as shown on the dossiers. The records of the Ministry of the Interior are not yet available.)

Lists. On none.

Arrests. Arrested by the Turkish Authorities early in 1919 and among those surrendered to the British Military Authorities on 28.5.19.

Petitions. None to date 12.12.20.

ACCUSATIONS.

5031. A. 11. b. Patriarchate List Part I. December 1918. "Un monster qui s'est distinguee pendant perquisitions et les supplices des détenus Arméniens."

5027. A. 14. Report from B.G.G.S. 'I' Tiflis of 9.6.19 wherein "MEMDUH BEY of Adrianople, Governor of Erzinjan is mentioned as one of those who formed a Committee which planned and carried out the massacres at Erzinjan in May 1915." Witness: Kourkin Kellerian, a merchant now (1919) in Constantinople in touch with Armenian Patriarchate, also others mentioned in Lt. Col. Saunders letter 1/3595 of 25.5.19.

5027. A. 33. Long detailed account of the massacres in and near Erzinjan in the early summer of 1915 when MEMDUH was Mutessarif, by the above mentioned witness, Kourkin Kellerian, now living at Rue Yoghourthane No. 22, Tarla Bachi, Pera and dated 2.9.20.

The witness was acting at the time as orderly to a Turkish officer. As organisers of these officially conducted massacres (probably tens of thousands massacred) the witness mentions the governor of the sanjak, MEMDUH BEY; the deputy for Erzinjan, Halet; the chief of gendarmerie, Ismail Hakki; the C.U.P. secretary Madjid Bey (at Malta); Ejzaji Mehmet (at Malta).

'Renaissance' 14.6.19. From Erzinjan after the massacres, MEMDUH was transferred to Bitlis. In conjunction with Nazim Nazmi he murdered all Armenians remaining over from the first massacres. He was later transferred to Bagdad. He was then made Vali of Mossul and Nazim Nazmi went to Mossul with him as Officer Commanding Battalion of Gendarmerie. Together with Nevzade, Commandant de la Place, they organised and carried out the massacre of the Armenian Labour Corps men. The Article is signed "M.B." (Mihran Boyadjian), a civil inspector, see below.

5035. A. 68. Mentioned in report by the (Armenian) Director of Personnel in the Ministry of the Interior, per Mr. Ryan on 8.8.19. (SECRET).

5027. A. 20. Complicity with Vali Tahsin Bey in extortion.

5035/48. Extract from Annex A. to Mr. Alfred Rizzo's letter to the High Commissioner of 16.10.19 on behalf of his client Sympath Kerkoyan, late merchant of Bitlis:-

"In 1916 when the Russians were on the point of entering Bitlis, the Vali, MEMDUH BEY, went personally to the building of the American Mission, which had been turned into a Hospital, and ordered the then doctor in chief, Mustafa Bey, to kill all the Armenian women and children serving (sic) therein, but the doctor did not carry out the order.

In 1917/18 the said MEMDUH BEY, then Vali of Mossul, in agreement with Halil Pasha, Commandant of the 6th Army Corps, and with Nevzade, the Merkez Commandant, had 600 Armenians, amongst whom were Sympath Kerkoyan and some old men and children, sent to Zoho, where they were compelled to work in the Labour Corps. More that 450 of them perished from ill-treatment and starvation."

B. 16.

A. Statement of 15.3.19 by Sahak of Erzinjan, now (1919) of the Russian Monastery, Galata, denouncing the Mutessarif of Erzinjan as a massacrer. Giving names of three other male witnesses: Mofsess, in Constantinople; Shahin Ohannes, in Odessa; and Erria Joroussian, in Constantinople.

B. Statement of 14.3.19 by Missak Tchiknavourian of Erzinjan, now (1919) living in the Russian Monastery, Galata, describes as an eye-witness the massacre and drownings in May 1915 which took place to the west of Erzinjan about one hour from the city. Witness' wife Agavni, also an eye-witness, is alive in Constantinople.

Statements A. and B. are unsigned, but appear to have been taken down in the High Commission.

C. Information from the Armenian Information Office, dated 15.3.1919, as follows:[*]

"MEMDUH BEY, one-time Mutessarif of Erzinjan and ex-Vali of Moussoul organised not only the deportation and massacre of the Armenians in Erzinjan, but also organised the massacre of the Armenians of Erzeroum who were crossing the territory of his Sanjak.

Together with the deputy of Kemakh, Halet, he has acquired a most terrible reputation in this activity of extermination.

He is known to have looted the houses of the Armenians after their deportation.

We can quote one instance of his horrible atrocities – after giving water to some 1,400 children who were crying "water water", he had them all buried alive. When he was promoted to the rank of Vali of Bitlis, he literally exterminated the entire Armenian population of Moush. When Bitlis fell, he went to Constantinople and became the head of the Government of Bagdad after the occupation of this city by the English Army. He was the appointed Vali of Moussoul when he pursued his sinister work of extermination together with a brigand named **Nazim Nazmi,** commander of the Police Force and also such men

---

[*] The statement appears in French and has been translated into English –WCB.

as Halil Pasha, military commander and Nevzat, the Military Commander of the City of Moussoul.

MEMDUH BEY went on persecuting Armenians deported from other localities. He organised males aged 10 to 70 into squads of workers and later exterminated them to the last man.

Witnesses:

1. Mrs. Satenik Garabedian, Armenian Hospital at Yedikoulé

2. Mr. Mihran Boyadjian, first class civil inspector, living in Pera, Pangalti Djadessi, No. 115."

B. 16.

D. Further information from the Armenian Information Office, dated 15.3.1919:[*]

"We believe it is our duty to draw your attention to the following information supplied by Mrs. Satenik Garabedian concerning MEMDUH BEY, Tayyard Oghlou, the Mutessarif of Erzinjan during the deportations, later on Vali of Bitlis, of Moussoul and at present detained with the other Unionists.

On June 2nd, 1918, he sent to his family in Constantinople by means of Mrs. Satenik who was employed by him as a servant, 800 Turkish gold pounds and 5,000 Turkish pounds in paper-money which he had taken from the Armenians established in Moussoul.

He also brought to Constantinople with him, according to Mrs. Satenik, a large quantity of gold and silver ornaments, rings and precious stones, all taken from the Armenians in Erzinjan. MEMDUH BEY hid them in a trunk covered by deer-skin in the first room on the left on the third floor of his house in Boyadji-Keuy, opposite the pier.

If, as a result of his arrest, these objects have been taken elsewhere, a search should be made in the house of his brother-in-law, one-time Mutessarif of Dardanelles and who lives in Bébék."

C. 21. Extract from a statement made at the High Commissioner by Mrs. Nuvart Mahokian, widow of Onnik Mahokian of Trebizond, merchant. (Mrs. Mahokian is an educated eye-witness speaking Armenian only. She gave a detailed account of her deportation from Trebizond to the Euphrates.)

"At Erzinjan we met a convoy of deportees from Erzeroum amongst whom were friends and relatives. Till then this convoy had been better treated than the first Trebizond one. I and six others of my family managed to join the Erzerum convoy. The Mutessarif of Erzinjan at the moment was MEMDUH BEY who afterwards became Vali of Mossul.

The first Trebizond caravan arrived at Erzinjan under Faik Bey's command on July 15th 1915. The caravan went on the next day on the Harput road via Khamack. I succeeded in joining the Erzerum caravan as conditions seemed to be better. Mushtak Bey was in command of this caravan; he was a gendarmerie officer but he left the caravan at Erzinjan.

On or about July 23rd the caravan moved on; it must have consisted of at least 15,000 men, women and children who had as yet neither been separated nor robbed. It was said

---

[*] The statement appears in French and has been translated into English –WCB.

that Tahsin Bey, Vali of Erzerum, later of Damascus (now at Malta), did not wish any atrocities to take place in his Vilayet. We took the same road as the Trebizond caravan had taken a week before. We marched along the banks of the Kara Su (Euphrates). Many of us were on horseback. All the way from Erzinjan to Kemakh I passed countless bodies of Armenians by the road and in the river. They belonged to previous caravans of deportees not to the Trebizond one which was not massacred till south of Harput. At one place before we got to Kemakh I saw a place where a large number of children had been buried alive in a large hole dug by the Armenians themselves. I saw there a number of Armenian women, ill or starving and dying; they told me that Memduh Bey himself had come out from Erzinjan and had ordered and assisted in this massacre."

5027. A. 9. This pack contains the evidence of several eye-witnesses of the Kemakh gorge massacres in the Sanjak of Erzinjan, all directly implicating the deputy of Erzinjan, Halet Bey. Also a memorandum by Professor Sarkiss Manougian of Sanssarian college, Erzerum, on the execution of Bishop Simpad Saadetian of Erzerum by MEMDUH BEY at Erzinjan, apparently by order of the Vali of the Province, Tahsin Bey (at Malta).

Also a memorandum by Dr. Armenag Madatian of Erzerum, now of Constantinople who saw the Bishop at the gate of the Armenian cemetery of Erzinjan just before his execution. The witness was in the last convoy of Erzerum Armenians passing through the city of Erzinjan.

N.B. Kemakh is [in] the sanjak of the Vilayet Erzerum, of which Tahsin Bey (now at Malta) was Vali.

5030. A. 18. Alleged copy of a Turkish official telegram dated 11.2.16 from the Vali of Bitlis (MEMDUH BEY) to the Mutessarif of Sairt (Serfitcheli Hilmi Bey). A free translation of this copy of a telegram is as follows.

It is undesirable that a single male Armenian should remain. It is required of you to plan their immediate destruction according to precedent. Make arrangements to this end.

The telegram is endorsed:- To the Commander of Gendarmerie and Commissioner of Police, given by hand, the 13th (of February 1916).

The original of this telegram is said to be in the possession of Djevdet Bey, late Mutessarif of Sairt, now (end 1919) of Amassia.

This copy was communicated by Mr. Mihran Boyadjian, late a 1st class Civil Inspector of the Vilayet of Bitlis and Mossul. As this gentleman's name frequently appears in the dossiers of prisoners who are alleged to have ordered or committed massacres in the eastern vilayets, it may be as well to quote the following minute, dated 31.1.20 by Lt.-Col. R. W. Graves, Head of the Armenian-Greek Section British High Commission:-

5030. A. 18. Mihran Boyadjian is personally known to me as a former Inspector of the Ministry of the Interior. He was, I believe, Mutessarif of one of the sanjaks of Bitlis and was to have accompanied Colonel Hoff, the Norwegian officer who was appointed Inspector-General of Reforms in Armenia in 1914. As his Assistant he bore a very good character, and any information supplied by him is likely to be authentic.

C. 1. M. Boyadjian's evidence before Court Martial on 3.5.19: MEMDUH arrived at Mossul on 17.9.17 (O.S.). He nominated Nazim Nazmi Commandant of the Armenian Labour Corps. (Nazim Nazmi was already a notorious massacrer.)

C. 27.

A. Statement by Ardachess Lepian, merchant of Erzinjan, taken down in Batum by Intelligence, Transcaucasia. Deportations took place from Erzinjan in May 1915.

Witness saw MEMDUH BEY and Ejzadji Mehmet on the road towards Kemakh; corpses on the road at the time. Witness also mentions MEMDUH and Madjid as on the directing committee organising the extermination of Armenians.

B. Statement by Hinganoush Bogossian of Erzinjan. Corroborates the above.

C. 27.

C. Statement by Memduhi Tomass[ian] of Erzinjan recorded 17.4.19 at Batum; corroborating.

G. XI. In Patriarchate's detailed List of September 1920. MEMDUH is duly listed as the chief official responsible for the massacres (west of the city of Erzinjan).

G. XIX. In the same list as above, MEMDUH is also listed under the heading of Mossul. MEMDUH succeeded Haidar Bey as Vali of Mossul.

IBRAHIM PIRIZADE SAIB BEY

Malta No. 2735

Interned 2.6.19.

Appointments. Senator.

Minister of Justice, 1915. President of the Council of State.

Lists. On List III, i.e. Mr. Ryan suggested his arrest to Grand Vizier on 27.3.19. His arrest demanded by French High Commissioner on 12.2.19 (despatch 269/1315, dated 5.3.19)

Arrests. Date of arrest by the Turkish Authorities is not known. He was among those surrendered to the British Military Authorities on 28.5.19.

Charge as reported to F.O. "Président du Conseil d'Etat, member du Cabinet de Guerre."

Petitions.

W. 1049/265. On 17.6.20. The governor of Malta recommended the sending of one of his servants. "He is over 60 years of age and weak . . . his character has been exemplary."

W. 3255. From wife of 9.10.20 asking to be permitted to go to Malta. Passed to Gov. Malta on [sic]/11/20. No further action taken (6/3/21).

N.B. In High Commissioner's despatch No. 1552/W/3667, dated 24/11/20 and covering report of special committee, it was recommended that IBRAHIM PIRIZADE SAID BEY should be detained until brought up for trial. In making this recommendation in the case of one who held high ministerial rank during the regime of deportations and massacres in 1915, the special committee was influenced in some measure by the following minutes:-

Commission:-

14.11.20. Minute by Mr. Ryan:

. . . In practice we have gone on the principle that a sufficient presumption of guilt to justify detention and ultimate prosecution existed against all members of the responsible Governments of Turkey at the time when the massacres and deportations took place and all persons so high in the councils of the C.U.P. as to be able to be credited with a share in directing its policy. If this is the principle, then it seems to me that all these people should stand their trial, and that (assuming none of them to have established their complete innocence e.g. by proving that they continually protested, that they were sick, that the Cabinet as a whole were ignorant of what was toward etc.), it would be for the judge or judges to consider whether the role played by particular individuals was so passive as to justify a lenient rather than a severe sentence.

. . . Pending further developments I think we should keep any ex-Ministers who certainly formed part of Turkish Cabinets when the deportation and massacre policy was adopted and carried out. This appears to me to be the only logical course, unless it is definitely laid down that a different principle applies viz. that acquiescence (with knowledge) is not to be regarded as a ground of accusation in the case of anyone, even Ministers or C.U.P. leaders and that some definite individual act immediately conducing to massacres must be forthcoming to justify prosecution. In one sense the question is a juridical one and not one of policy at all. So far as it **is** a question of policy I suppose it is one of Allied Policy. I take it that all prisoners now held on any ground connected with deportations and massacres must be regarded as held in trust for the Allied Powers.

15.11.20. Minute by Sir Harry Lamb:

I agree generally with Mr. Ryan, with whom I have discussed the question. It seems to me that we **have** adopted the principle of prosecuting the persons morally responsible rather than mere agents – excepting the most outrageous cases. That being so, we can not make much distinction between one member of the Cabinet and another, unless there were evidence that he offered strong opposition to the measures taken and merely yielded to a majority decision. Even then I think Mr. Ryan is right in considering that this should be a matter for appreciation by the Tribunal eventually constituted to try the cases, in mitigation of penalties and should not prevent the individual from being sent to stand his trial with the rest.

ACCUSATIONS.

5035/A/11.b. Patriarchate List 1919 Série II. "il a joué un role funeste dans les relations du Gouvernement avec le Patriarche Mgr. Zaven".

H. 6. Open letter in Turkish paper 'Sabah', addressed to the Senator IBRAHIM BEY, ex-Minister of Justice accusing him of being a puppet of Talaat's, of releasing criminals from the prisons in order that they might become tchetes wherewith to exterminate Armenians.

The organization of these tchetes carried out in the office of the Procureur Général de la Cour d'Appel, situated just above IBRAHIM's own ministerial room in the Ministry of Justice, etc.

G. 11. Armenian Patriarchate's denunciation, September 1920: "Ministre de la Justice. Exécuta sa part dans le crime en faisant relacher les criminels des prisons pour former les Tchétés du Teshkilat Mahsoussé. Il défendit aux fonctionnaires de la Justice d'intervenir dans les crimes commis. En déstituant les fonctionnaires chrétiennes pendant les deportations il fut cause de leur meurtre."

5031/A/7. Unsigned report through G.H.Q. 'I', dated 7.3.19 IBRAHIM is herein accused of having liberated criminals undergoing sentence, in order that they might be enrolled as Tchétes. For his good work in this connection he is alleged to have drawn £tq 15,000 from Secret Service Funds.

AHMED NESSIMI BEY
Malta No. 2736
Interned 2.6.19.

Appointments. Minister of Agriculture and Commerce, Minister of Foreign Affairs. Permanent Deputy for Constantinople. Permanent Member of C.U.P.

Lists. On List III i.e. his name was suggested for arrest by Mr. Ryan to Grand Vizier on 27.3.19. His name also occurs on list of French demands for arrest which was handed to the Grand Vizier on 12.2.19. (see High Commissioner's despatch of 5.3.19 in 1915).

Arrest. He was arrested by the Turkish Government early in 1919 and was among those surrendered to the British Military Authorities on 28.5.19 and deported to Malta.

Petitions. None to date (6.3.21).

N.B. High Commissioner's despatch (committee's report) No. 1552 of 24.11.20 recommended that he should be brought up for trial. In making this recommendation in the case of one who held high ministerial rank during the regime of deportations and massacre, the special committee was influenced in some measure by the following minutes by the 2nd and 1st Political Officers of the High Commission:-

14.11.20. Minute by Mr. Ryan:

... In practice we have gone on the principle that a sufficient presumption of guilt to justify detention and ultimate prosecution existed against all members of the responsible Governments of Turkey at the time when the massacres and deportations took place and all persons so high in the councils of the C.U.P. as to be able to be credited with a share in directing its policy. If this is the principle, then it seems to me that all these people should stand their trial, and that (assuming none of them to have established their complete innocence e.g. by proving that they continually protested, that they were sick, that the Cabinet as a whole were ignorant of what was toward etc.), it would be for the judge or judges to consider whether the role played by particular individuals was so passive as to justify a lenient rather than a severe sentence.

... Pending further developments I think we should keep any ex-Ministers who certainly formed part of Turkish Cabinets when the deportation and massacre policy was adopted and carried out. This appears to me to be the only logical course, unless it is definitely laid down that a different principle applies viz. that acquiescence (with knowledge) is not to be regarded as a ground of accusation in the case of anyone, even Ministers or C.U.P. leaders and that some definite individual act immediately conducing to massacres must be forthcoming to justify prosecution. In one sense the question is a juridical one and not one of policy at all. So far as it **is** a question of policy I suppose it is one of Allied Policy. I take it that all prisoners now held on any ground connected with deportations and massacres must be regarded as held in trust for the Allied Powers.

15.11.20. Minute by Sir Harry Lamb:

I agree generally with Mr. Ryan, with whom I have discussed the question. It seems to me that we **have** adopted the principle of prosecuting the persons morally responsible rather than mere agents – excepting the most outrageous cases. That being so, we can not make much distinction between one member of the Cabinet and another, unless there were evidence that he offered strong opposition to the measures taken and merely yielded to a majority decision. Even then I think Mr. Ryan is right in considering that this should be a matter for appreciation by the Tribunal eventually constituted to try the cases, in mitigation of penalties and should not prevent the individual from being sent to stand his trial with the rest.

ACCUSATIONS.

G. 11. The name of AHMED NESSIMI BEY occurs on the Patriarchate's detailed list of criminals of September 1920. The following biographical notice has also been received:

"AHMED NESSIMI BEY was born in Crete. He was, in the days of Sultan Abdul Hamid, a small employee in the Ministry of Foreign Affairs, viz a clerk in the Bureau of Correspondence. He was a secret affiliate of the C.U.P. and after the Constitution, he was elected member of their Central Committee. He became most influential among his fellow members, being considered as a specialist in European politics. Although he tried to reject subsequently, when cross examined, all responsibility in the misdeeds of the C.U.P., he is one of those on whose shoulders the responsibility falls heaviest.

Even the Turkish enquiry could not do otherwise, than admit his complicity and in the act of accusation read by the Imperial Prosecutor at the opening session of the trial of the Unionists on [27] 28 of April 1919, AHMED NESSIMI BEY is cited as responsible for the crimes committed by the Unionists. AHMED NESSIMI BEY was deputy of Constantinople. During the war he was in the Cabinet, first as Minister of Commerce and after as Minister of Foreign Affairs.

He was not only a party, but also a promoter of all the Turco-German acts against Humanity.

FAIK BEY

Malta No. 2737

Interned 2.6.19.

Appointments. Kaimakam of Merzivan in sandjak of Amassia in Vilayet of Sivas, 1915. Kaimakam of Shile. Kaimakam of Panderma, "from which post he was removed on account of abuses he had committed while he was kaimakam of Merzivan, abuses which were proved by enquiries made through Civil Inspections." The date of his removal is June 1918.

Lists. On List I i.e. his arrest was suggested to the Grand Vizier by Mr. Ryan on 23.1.19.

Arrests. He was arrested by the Turkish Authorities in January 1919 and was among those surrendered to the British Military Authorities on 28.5.19 and deported.

Petitions. W. 2606. Petition dated 28.11.19 from wife. In this petition the wife urges that FAIK BEY only carried out the orders of the Vali of Sivas (Ahmed Muammer Bey) when FAIK was kaimakam of Merzivan. She says that FAIK was tried four times by Court Martial and that he was released each time.

ACCUSATIONS.

A. 1. Signed statement, dated 26th November 1918, by Aznive Kasbarian of Chichli, Bomonti Djaddessi, Kurk sokak, Appartment Fernerdjian No. 6 sent under cover of a letter, dated 27.11.18 from Lt. General H. F. M. Wilson to High Commissioner. The statement contains a hysterical denunciation of FAIK BEY, the Kaimakam of Merzivan and Mahir Bey, the Gendarmerie Commandant (Mahir is on Foreign Office List).

C. 11. Detailed statement, made to British High Commission dated 3.2.20 by Mrs. Iskian of 8 Rue Anderlich, Pangalti. This statement, by an intelligent English speaking resident of Merzivan, gives a full account of the deportations and massacres of Merzivan whilst FAIK BEY was kaimakam in the summer of 1915. Besides the indirect implication of the Kaimakam, the witness directly implicates him in the massacres that were carried out in the valley of Teunek on the road to Chorum, close to Merzivan. See Appendix A.

5029. A. 7. (See Ahmed Muammer's dossier). Note by Dr. White, American Missionary at Merzivan: "He is equally guilty with Muammer Bey and he actually carried out the massacres and deportations on instructions from Muammer and he is credited with having done them extremely well."

5029. A. 11. Names of Armenian witnesses of Merzivan atrocities. Also list of names of principal agents employed still at large. (1.4.19)

APPENDIX A.

MERZIFUN AND ANGORA

Address: 8 Anderlich St. Pangalti, Pera. STATEMENT IN ENGLISH BY MADAME AROUSSIAG Y ISKIAN WIFE OF YERVANT ISKIAN. ANTIQUE DEALER OF ANGORA, DAUGHTER OF THE LATE BOGHOS TORIKIAN, MERCHANT OF MERZIFUN, MASSACRED NEAR AMASSIA ON 12th JUNE 1915 AND SISTER OF MRS. CAPTANIAN.

Statement made at the High Commission on 3.2.20.

"I was born in Merzifun (Merzivan or Mersovan); I had been living there since 1912 with my children who were being educated at the American College. Dr. White was Principal and Miss Charlotte Willard in charge of the girls' department; Dr. Mardin was in charge of the hospital. In May 1915 there were the first signs of something about to happen. MUAMMER was Vali of the Province. **Sirri** Bey was Mutessarif of Amassia and Faik Bey, now at Malta, was Kaimakam of the Kaza of Merzifun. **Mahir** Bey was in command of the troops and Major **Emin** Bey was his second in command. A lawyer, **Ahmed Effendi**, was also in close touch with this ruling gang. Fear began to fall on the Armenian population in Merzifun in May; it was felt or known that the Government was about to take measure against us. There was no question of a Turkish popular rising against us; the whole thing was done by Government order. The Turkish population remained gladly callous throughout. The deportations and massacres that ensued were carried out by the Government only through its officials, though of course very many Turkish men volunteered for the official job of butchering the Christians. In the country the Turkish peasants, men and women took an active part in massacring and torturing, but always with official sanction. Throughout the massacre period, there was never any excitement among the Turkish populace; all was cold blooded murder by official order or at any rate with official sanction.

One night in April, police and gendarmes arrested some 50 of the Armenian intellectuals and took them to prison. They were subjected torture and after some days sent to Sivas by night to prison. They have all disappeared. MUAMMER caused them to disappear. In May 1915 the Vali, MUAMMER, visited Merzifun. Just after he left 70 more young intellectuals were imprisoned and tortured. One of these is still alive and can give evidence; his name is Mr. Manuk Adjderian, Rue Anderlich, apartment House; near G.H.Q.

On June 12th (N.S.) the Government took away all the Armenian men of the town. My father was taken by night in his nightgown to gaol and placed underground. It was on a Friday night. Monday morning he was no longer in the barracks – then used as a prison. He had been made to disappear. Every night for a long time batches of men were taken out by night in different directions and massacred within a few hours of the town. They were always taken out to the place of massacre by gendarmes and police in uniform.

Mahir Bey gave me his signed permit to remain in Merzifun. It cost me Lt. 500 gold in jewels etc. given to **Faik, Mahir**, and **Emin** through the lawyer, to save my husband. Emin Bey once showed me a packet full of telegrams from MUAMMER and said that they in Merzifun were not properly carrying out the orders of the Vali; i.e. they were too lenient. Emin Bey gave permission for my husband and brother to go to Angora.

9. 2. 20. Since last speaking I have found out further details from Armenian friends from Merzifun who escaped massacre because they were rich, became converted to Islam and were friends of the Commandant, **Mahir** Bey.

My father was sent off on Sunday night together with about 200 others all roped together under an escort of gendarmes and police. Major **Emin** Bey, commanding the military was present at the departure of the convoy. The convoy took the road to Amassia. Near Amassia an escort from Amassia took over the convoy. In a valley near the fountain of Kaimakam Puna, they were all murdered by gendarmes and tchetes.

Sirri Bey, the Mutessarif of Amassia detained the Merzifun convoy some little time in Amassia so that the news should not be known at once in Merzifun. Before returning them he made them swear to keep the secret. The Police Commissaire of Merzifun at the time was **Salih** Bey.

After this first wholesale massacre the batches of those to be butchered were no longer directed to wards Amassia but were butchered close to Merzifun in a valley called Teunek on the road to Chorum, under the direct supervision of **Faik** and **Mahir**.

All men from boys to old men were massacred except those who could bribe sufficiently.

Mahir has himself boasted of his part in the massacre to one of my friends though he disclaims responsibility for the first massacre near Amassia. **Mahir** was a fanatice pan-Turanian. No one can tell where **Mahir** is now to be found."

SHUKRI BEY
(MUFTI ZADE SHUKRI BEY)

Malta No. 2738

Interned 2.6.19

Appointments. Was a Civil Inspector from October 1913 to Nov. 1914. Was in charge of "Emigration" in the Aleppo and Adana Vilayets from November 1914 to December 1915. Was a Civil Inspector, 1st Class, from December 1915 to (?) 1918, when he resigned.

Arrest. The date of his arrest or by whom is not known. In the 'Renaissance' of 4.4.19, it was reported that SHUKRI BEY had been brought from Smyrna to Constantinople under arrest. He was amongst those surrendered to the British Military Authorities on 28.5.19.

Accusation as reported to F.O. "Attentat commis à l'occasion de déportation."

Domicile. The house of his father-in-law: Arif Pasha.

Petitions. W. 1315 D.

1. On 7.2.20 the Minister for Foreign Affairs requested his release since the Turkish Court Martial had decided in his favour.

On 25.2.20 High Commissioner replied in the usual form saying that pending a decision of the Peace Conference High Commissioner is unable to comply with the request.

2. Petition of 21.4.20 from SHUKRI BEY, through Governor, Malta saying that it is considered unnecessary to return any reply to the petitioner.

3. Petition of 7.8.20 from wife.

4. **W. 3255**. Petition of 23.9.20 from him asking for permission for wife and daughter to come to Malta. Forwarded under cover of Malta's 11834/1564 (A) of 22.10.20.

ACCUSATIONS.

R. 2714. Translation of decyphered captured telegram, from Talaat Pasha to the Mutessarif of Aintab (i.e. notorious Ahmed Bey who was specially sent to Aintab for deportation purposes, 29.8.15 to 14.5.16; now at Malta), dated 18.9.15:

"SHUKRI BEY, Director of the Refugees Department has been detailed and sent by the Ministry to deal with the regular deportation of the Armenians to the assigned districts and to investigate and ensure that everything required for the purpose is in order. Please take any step which SHUKRI BEY may deem necessary on his arrival."

Naim's memoirs p. 8. SHUKRI BEY was General Supervisor of deportees, arrived in Aleppo early summer of 1915, . . . was organising the plan of the deportations and massacres. As long as Djemal Bey was Vali, i.e. to June 1915 and Bekir had i.e. to October 1915, SHUKRI could do nothing. His accomplice then was Djemal Bey

(C.U.P. Secretary). Not till the appointment of Mustafa Abdul Halik in October 1915 could SHUKRI get to work.

Renaissance 22.10.19.[*] "The wife of SHUKRI BEY, Director General of the Administration of Refugees during the Unionist regime and sent to Malta with the Unionist leaders, had presented a request to the Court Martial in which she declared that her husband was innocent and she asked that he be sent back to Constantinople. The Commission of Inquiry of the Court Martial, having examined the file of SHUKRI BEY, establishes that he had played an important role in the deportation and massacre of Armenians, and specially in Aleppo where he had personally directed the deportation of the Armenians. For these reasons, SHUKRI BEY's wife was told that it was impossible to undertake any necessary steps in her husband's favour with the representatives of the Allies.

It has been announced, however, that she has seen the Minister of War who has formally requested to find a satisfactory solution to her request."

N.B. (The dossiers of the Turkish Court Martial and other official documents bearing on this case have not yet been demanded of the Turkish Government under Art. 228 of the Treaty of Sèvres.)

K. 5. Patriarchate report of 26.2.21 on Bekir Sami Bey, Vali of Aleppo during the deportations. In this report it is stated that Bekir Sami (Chief Kemalist Delegate to Conference of London) was dismissed from his post as vali of Aleppo at the insistence of SHUKRI BEY, Director of Emigration, because Bekir Sami would not fall in with the Policy of the C.U.P. of extermination. SHUKRI BEY had been specially sent to Aleppo by the C.U.P.

---

[*] The original article appears in French and has been translated into English –WCB.

FEZI BEY
(ARIF FEZI BEY)

Malta No. 2743

Interned 23.7.19

Appointments. Deputy for Diarbekir.

Lists. On Lists I and III, i.e. his name was suggested by Mr. Ryan to the Grand Vizier on 23.1.19 and again on 27.3.19.

Arrest. Appears to have been arrested on our formal written demand on 28.1.19. He was handed over by the Turkish Authorities to the Egyptian Expeditionary Force and deported to Egypt. From Egypt he was transferred to Malta in July 1919.

N.B. In despatch 4316/M.E. 58, dated 7.3.19, the S. of S. writes to the High Commissioner:

"You should urge the Turkish Government to arrest the persons named in Mr. Ryan's report" i.e., among those named was FEZI BEY; see 5030 A.1. below.

Petitions.

1. **5030. A. 26.** Petition of 8.9.20, through Governor of Malta on 10.9.20. No action.
2. do. Petition of 23.9.20, asking to be allowed out on parole.

N.B. W. 2178. On 30.11.20. (No. 2647 'I') G.O.C. informed High Commissioner that Egyptian Expeditionary Force was releasing him on account of lack of evidence. Has High Commissioner any objection to his liberation on arrival at Constantinople?

In High Commissioner's despatch No. 1552/W.3667 dated 24.11.20 and covering report of special committee, it was recommended that ARIF FEZI BEY be detained at Malta (as a High Commissioner internee) until brought up for trial.

ACCUSATIONS.

5030. A. 1. Account of Diarbekir massacres in 1915 given by a Moslem deputy to Mr. Ryan on 23.1.19. This memorandum was sent to the Foreign Office under cover of Despatch 113/1212 of 3.2.19. The main points in this memorandum are:

A. FEZI's influence in Diarbekir 'rampant' at the end of 1918. "The Government is powerless and nothing can be achieved locally except by our sending a commission of enquiry backed by sufficient force to intimidate persons responsible for the massacres and to encourage well disposed persons to testify."

B. Deportations began in May 1915. "When the number was about 680 a party was sent down the river. This first party consisted altogether of men. Arrangements had been made with certain notorious malefactors and the party were massacred on the riverside some way down. Corpses were stripped of everything and proceeds handed over to the Vali. A reign of terror began in Diarbekir itself. Numerous parties of Armenians of both sexes and all ages were sent away and massacred at places which gradually became nearer and nearer to the town. Diarbekir and the neighbourhood became a massacre centre for deported persons from other provinces. A certain amount of killing was no doubt done on the line of the route in the other provinces themselves, but the main work of massacre was accomplished in or near Diarbekir. Informant said that this state of affairs lasted until late in the autumn when the Vali Rechid was recalled. It then came to an end. Informant was himself in Diarbekir until September 1915 when he left for Constantinople as he had broken with the Vali owing to his disapproval of the latter's proceedings and had reason to fear for his own life. Early in the period certain Sub-Governors who refused to carry out orders were dismissed and two were done to death. These were Nessimi Bey, Governor of Lidje and Sabit Soueidi, Governor of Bisheri."

C. "Informant mentioned the following as having played a very leading part, but did not give the list as a complete one":

Reshid Bey.	Vali of Diarbekir (Committed suicide to avoid arrest)
Fezi Bey.	Deputy for Diarbekir. A person then and now of enormous local influence. (Detained at Malta).
Rushdi Bey.	Commandant of the Gendarmerie (on Foreign Office List for surrender by the Turkish Government)
Shakir Bey.	Captain; A.D.C. to the Vali. (Arrested but escaped on his way under escort to Constantinople)
Bedri Bey.	(Ibrahim Bedreddin Bey). Provincial Secretary. (Detained at Malta)
Harum Bey.	Officer of Gendarmerie. (On Foreign Office List for surrender by Turkish Government)
Hussein Bey.	Director of Police. (On Foreign Office List for surrender by Turkish Government)
Memduh Bey.	Commissioner of Police. (On Foreign Office List for surrender by Turkish Government)
Sherif Bey.	Cousin of Fezi Bey. (On Foreign Office List for surrender by Turkish Government)
Shevki Bey.	Officer of Militia i.e. Tchetes. Relation of Fezi Bey. (On Foreign Office List for surrender by Turkish Government)
Sidki Bey.	(Birindjizade Sidki). Notable and mayor of Diarbekir. Cousin of Fezi Bey. (On Foreign Office List for surrender by Turkish Government)
Emin Bey.	Officer of Militia.

"Informant said that Zulfi Bey Deputy had not played an active part. He had disapproved like himself of the massacres.

Informant said that the massacres had been carried out by the Gendarmerie and the Milice. The former was strengthened by a considerable element of Circassians, compatriots of the Vali, imported by him. The Milice [irregular forces, including released criminals] was a sort of volunteer force organised specially for the purpose. It was officered by local notables. The rank and file were recruited from the worst elements including released criminals from local prisons."

'Renaissance' 25.6.19. Mihran Boyadjian, ex-Inspector de 1re class des Vilayets de Bitlis et de Mosul (personally known to us) refers to FEZI BEY in connection with Dr. Reshid (now dead) ex Vali of Diarbekir. M. Boyadjian met him in 1918 at Djizre, on the R. Tigris, inciting the people against the Christians.

A. 21. Statement of 16.1.19 by Mrs. Seyahi, nee Kazazian.

Murder of her father and her girl cousin (16 years). Circumstantial and hearsay. Vali Dr. Reshid when in prison here had told Mrs. Seyahi's husband that FEZI had ordered the murder. (Dr. Reshid since committed suicide). Mr. Kazazian was the owner of a large house property in Diarbekir. Twenty years ago Mr. Paul Cambon had saved his life. (Names and addresses available).

A. 22. Reported words of FEZI's; apparently at Diarbekir inciting to massacres.

(Pera: name and address).

A. 23.

A. Account of Diarbekir atrocities in May 1915, by Agop Minas Berberian (20) of Diarbekir, dated 24.1.19. then living at Mgr. Dolci's orphanage.

Hearsay regarding the drowning from reports of some 1,500 men near El Djezire, by order of Dr. Reshid and the Deputy FEZI BEY.

B. Account of same, also hearsay, by Fouroudjian (18) of Diarbekir; also eye witness of massacre of some 200 deportees by gendarmes on the road from Diarbekir to Jerusalem.

C. Account by Hanna Hanum (21) of Diarbekir now of Pera. Numbers of men given as seven to eight hundred not "about 1,500". Rather more circumstantial.

A. 24. Illegible scrawl in pencil.

5030. A. 8. Merely a Patriarchate list of 20.1.19 of "the Criminals of Diarbekir".

D. 29. "Faits et Documents" – pamphlet.

p. 8, p. 14 FEZI BEY was Vice President of the Medjlissi Ali of Diarbekir with Reshid Bey, the Vali, as President.

p. 20 FEZI enrols the Kurd brothers Eumerki and Mustafa sons of Perihan, chieftains of the Raman tribe, of the Kurdish village Chkavtan, to massacre the deportees (May 1915).

p. 50 from Ras-ul-Ain his executioners sent him a rope of women's hair.

D. 29 p.53 FEZI's father was Birinjizade of Arif, a distinguished massacrer of 1895.

5030/A/8. Patriarchate List of 20.1.19, being a list of the Diarbekir Massacres.

H.2. Extract from a statement made at the High Commission by Shefik Bey, late a Kaimakam in the eastern vilayets. In the Mardin district FEZI the deputy had great influence with the Kurds and Circassians. He was Dr. Reshid's right hand man in the massacres of Diarbekir.

C. 19. Signed statement by Monsieur Mihran Boyadjian, late a 1st Class Inspector of the vilayets of Bitlis and Mossul.*

The deputy FEZI BEY, one of the most fanatic members of the party of Union and Progress, having taken part in the secret meetings of the Central Committee, had just left Constantinople, after the end of the Parliamentary session and gone to Diarbekir. His intention was to encourage the Vali, Dr. Reshid and personally take part in the massacres of the 120,000 Armenians, Syrians and Chaldeians of the vilayet of Diarbekir.

I left Constantinople on the 15th of July, 1914, and via Egypt arrived in Aleppo, from where on the 7th of August together with the Diarbekir deputies FEZI, Zulfi and Kiamil Bey who had all arrived from the capital, we set off for Diarbekir.

On the way, we got around to talking about politics. In his conversation, FEZI BEY made threatening allusions to the Armenians. 'The Armenians,' he would repeat with bitterness, 'behaved badly towards us in our days of distress during the Balkan War. Zaven, the Catholicoss of Etchmiadzin and Nubar tried to get foreign intervention. You will pay a high price for it, my friend; your future is in danger.'

In vain I ventured to show him that the reforms that were being called for favoured more the Turks and the Kurds than the Armenians. He refused to understand. When we arrived at Ourfa, I was overjoyed to hear the **destitution** of Messrs. Hoff and Vestining who were charged with the inspection of the six oriental provinces. It was Hussein Djelal Bey, resigned Vali of Diarbekir (present Vali of Adrianoplis) who gave us the news.

It was the first month of the Great War. FEZI BEY was jubilant. 'You are going to see now what it means to ask for reforms' he told me in a mocking tone.

On the 10th of August we arrived at Diarbekir and found the smouldering ruins of the Bazar. A fire had reduced it to ashes a couple of days before our arrival. The Police Commissioner Memdouh Bey had been charged and was in prison. FEZI BEY had him set free. This Memdouh was to play a most sinister role in the massacres and the looting of Diarbekir and Mardin.

During the month of February, 1915, while engaged in my duty as inspector in the Sanjak of Seghert, I received from Constantinople two coded messages instructing me to hasten my inspection and go, urgently, towards the end of April to Mossoul. In accordance with my orders, I set out and arrived in Djiziré, on the 25th April. The panic of the Christian population had reached its limit; they were all terrified of massacres. Many of the notables came to me and implored my help. I appealed to the Kaimakam, Halil Sami. He informed me that the deputy FEZI BEY was in Djiziré since a fortnight, entrusted with a special mission by the Vali of Diarbekir. On the 27th of April, the day His Majesty acceded to the throne, FEZI BEY had invited the Chiefs of the Kurdish tribes to Djiziré and had declared to them that it was a religious and patriotic duty to massacre the Christians, that stealing the property of the Giavours was 'hellal' (that is to say, duly authorised by the Islamic law of Sheriat). Apparently, the Kaimakam had refused to help the bands of brigands and to dismiss the Armenian and Chaldean civil servants.

Reshid Bey, the Vali of Diarbekir, having telegraphed him to obey the orders of his repre-

---

*The statement appears in French and has been translated into English –WCB.

sentative FEZI BEY, dismissed him some days later, on the 1st of May, 1915. Upon three successive and very urgent cables from the Vali Rechid, FEZI BEY left Djiziré on the 24th April, one day before my arrival in that town, and went to Diarbekir.

In order to organise and begin the deportation and the massacre of the Armenians, Dr. Reshid was completely dependent on the help of FEZI BEY who brought with him, as honorary assistance, the two famous brigands, Perikhan Oghlou Omer and Mustafa who for 20 years had terrorised the country around Djeziré and who in their absence had been condemned to death several times.

And it is to these two honorary brigands that FEZI BEY confided the 670 Armenian notables and intellectuals of Diarbekir, to be taken to Chelikian, some 30 kilometers from the city, in the district of Becheri, and to be brutally massacred there. The job done, FEZI received them on their return with the question: "Speak up my good men, what have you done?" The brigands answered him: "We swear on your head, bey effendi, that not a single man escaped the two massacres."

Arriving in Diarbekir from Djeziré, FEZI BEY supported whole-heartedly the Vali Dr. Reshid and encouraged him as best he could. It was he who set up the "Teshkilat Mehsousé" (special organization) which included Rushdi Bey, the Commander of the Gendarmerie, his nephew Pirindji Zadé Sedki, the Mufti Zadé Shérif, Harpoutli Hussein, Attar Haki, the Chief and the Secretary of Union and Progress, Yassin Effendi Zadé Shefki, Veli Nedjet, (who is presently employed in the Department of Immigration) Moussouli Mehmed, Djergis Agha Zadé Keur Youssouf, Hadji Bakir, Hadji Gani Zadé Servet, Djergis Agha Zadé Abdulkérim, Direkdji Tahir, etc. It was these men who first started to massacre the 120,000 Armenians in the vilayet of Diarbekir and with such savage zeal and such fury that even the vandals would feel ashamed to listen to all those stories of atrocity. One example: The Armenian Bishop Tchilgadian was first tortured in the prisons for a long time, then upon the orders of FEZI BEY, was slowly burnt alive with petrol dropped on his head, drop by drop. The pharmacist Manssour, the Chaldean, was an ocular witness of this scene of horror. He lives now in Constantinople.

This then is the result of the famous sentence that FEZI BEY kept repeating during our trip from Aleppo to Diarbekir: 'My friend, your future is in danger; you are going to see what it means to ask for reforms.' According to my information, the deputy Zahdi maintained a cold neutrality during the massacres while Kiamil Bey risked his life in opposing these evil-doers. He even came to Constantinople and complained bitterly to Talaat Pasha who threatened him with death if he did not keep silent.

FAKHRI PASHA, General

Malta No. 2752

Interned 5.8.19 from Egypt

Copy in W 3255/5.

Appointments. Chief of staff to Djemal Pasha in 1915. Later commanding Expeditionary Force in the Hedjaz and defender of Medina until after the Armistice.

Lists. On none.

Arrest. FAKHRI PASHA surrendered personally to the Arabs at Bir Derwish on January 10th 1919. He was handed over to the British and interned in Egypt until August 1919, when he was transferred to Malta.

R. 1315. On 9.12.19. The General Office Commanding in Chief, Egyptian Expeditionary Force informed the High Commissioner that FAKHRI PASHA had been interned "Accused of complicity in the massacre of Armenians."

Petitions.

1. **R. 1213.** On 4.11.19. The Sublime Porte petitioned on behalf of wife for FAKHRI's repatriation from Malta. Copy of this petition was sent to Egyptian Expeditionary Force on 13.11.19.

2. **R. 2826.** On 27.2.20. General Office Commanding in Chief, Army of the Black Sea forwarded to High Commissioner two petitions: (1) of 18.2.20 from the Turkish Minister of War, and (2) of 15.2.20 from Aishe Sadika, wife of FAKHRI PASHA.

High Commissioner thereupon sent the usual formula to Minister for Foreign Affairs and General Officer Commanding in Chief.

3. **W. 3255/5.** Petition of 14.7.20. from wife to join husband in order to see him through an operation. Governor of Malta informs High Commissioner that no operation necessary and on 16.9.20 Secretary so informs wife.

4. **W. 3255/5.** On 19.10.20 Damad Ferid appeals through Mr. Ryan on behalf of Sultan and FAKHRI's wife, for release on ground of bad health of FAKHRI PASHA.

5. **606/24.** Wife's petition of 17.1.21. No action.

6. **860/24.** Wife's petition of 17.1.21. through French High Commissioner of 22.1.21.

N.B. High Commissioner's despatch 1552/W3667 of 24.11.20, covering report of special committee, recommends his detention for trial.

ACCUSATIONS.

5033/A/3. An account of the bombardment of the Armenian town of Urfa in October 1915 by W. S. Holloway of 53 Victoria Street S.W.1. who was interned at Urfa from July 1915 to January 1916. The Turkish Commanding officer was FAKHRI PASHA, Chief of Staff of Djemal Pasha, IVth Turkish Army, assisted by a German officer.

5033/A/3. Evidence of Dr. Armenag Alen Hayatian of Urfa against Franz Eckart, implicating FAKHRI PASHA in the massacre of some 200 boys and men on the hill Tell Fuder close to Urfa.

Treatment of Armenians. Viscount Grey. Descriptive accounts of the defence of Djebal Mussa, from July 21st 1915 to September 12th when the Armenians numbering 4,058 were rescued by the "Guichen" and other ships. On p. 525 the Turkish Commanding Officer is given as Captain Rifaat Bey. "Treatment of Armenians" also gives long descriptive accounts of events at Zeitun in spring of 1915 and at Urfa in autumn of 1915.

R. 2498. Summary of Statements sent under cover of General Officer Commanding-in-Chief Egypt Expeditionary Force, letter dated 6.3.20:

1. By Mustapha Shevket Bey, Kadi of Urfa, describing events at Urfa between middle of August 1915 to beginning of November 1915. General Fahreddin Pasha, temporary Commanding Officer IVth Army arrived at Urfa on 2.10.15. The Mufti, ordered to issue fetwa authorising the bombardment of the Armenian quarter, refused. Bombardment and siege began on 5th October, directed by Major Von Graft, Chief of Staff and Ali Ghalib Bey, commanding the 132nd and 133rd Infantry Regiments.

On the surrender of the Armenians Ali Ghalib shot all the men as ordered by FAKHRI PASHA.

2. By Doctor Farajallah on 18.6.19. Personal witness to bombardment. Captain Salih Bey, Officer Commanding Artillery, showed him the order signed by FAKHRI PASHA. 2,000 victims, Deportation of 1,700 women and children under Fobeir (sic) Bey.

3. By Dr. Armenag Abu Hayatian, of Urfa, on 20.4.19. "On 15th September 1915 at Urfa the Tchetes and Gendarmes . . . were let loose . . . FAKHRI PASHA and Ghalib Bey rushed up three battalions of Nizamieh, 3 guns and one machine gun from Aleppo." The note goes on with an accusation against Echkardt. Mr. Gracey, British, then in Belfast, Director of the Industrial Section of the Mission had his house destroyed and looted.

4. By Dr. Farajallah, Captain attached 133rd Artillery Regiment 23.3.19.

FAKHRI PASHA was ordered by Djemal Pasha, commanding the IVth Army of Syria, to reduce the Armenians of Urfa. Heard the orders given by FAKHRI PASHA to the officers commanding the Artillery.

5. By Captain Wetherel, General Staff 30.1.19 FAKHRI PASHA surrendered personally to the Arabs at Bir Derwish on January 10th 1919. He was then General Officer Commanding Hadjaz Force and Military Governor of Medina. From June 1915 to May 1916 he was General Officer Commanding XIIth Army Corps with his headquarters at Aleppo. In character he is very obstinate and a fanatical Mohammadan. This led to his delaying in every possible way his compliance with the terms of the Armistice regarding the surrender of the Holy City and its garrison, although he had received direct orders from his Government on the subject. Finally he was compelled to hand over his command under pressure of officers of his own staff and his subordinate commanders.

ABBAS HALIM PASHA

Malta No. 2754

Interned at Mudros on 29.5.19, transferred to Malta in September 1919.

Appointments. Minister of Public Works in 1915. (brother of Said Halim Pasha, Grand Vizier in 1915).

Lists. On none.

Arrests. Nothing is known as to his arrest by the Turkish Government.

Deportation. He was surrendered by the Turkish Government to the British Military Authorities on 28th May 1919 and deported to Mudros; thence to Malta.

Offence. Offence as reported to the F.O.: "Faire partie des Ministres responsible de la Destiné de l'Empire."

Egyptian Nationality, W. 2582.18/8/20. He and his brother Said Halim claim Egyptian Nationality. Telegrams, minutes and correspondence thereon.

Petitions. None to date, 7.3.21.

N.B. W. 2178. High Commissioner's despatch 1357 of 30.9.20 recommended his release on the Treaty coming into force. **W. 3667.** High Commissioner's despatch 1552 of 24.11.20 (Committee's report) recommended that he should be brought for trial. (See Mr. Ryan's and Assistant High Commissioner's views on 1915 War Cabinet Ministers in Appendix A).

ACCUSATIONS.

No specific accusation has been made.

He was a member of the cabinet which ordered the deportations entailing the massacre of hundred of thousands of Christians.

Appendix A.

14.11.20. Minute by Mr. Ryan:

. . . In practice we have gone on the principle that a sufficient presumption of guilt to justify detention and ultimate prosecution existed against all members of the responsible Governments of Turkey at the time when the massacres and deportations took place and all persons so high in the councils of the C.U.P. as to be able to be credited with a share in directing its policy. If this is the principle, then it seems to me that all these people should stand their trial, and that (assuming none of them to have established their complete innocence e.g. by proving that they continually protested, that they were sick, that the Cabinet as a whole were ignorant of what was toward etc.), it would be for the judge or judges to consider whether the role played by particular individuals was so passive as to justify a lenient rather than a severe sentence.

. . . Pending further developments I think we should keep any ex-Ministers who certainly formed part of Turkish Cabinets when the deportation and massacre policy was adopted and carried out. This appears to me to be the only logical course, unless it is definitely laid down that a different principle applies viz. that acquiescence (with knowledge) is not to be regarded as a ground of accusation in the case of anyone, even Ministers or C.U.P. leaders and that some definite individual act immediately conducing to massacres must be forthcoming to justify prosecution. In one sense the question is a juridical one and not one of policy at all. So far as it is a question of policy I suppose it is one of Allied Policy. I take it that all prisoners now held on any ground connected with deportations and massacres must be regarded as held in trust for the Allied Powers.

15.11.20. Minute by Sir Harry Lamb:

I agree generally with Mr. Ryan, with whom I have discussed the question. It seems to me that we **have** adopted the principle of prosecuting the persons morally responsible rather than mere agents – excepting the most outrageous cases. That being so, we can not make much distinction between one member of the Cabinet and another, unless there were evidence that he offered strong opposition to the measures taken and merely yielded to a majority decision. Even then I think Mr. Ryan is right in considering that this should be a matter for appreciation by the Tribunal eventually constituted to try the cases, in mitigation of penalties and should not prevent the individual from being sent to stand his trial with the rest.

SAID HALIM PASHA

Malta No. 2755

Interned at Mudros on 28th May 1919. Later transferred to Malta.

(Uncle of the ex-Khedive, Abbas Halim Pasha)

Appointments. Grand Vizier in 1915-17. He succeeded the murdered Mahmud Shevket Pasha.

Lists. On List III., i.e. his name suggested for arrest by Mr. Ryan to the Grand Vizier on 27.3.19. "As Grand Vizier in 1915-17 must share responsibility for massacres." His name is also on the list of French demands for arrest presented in writing to the Grand Vizier on 12.2.19. (See despatch 269 of 5.2.20. from High Commissioner to Foreign Office.)

Arrest. Arrested by Turkish Authorities on 10.3.19. (telegram 529 of 11.3.19 to Foreign Office,) and surrendered to the British Military Authorities on 28.5.19. and deported to Mudros.

Petitions.

R. 1315. D. Petition from him, sent on to F.O. in Aug. 1919. Petition from him, to Mr Lloyd George dated 12.8.19. Petition from him through Governor of Malta on 4.11.19.

W. 2582. Telegram of 28.7.20 from High Commissioner Egypt. Assistant High Commissioner minutes on 3.8.20 that SAID HALIM wrote a letter of thanks for removing him from the Turkish Government (in spring of 1919). He and Abbas Halim claim Egyptian nationality.

N.B. W. 3667. In despatch 1552 of 24.11.20 High Commissioner recommended his prosecution, (report of special Committee) See 2nd and 1st Political Officers' views in Appendix A.

ACCUSATIONS.

Naim's Memoirs. p. 48. On April 11th 1915 (O.S.) the Armenian Patriarch had made representation to the Grand Vizier. SAID HALIM's reply was as follows: Before the War you approached the Entente Powers wishing to sever yourselves from the Ottoman Empire. What is happening to the Armenians is the outcome of a scheme which will be carried out.

5035/A/11.e. Patriarchate Report of January 1919. SAID HALIM is said to have presided at the meeting of the C.U.P. which decided on the extermination of the Armenians.

G. II. Listed on Patriarchate's detailed list of criminals of September 1920.

"SAID HALIM is the uncle of Abbas Halim, former Khedive of Egypt. He was born in Egypt but has long been established in Constantinople. He is the husband of the sister of Sherrif Pasha, an old spy of Abdul Hamid (Sultan). This Sherrif Pasha after the Constitution ran away from Turkey and began in Paris a strong campaign against the Unionists.

SAID HALIM was a member of the State Council (Conseil d'Etat) during the days of Abdul Hamid. After the Constitution he deliberately sided with the Unionists, never missing an occasion to show the greatest enthusiasm for them. When HALIL BEY was

Minister of the Interior he was nominated chief of the Municipality of Yenikeuy, but he showed himself so deficient in this post that he was discharged by Hussein Kiasim Bey for incapacity.

He was always helping the Unionists by loans of money and at one time, when the Itilaf Party was in power the Tanin, the official C.U.P. paper, being in bad financial straits he made it possible to continue its publication by a grant of 2,000 ltq. in gold. He is said also at the same period to have prevented Nazim Pasha from acting energetically against the Unionists. Nazim Pasha was indebted to him for pecuniary services and obeyed his entreaties to leave the Unionist Chiefs alone.

Tremendously ambitious, fanatical and of a very middling intellectual capacity, he was with his name and great wealth a ready tool in the hands of the C.U.P.

After the Turkish Riot of 1913 when the Unionists came again into power, he was nominated Minister of Foreign Affairs in the Cabinet of Mahmoud Shevket Pasha, and [when] Mahmoud Shevket Pasha was murdered some time after he was nominated Grand Vizier. At that time he is accused of being the cause of the hanging of Salih Pasha, with whom he had a private feud.

He remained at this post for more than four years and during his Grand vezirat, the worst political crimes were perpetrated; persecutions against the Greeks, nefarious alliance with Germany, ransacking of the country under the name of military requisitions, deportation and slaughter of the Armenians, of other Christians and Kurds and Arabs, himself always readily signing all orders for the execution of these crimes and showing himself a ready defender of his fellow members of the Committee before public opinion, for he was whole-heartedly in sympathy with them.

Notwithstanding all his fawnings on the C.U.P. his influence among its chiefs was small, since Talaat easily discharged him the day he got in his head to become Grand Vizier himself. His responsibility in the Armenian atrocities is more than moral, and must be considered as of a provocative agent's kind. Already before his grand vezirate had published fanatical pamphlets pointing out what he was calling the danger of the six provinces.

In the act of accusation read by the Imperial Prosecutor at the trial of the Unionists on the 28th April 1920, he is cited as fully responsible and his accusation recommended.

APPENDIX A.

14.11.20. Minute by Mr. Ryan:

... In practice we have gone on the principle that a sufficient presumption of guilt to justify detention and ultimate prosecution existed against all members of the responsible Governments of Turkey at the time when the massacres and deportations took place and all persons so high in the councils of the C.U.P. as to be able to be credited with a share in directing its policy. If this is the principle, then it seems to me that all these people should stand their trial, and that (assuming none of them to have established their complete innocence e.g. by proving that they continually protested, that they were sick, that the Cabinet as a whole were ignorant of what was toward etc.), it would be for the judge or judges to consider whether the role played by particular individuals was so passive as to justify a lenient rather than a severe sentence.

. . . Pending further developments I think we should keep any ex-Ministers who certainly formed part of Turkish Cabinets when the deportation and massacre policy was adopted and carried out. This appears to me to be the only logical course, unless it is definitely laid down that a different principle applies viz. that acquiescence (with knowledge) is not to be regarded as a ground of accusation in the case of anyone, even Ministers or C.U.P. leaders and that some definite individual act immediately conducing to massacres must be forthcoming to justify prosecution. In one sense the question is a juridical one and not one of policy at all. So far as it is a question of policy I suppose it is one of Allied Policy. I take it that all prisoners now held on any ground connected with deportations and massacres must be regarded as held in trust for the Allied Powers.

15.11.20. Minute by Sir Harry Lamb:

I agree generally with Mr. Ryan, with whom I have discussed the question. It seems to me that we **have** adopted the principle of prosecuting the persons morally responsible rather than mere agents – excepting the most outrageous cases. That being so, we can not make much distinction between one member of the Cabinet and another, unless there were evidence that he offered strong opposition to the measures taken and merely yielded to a majority decision. Even then I think Mr. Ryan is right in considering that this should be a matter for appreciation by the Tribunal eventually constituted to try the cases, in mitigation of penalties and should not prevent the individual from being sent to stand his trial with the rest.

MIDHAT SHUKRI BEY

Malta No. 2756

Interned at Mudros on 29.5.19. Later transferred to Malta.

Appointments. Minister of Education, 1915. Deputy for Burdone. **Secretary General of the Central C.U.P.** to 1918, succeeding Eyub Sabri and Hadji Adil.

Lists. On List III., i.e. his name was suggested for arrest to the Grand Vizier by Mr. Ryan on 27.3.19.

Arrest. He was arrested by the Turkish Government on 30.1.19. for "being implicated in deportations and massacres", (see Turkish list in 5035/A/67). He was examined by the Turkish Court Martial. He was among those surrendered to the British Military Authorities on 28.5.19. and deported to Mudros.

Petitions. None to date (7.3.21).

N.B. The High Commissioner in his despatch No. 1552/W.3667, dated 24.11.20 and covering report of special committee, recommended that MIDHAT SHUKRI be detained at Malta until brought up for trial. For the views of the 1st and 2nd Political Officers on the responsibility of the 1915 Cabinet Ministers, see Appendix A.

ACCUSATIONS.

G. 11. In the Patriarchate's detailed list of those responsible for the massacres, dated September 1920, MIDHAT SHUKRI's name occurs fifth on the list of supreme heads of the C.U.P.

5014/6. He was one of those who connived at the escape of Dr. Reshid in January 1919.

Following biographical notice has been supplied by the Patriarchate:

"MIDHAT SHUKRI is a native of Salonika. His training was very deficient for he graduated only from a preparatory school and could not complete his courses at the Lyceum. Before the Constitution he was employed as an accountant in the General Direction of Instruction in Salonika. He was a secret affiliate of the Committee of Union and Progress. After the Constitution he became a most prominent C.U.P. leader. He succeeded Eyoub Sabri and Hadji Adil in the general secretaryship of the C.U.P. at Constantinople. He remained at this post until the Armistice.

An intimate and a worthy friend of Talaat, Enver, Behaedine Shakir and Dr. Nazim, he shares with them the full responsibility of all the misdeeds of the C.U.P. He made several journeys to Berlin, sent on secret missions. Under a gentle and refined appearance, he was the most cold blooded deviser of the worst schemes for suppressing in Turkey the Christian element, whom he considered the greatest drawback for the accomplishment of the Pantouranistic ideals of which he was a rabid promoter.

The record of his misdeeds against the Christian element is heavy and among them must be cited his doings of the period immediately following the Constitution, in the districts of Kassandra and Catherine to adopt the measure of deporting the whole village of

Christians if a single fire arm was found there. The atrocities committed under the provisions of this law by MIDHAT SHUKRI assisted by Dr. Nazim were a prominent factor of the cause of the Balkan War.

MIDHAT SHUKRI after the war, turned all his hatred against the Armenians. After the Armistice he made to disappear the greater part of the documents of the C.U.P.

In the act of accusation read by the Imperial Prosecutor at the opening session of the trial of the Unionists on the 28th of April 1919, he is cited as responsible for the crimes committed against the Armenians.

APPENDIX A.

14.11.20. Minute by Mr. Ryan:

... In practice we have gone on the principle that a sufficient presumption of guilt to justify detention and ultimate prosecution existed against all members of the responsible Governments of Turkey at the time when the massacres and deportations took place and all persons so high in the councils of the C.U.P. as to be able to be credited with a share in directing its policy. If this is the principle, then it seems to me that all these people should stand their trial, and that (assuming none of them to have established their complete innocence e.g. by proving that they continually protested, that they were sick, that the Cabinet as a whole were ignorant of what was toward etc.), it would be for the judge or judges to consider whether the role played by particular individuals was so passive as to justify a lenient rather than a severe sentence.

... Pending further developments I think we should keep any ex-Ministers who certainly formed part of Turkish Cabinets when the deportation and massacre policy was adopted and carried out. This appears to me to be the only logical course, unless it is definitely laid down that a different principle applies viz. that acquiescence (with knowledge) is not to be regarded as a ground of accusation in the case of anyone, even Ministers or C.U.P. leaders and that some definite individual act immediately conducing to massacres must be forthcoming to justify prosecution. In one sense the question is a juridical one and not one of policy at all. So far as it **is** a question of policy I suppose it is one of Allied Policy. I take it that all prisoners now held on any ground connected with deportations and massacres must be regarded as held in trust for the Allied Powers.

15.11.20. Minute by Sir Harry Lamb:

I agree generally with Mr. Ryan, with whom I have discussed the question. It seems to me that we **have** adopted the principle of prosecuting the persons morally responsible rather than mere agents – excepting the most outrageous cases. That being so, we can not make much distinction between one member of the Cabinet and another, unless there were evidence that he offered strong opposition to the measures taken and merely yielded to a majority decision. Even then I think Mr. Ryan is right in considering that this should be a matter for appreciation by the Tribunal eventually constituted to try the cases, in mitigation of penalties and should not prevent the individual from being sent to stand his trial with the rest.

MAHMUD KIAMIL PASHA

Malta No. 2758

Interned at Mudros on 29.5.19; later transferred to Malta.

Appointments. Commanding 5th Army. Commanding 3rd Army; Headquarters Erzerum. Under Secretary of State for War.

Lists. On none.

Arrest. Arrested by the Turkish Government on 30.1.19 and among those surrendered to the British Military Authorities on 28.5.19. He apparently was brought before the Turkish Court Martial (Renaissance 15.5.19).

Petitions. 8/8/24. From Italian High Commissioner of 22.1.21.

ACCUSATIONS.

"Renaissance" 18.1.19. 1.5.19. Refers to MAHMUD KIAMIL's telegram to the Provinces re the hanging of such Moslems as might give help to Christians, mentioned by the Public Prosecutor in his opening statement.

G. XVI. In the Patriarchate's detailed list of September 1920 MAHMUD KIAMIL is referred to, under the heading of Muammer, Vali of Sivas, as presiding at a meeting held at Erzerum for the purpose of concerting inter-provincial measures for the extermination of the Christian element.

G. XI. MAHMUD KIAMIL is listed under the heading "Erzerum 1915" with the mention: Commanding the Army Corps of the Caucasus.

E. II. In the Patriarchate's report dated 8.9.20, on Suleiman Faik Pasha, the latter is referred to as following to the letter the orders given by MAHMUD KIAMIL, Commanding the 3rd Army Corps as to the massacre of Armenians.

Henry Barby. In "Au Pays de l'épouvante", on page 22 and 34 there are several mentions of MAHMUD KIAMIL. The author of this book came into Erzerum with the Russian Army in 1916.

A. 8. Statement, dated 29.1.19, by Dr. Micael Kechichian, late of the 3rd Army Corps, now of Batum, Banque du Caucase. The witness was in Erzerum in 1915 and accuses MAHMUD KIAMIL of being the organiser of the massacres in the vilayet of Erzerum.

5027/A/14. Kellerian's account of Erzingan massacres; MAHMUD KIAMIL was at Erzerum during the deportation of Armenians thence and subsequently ordered the massacre of Armenian soldiers.

5029/A/12. Statement made at Sivas by Eghia Bakalian and submitted by Major Hurst on May 9th 1919. "The informant had seen the official order sent by MAHMUD KIAMIL Pasha and personally heard from the lips of Pertev Bey, the Acting Commander of the Sivas Division of the 3rd Army Corps, how fully this order was executed in the vilayet of Erzerum."

Informant is ready to testify before an international court.

J. 137 et sq. Telegram of 4.8.15 from MAHMUD KIAMIL, Commanding 3rd Army to Halil Redjai, Officer Commanding 5th Army Corps at Angora: Am informed that an Armenian Medical Officer belonging to the Workmen's Battalion at Nigde opposes the sending away of soldiers (of the Battalion).

Patriarchate's biographical notice, dated 2.12.20: MAHMUD KIAMIL Pasha was born in Aleppo and is an Arab. He had the usual training of a Turkish officer, passing through the preparatory school of the Province, and finally reaching the Kuleli school at Constantinople, to be transferred from there to Harbié, from where he graduated in 1901 as a staff officer.

He was a promotion comrade of Enver. During all the pre-Constitution time he progressed in his military career in different regiments.

After the Constitution, Enver being his friend, his promotion was more rapid. During the war he was military commandant of the third army corps, having its seat in Erzerum.

Cruel, of the worst moral character, he was the trusted agent of the C.U.P. for the work of suppressing the Armenians. After his secret councils with Behaedine Shakir and Doctor Nazim who had come to Erzerum especially to decide on the measures for the deportation and massacres, he gathered together on three occasions the valis of the Armenian provinces and arranged with them the plan of the wholesale eviction and massacre of the Armenians.

The dreadful results of these councils are now historical facts. Perhaps one of the strongest against MAHMUD KIAMIL, will be the telegram signed by him and sent to all the circumscriptions depending on his military command, in which he proclaimed that every Moslem who would shelter an Armenian would be hanged before his door and have his house burned. This telegram is textually cited in the act of accusation read by the Imperial Prosecutor on the opening session of the trial of the Unionists on the 28th of April 1919.

As a reward he was afterwards nominated under-secretary of State in the War Office. (Harbié Musteshari).

HALIL BEY

Malta No. 2760

Interned at Mudros on 29.5.19; later transferred to Malta.

Appointments. Minister of Justice. President of the Chamber of Deputies, 1914 – 10/1915. President of the Council of State, 1915. Minister of Foreign Affairs, 10/1915, succeeded by Ahmed Nessim Bey. Minister of the Interior, Deputy for Constantinople. Member of the C.U.P.

Lists. On none.

Arrest. HALIL BEY was arrested by the Turkish Government and was among those surrendered to the British Military Authorities on 28th May 1919 and deported to Mudros. His name appears on the French list of demands for arrest which was handed to the Grand Vizier on 12.2.19 (High Commissioner's despatch to Foreign Office No. 269 of 5.3.19.)

Petitions. Petition, dated 31.7.19, giving a summary of the reasons why Turkey entered the War.

To Foreign Office on 11.8.19.

5014/21. Petition from his wife reviewing his political career.

N.B. High Commissioner's despatch 1552/W.3667, dated 24.11.20 (Committee's report) recommended his being brought to trial. For the views of the 2nd and 1st Political officers on the responsibility of the 1915 Cabinet Ministers, see Appendix A.

ACCUSATIONS.

A. 16. Fiche: A Bochophile; instigator of atrocities. Upheld the abrogation of the Patriarchate's privileges.

5035/A/11.e. Patriarchate reported, 1919: "He has had one of the principal parts in the Armenian extermination deed."

G. II. Listed on Patriarchate's list of September 1920. Also Patriarchate's biographical notice, as follows:

HALIL BEY was born in Milas, in the Vilayet of Smyrna. His early training has been very deficient. Belonging to a family owning great agricultural properties, he entered the agricultural school of Halkali, but was too lazy to successfully finish his studies there. He was sent by his parents to Paris, to follow the courses of the Ecole des Hautes Etudes Politiques, but he came back from there without having completed his studies.

In the meantime he had made acquaintance with the agents of the Young Turk Party, so that after the Constitution of 1908 he was elected Unionist Deputy of Menteshé in the Vilayet of Smyrna. His election was made difficult by Hussein Kiazim Bey, who stirred up public opinion against him by arguing of his incapacity. A thorough Unionist, member of the Central Committee, he became quickly a "Persona grata" among the most powerful circles of the C.U.P. and one of their leaders.

He occupied, afterwards, often the post of Minister in charge at different ministries.

After the death of Emroullah Effendi he was Minister of Public Instruction. Afterwards he occupied successively the posts of Minister of Interior and Minister of Justice. He was President of the Parliament, when Moukhtar Pasha dissolved the Chamber.

During the early part of the Balkan War he was obliged to hide himself from the Itilaf Party. He had then taken refuge in the house of the Armenian deputy, Zohrab, the same who was murdered in 1915 by a decision of the Central Committee of which HALIL BEY was a prominent member. HALIL allowed him willingly to be murdered, remaining deaf to the entreaties of the family of the Deputy.

After the Young Turk Riot of 1912, the murder of Nazim Pasha and accession again of the C.U.P. to power, he was elected again deputy.

In 1914 at the declaration of war he was president of the Turkish Parliament, and one of the chief propagandists to urge the entering into the war on the side of Germany. He was sent on a mission to Germany at the declaration of war and negotiated Turkish participation in the war, direct, with the Emperor. They nominated him again in 1916 Minister of Foreign Affairs. Ahmed Nessim Bey succeeded him and HALIL became Minister of Justice.

Although very clever in hiding his responsibilities, HALIL BEY as one of the leaders of the C.U.P. has the fullest responsibility in all the crimes that were committed.

Talaat, Enver, Ibrahim Pirizadé, Hairi, and HALIL used to hold private meetings during the war at the palace of Enver at Couroutchesmé, and settle the political misdeeds.

He had among his fellow members the reputation of knowing Europe thoroughly and his secret assertions that he would be able to screen the C.U.P. before the European public without any restrain at all.

In the act of accusation read by the Imperial Prosecutor at the opening session of the trial of the Unionists, on 28th April 1919, he is cited as responsible for the crimes committed against the Armenians.

APPENDIX A.

14.11.20. Minute by Mr. Ryan:

. . . In practice we have gone on the principle that a sufficient presumption of guilt to justify detention and ultimate prosecution existed against all members of the responsible Governments of Turkey at the time when the massacres and deportations took place and all persons so high in the councils of the C.U.P. as to be able to be credited with a share in directing its policy. If this is the principle, then it seems to me that all these people should stand their trial, and that (assuming none of them to have established their complete innocence e.g. by proving that they continually protested, that they were sick, that the Cabinet as a whole were ignorant of what was toward etc.), it would be for the judge or judges to consider whether the role played by particular individuals was so passive as to justify a lenient rather than a severe sentence.

. . . Pending further developments I think we should keep any ex-Ministers who certainly formed part of Turkish Cabinets when the deportation and massacre policy was adopted and carried out. This appears to me to be the only logical course, unless it is definitely laid down that a different principle applies viz. that acquiescence (with knowledge) is not to be regarded as a ground of accusation in the case of anyone, even Ministers or C.U.P. leaders and that some definite individual act immediately conducing to massacres must be forthcoming to justify prosecution. In one sense the question is a juridical one and not one of policy at all. So far as it **is** a question of policy I suppose it is one of Allied Policy. I take it that all prisoners now held on any ground connected with deportations and massacres must be regarded as held in trust for the Allied Powers.

15.11.20. Minute by Sir Harry Lamb:

I agree generally with Mr. Ryan, with whom I have discussed the question. It seems to me that we **have** adopted the principle of prosecuting the persons morally responsible rather than mere agents – excepting the most outrageous cases. That being so, we can not make much distinction between one member of the Cabinet and another, unless there were evidence that he offered strong opposition to the measures taken and merely yielded to a majority decision. Even then I think Mr. Ryan is right in considering that this should be a matter for appreciation by the Tribunal eventually constituted to try the cases, in mitigation of penalties and should not prevent the individual from being sent to stand his trial with the rest.

MUSTAFA KEMAL BEY (KARA KEMAL)

Malta No. 2761

Interned at Mudros on 29.5.19; later transferred to Malta.

Appointments. Minister for Food Supplies. Permanent member of the Central C.U.P.

Lists. On none.

Arrest. Arrested by the Turkish Authorities on January 30th 1919 for being implicated in massacres (Turkish list in 5035.A.67). He was among those surrendered to the British Military Authorities on 28.5.19.

Petitions. None to date. (8.3.21)

N.B. High Commissioner's despatch 1552/W. 3667 of 24.11.20, covering report of special committee, recommended his detention until brought up for trial. For views of the 2nd and 1st Political officers on the responsibility of the 1915 Cabinet Ministers, see Appendix A.

ACCUSATIONS.

5035.A.11.b. On Patriarchate's first list of Hundred Guilty Turks dated 27.12.1918.

A. 16. Unsigned fiche. He instigated measures of oppression and boycott against the trade of Christians.

G. II. On Patriarchate's detailed list of September 1920, he is noted as one of those who voted the deportations.

R. 1213. Commanding Officer, Moda, 23.12.19 reports the release (sic) of Kara KAMAL as one of the topics of the day. 'Intelligence' of 28.12.19 in forwarding report states: known as the one capable C.U.P. Financier.

During the War was appointed Iashe Naziri (Food Controller) and thus made an immense fortune . . . It is known that there is a very large quantity of C.U.P. money in various German banks under his name.

APPENDIX A.

14.11.20. Minute by Mr. Ryan:

. . . In practice we have gone on the principle that a sufficient presumption of guilt to justify detention and ultimate prosecution existed against all members of the responsible Governments of Turkey at the time when the massacres and deportations took place and all persons so high in the councils of the C.U.P. as to be able to be credited with a share in directing its policy. If this is the principle, then it seems to me that all these people should stand their trial, and that (assuming none of them to have established their complete innocence e.g. by proving that they continually protested, that they were sick, that the Cabinet as a whole were ignorant of what was toward etc.), it would be for the judge or judges to consider whether the role played by particular individuals was so passive as to justify a lenient rather than a severe sentence.

. . . Pending further developments I think we should keep any ex-Ministers who certainly formed part of Turkish Cabinets when the deportation and massacre policy was adopted and carried out. This appears to me to be the only logical course, unless it is definitely laid down that a different principle applies viz. that acquiescence (with knowledge) is not to be regarded as a ground of accusation in the case of anyone, even Ministers or C.U.P. leaders and that some definite individual act immediately conducing to massacres must be forthcoming to justify prosecution. In one sense the question is a juridical one and not one of policy at all. So far as it **is** a question of policy I suppose it is one of Allied Policy. I take it that all prisoners now held on any ground connected with deportations and massacres must be regarded as held in trust for the Allied Powers.

15.11.20. Minute by Sir Harry Lamb:

I agree generally with Mr. Ryan, with whom I have discussed the question. It seems to me that we **have** adopted the principle of prosecuting the persons morally responsible rather than mere agents – excepting the most outrageous cases. That being so, we can not make much distinction between one member of the Cabinet and another, unless there were evidence that he offered strong opposition to the measures taken and merely yielded to a majority decision. Even then I think Mr. Ryan is right in considering that this should be a matter for appreciation by the Tribunal eventually constituted to try the cases, in mitigation of penalties and should not prevent the individual from being sent to stand his trial with the rest.

ALI MUNIF BEY

Malta No. 2762

Interned at Mudros on 29.5.19 and later transferred to Malta.

Appointments. Under Secretary for the Interior under Talaat, September 1913 to August 1915.

Vali of Lebanon, after suppression of autonomy, September 1915 to January 1916.

Minister of Public Works, January 1916 to October 1918.

One of the principal members of the Central C.U.P.

Lists. On List II and III, i.e. his arrest was suggested to the Grand Vizier by Mr. Ryan in February 1919 and again in March 1919. His name also occurs on list of French demands addressed to Grand Vizier on 12.2.19. (See despatch to F.O. 269 of 5.3.19. in 1315).

Arrest. Arrested by the Turkish Authorities on 30.1.19 and among those surrendered to the British Military Authorities on 28.5.19 and deported to Mudros. In September 1919 he was transferred to Malta.

Petitions.

1. **5053/A/13.** Petition from wife of 10.6.20.

2. Petition per Professor Huntingdon, apparently by Mrs. Manek Tchetchegan.

3. **W. 2869.** Petition of 19.10.20, through Governor of Malta of 26.10.20. (Malta has sent copies of the petition to Foreign Office and War Office direct.)

ACCUSATIONS.

5035.A.11.b. On Patriarchate's List of First Hundred of Guilty Turks.

Mr. Philip [Perceval] Graves says he is responsible for inducing the famine in the Lebanon with the follow-ing note:- as Vali of the Lebanon he committed the cruellest atrocities on the Maronites.

H. 10. In Patriarchate's report of 22.12.20 on Mustafa Reshad Bey and the police organisation at Constantinople, Ali Munif is mentioned as employed on special missions carrying out measures of terrorism. He was at the time Mushtessar of the Ministry of Interior.

H. 16. Extract from Patriarchate's report on Nedjati Bey, chief organiser of the massacres in vilayet of Angora (on F.O. list, not yet arrested), Ali Munif, then Mushtessar [undersecretary of state] of the Ministry of the Interior, is mentioned as having accompanied Nedjati to Yozgad, which visit resulted in the notorious massacres under the Kaimakam Kemal, known as the Butcher Governor. (Hanged by the Turkish Court Martial on 10.4.19)

APPENDIX A.
EXTRACT FROM APPENDIX C. TO AKDAGHLI OGLOU MEHMET'S DOSSIER? BEING A REPORT FROM THE ARMENIAN PATRIARCHATE UNDER COVER OF THEIR LETTER OF 13.1.21 IN 570/24

"In 1915, when the propaganda began against the Armenians there was at Yozgad an honest governor, Mouhedine Pasha, who was refusing to set the Moslems against the Christians. He was for this reason discharged on May 16th 1915, by the C.U.P. and replaced by Djemal Bey.

Nedjati Bey responsible delegate for the C.U.P. for Angora, and Ali Munif who was then Secretary for the Interior, came on a tour to Yozgad, to organise the deportation and the slaughter of the Armenians. During their stay at Yozgad, they were the guests of Auzoun Ahmed and Behdjet.

They wanted to impress on Djemal Bey, the necessity of not only deporting Armenians, but also of slaughtering the convoys on the way, but Djemal Bey did not agree with their views. He is said, by a Turkish witness to have uttered these words, "I will never allow the gendarmes to kill the deported, you have better release all the convicts and allow them four days to murder the Armenians, and after allow me to catch, with my gendarmes, all the convicts and have them killed by my gendarmes." As in fact, the search for arms among the Armenians and the expedition of the first convoys of deportees, by Djemal Bey, were done without atrocities being committed on them.

This of course was not what was wanted by the C.U.P. so they had Djemal discharged, and replaced him per-interim by Kemal Bey, the Kaimakam of Boghazlian, and formed the Endjumen or secret council for exterminating the Armenians and the Teshkilati Mahsouseé of gangs of volunteer murderers."

Petition of 19.10.20

F.O. 371/5091 COPY

From:- Governor and Commander-in-Chief. Malta.
To:- Secretary, War Office, London. S.W.1.
CR. Malta 11834/1670.

MALTA, 26th October, 1920.

Sir,
I have the honour to forward, for such action as may be desirable, letters addressed to the Secretary of State for War and the Secretary of State for Foreign Affairs from No. 2762, Ali Munif, a Turkish Political prisoner interned at Malta.

An identical letter has been forwarded to the High Commissioner, Constantinople.

I have the honour to be,
Sir,

Your obedient Servant,
(Sd) A. F. W. Green Colonel
i/c Administration.

For Governor and Commander-in-Chief.
MALTA.

Polversita.
Malta, 19th October 1920

To His Excellency the Secretary of State for Foreign Affairs,
Foreign Office, London.

Your Excellency,
More than sixteen months ago, I was taken by the British military authorities in Constantinople and deported first to Mudros and then to Malta.

Some of my comrades who shared my fate have asked several times for the reason of such a treatment, but nobody ever received any reply. Only once information was obtained about our cases. It was when His Majesty's High Commissioner His Excellency Admiral de Robeck was passing from Mudros. The information was to the effect "that the Peace Conference would decide our cases." Therefore, expecting the conference's decisions about us, I have not applied till now, to anywhere regarding my personal case. But Your

Excellency knows very well that the Peace Treaty with Turkey is now signed and that it includes clauses, making clear the point of view of the Peace Conference about those supposed to be guilty of war crimes. In this clearer situation, I feel the need of submitting to Your Excellency the present petition, asking Your Excellency's kind intervention.

According to the clauses of the Peace Treaty with Turkey regarding the war guilty, the Allies demand from Turkey the surrender of two categories of persons:

1) The persons accused of acts of violation of the laws and customs of war.
2) The persons responsible for the massacres committed in the territory of the Turkish Empire in 1914.

As far as I am concerned, I beg to point out that from the beginning to the end of the war I had no functions connected with the war and I had nothing to do with soldiers, prisoners or subjects of Entente Powers.

Consequently, I can not be considered as guilty of ill-treatment of prisoners. As to the massacres, which took place in 1915, I was not in a position at that time neither to decree nor to commit, directly or indirectly, these acts. Consequently I cannot be held responsible for them, neither as a decreeing power, nor as an executing capacity. My being a member of the Ottoman Cabinet only towards the middle of 1917, as the Minister of Public Works, as well as my other former functions, cannot constitute in themselves any reason to be held responsible for the events of 1915, or the ill-treatment of prisoners.

As a result, I can pretend that no responsibilities can lie with me regarding the charges to be tried either before the military tribunals of the Allies or before an international court to be designated by the Allies or formed by the League of Nations.

Under these circumstances, I am at a loss to understand the reason of my being detained at Malta indefinitely. There is, of course, the remote possibility that we are held here for the account of the present partisan government in Turkey. As a matter of fact, that government speaks in a recent law "of the persons detained in Malta for having acted contrary to the high interests of the country (Turkey)." It is, however, very hard to believe that Great Britain would act blindly as a gaoler for the good pleasure of the Turkish government. Therefore, this possibility must be dismissed from the mind.

We were taken to Malta directly by the British military authorities, pending the decisions to be reached by the Peace Conference.

Well, the Peace Treaty is now signed, and is being carried out in many of its important provisions. If the British authorities have been waiting for this treaty in order to clarify the situation in our regard, they should have proceeded long ago to establish the kind of treatment to be accorded to every individual.

In this situation, I am taking the liberty to make the following request to Your Excellency –

If I am charged, in spite of every logical expectation of the contrary, with some guilt involving the jurisdiction of the Allied military courts or an international tribunal, I should like very much to be informed at once of the nature and the detailed circumstances of the charges, in order I may avail myself of the right of self-defence, granted by the peace treaty. In this case, I should be taken immediately under trial, as the financial difficulties and moral sufferings since two years have reached a degree which I can hardly endure any more. In case there is no charge against me involving the jurisdiction of those courts, then I beg to be released without being further deprived unnecessarily of my liberty.

Hoping that Your Excellency will not withhold his gracious attention from my case, and will favour me with an early reply, I remain

Your Excellency's

Most obedient Servant.

[Signed: Ali Munif, Former Turkish Minister of Public Works, detained in Malta]

SHUKRI BEY (AHMED SHUKRI BEY)

Malta No. 2763

Interned at Mudros, 29.5.19. Transferred to Malta in September 1919.

Appointments. Minister of Education, 1915. Deputy for Kastamuni. Editor of Turkish paper "Zeman". (Brother-in-law of 2784 Suleiman Nazif).

Lists. On List III, i.e. his arrest was suggested by Mr. Ryan to the Grand Vizier on 27th March 1919.

1315. Part I. SHUKRI BEY was amongst those whose arrest was demanded of the Turkish Government by General Franchet d'Esperey on February 12th 1919. (See despatch 269 to F.O. dated 5.3.19).

Arrest. Arrested by the Turkish Government on a date not known.

Deportation. Taken over by British Military Authorities from Turkish Authorities on 28th May 1919 and deported to Mudros, thence to Malta.

Charge. The charge as reported to the F.O. was: "His position as a minister". On List III, this is amplified as follows: "ex-Minister for Education in 1915. Must share responsibilities for massacres."

Petitions.

R. 1128. Memorandum, dated 24.7.19, in praise of the C.U.P. addressed to Mr. Lloyd George. Sent on to the Foreign Office on 9.8.19.

N.B. The High Commissioner in his despatch No. 1552/W.3667 dated 24.11.20 and covering report of special committee recommended the detention of AHMED SHUKRI BEY at Malta until he be brought to trial. For views of the 2nd and 1st Political officers on the responsibility of the 1915 Cabinet Ministers, see Appendix A.

ACCUSATIONS.

There is nothing specific against AHMED SHUKRI BEY.

5035.A.11.b. He is mentioned in Patriarchate's list, dated 27.12.18 as one of the organisers of the extermination of the Armenians.

5035.A.11.e. Mentioned in another such list of "some notorious criminals."

Patriarchate's biographical notice, dated 2.12.20:

AHMED SHUKRI is a native of Castamouni. He was sent to Constantinople in his early youth and graduated at the school of Dar-ul-Mualimin. For a time he was employed as accountant at the Dar-ul-Hair, a bureau attached to the Evkaf. His training in these religious Moslem surroundings had developed in him his inherent fanatical propensities and through all his career he always made himself noted for his anti-Christian feelings which later on were enhanced by his panturanistic ideals. As to his moral character, apart from his being an inveterate drunkard, he always showed himself devoted to all kinds of vices. In every post that he occupied in schools and afterwards as supreme chief of the educational establishments, he left a notorious renown.

He became there a secret affiliate of the Union and Progress. This secured for him his nomination as Director of Public Instruction at Salonika. In 1908, after the victory of the Union and Progress, his C.U.P. friends had him nominated governor of Seres in 1909. Afterwards, he was sent in the same capacity to Magnesia.

During the Ministry of Kiamil Pasha, the Minister of Interior Reshid Pasha discharged him for his immorality. His C.U.P. associates, when in power, managed to have him elected deputy of Castamouni, and in 1915, entrusted him with the Ministry of Public Instruction. At the same time he was given the Posts and Telegraphs Ministry per-interim, to reward him for his ardent propaganda of the war and for the development of the panturanistic idea, which he had been making through the newspaper he was publishing, the 'Zeman'.

He is responsible for the Armenian atrocities.

1. As having decided with his colleagues of the Union and Progress on the deportations.

2. His personal share in this crime being the discharge of all the Armenian professors in the provincial Turkish schools and lyceums at the time of the deportations, rendering thus their murder more easy, by depriving them of their official capacity.

3. He never allowed the Ministry to make an enquiry about the fate of these murdered officials.

When he was acting as Minister per-interim of the Posts and Telegraphs he discharged all the Armenian officials, working on the cable, Constantinople-Keustendjé.

Being, as we have already said, a fanatical panturanian, he put a hand on all Allied Establishments of Education in Turkey as soon as the war broke out between the Allies and Turkey and tried to transform all these establishments into Turkish faculties.

This task made him ridiculous because all the bogus schools he established were deprived of genuine students, Turkey lacking the preparatory schools for these faculties. The only result was that all these Allied establishments which had cost so much money and effort were plundered and wrecked.

AHMED SHUKRI BEY also made himself notorious by his dishonest dealings during his ministry, especially at the Posts and Telegraphs, where he was responsible for the great robberies in the parcel-post department.

The scandal of his unlawful speculations in sugar became so great that after an altercation with Djavid Bey in 1917, he was obliged to give in his resignation. He opened then a business bureau in Stambul, where with the aid of his C.U.P. friends he continued his dishonest dealings.

Ardent C.U.P. propagandist, he made journeys in Germany and Austria. In his last journey to Austria he was operated on for his eye.

APPENDIX A

14.11.20. Minute by Mr. Ryan:

... In practice we have gone on the principle that a sufficient presumption of guilt to justify detention and ultimate prosecution existed against all members of the responsible Governments of Turkey at the time when the massacres and deportations took place and all persons so high in the councils of the C.U.P. as to be able to be credited with a share in directing its policy. If this is the principle, then it seems to me that all these people should stand their trial, and that (assuming none of them to have established their complete innocence e.g. by proving that they continually protested, that they were sick, that the Cabinet as a whole were ignorant of what was toward etc.), it would be for the judge or judges to consider whether the role played by particular individuals was so passive as to justify a lenient rather than a severe sentence.

. . . Pending further developments I think we should keep any ex-Ministers who certainly formed part of Turkish Cabinets when the deportation and massacre policy was adopted and carried out. This appears to me to be the only logical course, unless it is definitely laid down that a different principle applies viz. that acquiescence (with knowledge) is not to be regarded as a ground of accusation in the case of anyone, even Ministers or C.U.P. leaders and that some definite individual act immediately conducing to massacres must be forthcoming to justify prosecution. In one sense the question is a juridical one and not one of policy at all. So far as it **is** a question of policy I suppose it is one of Allied Policy. I take it that all prisoners now held on any ground connected with deportations and massacres must be regarded as held in trust for the Allied Powers.

15.11.20. Minute by Sir Harry Lamb:

I agree generally with Mr. Ryan, with whom I have discussed the question. It seems to me that we **have** adopted the principle of prosecuting the persons morally responsible rather than mere agents – excepting the most outrageous cases. That being so, we can not make much distinction between one member of the Cabinet and another, unless there were evidence that he offered strong opposition to the measures taken and merely yielded to a majority decision. Even then I think Mr. Ryan is right in considering that this should be a matter for appreciation by the Tribunal eventually constituted to try the cases, in mitigation of penalties and should not prevent the individual from being sent to stand his trial with the rest.

AHMED AGAYEFF

Malta No. 2764

Interned at Mudros on 29.5.19, later transferred to Malta.

Race.

1. A Tartar of Jewish origin, professing Islam. A Shi of Azerbaidjan, 56 years old.

Nationality.

2. Born a Russian subject. In 1909 he became an Ottoman subject "for his services to Islam", and thence forward called himself Agha Oghlou Ahmed. In 1918 he alleges that he became a subject of the Republic of Azerbaidjan and resumed his name of AHMED AGAYEFF.

Occupations.

3. Originally an agent provocateur in the Oukrania, later a leading member of the Central C.U.P., he became Deputy for Afion-Kara-Hissar in 1918. He was the chief Editor of the pan-Turkish newspaper **Terjiman Hakikat** from January 1916 to May 1918. Well known propagandist. After the Armistice he was elected member of the Azerbaidjan Chamber and nominated member of that State's delegation to the Peace Conference.

Arrest.

4. In January 1919 the Azerbaidjan Delegation to the Peace Conference arrived in Constantinople, AHMED AGAYEFF was one of the Delegates. The Delegation was furnished with: (a) a diplomatic passport issued by the Azerbaidjan Government, dated January 8th 1919; (b) an instrument giving power to the Delegation to treat with the Allies, dated 13th November 1918; (c) a note requesting the Military Attaché to the British Embassy, Paris, to facilitate the object which the Delegation has in view, signed by Major General W. M. Thompson Commanding Troops Baku on January 3rd 1919. On January 25th General Staff Intelligence telegraphs to D.M.I. " . . . I am detaining AGAYEFF". In February his name was suggested by Mr. Ryan to the Grand Vizier for arrest (List II) and again on 27th March 1919 his name was suggested (List III). According to his own story he was arrested by the Turkish Police by order of General Franchet d'Esperey and imprisoned on 14th March 1919.

There is no official record on file of the date and manner of his arrest, but it is believed that his arrest was made on 20th January 1919 by . . . ? he was among those surrendered by the Turkish Government to the British Military Authorities on 28th March [sic, May] 1919 and deported the same day to Mudros as a political undesirable.

Charge as given to F.O.

5. The accusation against him, as given in despatch to Foreign Office 1023/A/1315/D of 17th June 1919, is "avoir trouble la sécurité publique".

Petitions.

6. The following petitions have been received:
  (a) From AHMED AGAYEFF, dated Constantinople, Military Prison, 16th April 1919.

Appendix "I" 223

(b) From the same, dated Mudros, 5th June.

(c) From Sitare Agayeff, his wife, dated Constantinople 7th July.

(d) From AHMED AGAYEFF to the Lord Chancellor, dated Mudros, 19th July. Copies of all the above documents and enclosures were sent to the Foreign Office under cover of despatch of 9th August, the reply to which was: "such petitions as this need not be forwarded".

R. 2582.

(e) 2nd petition from wife, dated 22.9.19.

(f) 3rd petition from wife, dated 2.10.19.

(g) 4th petition from wife, dated 22.11.19.

(h) 4th petition from AGAYEFF, dated 20.10.19.

(i) 5th petition from wife, dated 12.1.20.

731/24.

(j) 6th petition from wife, dated 18.1.21.

On 6th petition, wife informed that no action could be taken (22.1.21).

1805/24.

(k) 7th petition, undated, from wife, passed by General Officer Commanding-in-Chief on 14.2.21.

Proposed release.

6.a. **R. 2498.** Letters of 8th and 17th December 1919 from the British Chief Commissioner in Trans-Caucasia. (No importance.)

R. 2582. Foreign Office telegram of 31.3.20: Colonel Stokes (Tiflis) advocates release; would have good effect in Azerbaidjan.

Do. Telegram of 5.4.20. High Commissioner to Foreign Office: I consider that he should on no account be released.

R. 2498. Minute by Admiral Webb, dated 5.1.20: "It is well that he should remain in custody for as long a period as possible."

W. 3667. High Commissioner's despatch No. 1552 of 24.11.20, covering report of special committee, recommends that he be detained at Malta and brought up for trial.

ACCUSATIONS.
Intelligence Reports.

7. The following are extracts from reports, High Commissioner's despatches and minutes:-

Naval G.S. of 28.1.19. Also 5035/A/11.c. "A low down character, strong C.U.P., a pan-Turanian Journalist, well paid by Huns. He collaborated with Zia Bey ([Gök] Alp) in arranging massacres in the Caucasus, also atrocities and oppression of Arabs, Greeks and Armenians. He made several trips to the Caucasus and Azerbaidjan for which Enver kept him very plentifully supplied with funds."

Naval G.S. 23.1.19. 5031/E/1.

8. "Went to Mecca where because of his relations with certain Egyptians he became an object of suspicion with the British Authorities in Cairo. He was in very close touch with the Ulema of the Al Azhar."

H.C.'s despatch, 102/1289 of 2.2.19.

9. "The selection of 'Monsieur' AHMED AGAYEFF as a delegate was also unfortunate in view of his past intimate connection with the late Government of Turkey . . ." "Ali Mardan Bey said that AGAYEFF was an Azerbaidjan subject, but that if there was any objection to him he need not be included in the trip to Paris."

Mr. Ryan. 18.4.19.

10. "AHMED AGAYEFF has a thoroughly bad reputation . . ."

Capt. Raikes. G.S. 'I' 23.4.19.

11. (a) AHMED AGAYEFF's paper stated to have been German subventioned. (b) Until recently AHMED AGAYEFF was an Ottoman subject. (c) German agent reported that he received Enver at his house in the Caucasus. Also paid to have taken Lt. 10,000 to the Caucasus with him for running a Turk Propaganda paper. (d) Reported on 1st April 1919, that two Azerbaidjan officers had brought money to Constantinople, one half of which was for AHMED AGAYEFF and the remainder for Bolshevik leaders in Constantinople.

Mr. Ryan. 13.6.19. "This is one of those awkward cases in which the man has the worst possible name. . ."

G.S. 'I' on14.7.17. in R. 1723.

12. "When Turkish [troops] arrived in Caucasus he went to Azerbaidjan and is accused of promoting massacres in Baku.

H. 15.

13. Articles and notices that appeared in the 'Renaissance' of 24.1.19, and 5.2.19. Also in 'Stamboul' of 29.1.19 giving an account of the career and activities of AHMED AGAYEFF and urging his arrest.

G. II.'s

14. Patriarchate's detailed list of September 1920 AHMED AGAYEFF's name appears as editor of the "Terdjiman Hakikat" under the general heading: Constantinople; influential members of the committee for propaganda who participated in the organisation of the massacres. The other names given under this heading are:- Kutchuk Nazini, Yunus Bey, editor of "Tasfiri Efkiar" (on Kemalist delegation to London Conference); Zia Geuk Alp (at Malta); Selah Djimoz Bey (at Malta); Hussein Tussum Bey, Director of the Milli Agency (at Malta); Atif Bey of Makrikeui (at Malta).

YUSSUF TSAWISH IBN NOURI BITLISSI
Malta No. 2768
Interned (from Egypt) on 28.1.20.

Appointments. Sergeant of Gendarmerie at Mardin.

Lists. On none.

Arrest. Arrested by Egyptian Expeditionary Force early in 1919. Interned in Egypt and transferred to Malta on 28.1.20.

Petitions.
None to date 8.3.21.

ACCUSATIONS.

From the attached information, appendix A, the accusation appears to be one of complicity in the massacre of the Armenians of Eksor, near Mardin, in June 1915.

R. 2498. The summary of evidence was sent to the High Commissioner under cover of General Commanding, Egypt Expeditionary Force B/19928, dated 6.3.20.

APPENDIX A.   J.T. 192

Original in R 2498   Copy in D 18

D.A.Q.M.G.

5th Cavalry Division

Reference YUSSEF SHAWISH.

Herewith please find summary and copy of statements in this matter. As reported on several occasions the delay in taking the summary in this case has been due to the difficulty of obtaining witnesses from MERDIN and EKSOR.

I informed Descrops that these witnesses were unwilling to come to Aleppo until the harvest was finished. Finally I was able to send a message to Manour Jabouri Kanou of Mardin who owns the village of Eksor and he sent down three witnesses. I was also informed that several other witnesses would have been prepared to come to Aleppo if the recent release of Abdul Vehab and 3 others and the release on bail of Sheikh Muslim had not frightened them owing to their being in Turkish territory.

As will be seen by the Summary there is no direct evidence against YUSSEF SHAWISH as to the murder of British prisoners of war, but one witness considers that direct evidence of this could have been obtained prior to the release of the Kurd prisoners (i.e. Abdul Vehab and others).

It seems to have been a matter of common knowledge that YUSSEF did cause the death of these prisoners but I think that any witness who did see it would now probably deny having done so for fear of the accused being released.

I am forwarding statements in this case to give a better idea of the evidence that would be obtained against this man if witnesses could be persuaded to come to Aleppo. There seems to be no doubt that YUSSEF SHAWISH while in command of men ostensibly for protection of EKSOR, was mainly responsible for the massacres of the inhabitants.

C. M. Buildings. Aleppo 16/8/1919

/S/

C. I. BAKER (?) Contain MILITARY COURT

YUSSEF SHAWISH IBN NOURI EFF. BITLISSI, a gendarme of Mardin, was entrusted with a gendarmerie and militia of 100 men, for the deportation of the Armenians and the care of the Christians of Eksor village in particular.

He robbed the Christians, raped and carried away their virgins, and had a great part in the massacres.

From Mardin we watched the burning down of Eksor. One of the Christians of this village [who] escaped to Mardin reported to us that the Kurds had attacked and massacred the Christians, being assisted by YUSSEF SHAWISH, who also took part. A few hours before the Kurds attacked, he was seen to have gone to their camp and made the necessary arrangements. That was in June 15. When these massacres had settled down he returned to Mardin and used to tell us how he persecuted the Christians and how he had made £3,000 because his arms were long for their persecution. There are many to witness against YUSSEF SHAWISH for his responsibility for the lives of the 4,000 Christians of Eksor.

(Signed)   1. JIRJIS MELKON MAKDIS   OF MARDIN
           2. ABDUL AZIZ YACUB   OF DIARBEKIR
           3. JIRJIS YUNAN   OF MARDIN
           4. YACUB ABDUL MESIH SHALMI OF MARDIN

date. 4/2/19.

Address: c/o Syrian Church Aleppo

N.B. Above is condensed from attached 4 accusations.

YUSSEF SHAWISH, son of Nouri Eff., Gendarmerie Sergeant being at Tel Eorman, Geulliyes, two villages belonging to Mardin; this man was the principal agent of 3 thousand Armenian Catholics of Tel Erman village, where he killed by his own sword children, young girls, whose mothers are now at Mardin. He killed them with his own hands. He killed the father named Ibrahim, Syrian Orthodox priest, after having violated his daughter in front of his eyes.

The British prisoners, on their way from Mosul to Ras ul Ein were – 3 of them – caught by this brigand, ransacked, killed and their bodies thrown in the wells of the Geulliyes village near Mardin.

4/2/1919

/s/s JOSEPH TFINKDJI

[Chaldean] priest, Aleppo.

Mohammed Haj Yussef, Arab of Mardin gives the following evidence against YUSSEF SHAWISH BITLISSI

YUSSEF SHAWISH BITLISSI, Gendarmerie Sergeant of Mardin, son of Nouri Eff., Officer Commanding Gendarmerie of Mardin (latter now holds the same post in Marash).

During the Armenian deportations YUSSEF SHAWISH used to escort the parties of refugees sent out from Mardin. Informant always heard that YUSSEF SHAWISH used to massacre and rob the Armenians, together with his gendarmes. He is well known for his cruelty to Moslems as well as Christians. It is said that at Mardin he received more bribery than any other Government employee. Poor before the Armenian massacres, he is very rich today.

He and his father compelled several Armenian girls to live in their houses. Informant says that YUSSEF SHAWISH has committed all kinds of atrocities. He is capable of all cruelty.

YUSSEF SHAWISH was sent to Eksor village with 40 of the Mardin Militia. In one night 4,400 Syrian Christians of Eksor were handed over to the Kurds, who together with YUSSEF SHAWISH and his 40 men, massacred all those 4,400 Christians.

Because of his cruelties and misbehaviour while on duty, the Turkish Government arrested him and he was condemned to death. He was escorted to Diarbekir and Kharput. Finally he was liberated and drafted in the regular Army. Finally he managed to be enlisted gendarmerie sergeant at Antioch where his atrocities are well known by all the inhabitants of that town.

Aleppo 4.2.1919.
/S/ MOHAMMED YUSSEF of MARDIN.

SUMMARY OF EVIDENCE IN THE CASE OF YUSSEF IBN NOURI SHAWISH

PROSECUTION

1ST Witness. Abdullah Georgis, Christian of Eksor, living at present with Abdul Kareem, Azizieh Quarter, Aleppo, having been duly warned, states:-

In 1915 I was in Eksor. About the beginning of July the accused came to Eksor in command of about 40 gendarmes and 100 soldiers to protect the place against the Kurds. As soon as he arrived he posted his men all round the village to prevent anybody leaving the place.

I saw some people who were afterwards killed leave the village to go to Merdin after YUSSEF arrived, but about fifteen minutes later YUSSEF sent some of his mounted men after these people and they were brought back.

About 3 p.m. I saw YUSSEF leave the village accompanied by two soldiers and go in the direction of the Kurds. He returned after about half an hour accompanied by two Kurd chiefs who went away when they reached the village. YUSSEF then issued orders that all the people of the village were to gather either in or rounds Garbouri's house where he was living as that would be the safest place for them during the night.

Later I overheard YUSSEF talking to one of his corporals on the lower roof of the house. He said that the Kurds were going to attack the village that night when the moon was shining and that the soldiers and gendarmes were not to fire their rifles unless it was light enough to see whom they were firing at or words to that effect.

About 8 or 8:30p.m. the two Kurd Chiefs who had accompanied YUSSEF in the afternoon came back and YUSSEF had an interview with them on the roof of the house. I heard him telling them that they would make their attack that night and that he would give them a signal by blowing a trumpet when the time came for the attack. The Kurd chiefs then left the village. By this time practically all the people of Eksor were gathered either in the house or the courtyard of Garbouri.

That night when the moon was shining some time after midnight somebody blew a trumpet on the roof of Garbouri's house. At once all YUSSEF's soldiers and gendarmes gathered round Garbouri's house. The trumpet was then blown again and the Kurds began to make their attack entering the village and firing at the people.

Just after the trumpet was blown for the second time the Kurds started firing into the air and the soldiers and gendarmes also were firing into the air, but when the Kurds entered the village I heard YUSSEF order his men to fire at the people. I actually saw YUSSEF firing at the people with a rifle. When the Kurds arrived in the village they and YUSSEF's men joined forces and a general massacre ensued. I remained in the house for about another hour passing myself off as a Kurd, but when I tried to escape from the roof I was wounded in the shoulder by a Kurd with a dagger. I then got two beds and put them on my shoulder and managed to escape from the village by pretending to be a Kurd looting.

Just before I left the village it was set on fire by the Kurds and soldiers. About 3,000 people had been killed when I left. I managed to make my way to Mardin where I was treated by an American doctor.

The day before the night of the massacre I heard the three sons of Garbouri, Mikhail, Elia and Yussef asking the accused for permission to go to Mardin and an escort to accompany them. YUSSEF SHAWISH refused to let them go and they were killed during the massacre.

As far as I know the total number of people killed in Eksor at that time was between 5,000 and 6,000.

Question.   What was the exact time at which I arrived at Eksor?
Answer.   Between 12 noon and 3 or 4 o'clock p.m.
Question.   Before I arrived at Eksor was there in the village a party of 15 or 20 men with a Captain?
Answer.   I did not see them.
Question.   On the day that I arrived in Eksor what was I wearing and what was the colour of my horse?
Answer.   You were dressed as a Bach-Caoush but your tunic was very dark nearly black. Your horse was something like a light bay.
Question.   What were the numbers of the Kurds who attacked the village?
Answer.   I don't know.
Question.   Do you know the corporal to whom you say I gave orders?
Answer.   No I do not know him or his name, but he had two stripes on his shoulder.

The evidence is read to witness and acknowledged correct. The accused declines further to cross-examine the witness who withdraws.

2nd Witness. Mikhail Ibn Hanna of Eksor living at present with Abdul Kareem, Azizieh Quarter, Aleppo, having been duly warned, states:-

In 1915 when I was in Eksor we had for our protection about 8 gendarmes and about 20 soldiers with an officer. The local tribes of Kurds and Arabs tried to raid the village two or three times, but were prevented mostly by the gendarmes. In June we sent to Mardin asking for further protection and near the end of the month the accused arrived with about 40 gendarmes and 85 or 90 soldiers. He arrived about 1 p.m. and the first thing he did was to give his soldiers orders to surround the village and allow nobody to leave.

I saw many people try to escape from the village, but they were all brought back by the soldiers and gendarmes.

The Mukhtar and the old men and three sons of Garbouri then asked YUSSEF on behalf of the entire population of Eksor for permission to go to Mardin but this was refused and everybody had to remain.

During the afternoon YUSSEF left the village with 4 or 5 soldiers, and went off after the Kurds and Arabs who had withdrawn when they first saw YUSSEF's force. After about half and hour he returned to Eksor and went to Garbouri's house where he was staying. I then heard him tell the people that they had better come and spend the night in Garbouri's house as that would be the best place for his men to defend them in case of need.

He remained in Garbouri's house till about one hour after sunset and then calling one of his soldiers to him ordered him to go out to the Kurds and bring two of the chiefs Khalil Baialo and Saido Ibn Hami Hasso. I then heard this soldier go just a little way out the village and call to some of the Kurds who were quite near that YUSSEF wanted to see these two men. After a little while these two men came and I saw YUSSEF go and talk to them just outside the village. I did not hear what they said.

When YUSSEF returned he went on to the lower roof of the house and I heard him telling some of his corporals that the Kurds were going to attack the village that night when the moon was shining and that they were not to fire at the Kurds but up into the air until it was light enough to see who were Mohamedans and who were Christians and that anybody who disobeyed his orders would be shot.

He also told them that he had arranged to give the Kurds a signal for them to attack and would give another signal when they got into the village signifying that they surrendered to the Kurds or words to that effect.

By this time practically all the people of Eksor were in Garbouri's house but nobody was sleeping as we were all afraid. The accused was on the roof with his soldiers all night, and about 2½ or 3 hours before sunrise when it was quite moon-light somebody blew a trumpet and all the soldiers and gendarmes round the village came to Garbouri's house, pretending to be defending the village against the Kurds.

After a few minutes the trumpet was blown again and at once the soldiers began to fire indiscriminately at the people. I also saw YUSSEF himself firing a rifle at the people. The Kurds then advanced into the village and began massacring the people and were joined by the soldiers and gendarmes led by YUSSEF.

I was hiding in a small room in the house with my father and three of the Kurds came in and found us. They killed my father and robbed me leaving only my trousers. They were going to kill me but other men came in and demanded my jacket and they all began fighting. The three wounded the last comer who began calling for his friends and being afraid they all went out of the room.

I lay there shamming death and some more Kurds came in and after having killed a small boy and a woman started arguing as to whether I was dead or not. To settle the matter one hit me on the head with a big stick and another with an axe and they went away leaving me for dead.

I fainted and recovered consciousness about noon the same day. I saw that some soldiers and the Rais el Mahkemi from Merdin were there with a lot of people busy looking for dead bodies. Before I was hit on the head the village had been set on fire and Garbouri's house burnt.

I was then taken to hospital in Merdin and treated by an American doctor.

The total number of people who perished in the massacre was about 5,500.

Question.   Was there anybody senior to me who came with the party from Merdin?
Answer.   I did not see anybody.

Question.	Do you know the soldier whom you say I sent to call the Kurd chiefs?
Answer.	I do not know him.
Question.	Were any of the soldiers, gendarmes or the attacking Kurds and Arabs wounded or killed?
Answer.	I did not see.

/S/ MIKHAIL HANNA

The evidence is read to witness and acknowledged correct. The accused declines further to cross-examine the witness who duly withdraws.

3rd Witness. Georges Bahnan, Christian of Eksor, living at present with Abdul Kareem, Azizieh Quarter, Aleppo, having been duly warned, states:-

About the end of June 1915 I was living in the village of Eksor. At that time there were 20 or 25 soldiers in the place to protect us against the neighbouring tribes of Kurds and Arabs, who seemed likely to attack the village, but as they were not strong enough we applied to the authorities at Merdin for further protection. They sent us the accused YUSSEF SHAWISH in charge of a party of about 30 gendarmes and about 100 soldiers.

They arrived about noon or 1 p.m. one day and the first thing that YUSSEF did was to surround the village with his men. He then went to Garbouri's house and took up his residence there. He then told all the people of the village that they were on no account to leave the place and that anybody who disobeyed his orders would be perished. I heard Elia Garbouri asking YUSSEF for special permission to go to Merdin which YUSSEF refused to give saying that he was responsible for the safety of everybody in the village or words to that effect.

About 4 p.m. YUSSEF sent two of his soldiers out to the Kurds, I overheard his instructions to them which were to go out and tell two of the chiefs Khalil Baislo and Saido Ibn Hami Hasso that he YUSSEF desired to speak to them. The two soldiers went out and told the chiefs and then came back, and told YUSSEF that they would not come, they were afraid to come right into the village, but that they were quite willing to meet him outside the village.

A little while after sunset these two Kurds chiefs came in sight outside the village and YUSSEF went off to meet them unarmed.

He spoke to them for 15 or 20 minutes and then came back to Garbouri's house.

He was then on the lower roof of the house with 4 or 5 of his men talking to them. Mikhail was there and I was there as well, and overhear YUSSEF telling his men that the Kurds were going to attack the village that night, that they were going to wait until the moon was shining so as to be able to distinguish the soldiers from the civilians, that when the attack was made his men were to fire not at the Kurds but in the air, and that he had arranged to give the Kurds two signals by sounding a trumpet the first when the time was ripe for them to attack and the second to signify that the soldiers and gendarmes would surrender or words to that effect.

Previous to this YUSSEF had issued orders that all the people of EKSOR were to come to Garbouri's house for the night as that would be safest place for them so they all came along.

A little later YUSSEF gave his men orders to begin firing into the air and they kept up a desultory fire during the night. After the moon rose somebody on the roof of Garbouri's house blew a trumpet and all the soldiers and gendarmes round the village came to Garbouri's house.

The trumpet then blew again sounding the surrender and I heard YUSSEF order his men to fire at the people of the village. The soldiers and gendarmes started to fire on the people and YUSSEF seizing a rifle started firing at them himself. I actually saw YUSSEF fire at and kill Mikail Elia and Yussef Garbouri. Others also fired at them.

The Kurds by this time had advanced on the village and entered it and started massacring the people.

I jumped down from the roof and mingling with the Kurds passed myself off as one of them. I then escaped from the village and hid myself among the wheat a little distance away. At the sunrise I saw smoke rising from the village which had apparently been set on fire. I remained hidden in the wheat all day long and the same night about 9 p.m. escaped to Merdin. The total number of people killed in Eksor was about 5,500. In August 1917 I was travelling from Merdin to Rasseline by road to deliver to the Bagdad railway Co. some grapes. At Bonias I met a Kurd whose name I do not know but whom I could recognise if I saw. (In the course of conversation he told me that YUSSEF CHAAOUISH had murdered three British prisoners of war in Arada near Rasseline.)

Question.	When I came to Eksor was I in sole charge of the party?
Answer.	Yes you were.
Question.	When I gave the order to my men to fire in the air how did I give it, and where were the soldiers?
Answer.	You gave the order only to the soldiers near you, who fired. The others round the village did not fire until they came to the house.
Question.	When Elia Garbouri came and asked me for permission to go to Merdin he mentioned another man also. Do you know this other man's name?
Answer.	Yes, Sheikh Kassim.
Question.	When permission was asked to go to Merdin were not the people afraid of meeting the Kurds?
Answer.	The Kurds had withdrawn at that time and we were not afraid.

/S/ GEORGES BAHNAN

The evidence is read to the witness and acknowledged correct. The accused declines further to cross-examine the witness who withdraws.

4th Witness. Abdul Kareem Kanou, Azizieh Quarter, Aleppo, having been duly warned states:-

In 1915 about the beginning of July I was in Merdin. Orders were received that no more Syrians were to be killed and in consequence of this my uncle Mansour and my brother Abdul Lahaat who were in prison were released. After this my uncle Mansour fearing that the Kurds would attack Eksor went to the Governor of Mardin and asked for more protection. In consequence about 100 soldiers of the "Mellico" were sent down to Eksor and were followed by YUSSEF and about 25 gendarmes. YUSSEF was in command of all the soldiers and gendarmes.

The same night I saw rifles flashing in the direction of Eksor and in the morning saw the village burning.

There were about 5,000 people all Syrians in Eksor, and only about 15 or 16 persons escaped and came to me in Mardin and told me what happened.

(I heard in 1917 that YUSSEF had murdered 3 British prisoners of war but do not know anything more about it.)

My three uncles Elia, Mikhail and Yussef were all killed in Eksor by YUSSEF's order.

/S/Abdul Kanou

The evidence is read to witness and acknowledged correct. The accused declines to cross-examine the witness who withdraws.

Appendix "I"

COPY OF STATEMENT BY FATHER JOSEPH TUFENKDJI, Chaldean Priest of Aleppo.

YUSSEF SHAWISH IBN NOURI BITLISSI was chief of the Gendarmerie at Golieh and the neighbourhood.

About August 1916 some British prisoners were travelling by train from Mosul to Ras el Ain.

They were dispersed along the line to work on the railway, and one Englishman and two Indians were left at Golieh.

In October 1916 I went from Sangar to a village near Golieh and there met an Indian Prisoner of War. This Indian told me that YUSSEF SHAWISH had taken all the cloths from these three Prisoners and had murdered them, and had thrown their bodies into a dry well.

Nouri Bitlissi, father of YUSSEF, told me that his son had murdered British prisoners.

When I was a prisoner at Mardin I heard the Turkish Guards saying that Nouri's son had killed three British prisoners at Golieh and two were at Nissibine.

/S/ FATHER JOSEPH TFINKDJI
Original taken down by me at Beirut this 3rd day of July 1919.
/S/ J.cR. WARE, Captain
D. A.P . H., Beirut

YUSSEF UBN NOURI EFF. BITLISSI

Statement of Jijis Melkon Mano of Mardin. Taken by Captain Butler.

YUSSEF for about a year was a Cavalry Sergeant in charge of 15 to 20 gendarmerie at Mardin. In June 1915 when about 600 Christians were massacred outside Mardin he took part in this under the orders of Mamdouch Bek the Chief Commissaire coming from Diarbekir to Mardin. After this massacre orders were published by the Turkish Authorities in Mardin that the Sultan had given orders that no more Assyrians were to be killed. I did not hear this order myself but there were many who did. In consequence of this order Mansour Jarbouri Kanou (the chief man of the village of Eksor) applied to, the Turkish Authorities for police protection for the village as they were frightened of the Kurds. YUSSEF was sent with 20 men, Mansour again applied for more men as this was not enough and YUSSEF's command was finally increased to 100 or 150. One night I heard shots being fired from the direction of Eksor and saw the village burning. In the morning I saw that the village was surrounded with men and shots were being fired as people came out from the burning village, a few escaped. About 5 or 6 women and one man are, I believe, all that escaped, over 3,000 must have been killed. One of the Jarbouri family, a woman of about 35, is the only one I know of by name, she is now living in Mardin and Mansour could find her for you.

After this YUSSEF when he returned to Mardin levied extortion from Christians and he took and kept in his house 4 girls from leading families.

YUSSEF found with 3 bombs on his pocket on day Allenby arrived.

Abdul Aziz Yacub of Diarbekir. Employed in Public Debts Office, Aleppo, states:

After the massacre of about 600 prisoners in June 1915, the Turkish Authorities verbally published an order that no more Syrians should be killed. Then Mansour Jarbouri Kanou applied to the Authorities for protection for his village of Eksor against the Kurds. YUSSEF with 20 or 30 gendarmerie was sent. Jarbouri applied for further protection, and YUSSEF's command was made up to about 150 men. About 19:30 one evening I saw the flashes of many rifles in the village of Eksor and that continued till about midnight when I went to my room. Early next morning when I looked towards Eksor I saw that the village was burning. I watched through a telescope. The village was surrounded by men, others were apparently looting that part of the village which was not yet burnt. When they came out into the open I could distinguish the difference between gendarmes, soldiers and Kurds, they were mixing together and not fighting and they were, most of them carrying something which they had looted. About 17:00 that day I saw a number of soldiers who had been at Eksor in Mardin. There were about 3,000 persons in Eksor and only one man and 7 or 8 women escaped. The man was a member of Mansour Jarbouri's family. I hear that he later wiped out the village of Ibrahimieh; he used to plunder the immigrant trains. He kept 6 of the best looking Armenian girls, one of them is still in Mardin in the house of Suleiman Gamsurli (the brother of the chief of the Municipality). Her name I believe is Zabel, and she is of the best family.

I know he robbed many people.

(Further particulars of Zabel see Minas Minassian, Aleppo)

Jirjis Jarbouri Kanou of Eksor village. Now in Cerole Egyptian Bab el Farag:

About June or July 1915 I was living in the village of Eksor when YUSSEF SHAWISH arrived in charge of 20 Gendarmerie. Mansour Jarbouri, my uncle, and the chief man of the village did not consider these enough to protect them against the Kurds. He paid the Turkish Authorities a considerable sum to increase the number. Additional men were then sent bringing the number up to about 150 men. When he first arrived he told the inhabitants that he was there to protect the village and there was no need to be afraid of the Kurds. I was there when he told my father this. About sunrise the day before the massacre I saw YUSSEF go out of the village and speak to Kaalil Dillala, Sardou Bin Chasou, Sheikh Ibrahim, Kalil Abdullah, who were the 4 chief men of the neighbouring Kurds, about 300 yards outside the village. I and three others walked towards them to see what was being done but YUSSEF ordered us away. The three with me (my brother-in-law, father and my uncle) were all killed that night. We became frightened at this and many of us tried to leave the village almost immediately afterwards but everywhere round the village we found YUSSEF's men who turned us back again. About 10:00 fearing that YUSSEF was going to massacre us, I dressed like an Arab and crept out of the village. I was stopped at the first Caracol [police station] but my father bribed the chief of the Caracol to let me pass. After that I managed to pass the other Caracols as I was not known. I then went to Mardin, about 01:00 I saw the flash of rifles at Eksor at first scattered but gradually increasing, by midnight the firing was at its height and the flashes seemed continuous. Then it suddenly slackened and practically stopped except for an occasional shot and I knew they were in the village using their knives. About 03:00 or 04:00 I saw fire break out in the village and after sunrise I saw it burning fiercely. I was unable to see with the naked eye what was being done. About 10.00 I saw YUSSEF riding back at the head of his men none of whom appeared to be wounded or killed though their clothes were spattered with blood. When he arrived at the Serai, my brother-in-law Elyas Armoun went up to him in my presence and said "What has happened" YUSSEF said "it is all over, they are all killed, I was unable to protect them."

Afterwards [sic] my uncle Mansour used to pay YUSSEF money and make him present so that nothing should happen. Several times I have been to YUSSEF's house and each time there would be new Christian girls there, sometimes we were able to have a few hurried words with them and they all told us that YSUSEF had taken them from immigrant trains and was using them as mistresses for himself and his friends. I do not know what happened to them after he had had them a week for they always seemed to be changing. I went to his house 12 or 15 times during/about 3 months and must have seen 50 different Christian girls, all good looking.

YUSSEF then saw my father and told him that he would try to save him and his family from the Kurds that night. My father in my presence paid him £500 in gold.

Abdullah Ghuarges	left for dead.
Mansour Ibn Ibrahim	(Eksor village) Galloped off on a horse.
Mikhail Ibn Hanna	(Eksor village) left for dead.

Mejider Bint Faris   (Eksor village) captured by Kurds.

Jirjis Bin Isaac   (Eksor village).

All these escaped from Eksor. Medjider had to be brought back from the Turks.

Farah Allah Hadaieh. (of Mardin) Sedieh Quarter, Abu Aggoor Street.

In June 1915 I was imprisoned with all the notable Christians of Mardin. There were 485 in there with me. They then separated 83 Syrians and the remainder were taken out and massacred. About 3 days later Mandouk Bey, the chief police, entered the barracks. I was told to go round all the Syrians and see that no Armenians were amongst them. When I had reported that they were all Syrians I and several leading inhabitants were brought up before the Governor (Raouf Bey I think his name was). He then told us in the presence of Mandough Bey and the chief of the police that the Sultan had given order that no more Syrians should be exiled or massacred as they were good citizens and faithful to the Turkish Empire. The inhabitants of Eksor were Syrians. I saw YUSSEF return at the head of his men from Eksor and did not appear as though any of them had been fighting.

20.5.1919.

/S/ FARGALLAH HADAIEH

Jacub Adbul Messih Shalmi. Hearsay evidence.

Joseph Tfinkdji.

In June 1915 he was at Mardin and heard of the order that no more Syrians should be killed in spite of which YUSSEF SHAWISH superintended the massacre of them at Eksor.

About 18 girls escaped from YUSSEF and came to my Church for protection, but were all recaptured. These girls told me of all sorts of beastly atrocities committed by YUSSEF and his friends and in some cases girls died within 24 hours of their arrival whether by their own accord or by YUSSEF's acts I do not know. They had all been taken from immigrant trains by YUSSEF. I can only remember the names of three girls who escaped to our church, Nejimen who died in the church, Zekia who was recaptured and presented to Mahmoud Shavket Bey and is still with him at Nesebin Street and Arshalous who was recaptured.

In all YUSSEF must have had over 40 girls passing through his hands during the 8 months after June 1915.

Shamoon the butcher in (Eksor)

Jeje Uskar still in Eksor, were of those who escaped the massacres.

Yussef Aboud, Syrian Catholic priest, now residing in Eksor, can supply names and information though not present at massacres.

Abdullah Georgis. Of Eksor, living at present with Abdul Kareem, Azizieh Quarter, Aleppo, states:-

In 1915 when I was in Eksor we heard that Nouri Eff. the Gendarmerie Cavalry Commander and father of YUSSEF SHAWISH had received orders from Andul Kadir Pasha to destroy the villages round Mardin. Soon after this YUSSEF SHAWISH came to Eksor with about 50 Gendarmes and 100 soldiers, ostensibly to protect the place against the Kurds. One day about 3 p.m. he had an interview with the chiefs of the Kurds and other tribes near Eksor.

I was not present at the interview but when YUSSEF returned I overheard him speaking to one of his Corporals.

He said that he had arranged that the Kurds and Arabs would attack Eksor on moonlight night. He also told the Corporal to tell his men not to fire their rifles when it was dark, but to wait for the moonlight so as to be able to avoid shooting Mohamedans.

The same night which was a bright moonlight night, a little after midnight someone from the house of Garbouri Kanou in which YUSSEF was living blew a trumpet and all YUSSEF's soldiers and gendarmes that were in the village gathered round this house.

At that moment the Kurds attacked the village and began firing their rifles. The soldiers and gendarmes also began to fire from the roofs into the air, thus making a pretence of defending Eksor, but as far as I could see none of the attackers were killed or wounded. The Kurds then came into the village and were joined by the soldiers and gendarmes headed by YUSSEF, and the whole crowd began massacring the people.

Just before the Kurds arrived in the village I actually heard YUSSEF SHAWISH give an order to his men to fire at the people of Eksor.

Before the Kurds attacked, YUSSEF had told the people that the safest place for them would be near the house of Garbouri, so that when the massacre actually started they were all gathered together like sheep ready to be killed. During all this time I was in Garbouri's house and because I can speak Kurdish I succeeded in passing myself off as a Kurd. I remained in the house for about 1½ hours after the massacre started during which time I saw YUSSEF firing from a roof with a rifle at the people prior to his joining in with Kurds.

I then made my escape, from Eksor and as I left the village was set in fire, but by whom I do not know. When I left about 3,000 people had already been killed and I myself had received a wound in the shoulder with a dagger by a Kurd when leaving Garbouri's house.

I managed to make my way to Mardin where I was treated by an Armenian doctor. I heard Mikhail and Elia and Yussef sons of Garbouri on the day of the massacre, asking YUSSEF SHAWISH for permission to go to Mardin, but this was refused by YUSSEF and they were massacred the same night.

The total number of people killed in Eksor was between 5,000 and 6,000.

Mikhail Ibn Hanna. Of Eksor, living at present with Abdul Kareem, Azizieh Quarter, Aleppo, states:-

In 1915 about August when I was in the village of Eksor we were attacked one day by the Kurds. We succeeded in defending ourselves and afterwards applied to the Authorities at Mardin for protection. They sent us YUSSEF SHAWISH in charge of about 90 soldiers and 40 gendarmes. They arrived during the afternoon one day and a little later went out of Eksor and had an interview with the chief men of the Kurds. When YUSSEF returned I heard him telling his men that the Kurds would attack the village during the night when the moon was shining and that they were not to fire at the Kurds but into the air, and that anybody who disobeyed his orders would be shot at once. He also said that they would wait for the moon so as to be able to distinguish between Mohamedans and Christians.

YUSSEF was living in the house of one Garbouri and he told the people of Eksor that it would be safer for them if they spent the night near this house so that his soldiers could protect them, so we all gathered near, I was in Garbouri's house upstairs.

Some time after midnight somebody blew a trumpet from the roof of Garbouri's house, and immediately the Kurds opened fire on the village. I heard YUSSEF order his men to fire on the people from the roofs and then to go and break into the houses and massacre them all. After a while the Kurds came into the village and also began massacring the inhabitants. They came and broke into the room where I was with my father, killed him and robbed me, and while they were quarrelling over my things I escaped from the house and hid myself among the corpses. About 8 a.m. two or three Kurds came along and seeing I was not dead one of them hit me on the head with an axe and left me for dead.

About an hour later the village was set on fire.

I remained there for about three hours and then the Rais el Mahkemi and some soldiers came and the Kurds escaped and I was taken to the Hospital in Mardin.

The people killed in Eksor on that occasion numbered about 5,000.

Date of YUSSEF's arrival in Eksor 27.6.1915 approx.

Georgi Behnen. Of Eksor, living with Abdul Kareem, Azizieh Quarter.

About June 1915 I was living in Eksor. At that time about 25 or 20 soldiers were there to protect us against the Kurds. The day before the massacre in the morning YUSSEF SHAWISH arrived with an additional 100 men (gendarmerie and the "fifty").

During the afternoon I saw YUSSEF go out and have an interview with the Kurdish Chiefs around at a place about 10 or 15 minutes away. I saw the meeting. YUSSEF was unarmed. About 5 p.m. YUSSEF returned. Mikhail and myself hid behind a house and overheard YUSSEF talking some of his N.C.O.s

He said that he had told the Kurds that if they wanted to attack Eksor they must wait for the moon to come up, not attack in the dark, and then they would be able to discriminate between Christians and Mohamedans. He also said that the Kurds would attack the village that night and that he had arranged to give them a signal when the time was ripe by blowing a trumpet.

YUSSEF then told the people of Eksor that the safest place for them that night would be the house of Garbouri, where he himself was living, so they all collected either in or near Garbouri's house.

About half an hour after the moon rose, which was not long before the dawn, someone blew a trumpet from the roof of the house. The Kurds started firing in the air and advancing towards the village. YUSSEF then ordered his men to fire on us, which they did. I saw YUSSEF himself shoot at and kill Mikhail, Elia and Yussef Garbouri, the sons of the owner of the house. When I saw this I jumped from the roof where I was to the yard and mingled with the Kurds, passing myself off as one of them. The Kurds were all coming into the town to massacre the inhabitants and I escaped and hid myself among some wheat, some little distance away. About 2 hours later I saw the smoke from Eksor, which had been set on fire. About 9 p.m. the following night I escaped to Mardin.

The number of people killed in Eksor were somewhere about 5,000.

TAHSIN BEY (HASSAN TAHSIN BEY)

Malta No. 2774

Interned 22.3.20.

Appointments.

Vali of Van	27.3.13 – 30.9.14
Vali of Erzerum	30.9.14 – 10.8.16
Vali of Syria	10.8.16 – 20.6.18
Vali of Smyrna	30.10.18 – 22.11.18

(Son-in-law of Hulussi Bey).

In December 1919, Tahsin Bey was returned as Deputy both for Van and Smyrna; he opted for Smyrna. At Van during the Balkan War, his actions appeared to be Armenophile. Whilst Vali of Erzerum, during the whole period of the deportations, he had under his orders the notorious deportee, Memduh Bey, Mutessarif of Erzindjan. As Vali of Syria, TAHSIN was the associate of Djemal Pasha, the Virtual Military Dictator south of the Taurus.

2. **Previous suggestions for arrest List II, III, VI, VII.** His name was suggested for arrest to the Grand Vizier in February 1919 and again on March 20th 1919, but though he was living on the Bosphorus, the Sublime Porte took no action. (Lists II and III). His name was again suggested for arrest to High Commissioner on August 15th, but though approved, High Commissioner on September 9th decided the matter should remain in abeyance. (List VI). On September 19th 1919 the question of his arrest by the Interallied Police was again brought forward, but on October 5th the High Commissioner gave instructions for his name to be placed on the list of those to be arrested and tried under a clause of the Peace Treaty. (List VII).

3. **Trial by Court Martial.** TAHSIN Bey appears to have been tried by Turkish Court Martial but "grâce aux certificates qu'il avait pu obtenir des Arméniens à Erzerum et à Damas et grace au concours de certains journaux turcs et Arméniens il fut pour le moment acquité." (Note from a reliable source, in C. 14).

4. **Domicile.** TAHSIN owns a konak at Buyuk Déré, which he is said to have bought at a cost of LT. 40,000, part proceeds of the extortion and loot brought back by him from Syria.

5. **Arrest.** Arrested as a Nationalist leader by British Military Authorities on 16.3.20 and deported to Malta. He was definitely transferred from General Officer Commanding-in-Chief's List to High Commissioner's List on 5.2.21. (1316/24).

Summary of recent correspondence. In High Commissioner's despatch 1552/W. 3667 of 24.11.20, covering report of special committee, it was recommended that he be detained at Malta until brought up for trial.

W. 2178, 5897/2 'T'. On 23rd November 1920 General Officer Commanding-in-Chief recommends his release as a Nationalist arrested by his orders.

297/24. In General Officer Commanding-in-Chief's 3211 'I' of 7.1.21, he is listed for trial, but whether on a military charge or not is uncertain.

297/24. To General Officer Commanding-in-Chief on 20.11.21 requesting his definite transfer to High Commissioner's list.

1316/24. General Officer Commanding-in-Chief of 5.2.21 acquiescing.

Petitions.

1. **1651/24.** Petition of 1.2.21, through Governor of Malta of 7.2.21, asking to be permitted to join his wife about to undergo an operation.
2. **1739/24.** Petition of 18.2.21 from wife, complementary to above.

ACCUSATIONS.

5. [sic, 6] Through Mr. Ryan on 19th September 1919: on TAHSIN's transfer as Vali from Van to Erzerum, he began the pillaging of Armenians under cover of military requisitions. He was a leading spirit in the councils held at Erzerum to decide on the measures for the deportation and massacre of Armenians. These councils were presided over by Doctor Behaeddin Shakir, delegate of the central C.U.P., Muammer (a deportee), Vali of Sivas, Djevdet (a deportee) Vali of Van, and Mustafa Abdul Malik (a deportee) Vali of Bitlis. (All the very worst of criminals).

7. **5027/A/20.** Through Mr. Ryan on 16th September 1919, from a known reliable source:-

   (a) Deportation and massacre of 400 Armenians from the Kaza of Baiburt (Erzerum Vilayet) not one of whom is now alive. (See also para. 12 and 14).

   (b) TAHSIN matured and carried out the coup d'etat resulting in the downfall of Kiamil Pasha.

   (c) Was Vali of Erzerum, with Memduh as his Mutessarif of the Sanjak of Erzindjan, when massacres were at their worst, (i.e. summer of 1915).

   (d) As Vali of Syria he acted as a shield to Djemal Pasha's atrocities and pillaged very successfully.

   (e) Extortion of LT. 5,000 gold from an Armenian girl and murder of her parents.

8. **5027/A/14.** Evidence of Kellerios Kurkin as given to 'Intelligence', Transcaucasia.

May 1919: He TAHSIN Bey – personally accompanied deportees from Erzerum to Erzinjan and had them massacred. (See para. 16).

9. **5027/A/6.** A "Bureau d'Information Arménien" report on Baiburt (Erzerum Vilayet) massacres. (paras. 11 and 16).

10. **"Treatment of Armenians Miscl. No. 31 (1916)".** Viscount Bryce, p. 221 – Considers that 98% of the Armenians of the Vilayets of Erzerum and Bitlis were deported or massacred previous to the Russian occupation, i.e. 8 to 10,000 survivals out of an Armenian population of 400,000. The deportations began in May 1915.

11. **Page 222.** Rev. Robert Stapleton residing at Erzerum until after the Russian occupation:

(a) Hanging of the three Armenian servants of the Russian Consul in November 1914.

(b) Massacre of Khnyss by Kurds on 19th May 1919 [1915].

(c) Deportation and massacres of the countryside Armenians. Inhabitants of 100 villages deported by order of the Government at two hours notice. Total number between 10,000 and 15,000. Of this number very few returned and very few reached Erzingan. They were escorted by gendarmes, but the people responsible for the massacres would probably be tchetes or Hamidia ... These massacres occurred in June 1915.

(d) On June 9th 1915, TAHSIN Bey issued an order that the whole civil population were to leave the city of Erzerum.

(e) The first caravan of Armenians consisting of 40 families mostly belonging to the prosperous business community, left Erzerum on June 16th 1915, taking the road to Diarbekir via Kighi. The whole of this caravan was massacred between Kighi and Palu (on the borders of Erzerum – Diarbekir Vilayet). Only one man and 40 women and children survived.

(f) On June 19th the second caravan, consisting of 500 Armenian families left the city of Erzerum. They were permitted to transport and a time given to them to prepare for the journey. They took the road to Erzingan via Baiburt. At Baiburt the caravan numbered some 15,000. At Erzingan (Vilayet of Erzerum) the caravan was not permitted to proceed by the carriage road to Sivas but was turned onto the paths via Kemakh, Egin and Arabkir. Consequently they were deprived of all transport at Erzingan where TAHSIN Bey was at the time. At Kemakh 12 hours from Erzingan, the first regular massacre of men took place. (See para. 16)

(g) In February 1916, 50 Armenian masons who had been employed in building a club house for the Turks in Erzerum were deported to Erzingan and shot there. Four escaped by shamming death.

(h) TAHSIN Bey left Erzerum on (or about) 15th Feb. 1916 on the arrival of the Russians. On that day there were about 22 Armenians (girls) in the town.
(Note: Mr. Stapleton does not directly implicate the Senior Government Official, the Vali of the Province – but that is understood to be the attitude of American missionaries. The account of the Erzerum deportations was given by Mr. Stapleton to the Rev. H. T. Buxton in 1916).

12. **p. 233.** Report by Dr. V. Minassian, published in Armenian journal "Nabak" of Tiflis, 8th March 1916. Describes (from reports to him) the deportation from Baiburt, rapings, extortions, murders that took place on the road to Kemakh, (all in Erzerum vilayet) and final massacre near Kemakh, where the women were thrown into the Euphrates (see paras. 16 and 17). He also implicates the German Consul in Erzerum, (?) Anders, and says that German officers helped to organise the deportations and took their share of booty, i.e. moveable goods including girls.

13. **p. 236.** Mr. Saprastian's report dated Tiflis 15th March 1916. Murders and tortures of prominent Armenians in Erzerum city early in 1915, previous to deportations. Massacres of the 'peasant' Armenians in the Kemakh gorge by their escort consisting chiefly of criminals released from prison for the purpose. Some 15,000 massacred. Account of the deportation of the first caravan from the city of Erzerum. TAHSIN Bey received

LT. 1,000 for their safe conduct. Abduction by force of Armenian women by German officers.

Bishop Sempad was sent off from Erzerum alone in his own carriage and never heard of again.

14. **p. 242.** Narrative of the Baiburt massacres and hanging of Bishop Anania Hazarabetian and other notables.

15. **p. 244 to 255.** Further narratives of massacres in the Erzerum vilayet, but no names mentioned.

16. **Mme. Zarouhi Capedjian. C6.** On January 27th 1920 Madame Zarouhi Capedjian, widow of Abram Capedjian, glass merchant of Erzerum massacred near Malatia, made at the High Commission a long statement, as an actual eye witness, describing in detail the massacres and sufferings of the second caravan of Armenian deportees from Erzerum city. Between Ashkala and Erzingan, especially between Baiburt and Erzingan, she passed hundreds of corpses, several with their eyes gouged out. This was specially the case with the bearded corpses, i.e. those of Armenian priests. At Ashkala a number of young men were separated out in order, it was said, to be drafted into a labour battalion; none of these young men have since been heard of.

TAHSIN Bey, the Vali, was in Erzingan when she arrived outside the town. Here, the witness, together with all those comprising the caravan were deprived of all means of transport. Instead of taking the carriage road to Sivas, the caravan was herded onto the path leading to the Valley of the Kara Su. Between Erzingan and Kemakh the witness passed countless corpses. At Kemakh, as the many thousands of deportees crossed the bridge, a large number of men were separated out and have since disappeared. The caravan was finally wiped out between Malatia and the Euphrates, but all the place names mentioned above all in the vilayet of Erzerum, over which TAHSIN Bey was **Vali.**

17. **Other statements.** Mrs. Capedjian's statement is fully corroborated by other statements made by Armenian deportees. See C. 21 and C. 27.

18. The following is a copy of a translation of an alleged original telegram which was communicated to the High Commission. Original believed to be in Turkish 1st Court Martial records.

H. 4. Telegram No. . . dated 16th July 1915, from TAHSIN Bey Vali of Erzerum to Sabit Bey Vali of Mamuret-ul-Aziz. The details given by Your Excellency on the 13th July 1915 have made a great impression on us, the state of things described amounts to anarchy and it is contrary to the wishes of the Government and of our Party. I have communicated to the Minister Talaat Bey your statements as well as all that I have seen and heard. The welfare of the country requires that everyone at all responsible should be at once withdrawn. Everywhere I am saying that whatever we did, we have not done it in order to fill with money the pockets of some persons. It is because we are after the salvation of the Government that we are deporting the Armenians to the south. This is the sole object. It is advisable that you too should write in this sense to the Ministry. Anyhow, please, send the deported groups of Erzerum via Malatia. It may be, that they will be attacked at Eghin. Please send trustworthy officials to the district between Kemakh and Eghin; it is necessary that officials should know the object and intentions of the Governments. The Army advances with full success. I am going to inform you that 800 prisoners were taken.

(**N.B.** The route taken by the majority of the Erzerum deportees was via Erzingan (then a sanjak dependent on Erzerum), down the valley of the Kara Su, past Kemakh and Eghin, to Arabkir, Malatia and the south. Very large numbers were duly massacred between Kemakh and Eghin (under instructions from TAHSIN and his Mutessarif of Erzingan, Memduh Bey). The boundary between Erzingan and Mamuret-ul-Aziz is just north of Eghin.)

19. **G. XI.** In Patriarchate's detailed list of criminals of September 1920, TAHSIN is duly listed as the Vali responsible for the deportations in Erzerum Vilayet.

20. The Armenian Patriarchate has also supplied the following biographical notice on TAHSIN Bey:-

"TAHSIN Bey was born in a village near the town of Salonika. His early training was very deficient having only followed the courses of the Preparatory School of Salonika. He was sent away from this school for gross immorality.

In 1904 he was nominated, through the protection of his powerful friends, Nahie Mudiri (Governor) of the circumscription of Negritia in Salonika. He was then in secret intercourse with the C.U.P.

In 1908 he was promoted Kaimakam of Katherina and when the Constitution was proclaimed he became a most enthusiastic Unionist. As a reward he was again promoted to the Mutessarifat of Seres. In 1913 he was nominated Vali of Van and a year later Vali of Erzerum.

The fact that at that time the adoption by Turkey of the plan of reforms for the six Armenian provinces was been energetically urged on Turkey by the Powers and secretly opposed by the Young Turk Party shows what reliance the C.U.P. had on the cunning abilities of TAHSIN Bey in selecting him to counteract any scheme put forward for the benefit of the Christians and make them fall through under a show of readiness to accept them and to act righteously.

The opportunities for doing all the harm he could were not missed by TAHSIN Bey. After the declaration of War, with the full approval of Mahmud Kiamil and in obedience to Behaeddine Shakir and Dr. Nazim, he lent a willing hand to the deportation of the Armenians taking due care in the meantime, by appropriate telegrams to secure future cover in order to save himself from responsibility. These attempts to cover himself will not of course be of any avail before the Tribunal of Equity, since the Province of Erzerum, where he was Vali, has been one of the regions where the massacre and deportation of Armenians was most ruthlessly carried out.

The town of Erzerum was moreover the great centre for the preparation of the plans for the annihilation of the Armenian population. It was there that several councils of the Valis of the Armenian provinces were held under the presidency of Mahmud Kiamil. At every one of these councils, TAHSIN Bey was present.

Although he managed to have the Armenians of the town of Erzerum slaughtered outside the borders of the Erzerum province, in the sanjak of Malatia, the enormous Armenian population of the districts of Baiburt, Erzingan and Keghi was slaughtered in these localities under the guidance of his subordinates, the governors of these districts.

TAHSIN Bey remained the Vali of Erzerum until 1917 and having enriched himself of the spoils of the Armenians, he was after this date nominated Vali of Damascus.

At Damascus following always his secret aim of suppressing as many Armenians as possible, without incurring any responsibility, he was the cause of death by starvation of 150 Armenian orphans in the orphanage of Damascus. Tcherkes Massan Bey, in charge of the Armenian refugees and orphans of that region, has brought definite accusations against him and cited eleven witnesses in proof of his accusation."

DEFENCE

21. The telegrams mentioned below are said to be translations of originals. The translations only have been communicated. They are quoted here as apparently being in TAHSIN's favour.

J. 25. Telegram of 11.5.15 from TAHSIN to the Minister of the Interior, Talaat Pasha, protesting against the deportations.

J. 26. Telegram of 13.5.15 from TAHSIN to the Commander of the IIIrd Army.

J. 27. Telegram of 27.5.15 from TAHSIN to the Minister of the Interior, apparently implicating Vali Sabit Bey of Mamuret-ul-Aziz in certain acts of brigandage committed by Kurds in Dersim.

J. 76. Telegram of 10.7.15 from TAHSIN to Djemal Azmi, Vali of Trebizond protesting against the method of deportation, after himself seeing deportees on the road.

HILMI ABDUL KADIR, Colonel

Malta No. 2789

Interned at Mudros on 15/3/20; Transferred to Malta on 31/3/20

Appointments. Adjutant-Major d'Etat Major en retraite.

Engineer, Public Works, Kirkuk, Mossul Vilayet. Commanding the Labour Battalion at Mossul in 1918.

Lists. On none.

Arrest. Arrested by the British Military Authorities in Batum on 13.4.19 as a notorious massacrer in the Eastern Vilayets and in Persia. On or about 6.2.20 he was transferred to Chanak and from Chanak to Mudros on 15.3.20. The following minutes appear on correspondence.

R. 1956. G.O.C.-in-C. 11.12.19. "There appear to be difficulties in the way of ABDUL KADIR's trial in Persia and I therefore propose to sanction his release unless you have any other views regarding his disposal." This occurs in covering letter to copies of the accusations received by G.O.C.-in-C. from Batum.

Military Attache's Minute of 20.12.19. "Yes. He should certainly go to Malta. It will probably be a difficult case in which to get a conviction, but he should in any case be kept a prisoner as long as possible."

Assistant High Commissioner's Minute of 23.12.19. "Concur: this seems very necessary."

H.C. to G.O.C. 24.12.19. Asking that HILMI Bey may be transferred from Batum to Constantinople in custody: for deportation to Malta. Malta refuses to receive any more prisoners. Assistant High Commissioner sends copies of Correspondence to Foreign Office on 21.1.20.

Prisoner's Cash. W.R. 1956. On 7.2.20 a sealed bag of money, the property of HILMI Bey, was handed over by the Deputy Provost Marshal and is now in Chancery safe.

Petitions. W.R. 19156.

1. From Minister for Foreign Affairs on 2.10.18 requesting the transfer of HILMI Bey to the Turkish Court Martial. On 28.2.20 High Commissioner answered in the usual formula.

2. From son, dated 14.2.20. No action.

3. From General Ahmed Hamdi Pasha, President of the Anglophile Society, dated 14.2.20. No action.

4. Petition by Lt. Col. Kiemal of the Armistice Commission dated 15.2.20. "HILMI Bey of Kastamuni was brought from Batum and interned in Arabian Han. He is a retired officer of the Balkan War and was formerly Staff Captain. The reason of his retirement was his opposition to the U.P.C. [C.U.P.] and he was the chief person in Alaskar group. After the Balkan War he went to Anatolia and then to Persia for commercial purposes. . . ." No action.

5. Petition of 10.4.20 asking for return of his money (now in Chancery safe) described as £T. 140 gold and £T. 320 paper and cheque for (?) £T. 2,000. No action.

6. Further petition of 2.6.20 on same subject (17.6.20) drafted letter to Governor of Malta informing HILMI that request can not be entertained until decision of Court is made known).

ACCUSATIONS.

W. 1956. G.O.C.'s 3868 "I" of 11.12.19. On 26.11.19 the Military Governor of Batum wrote that HILMI ABDUL had been arrested on accusations of being concerned in atrocities of Mriandab, Sajbulak and Maragha in Persian Azerbaidjan.

Do. Note by Major Warburton dated 7.10.19. Enquiries made by Major Bryan at Tabriz, Maragha and Mriandab and by Major Warburton at Tiflis and Tabriz. The conclusions to the "Note" are:-

"It is clear that there are good cases against HILMI Bey in respect of his

(a) Murdering at Maragha the two Persian Governors Muhammad Hussein Khan, Acting Governor of Sanj Bulagh, and Seifeddin Governor of Sakhiz.

(b) Burning houses at Maragha and extorting money there.

(c) Extorting money from various persons at Tabriz. All these offences were committed in Persian territory late in 1914."

C. 25. 25.2.20. Notes from information supplied by Mihran Boyadjian late a 1st Class Inspector of the Vilayet of Bitlis and Mossul.

HILMI Bey was in 1914 a retired Staff Colonel, and was sent by the C.U.P. as an undesirable to Mossul. Here the Vali made him Engineer, Public Works Department, at Kirkuk. Towards the end of 1914 Suleiman Nazi Bey, then Vali of Mossul, later Vali of Bagdad, nominated Ibrahim Fezi Deputy for Mossul* and Colonel HILMI Bey of the Public Works Department to take command of the irregular troops on the Persian frontier; Fezi as Chef de Mission and HILMI as Military Commander. (For the career of these two men in Persia see C. 24)

HILMI and Ibrahim Fezi ravaged the district of Urmia as far as Tabriz and massacred a great part of the population without distinction of race or religion. HILMI thus amassed wealth. Later the Commander in Chief Halil Pasha, rewarded him by transferring him as Engineer of Public Works for the Vilayet of Mossul.

In 1915 HILMI Bey accompanied the Vali Haidar Bey (List VII) on three occasions on his expeditions against the Nestorians. On these occasions HILMI Bey had the rank of Officer Commanding Artillery.

In 1917 when Memduh (Malta) was Vali of Mossul; Halil Pasha, Military Commander; Nazim Nazmi (Erzerumli Nazmi) commanding the Gendarmerie, and Nevzade (Malta) Commandant de la Place de Mossul; HILMI Bey was entrusted with the extermination of the men of the Armenian Labour Corps. Of a battalion of 400 there remained 60 to

---

* Bitlissi Ibrahim Fezi also commanded the Gendarmerie in Mossul and was later Mutessarif of Sulimaniya.

80 when the British entered Mossul in December 1918. The balance had been killed by massacre, hunger or sickness.

HILMI Bey himself had five Armenians shot without trial of any sort at Zacho.

Among his lesser crimes was his predilection for sodomy. Armenian boys of 10 to 15 were his victims. Besides this vice there is a notorious case of his rape at Mossul of an Armenian girl from Yalova.

Annexed hereto (Appendix A) is an article which appeared in the Kurd organ "Ginne" of November 20th 1919, signed by Hulmuz Bari and giving an account of the ravages committed by Ibrahim Bey and his "Bimbashi", i.e. HILMI Bey, in the district of Urmia.

5035/A/36. Signed statement of 23.4.19 by Vartan Tekerian of Pera, accusing HILMI Bey of murder near Mossul in 1918. Probably a murder of one of the Labour Corps in May 1918.

Do. Information of 22.4.19 by Yalova people; accusations of theft, rape and murder.

5030/A/21. Simpat Kerkoyan on 19.5.20 in Labour Battalion under Colonel HILMI. Deprivation of food, theft, shootings from May to October 1918. Of 600 men, 100 now alive.

H. 2. Statement made verbally at the High Commission by Shefik Bey, late Kaimakam in the Eastern Vilayets.

I know HILMI ABDUL KADIR personally. He had been a Junior Staff Officer; he got into trouble with the C.U.P. and was exiled to Mossul in 1914. He became engineer to the Municipality of Kirkuk. When in October 1914 Halil Pasha, in command of the expeditionary force crossed into Persia, HILMI ABDUL KADIR and Ibrahim Fezi, Major of Gendarmerie and Deputy for Mossul, were appointed by Suleiman Nazif Bey, the Vali of Mossul, to accompany the force charged with the organization of irregular levees (tchetes) in northwest Persia they were the chief massacrers, HILMI the worst. He became enormously rich as the result of this expedition. He used to boast of the hanging of two Khans at Maragha. He himself told me in Mosul that he had hanged those two big men in order to advertise himself.

He was known in Persia as Erkhan Pasha (Pasha of the General Staff). In the northwest of Persia he is extremely well known for his atrocities and his tyranny. His reputation in Mossul as a debauchee was of the worst.

When I was Kaimakam of Ghevaz I once sent him 400 sheep for his tchetes on his instructions. Later when I was at Ras-ul-Ain, HILMI became Commandant of a Labour Battalion in the Mossul Vilayet. This was a reward for his zeal; he had also affiliated himself to the C.U.P. by then, as I know by a letter HILMI entrusted to one Mehmed Bey, a friend and compatriot of mine, who was to deliver this letter to his (Mehmed's) brother who at the time was Minister of Education.

As Commandant of a Labout Battalion the C.U.P. entrusted him with the disappearance of the Christians composing the Battalion.

N.B. The informant Shefik Bey appeared to be an intelligent man with a wide knowledge of the Eastern Vilayets, he impressed me as one speaking the truth, discursively, and making mistakes as to dates, still the truth as he remembered it. His information is fully borne out by other information on file. He appeared to be dispassionate and to have no grudge against particular persons, only against the C.U.P. Shefik Bey was not reluctant to speak; he is the first Turk or Circassian to come forward.

K. 4. On 26. 2 21 the Patriarchate furnished the following information:-

Colonel ? (adjutant Major HILMI) of the staff, who had been arrested by the British Military Authorities at Batum, and is presently in Malta, was born in the town of Castamouni. Formerly he was an officer devoted to the Hamidian "regime", and at the beginning of the Balkan War, when the star of the Unionists seemed to have declined, he was one of the numbers of the committee of Haliskiaran, a secret committee of officers formed in the army to evict the Unionists. With the coming again into power of the Unionists, after the murder of Nazim Pasha, he was sentenced to degradation and dismissal from the ranks of the Turkish army.

Left without any resources, he sought the protection of Shukri Bey, Minister of Public Instructions, presently also in Malta, whose great influence as a Unionist chief he was well aware of.

Shukri Bey, being a native of the same town of Castamouni, and knowing HILMI well, took him under his protection, and as, at that time, beginning of 1914, his brother-in-law, Suleiman Nazif was Vali of Mossul, he sent HILMI to Mossul, recommending him warmly to Suleiman Nazif. There HILMI won the goodwill not only of Suleiman Nazif, but later on also of Lieut. Colonel Basri Bey (also at Malta).

Having thus made not only his peace with, but also his show of devotion to the C.U.P. chiefs, he was ripe for executing all the dishonest or cruel missions, that would be confided to him.

He was given the "bogus" title of "Engineer of Public Works" of the Vilayet, getting a salary and being thus at the disposal of the Vali.

His misdeeds must be separated into two heading:-
1. Those related to the atrocities on the Eastern Frontier.
2. Those related to the atrocities perpetrated against the Armenians in Mossul.

It is proved now in the documents to be found in the secret correspondence and by cipher telegrams between Suleiman Nazif and the Harbié, that the work of preparing bands for invading the Persian frontier, for exterminating the Christians there, and for preaching the holy war against the "Kiafir" Ententists, had begun long before the entrance of Turkey into the war. In fact these telegrams begin from the 4th of September 1914.

Suleiman Nazif was on of the chief organisers and he had entrusted this kind of work to a native of Bitlis living in Mossul and the worst unionist of the town, Ibrahim Feizi.

On account of his past military career, HILMI was given as a help to Ibrahim Feizi, and when the time came, after the proclamation of the Djehad following the declaration of the war, to go and invade the north-western part of Persia and commit all kinds of atrocities, HILMI was one of the Tchetebashis of Ibrahim Feizi during the expedition which, in the month of December 1914, met with an overwhelming repulse from the Russians.

HILMI, although under a cloud as Ibrahim Feizi was, for his atrocities against Persian governors, managed to escape punishment owing to the protection of Suleiman Nazif and other officials.

His bogus title of Engineer of Public Works of the Vilayet was going to give him the opportunity of showing, some months later, all his capacity for harm against the Armenians.

In the latter half of 1915, when all the poor remnants of the huge caravan of deportees, that could reach Mossul, began to crowd in the town, Lieut.-Colonel Bassri, Nevzade, and the Vali who had succeeded Suleiman Nazif (i.e. Haidar Bey, on Foreign Office List) began to think of the means of exterminating these Armenians.

The means found was to enlist these deportees, starved and nearly dead of exhaustion, from the age of ten or twelve to sixty, and send them to work in the labour battalions for the construction of the road of Zacho. The care of enlisting these Armenians, making them work, or in other words exterminating them through starvation and exhaustion and even very often by direct murder, was entrusted to HILMI, who accepted this task and executed it most willingly. His victims are numbered by tens of thousands. He used also to pick up among the deportees the good looking girls and he carried them to Mossul to be put in the "Lupanars" [brothels] which he had, as Engineer of Public Works in charge of the embellishment of the town, devised in the different quarters of Mossul for the use of the military.

The opening of the "Lupanars" was announced in official communications from the military government of the town. The stories of many of these unfortunate women, thus condemned to the most dreadful degradation and who committed suicide to escape from this earthly hell wherein they found themselves, form another chapter of the heart-rending tales of the deportations which are now falling into oblivion.

This is only one part of the accusations against HILMI. As an acolyte of Basri and friend of Nevzade, he is also responsible in Mossul, for atrocities committed against the Kurds, the Sheik Abdul-Rezak in particular, and also against war prisoners.

His case must be judged with that of Nevzade for his misdeeds in the Vilayet of Mossul. Already in the trial of Nevzade before the first Court Martial his name was always mentioned, and this dossier of the Mossul trial, when consulted, will bring out evidence against him. On the other hand his case is to be judged with that of Suleiman Nazif and Ibrahim Feizi for his misdeeds at the Eastern Frontier, and the consultation of the secret dossier at the Ministry of War relating to the Iran expedition will bring the necessary evidence against.

During all his stay in Mossul, HILMI had never neglected the practice of robberies on a huge scale and at last he returned to Constantinople and established himself as an honest banker. It was after the Armistice when he was engaged on speculations over the exchange between the value of the English pound and Russian rouble, which made it necessary for him to go to Batum, that he was arrested there by the rightful hand of the British Military Authorities and sent to Malta.

The case of HILMI presents another difficulty, as there are two other HILMIs, the one another Colonel **HILMI** Abdul Kadri who also held official posts at Kerkuk in Mossul vilayet and who also played a prominent part in the atrocities committed in the Eastern

Vilayets. Testimonials against these Hilmis are bound to get mixed, owing to the fact that the Turks have not the custom of using family names.

In order to prevent any confusion we will give some particulars about the two other Hilmis, (filed in High Commission).

It must be noted that the HILMI in Malta, whom we have dealt with, is a native of Castamouni. Of the two other Hilmis, the military Hilmi Abdul Kadri is a native of Aintab and the third, a native of Serfidjé.

APPENDIX A

Summary of an article on IBRAHIM FEVZIE BEY, published in the Turkish newspaper GINE, of Thursday, November 20th 1919. Original in K. 4.

BITLISLI IBRAHIM FEVZI BEY, who pretends to be a Kurd, is not known by any one of his compatriots of Bitlis. He was originally a Gendarmerie Captain, and owing to his connection with the C.U.P. he became a Major. When he was named a deputy, he was Gendarmerie Commander at Mossul. Although he was born at Bitlis, he passed all his life in Irak, among the Arabs; so he has absolutely no connection whatsoever with Kurdistan. The actions of this man are a stain not only for Islamism, but also for every other Nation to which he may belong. The only advantage he possesses, is that he applauds to every single crime, considering it to be justice. Thanks to the influence of his post, he perpetrated unreckoned evils to thousands of persons, he used his being a deputy as a profiteering organ, and thus he became the owner of a colossal wealth. He was the C.U.P. chief organ during the War and he was sent as Governor in the Sandjak of SOULEIMANIE in the Vilayet of MOSSUL. There he calls near him the notable Cheikhs of the place, who had a great influence over the different tribes of Persia. Fevzi Bey declares to them that he was named with the duty to suppress the influence of the Russians, and if necessary to occupy the whole of Persia. Hence he proposes that troops be given to him. The Cheiks reply that such a movement towards Persia would provoke great inconveniences. Fevzi Bey gets furious and begins to threaten. So the Cheiks follow him by force and arrive to the Kassaba [small town] of BANA in Persia. There they are received by Mehmed Khan, the distinguished judge of BANA, who gives them a very warm hospitality. Profit-ing of this Fevzi Bey proposes to Mehmed Khan to give him troops. Mehmed Khan con-sidering the great responsibility of such a measure, does not attach much importance to Fevzi Bey's persistency, and even puts off the gathering of the troops. Finally, Fevzi Bey seeing himself found in the presence of a categorical refusal, returns to SULEIMANIE, takes with him a battalion of regular troops and comes back to BANA. The first thing he did was to arrest all at a sudden, Mehmed Khan, whose guest he was for days long, to hang him right away and to confiscate and plunder all his property; he then begins to attack all the surrounding villages and kassabas. Both he and his assistant were finding no more opposition in the execution of their plans. He then proceeds to the Kassaba SAKIZ and he spreads about the news that he arrived with an extraordinary mission by the Kha-lif with an authority to hang in Persia any persons he wished. Thereupon the officials and the people of the district in compliance with their habits, slaughtered hundreds of sheep and cows, in order to appear agreeable to that monster. The latter however got more encouraged by this treatment, and similar to the martyr Mehmed Khan, he decided to do the same thing with Medjid Khan Zade Seifeddin, judge of SAKIZ. But seeing that Seifeddin Khan was richer, more influential and much stronger, he behaved here in a more friendly manner; besides he was rather afraid of the revenge of SERDAR HUS-SEIN KHAN, judge of Savoutchouplak, and chief of the big tribe "Moukeri". They again remain as guests for a few days in the house of Seifeddin Khan and in the mean-time they are preparing for their cursed plans.

Finally they invite SERDAR HUSSEIN KHAN also to Sakiz. Without suspecting anything, they take both of them to the Kassaba of BOUKIAN, and there in cooperation with the other monsters of their band, they shot both of them and they begin plundering all the surrounding villages.

After they perpetrated these two crimes, the Major Deputy with the Commander[*] of the band made up their minds to attack the cities MERAGA and TEBRIZ. So they started and through MEYANDOUAB, they came to MERAGA. On their way they drowned in the river TCHIFELOU all those unfortunate persons who were opposing their plans. They plundered MEYANDOUAB and they killed almost every single man there. Near TEBRIZ they fought with a small Russian detachment, and beating it, they took over 50 loads of precious objects and money, and thus they entered TEBRIZ. Here they began collecting from the people money for the would be needs of the War, but having come to conflict with the Russian forces, they leave the city without doing much.

Thus Major Deputy Fevzi Effendi, became an enemy to both Moslems and Kurds.

---

[*] Hilmi Bey.

EJZAJI MEHMET EFFENDI (MEHMET HASSAN)

Malta No. 2790

Interned at Mudros on 15.3.20; at Malta on 31.3.20.

1. **Appointments**. A notable of Erzinjan and leading member of the C.U.P. committee in 1915. Believed to have been a druggist – Major in the Army prior to 1915; hence perhaps his nickname Ejzaji, chemist.

2. **Lists**. On none.

3. **Arrest**. The British Military Authorities arrested him, as accused of massacre in Erzinjan in 1915, at Batum on 16.4.19. On 22.1.20 he arrived in Constantinople in custody, thence transferred to Chanak and on 15.3.20 sent to Mudros.

4. **Cash found on the prisoner.** On 23.1.20 a sealed packet was handed over by the Military Authorities, said to contain roubles and Turkish gold, which bag was deposited in the chancery safe.

5. **Petitions**. EJZAJI MEHMET being a rich man, with many creditors, 14 petitions had been received on his behalf up to 10.3.20.

W. 2890. 15th. From himself of 17.4.20.

6. **N.B. W.3667.** In the High Commissioner's despatch to Foreign Office No. 1552 of 24.11.20, covering report of special committee, it was recommended that EJZAJI MEHMET be detained and brought up for trial.

ACCUSATIONS.

7. **27.A.12.** The documents sent under cover of G.H.Q letter 'Intelligence' 2888/23 of 9.6.19 to Military Attaché are here summarised:

Cover from Intelligence Transcaucasia signed by Brig-Gen. W. H. Beach, dated Tiflis, 25.5.19. "Attached is a statement of charges against EJZAJI MEHMET of Erzinjan of complicity in the massacre of Armenians:

(a) at or near Erzinjan in May or June 1915.

(b) In the Sansa valley, between Erzerum and Erzinjan about April 1915.

(c) And of violation of Armenian women."

8. **See also para. 21.** Evidence of **Ardachess Lepian,** merchant of Erzinjan, then of Batum. Mentions Memduh and Madjid (both deportees) as the directing Committee. Early in 1915 Enver passed through Erzinjan going to Erzerum. Deportations from Erzinjan began in May, 1915, 20th to 28th May, towards Urfa. Witness saw EJZAJI MEHMET and Memduh on the road towards Kemakh; corpses on the road.

9. Evidence of **Haiganoush Bogossian** of Erzinjan, recorded 19.5.19 at Batum. Saw EJZAJI MEHMET and Memduh last days in May 1915 on road between Erzinjan and Kemakh; EJZAJI MEHMET was wearing military badges and was giving orders. Detail of Kemakh gorge massacre. Witness escaped by shamming death and some months later became a slave in Memduh's house, Memduh's mother being a kind-hearted woman. When in Memduh's house, meetings often took place at which Memduh, EJZAJI MEH-

MET "Defterdar", Halat Bey and the Vali, Tahsin Bey were present. EJZAJI MEHMET had such power that even Memduh was under his orders.

(**N.B.** The "Defterdar" seems to be Madjid Bey, the deportee)

10. **Memduhi Tomassian,** of Erzinjan; recorded 17.4.19 at Batum.

"In 1914 my father and uncle were taken away to Erzerum and hanged by order of EJZAJI MEHMET, Halat and others."

Kemakh atrocities, spring 1915; EJZAJI MEHMET, Halat, Memduh. Always refers to "EJZAJI MEHMET's soldiers"; e.g. they violated 250 women and children.

11. Makruhe Sarafian, 19, or Erzerum. Recorded at Batum on 20.5.19. In May 1915 some 300 families deported from Erzerum. Reached Erzinjan in 8 days without incident. Saw EJZAJI MEHMET first day out from Erzinjan ordering people about. Next day Kemakh massacres.

Thence on to Malatia where arrived about 25% of the deportees who had originally left Erzerum.

"I saw EJZAJI MEHMET again in Sivas: that was when the Russians came to Erzinjan. He rented a house and lived there with his family. I recognised him and often saw him. In Sivas he was engaged in business and did not wear uniform. In Erzinjan he was wearing military uniform."

12. **Khanganie Boyadjian,** 30 of Baiburt. Recorded at Batum on 20.5.19.

Deported from Baiburt to Erzinjan in June 1915. "At Erzinjan we were all assembled on an open space outside the city. There were no Christians left in Erzinjan. At this open space were the chief officials and leading men of Erzinjan, of whom I can only name EJZAJI MEHMET. They collected all the small children and babies and threw them in the river before our eyes. EJZAJI MEHMET sent one of my children to the river and gave three more of mine to other Turks. I have since recovered two of them. EJZAJI MEHMET sent me by a servant to his house. Many young women were taken away like this.

All the remaining males were taken down to the river and shot. Officers came and demanded money of my husband's brother; he had none left and they shot him. When I tried to take his ring from his finger they threatened to shoot me. There were hundreds of Armenians killed that day.

I was kept several days at EJZAJI MEHMET's house. I found there a very beautiful girl aged 20, the daughter of Sarkis Effendi, a rich Armenian of Erzinjan. EJZAJI MEHMET's wife opposed our coming and did not let EJZAJI MEHMET harm us. After some days he took us to a cloth factory where he kept me 14 months. He treated us both as mistresses, keeping us in one room. After one month he sent the girl away as she was always resisting him. I do not know what became of her. He brought another young woman to live in the room – an Armenian girl from the factory.

After two months EJZAJI MEHMET took me to Baiburt to find some money I had hidden there. Knowing I was rich he continually insisted and at last made me tell him of this money. I took out this money and gave it to him, 500 liras and 200 liras worth of ornaments. He kept all this. When he was leaving the city, seven days before the Russians came in, he gave me his decoration and said that whenever I brought it to him he would repay me. This is the decoration (produces a star bearing the inscription, "Ibret, Rahmat, Sidaquat.")

During my stay with him I got EJZAJI MEHMET to recover my little girl for me and I also recovered my little boy – but I kept this from him. When I went to Baiburt with EJZAJI MEHMET I enquired everywhere for my husband but could get no news of him. He had six shops there and a house. These were all taken by the Turks.

When the Russians came to Erzinjan, I went to Erzerum having been over a year in the keeping of EJZAJI MEHMET. I came to Batum a month ago.

13. **Sharan Mateossian**, 24 of Erzinjan. Recorded, Batum 21.5.19.

When the War began I was taken to work in a Labout Battalion at Sansa between Erzerum and Erzinjan. I knew EJZAJI MEHMET. He came several times to Sansa with the Governor of Erzinjan. During the 15 days I was there most of the young Armenians among us were taken away in parties of 15 and 20 with their hands bound and then we heard the sound of shooting. We used to see their dead bodies in the river or near the road on which we were working which was close to the river. More than 3,000 were taken away like this.

14. **Aram Bezigian**, 25 of Erzinjan. Recorded Batum, 21.5.19.

I was taken as a soldier in Erzinjan and sent to the Labour Battalion at Sansa. I knew EJZAJI MEHMET otherwise called MEHMED Effendi. This (on file) is his photo. I saw him 3 or 4 times there in 10 days. He was giving orders to our officers.

The Governor of Erzinjan came to Sansa with EJZAJI MEHMET but it was always EJZAJI MEHMET that was giving orders. Sometimes he wore uniform and sometimes mufti.

15. **Ardashes Kouyumdiyan**, 25 of Erzinjan. Recorded Batum, 21.5.19.

In 1914 I was taken as a soldier. In April 1915 I and 24 others were disarmed and sent to a Labour Battalion at Sansa. Sansa is a valley with a river running through it and we were working on a road beside the river. I was there 8 days. EJZAJI MEHMET and the Governor of Erzinjan came there, and spoke with our officers. After they came, our officers in the morning sent away parties of Armenian labourers as if for other work. Sometimes 20 or 40 or 100 were sent in a day with 8 or 10 "Chetes" as escort. They were taken in the Erzerum direction, i.e. upstream, and we used to see their bodies floating downstream. About the eighth day I and 20 others were taken, 15 Greeks from Sivas, and 5 Armenians. We were taken away some distance to the river bank and stripped and bound and shot down. But before I was bound I escaped and swam the river. I was fired on and thrice wounded, but reached the other side and got to a village where the villagers helped me and sent me to the interior of Dersim. The 20 men with me were killed.

16. **Lieutenant Kalust Sumanian**, of Erzinjan (now ? at Erivan). Recorded at Batum in April 1919.

I have known EJZAJI MEHMET since my childhood. I recognise his photograph.

Before the war when the C.U.P. was organised he had a special office and was the chief representative in Erzinjan. This would be in 1908 when he was a military officer with the rank of Major.

I served in the Turkish Army and in Feb. 1915 was wounded and was sent home to Erzinjan to be treated. When I recovered I was sent to Sansa where Armenians were being used for road repairs. I was put in command. Three Turks were appointed over the men. After a few days EJZAJI MEHMET, Halat and Memduh came to Sansa and had a meeting with the other three and many Turkish troops arrived. I was superseded and sent away. After this the 2,000 workmen were massacred. I saw the dead bodies myself.

17. **Lieutenant Hampartzum Topajian**, (?now in Erivan). Recorded at Batum in April 1919.

I was a teacher, but served in the Turkish Army during the war as an officer. I was in Erzinjan in August 1915, and January 1916. I saw EJZAJI MEHMET there. I identify his photo.

EJZAJI MEHMET was chief representative of the C.U.P. at Erzinjan. He was always meeting the Governor there and was always going to Erzerum. I often saw him with Halat Bey, the Chief of the Committee of Union and Progress, and also with Doctor Behaeddin Shakir who saw him whenever he came from Constantinople. I have often seen this myself. I have seen Halat, Memduh, EJZAJI and the Doctor together often. EJZAJI MEHMET commanded the gendarmes in the neighbourhood and the troops of the "Teshkilat mahsusse" (the special organisation for the massacre of Armenians).

I saw many dead bodies in the Erzinjan district, I heard an order given by the Town Crier in Erzinjan in August that everyone was to bring in Armenian babies protected by them. These were put in carriages and taken to the river and thrown in there. EJZAJI MEHMET supplied carriages for this purpose.

At Sansa I saw many Armenians massacred. I actually saw live Armenians buried.

18. **Dr. Yekishe Mugurdidian of Erzerum**. Recorded at Batum in April 1919.

I was a Captain in the Turkish Medical Service and was serving in the hospitals at Erzinjan. I recognise the photograph of EJZAJI MEHMET. I saw him working in charge of the troops in May 1915 when the massacres took place in the Kemakh valley.

19. **5027.A.12**. Enclosure to letter No. 2888/23 I. dated 15.12.19 from General Officer Commanding-in-Chief, Army of the Black Sea.

Extract of letter No.G.10/55 dated 26th November received from Military Governor, Batoum.

"EJZAJI MEHMET ("Pharmacist" MEHMED) arrived in Batoum by sea on 16th April, and was immediately arrested by Capt. Leahy, Intelligence Officer, on information of his having been concerned in the massacre of Armenians at Erzinjan in 1914 and 1915. Evidence was collected against him mainly in Batoum. He was shown to be a revolting scoundrel who had taken a leading part in the deportation of some thousands of Armenians from Erzinjan in the spring of 1915, and in their wholesale massacre in the neighbouring Kemakh valley. Copies of statements of witnesses, amounting to a complete brief for the prosecution of EJZAJI MEHMED, were sent by Intranscau to G.S. 'Intelligence' Constantinople in May or June last; and on this evidence his conviction on charges of wholesale murder would be certain: but the witnesses must certainly scatter and disappear in time, and their evidence melt away. In any case his indefinite detention in Batoum without a defininte charge being preferred against him is undesirable. The High Commissioner, Constantinople in his No. 5027/A/17 to the General Officer Commanding-in-Chief – Q. (forwarded with G.H.Q. 'I' No. 2888/23 'I' Constantinople, to collect enough of the witnesses whose evidence against him has been recorded; but I fear this will not always be possible."

20. **5027.A.12**. Signed statement, dated 5.8.19, by Mrs. Tacouhi Parseghian, c/o Dikran Yaldizjian, Direklet Arassi No. 28, Nouri Osmanie.

The witness at the time, i.e. June 1915, was living with her husband at Rafie, one hour distant from the city of Erzinjan. She describes EJZAJI (Chemist) MEHMET as "Captain, Military Chemist". Her statement is as follows:-

"During the Armenian deportation my brother-in-law, Abkar Effendi, had handed over the chemist shop together with his warehouse to EJZAJI MEHMET, one of the notables (Eshrafs) of Erzinjan. Later EJZAJI MEHMET had my brother-in-law exiled and murdered. My husband and myself were at that time in Rafie, an hour distant on horseback from Erzinjan; from there we were exiled and during this time my husband, Sarkis was killed. The chemist shop and warehouse at Erzinjan had a value at that time of 2,000 pounds Turkish gold. The household furnitures together with some more valuable drugs kept in the house, which had a value of 750 pounds Turkish gold, have been actually robbed by EJZAJI MEHMET.

21. **5027.A.12**. Signed statement, dated 6.8.19, Ardachess H. Lesbian, a merchant of Erzinjan, now living c/o/ Dikran Tanelian, Pershembe Bazar No. 28, next to Tijaret Han, Galata. Witness was in Erzinjan until 28.5.15. His statement is as follows:-

"EJZAJI MEHMET, being the leader of C.U.P. organised a special committee composed of Halat Bey, Medjid Bey, and Mehmet Bey, the Commandant of Gendarmerie in order to organise the Armenian massacres and deportation. He, under his own organization, caused the Armenians to be killed at a place about two hours from the town of Erzinjan. According to information I got from the Kurds, EJZAJI MEHMET caused Dr. Der-Stepanian, an important merchant to be murdered in order that he might take the whole property into his own possession. After I had been exiled, the said EJZAJI MEHMET seized our factory of Gingham (Manbussa) and also the whole of the contents, yarns, looms, etc., which at that time had a value of 4,000 pounds Turkish gold."

22. **5027.A.12**. Letter addressed to the High Commission, dated 25.7.19 from Kourkin A. Kellerian, late a merchant of Erzinjan now living at Dekirmen Sokaghi No. 1 Selamsiz, Scutari.[*]

"Some time ago, EDJZADJI MEHMED EFFENDI of Erzinjan has been arrested in Batoum by the English Police.

He is charged with participation in the Armenian massacres and the looting of their property, as testified and confirmed by the survivors in the presence of the Police Chief in

---

[*] The original letter appears in French and has been translated into English –WCB.

Batoum. The General Office in Tiflis has set of a special mission to study the case of EDJZADJI MEHMED EFFENDI.

Two months ago, when I was in Tiflis, I supplied all the information I had upon the orders of Col. Saunders, to Major Vendersend who was at the head of that special mission. I also presented my right to the 3,000 Turkish pounds that MEHMED EFFENDI owed me and which represented the value of the merchandise I had deposited with him in the eventuality of deportation.

According to my information, the police has confiscated the sum of 500,000 Nikolai roubles that MEHMED EFFENDI carried with him. Besides this sum, MEHMED EFFENDI has a great deal of money in the banks as well as much property. He is a man who made his fortune with the property stolen from deported Armenians, although some merchants have put in a demand claiming that the confiscated money belongs to them. I am sure that this is a plan aimed at misleading the judges.

I am ready to present to you the evidence that the 3,000 Turkish Pounds belong to me and I hope that the prisoner EDJZADJI MEHMED EFFENDI will admit my right to it.

Please inform me if you are willing to return to me the confiscated money as my state of refugee has left me, in the last four years, penniless. . . ."

23. **5027.A.12**. Signed statement, dated 10.7.19 by Madame Hadji Osanna Babiguian of 22 Rue Tourna, Pancaldi, making a claim for goods usurped by EJZAJI MEHMET from her father Meguerditch of Erzinjan.

24. **do**. Signed statement, dated 10.7.19, by Noig Der Stepanian of 12 rue Elma Daghi, 4th floor of the Appartement Nomico, Pancaldi, claiming LT. 20,000 gold, property usurped from his father, a rich merchant of Erzinjan.

25. **5027.A.12**. Further signed statement, dated 18.7.19, by Noig Der Stepanian, as follows:[*]

"EDJZADJI MEHMED EFFENDI was a simple tradesman in Erzinjan with a capital which at first amounted hardly to 500 Turkish Pounds. Having entered into the Committee of Union and Progress, he made a fortune of some 1,500 Turkish Pounds before the war. During the first four years of the war he increased his fortune to well over 300,000 Turkish Pounds. He was the closest friend of Djevat Bey, Commander of the troops in Constantinople. The Mutessarif of Erzinjan in 1915, Memdouh Bey, always acted upon the advice of MEHMED EFFENDI. According to the evidence of Armenians in Erzinjan, he was a very powerful man in that city. During the war, he went to Batoum and backed by Vehib Pasha, appropriated and brought back a large quantity of merchandise. A man, who during fifty years had hardly made a fortune of 1,500 Turkish Pounds, managed to make, during the four years of war, a capital of half a million Turkish pounds.

On April 24, 1915, I was exiled from Constantinople to Kenghri. While I was still there, my father and my entire family were deported, on the 18th of May, 1915, from Erzinjan. On the 28th of May, I received a cable from my father, sent from Eguine, which is a small

---

[*] The original letter appears in French and has been translated into English –WCB.

town some two days' distance from Erzinjan, telling me that he had put our shop, our home and all the furniture, in the trust of EDJZADJI MEHMET EFFENDI.

After 101 days of exile I escaped and returned to Constantinople. I appealed to him but he answered that the entire contents of our shop were hardly worth 1,000 Turkish pounds. I did not say anything to him, as the situation of the Armenians was very critical at the time.

My father was the biggest trader in manufactured goods, in Erzinjan, and our commerce was 150 years old. Our transactions in the Erzinjan and Constantinople market confirm that MEHMED EFFENDI has appropriated 20,000 Turkish Gold Pounds from our fortune. A certain Iydi Hodja of Erzinjan has revealed to Mr. Arshag Surmenian, a native of Erzinjan, that MEHMED EFFENDI has sold to the people of Kelkid (a small town near Erzinjan) the merchandise in the shop of Sarkis Der Stepanian, my father, for the sum of 18,000 Turkish Pounds."

26. **5027.A.12**. Signed statement dated 18.7.19, by [PENIAMIN] Metchiguian of Scutari, Idjadie-Arabzade Rue Berberoglou 18, claiming Lt. 2,000 gold on account of goods usurped from his brother; also accusing EJZADJI MEHMET of being the instigator of the deportation and murder of his two brothers, Nichan and Sebouh.

27. **do**. Signed statement, dated 18.7.19, by Ardaches Pachalian of Erzinjan, now in 103 Rue Tchimen, Pancaldi, claiming Lt. 15,000 gold on account of goods usurped from his father Hadjibab and his brother Sarkis in May 1915 at Erzinjan.

28. **5027.A.33**. Long detailed account of the massacres in and near Erzinjan in the early summer of 1915, by Kourkin Kellerian, now living at Rue Yoghourthane No. 22, Tarla Bachi, Pera, and dated 2.9.20. The witness was at the time acting as orderly to a Turkish officer in the Army.

As organisers of these officially conducted massacres (probably tens of thousands massacred) the witness mentions the Governor of the sanjak, Memduh Bey (at Malta); the deputy for Erzinjan, Halet Bey; the chief of Gendarmerie Ismail Hakki Bey; the C.U.P. Secretary, Madjid Bey (at Malta) and EJZAJI MEHMET, whom he saw once. The last is also mentioned again on page 16 of report.

Appendix "I"

*

No. 783/W.2890
British High Commission, Constantinople, 3rd June 1920
[Stamp of receipt: June 14 1920, 6369]
Enclosure.

My Lord,

I have the honour to forward, for Your Lordship's consideration, a copy of a letter dated 17th April 1920, which has been received from one, EDJZADJI MEHMET Effendi now detained at Malta.

2. Edjzadji Mehmet was arrested, as he states, by the British Military Authorities at Batoum on the 16th April 1919, on a charge of massacring Christian Ottoman subjects in the sandjak of Erzinjan in April, May and June 1915. In January 1920 he was transferred to Constantinople, thence to Chanak, thence to Mudros, and finally interned at Malta on 31st March 1920.

3. The charge of massacre was carefully enquired into by a qualified officer at Batoum, where a number of ocular witnesses were residing at the time. The charge has since been fully corroborated and further substantiated here.

4. On the prisoner's arrival here on 23rd of January 1920, his property in roubles and Turkish gold was handed over to me by the Military Authorities in a sealed bag, which is now lying with original seals intact in the Chancery safe in this High Commission.

5. As regards the petitioner's first question in the last paragraph of his letter: "to supply me with information regarding my possessions", I would submit that I may be instructed whether there is any objection to the petitioner being told that his money, as sealed by the Military Authorities in Batoum, is in safe custody here. As regards his other property, coal, etc., I suggest that the petitioner may be told that he might best apply to his commercial associates.

6. As regards the petitioner's second question: "to safe-guard my rights regarding the loss I had to sustain", I consider that the petitioner, having been arrested in time of war on a prime facie charge of massacre, will have no claim to compensation against His Majesty's Government whatever may be the eventual result of his arrest.

7. As the question involved is one of wide application and one of importance, I venture to submit this specific instance for Your Lordship's consideration.

I have the honour to be,
My Lord,
Your Lordship's obedient servant,
[Signature of Admiral de Robeck]
HIGH COMMISSIONER.

---

* F.O. 371/5089

Polverista. Malta. April 17. 1920.

To His Excellency,
The British High Commissioner,
Constantinople.

Your Excellency,

On April 2, 1919, I had left for Batoum on board "America", a steam-ship under the Russian flag which I had rented, after finishing all the necessary formalities and getting special permission from the British Port Authorities in Galata. I arrived there on 17 April. Three or four hours after my arrival I was arrested by the British Police. This arrest can only be the result of insinuations and intrigues against me arising merely out of commercial competition. I have been known for a long time to be engaged in honest business. My accounts could easily be investigated. When I was arrested, I was even withheld two hours' permission to settle my accounts. Therefore, I am in need of information upon the following subjects:

1. What has become of my merchandises, of coal in value of 2,000 pounds and transport payments amounting to 16,000 pounds in which my associates are also interested?

2. In my bag which I left in charge of Mr. Fostropoulo and of which the British Police took the key. There were Russian roubles (Nicola and Kerenski), to the amount of 500,000 as well as 300 Turkish pounds. What has become of the bag and money?

3. As a result of this illegal and unjust act, applied without any reason at all, I have lost my whole capital. My Russian money, having then a value of 20,000 pounds do not amount to more than 3,000 pounds with the present exchange rate.

I humbly request Your Excellency to give the necessary orders: (1). To supply me with information regarding my possessions, (2). To safeguard my rights regarding the loss I had to sustain, and (3). To investigate my case as soon as possible in order to set me in liberty as soon as possible.

Your Excellency's most obedient servant,

(SGD). EDJZADJI MEHMED EFFENDI.
2790.

---

* F.O. 371/5089

Appendix "I"

REFET PASHA (ALI REFET PASHA)

Malta No. 2792

Interned 13.4.20.

Appointments. Brigadier General on Retired List and Military Governor of Samsun District during the winter of 1916-1917. (There is also a Refet Bey, defender of the Gaza who also held a high military appointment at Samsun in 1918). ALI REFET Pasha is said to have succeeded Avni Pasha, transferred to Smyrna for not carrying out the order re the Greek deportations.

Lists. On List III, i.e. his name was suggested for arrest by Mr. Ryan to Grand Vizier on 27.3.19, but nothing was done. On List VI, i.e. his name was approved by Assistant High Commissioner, for arrest on 8.9.18, but the list remained in abeyance.

On List VII, i.e. on Foreign Office List.

Trial by Turkish Court Martial. C.26. On 3.3.20 REFET Pasha was condemned in contumaciam to two years' imprisonment and a fine of Lt.5,000. The charge is given as "accarpement".

Arrest. He was arrested by the British Military Authorities at Bostandjik on 18.3.20.

Domicile. Hadji Badem, Kadikeuy.

Petitions. None to date. (21.2.21)

N.B. In High Commissioner's despatch to F.O. 1552/W.3667 of 24.11.20, covering report of special committee, it was recommended that REFET Pasha should be detained at Malta until brought up for trial.

ACCUSATIONS.

I.C. 22/39 in R. 2908. "Born in Constantinople. He obtained his brevet of Staff Captain and was sent to Yemen. Later he was attached to the Corps sent to Albania to suppress that Albanian insurrection. He took part in the Balkan War and was promoted Major; at the second phase of the Balkan War he was appointed Base Commandant (Istamboul Merkez Commandant) by Mahmud Shevket Pasha and was holding this position when the latter was murdered. Later he was appointed Commandant of the 11th Division and took part with his Division at the Dardanelles during the general war. Later he was in Palestine and Syria. He is compromised in illegal profiteering and in deportations and was sentenced to two years' imprisonment and to the payment of Lt. 5,000. During Ahmed Izzet Pasha's Cabinet he was General Commandant of the Gendarmerie. Since the Armistice he is reported to be connected with the financing of the Nationalist movement." Control Officer, Samsun, reports him as a most dangerous man.

4029/A/26.

a. Unsigned fiche through Captain Perring on 1.8.19. He burnt over 80 villages "de mon arrondissement" and hunted out all the inhabitants during the height of the winter, January to March 1917. The greatest of criminals.

b. Letter from President of Armenian Council per Captain Perring on 31.7.19. REFET was not in Samsun during the Armenian deportations. The Greek deportations began shortly after his arrival. "Il a mené une vie princière, louche et mystérieuse avec les femmes et les filles, don't les mères et pères étaient expulses." His accomplices were Behaeddin Bey and Major Ihsan Bey, latter President of Court Martial in 1917.

(Ihsan Bey on Lists III and VII not yet arrested 2/21. Behaeddin Bey was the Inspector of Police).

5029/A/3. This is merely a long list of the perpetrators of the Samsun and Baffra atrocities and the names of certain available witnesses, dated March 1919.

A.H.C.'s Minute of 15.8.19.   5029/A/6. "He should be", i.e. noted for listing.

B. 2. Denunciation of 10.3.19 by Stylianos Papadopoulos. Atrocities at Samsun and Baffra, November 1916 to May 1917. REFET Pasha ordered:-

a. The evacuation of 220 Greek villages inhabited by 80,000 people.

b. Of these, he burnt 178 villages.

c. Deportation, commencing 27.12.[16], of all notables from Samsun, Baffra and Tcharshamba.

d. In conjunction with Major Ihsan Bey, President of the Court Martial, he hanged 200 Greek villagers on the charge of being deserters.

e. Of the deportees, 75% perished.

Address of witness: Haviar Han 81, Galata, tobacco merchant.

B. 3. Denunciation of 10.3.19 by Georges S. Mavrides, tobacco merchant, then of Tokatlian's Hotel, Pera. As above B.2.

C.26. "Renaissance" of 6.3.20, quoting from "Proodos" gives detailed accusation against REFET. Also against: Mustafa Bey, Mutessarif of Samsun; Baha, C.U.P. Delegate; Hussein Husni, Chief of Police, Samsun; Sabri, Police Commissioner; Major Ihsan, President of the Court Martial; Osman Bey, Mayor.

In these deportations some 30,000 Greeks perished, i.e. 60%.

Les Persecutions de l'Hellenisme en Turquie (1914-1918). This book was issued in 1919 by the ecumenical Patriarchate. It contains several pages dealing with the deportations, etc., of Greeks in 1916-1917 from Samsun, Baffra, Sinope and Amassia. The book is of no value from a juridical point of view.

5029/A/18. Statement by Mgr. Yervanos Caravangellis, Greek Archbishop of Samsun and Amassia, dated 1.8.19 re burning, without orders, 80 villages early in 1917 etc.

Captain Perring adds that much evidence can be had from the Phanar.

R. 2908. Letter from Mgr. Germanos Caravangellis, Orthodox Metropolitan of Samsun and Amassia, dated Constantinople 20.3.20, informing High Commissioner of REFET Pasha's arrest on 18.3.20. "Reconnu (a Bostandjik) par un émigré grec de Samsoun", urging the maintenance of the arrest and engaging to place at our disposal an infinite number of witnesses.

Greek H.C. of 3.4.20. Statement by the Comité des Originaires du Pont, describing the deportations under REFET's orders.

5029/A/20. Statement by Hagop H. Gueuvchenian; mention only of REFET Pasha.

This intelligent witness who was in Samsun throughout the Greek deportations is available.

G.10. In Patriarchate's detailed list of September 1920, the name of REFET Pasha is duly noted.

On 2.12.20 the Armenian Patriarchate supplied the following Biographical notice concerning REFET Pasha:

"REFET Pasha is of very poor extraction being the son of a Tartar refugee in Constantintople. After passing through the Preparatory school he went to the Kuleli Military School and from there to the Harbié, from where he graduated with the grade of a Staff officer. He was secretly affiliated to the C.U.P. and after the Constitution his promotion was very rapid. When Mahmud Shevket was killed, he was the Military Commandant of Stambul.

During the War he was commanding a division in Tchanak Kalé and afterwards he was sent to Samsun as Military Commandant. During his stay there he committed the worst persecutions against the Christian element and issued an order for the immediate deportation of the Christians on the 27th of December 1916.

All the Christian population of the littoral, from Samsun to Baffra, was evicted from their homes within two or three days. No mercy was shown by him, even the sick and the new-born children were deported.

Of this population of 40,000 nearly the whole died on the way from exposure and starvation in the cold winter. He had the villages, more than 100, burned. All the property of the Christians in these villages and in the town of Samsun was plundered.

Allied inspectors who went to Samsun after the Armistice have been able to ascertain these facts, and the Greek Metropolitan, Monseigneur Yermanos is the chief witness against REFET Pasha.

REFET Pasha was rewarded by the C.U.P. by being called to a more important military post in Syria.

He resigned after the Armistice and established himself in Constantinople as a merchant in order to put to some use the wealth he had gained.

He was brought to trial about the 9th March 1920, before the First Court Martial, presided by Essad Pasha, but this Court Martial decided to try him only for unlawful speculations on sugar, remaining deaf to the other more terrible accusations brought against him.

The British Military Authorities put a stop to this parody of Justice by arresting and sending him to Malta.

MEHMET KIAMIL

(Native of Tripoli in Barbary)

Malta No. 2795

Interned 11.5.20

Appointments. Journalist at Mossul in 1917 and 1918. An Employee at the Pera Municipality in 1920.

Lists. On List VII (additional). Despatch to F.O. No. 702/R.2178. of 16.5.20; copy the same date to General Officer Commanding-in-Chief.

Arrest. Arrested by Allied Police in Galata on 20th March 1920. (charged by Aharon Varjabedian and Mr. Tchakirian for participation in Mossul atrocities in 1917 and 1918 in complicity with General Halil Pasha (VII); Nevzade Bey (Malta) and Colonel Adbul Hilmi Kadir (Malta).

Petitions.

W. 2178. From wife of 15.4.20.

5027.A.26. From wife of 11.8.20.

ACCUSATIONS.

W. 2178.

A. Letter of 22.3.20 from Mr. M. Boyadjian, late a 1st class Inspector in the Vilayets of Mossul and Bitlis.

 a) Spy in Bagdad.

 b) Informer at Mossul, resulting in death of many.

 c) Informed against the baker Serope and his sister, as in British service; their execution.

 d) Because of him, no one could communicate with Mgr. Zaven, Armenian Patriarch, then exiled in Mossul.

 e) As editor of Government Newspaper; propagandist.

 f) Imprisonment of Mihran Boyadjian at MAHMET KIAMIL's instance; also imprisonment of Mr. Ackdjian, dragoman of the American Consulate at Alexandretta.

B. Statement by Aharon Varjabedian on 20.3.20, at the High Commission:

MEHMET KIAMIL was editor of the paper "Agence" in Mossul, notorious for its anti-Armenian propaganda. He was then in the service of Halil Pasha and Nevzade Bey. He denounced Armenians unless sufficiently paid not to do so. He was rationed and paid by the Turkish Authorities. Responsible for many deaths.

5027.A.26. Further signed information of 22.3.20 by Aharon Varjabedian of Ortakeuy, 17 Rue Kachadie. MEHMET KIAMIL was wont to hand over his victims to Hadji Tchaoushe for dispatch. Ravishing Armenian girls his habit. Occular witness. Gives names of Leon Abadjian and Haroutioun Paboudjian, now living in Ortakeuy Berracks, as other witnesses available.

5027.A.26. Minute of 24.8.20 by Sir H. Lamb:

" . . . There is a prima facie case . . ."

MUSTAFA RESHAD BEY

Malta No. 2798

Interned 31.5.20

Appointments. Director of Kismi Siyassi (Political Section) of the Prefecture of Police from May 1915, when he succeeded Madji Bey sent to Smyrna on a police mission, to the middle of 1917, when Tevfik Hadi Bey (No. 2682) succeeded him.

In 1917, 1918, he was successively Mutessarif of Aidin, of Changri and of Bolu. In 1918 he returned to Constantinople and engaged in commerce wherein he lost the money he made during his time as a police official.

At the Armistice he held the post of secretary of the Tailors Guild (Terziler Djemiti).

Lists. On Lists II and VII, supplementary, i.e. Mr. Ryan suggested his arrest to the Grand Vizier in February 1919. Again his name was included in the supplementary list of persons recommended by High Commissioner for Scheduling for Prosecution, which list was sent to the Foreign Office on 16.5.20.

Arrest.

A. By Turkish Government on 16.3.19. on charge of "exile and torture". Released (on bail) in October 1919 without previous reference to the High Commissioner.

B. By Allied Police on 29.4.20.

Petitions.

1. From Dr. Frew, undated (probably July 1919): RESHAD treated British subjects with consideration.

2. From the same dated 3.8.20.

3. From the same dated 30.4.20.

4. From the same dated 8.5.20.

5. From the same dated 8.6.20.

(All the above refer to the good treatment meted out to Dr. Frew himself by RESHAD.)

6. Petition of 30.6.20 signed by Mons. D. Arditti, Mons. Emile de Cand, and Mons. Joullie.

ACCUSATIONS

A. 5035.A.60. Signed statement by Shavarsh Missakian, Editor of "Djagadamart." Dated 25.7.20. (For copy see Appendix A).

B. do. Patriarchate report, dated 24.7.19. It was on his instigation that the C.U.P. decided to deport all Armenian batchelors and all Armenians native of Anatolia. It was he who sought them out by means of his agents, Topal Nureddin, Arab Enver, Papaz keze, Sheriff of Kassim Pasha and the renegade Hidayet.

The full and entire responsibility for these persecutions rests on MUSTAFA RESHAD and the Director of the Judicial Section, Tevfik Hadi Bey (Malta No. 2682).

C. do. Signed statement by Mr. Tchakirian, dated 1.8.19. Mr. Tchakirian is an official of the Armenian Patriarchate attached to the High Commission.

Organiser of the deportation of the intellectual youth of Constantinople and of their subsequent extermination. Over 300 publicists, priests, politicians, deputies, professors and scholars were exiled by him to Changri and Ayash (Angora Vilayet) and murdered. With the connivance of his chief Bedri Bey (one of the Principal Eight, now in flight) RESHAD submitted some of the Armenians living in Constantinople to torture. RESHAD's accomplice in these tortures was Ali Riza Bey, of the Police, now a merchant here. RESHAD had such influence that he could arrest Armenians after they had been acquitted by the Court Martial; he then had them murdered on the road on the other side of the Bosphorus.

The following are among the survivors of his atrocities:

Orchak [*sic,* Arshak] Moucheghian, Samuel Dikran, Baghos [*sic,* Boghos] Vartanian, Armenak Chaldjian, Madame Sona Tarpinian, Shavarsh Missakian, Samuel Tarpinian, Iknadios Andronian, Khossrov Babayan, Mlle. [M]eguerditchian, etc.

Of the 250 Armenians arrested on 24.4.15 only some 20 are now alive.

D. 5035.A.60. Petition, undated (1919) from Houliane and Hripsime Sarkissian asking for the restitution of three cases of books, the works of the murdered historian, Karekin Hajag, impounded in August 1916.

E. Do. Signed statement by Sdepan Damlayan, dated 8.8.19. he then being employed in the Armenian-Greek Section [of the High Commission]. Generally corroborating above listed statements. In particular the torturing and deportation of the writer's cousin's husband. Also refers to the tortures applied by RESHAD to Armenians at Ismidt. RESHAD had made a study of the Armenian language and of their political desires etc.

F. Do. Signed statement by Arshag Madatian of 5 Rue Fouroun, Feridis, Pera, dated 3.5.20, describing the tortures he was submitted to in May 1916 by RESHAD BEY.

G. Do. Signed statement, dated 20.4.20, by M. Sahakian. He has a copy of the secret order given to the escort by RESHAD to murder him and his fellow prisoners in January 1917. The writer escaped and finally reached Bagdad in British occupation.

H. Do. Signed statement by Arshak Mousheghian, c/o "Djagadamart", dated 3.5.20. Tortures whilst in prison at Stambul in April 1916. Suicide of his fellow prisoner, the engineer Mihran Jezairjian after torture.

I. Do. Signed statement, dated 2.5.20. by Dicran Vartanian of Rue Idjadie, Altoun Bakal, Pancaldi, describing the tortures he was submitted to in June 1916.

C.11. Name duly listed in Patriarchate's detailed list of massacres of September 1920.

Patriarchate's biographical notice and information, communicated on 22.12.20 as follows:

MUSTAFA RESHAD was born in Constantinople at Ortakeuy. After having followed the course of primary Turkish schools, in Constantinople, Erzinjan, etc. where his father acted at times as Governor, he was sent to the Mulkié, the Turkish normal school in Constantinople, and graduated from there in 1902.

In the Mulkié he had followed the courses of Armenian language and improved the knowledge of Armenian he had acquired when he was a child in the Armenian Provinces, and he kept improving it every time he had an opportunity to do so.

He had also learned English. After having finished his studies, he was for a time a functionary in the "Hazinei Hassa", (Sultan Hamid's private treasury). At that time living in Boyadjikeuy, he used to give, in the evenings, Turkish lessons to Armenian neighbours, and in return study Armenian from them. That explains his thorough proficiency in Armenian.

He numbered himself among the secret members of the Young Turk Party, and when the Constitution was proclaimed he came out as an enthusiastic member of the C.U.P. The Hazinéi Hassa in its old organization having then suppressed, the C.U.P. nominated him, on account of his knowledge of Armenian, Kaimakam in one of the Kazas round the town of Erzerum in 1910.

The Mutessarif of Bayazid, in the Vilayet of Erzerum, having then been killed in an affray, he was sent to Bayazid as Mutessarif per-interim. That region being in a very unsettled condition he was also himself wounded some time after, and he came back to Constantinople, with an aureola among members of the C.U.P. as an exceptionally deserving and energetic functionary, when his real qualifications seem to have been only to be as harsh as possible and to be deprived of all those diplomatic of tactfulness which make peace prevail among the different ethnic elements inhabiting those regions.

In Constantinople he remained quiet, at least apparently, during all the time that the C.U.P.'s power seemed to follow a downfall, i.e. during Kiamil Pasha's Cabinet and the beginning of the Balkan War; but in 1913 after the murder of Nazim Pasha and the rise again of the C.U.P. his fortunes became brighter, for he was the brother-in-law of Sezai Bey, a leader of the C.U.P.

Having the renown of knowing European languages, English and French, and being possessed of a thorough knowledge and conviction of the Turkish point-of-view of settling the Armenian Question, and all other questions arising from the strong influence acquired by European subjects in Turkey, he was entrusted in 1913 with the reorganization of the political department of the Police Administration.

A kind of Ministry with three departments in it was formed, with his collaboration and according to the plans that he had presented.

1. The Kismi Idaré (dealing with cases depending on the Police Tribunals.)
2. The Kismi Adli (dealing with cases depending on the law courts.)
3. The Kismi Siassi (dealing with cases considered as having a political character.)

This Kismi Siassi was itself divided into three sections:

1. Section dealing with Moslems.
2. Section dealing with Christians and Jews.
3. Section dealing with Foreigners.

This Kismi Siassi like the other departments had a mudir at its head, and this mudir was at the same time director of its first section, and as mudir had of course the higher supervision of the second and the third sections.

Bedri Bey was at the head of this powerful police organization, and he had MUSTAFA RESHAD as his assistant. The Kismi Adli department was entrusted to Tefik Hadi and Kismi Siassi to a certain Hadji Bey.

When Turkey entered into the war, a special council of terrorism was formed under the presidency of Talaat. The members of this council were:

1. Djambolat Bey: Prefect of the town, and Director of Public Security, i.e. Chief of the Police and Gendarmery organization for the whole of the empire.

2. Bedir Bey: Minister of Police for Constantinople.

3. Murad: Assistant of Bedri for administrative cases.

4. MUSTAFA RESHAD: Assistant of Bedri for political cases.

5. Tefik Hadi: Assistant of Bedri for legal cases.

6. Aziz Bey and Essad Bey: Chiefs of departments of the Public Security.

This council was planning all the measures of terrorism which were put into execution either by the Police Ministry, through the agency of Bedri and his assistants, or the Direction of Public Security, through the agency of Djambolat, Aziz and Essad, to whom must be added the special mission of Ali Munif acting as delegate of Talaat, of whom he was the councillor (musteshar) at the Ministry of the Interior. The members of this council, which was executing itself orders coming from the C.U.P. Central Committee, bear all the responsibility for the thousand and one acts of exile and murder on the highways of so many innocent Armenians, in which must be specially remembered the group of 220 Armenian notables, arrested in Constantinople at the end of April 1915.

The deportations or exile and confinement of the Allies' Subjects to the Interior or to the "danger-zones" of Tchanak-Kalé, were also executed by the orders of this council, Bedri and his assistant MUSTAFA RESHAD had the special mission of preparing the lists.

At the beginning of 1915, Hadji Bey, Director of the Kismi Siassi, was sent to Smyrna on a policy mission for the execution of which he could not come to an agreement with Rahmi Bey, the Vali of Smyrna. Owing to this failure he was discharged from his post and MUSTAFA RESHAD took his place at the head of the Kismi Siassi.

At this post until the middle of 1917, with his assistant Ali Riza, one of the worst types of Turkish police functionaries he committed all the abuses that were possible, arbitrary arrests, false accusations, sending thus a great number of men to exile and death on the highways of Anatolia. He has only to show to his credit some cases of rescuing people who had been falsely denounced by others and exiled and who had found the means of having themselves recommended to him and were able to propitiate him. For the greater part of this period, his private domicile was at Ortakeuy.

Towards the middle of 1917, after the departure of Bedri, from the Police Ministry, and when the persecutions against the Armenians had slackened MUSTAFA RESHAD was discharged from his post of Mudir of the Kismi Siassi and nominate mutessarif of Aidin. He went there but remained in Aidin only six days, as he was after this short period sent away by Rahmi, the Vali of Smyrna. He was later nominated mutessarif of Tchanguiri, but he refused to go there and was nominated mutessarif of Bolou. He went there but remained only a short time as the habits of omnipotence he had acquired during his administration of the Kismi Siassi were making his administration intolerable to the Moslem inhabitants. Returning to Constantinople he tried in 1918 to occupy himself in commercial pursuits but succeeded only in losing his dishonest earnings acquired during the time that he was in the Police Administration.

Finally he was obliged to accept the post of secretary of the Association of Tailors (Tarziler Djemieti), an employment which he held at the Armistice.

Additional. It must be noted that during his stay at the Police Ministry, either as assistant of Bedri or as Director of the Kismi Siassi, MUSTAFA RESHAD had the direct supervision of the work of torturing and robbing the Armenians who were gathered in Constantinople and sent in exile, to be for the most part murdered on the highways of Anatolia.

The Police Council of Terrorism, presided by Talaat, then Minister of the Interior, had decided that all the unmarried Armenians residing in Constantinople, who were natives of the provinces, should be exiled.

Bedri and MUSTAFA RESHAD with a great number of assistants, among whom the police functionaries Ali Riza, Mehmed Abeddine, and Eumer, are the most conspicuous, had taken in charge this huge work of noiselessly deporting thousands of men from Constantinople.

I. The unfortunate deportees were brought to the Police Ministry everyday in the latter half of 1915 by hundreds and they were deprived of all their valuables for which no receipt of any kind was delivered to them.

The jewelry and the money thus plundered was shared among Bedri and MUSTAFA RESHAD, who had the lion's share, and Ali Riza, Mehmed Abeddine, Eumer, and other minor satellites.

Apart from that when the deportee was a merchant Ali Riza, or one of the other trusted agents, were sent to plunder the shop.

It was much later on that the organization of the Emlaki Metrouké (abandoned property), for the property of Constantinople deportees was set up, and until that time Bedri and MUSTAFA RESHAD were left free to plunder at leisure the property of the deportees.

Ali Riza, Mehmet Abeddine and Muamer are actually in Constantinople, and if arrested and severly cross-examined and confronted before and Allied Tribunal, with the few survivors, who having passed through the clutches of MUSTAF RESHAD, have come back, would be obliged to own to their robberies or turn king's evidence against MUSTAFA RESHAD.

II. Many of the deportees were submitted by the orders of MUSTAFA RESHAD to tortures, flogging etc. at the Police Ministry. But the greatest sufferings endured by the deportees took place at their first station at Ismid. That task was confided to Ibrahim, Director of Prisons at Ismid, who was obeying MUSTAFA RESHAD's orders. The latter had made at the beginning of the deportations a special journey to Ismid in order to plan things with Ibrahim.

The first floggings were inflicted in the Armenian church of Ismid, by Ibrahim under the direct supervision of MUSTAFA RESHAD.

APPENDIX A

MUSTAFA RESHAD BEY.
Written statement by Shavarsh Missakian, Editor of 'Djagadamart'.

1. WHAT IS THE POLITICAL SECTION OF THE PREFECTURE OF POLICE?

After the declaration of war against the Entente Powers in 1914, the Turkish Police Direction was raised to the rank of a Ministry, without the name of one, but with full rights, de facto and de jure. Bedri Bey was the chief. The Direction had three branches: **Political Section** (Kismi Siassi), **Administration** (Kismi Idari), and **Judicial Matters** (Kismi Adil). As a matter of fact, the Political Section was the only one having the largest possibilities and empowered with extraordinary rights. MUSTAFA RESHAD BEY was its omnipotent chief until 1917, when he was succeeded by Tevfik Hadi Bey. The routine of arresting, deporting and exterminating the leading Armenians of Constantinople was entrusted to him, because he was well acquainted with Armenian life, he had some knowledge of the language, and was clever enough to be known as an Armenophile.

2. THE ACTIVITY OF RESHAD BEY.

The Political Section had at its disposal large sums of money from the Secret Funds of the Home Ministry and from the Service de la Sureté, spies and agents of various nationalities, interpreters and "Affairistes" of every type were paid and favoured in this Section, which was the nightmare of every honest citizen during the spring of 1915, when it began its activity on a large scale. RESHAD BEY was king in his own house. He had ready-made lists of Armenians of some influence, compiled by his agents since the beginning of the war; he had them classified and, on the night of 11/24 April 1915, by his orders 220 well known Armenians were arrested and exiled to Ayash and Changri (Kastamouni). This was only the signal. The same order was telegraphed to the provinces. The ghastly work went on according to the plans and caprices of RESHAD BEY, who was powerful enough to overlook the sentences of acquittal delivered by the Court-Martial of Stambul (Divani-Harb). As a matter of fact, he was the right man in the right place; and when his chief Bedri Bey, Director of Police and Vali of Constantinople, was appointed Vali of Aleppo, he remained in office and was as independent as ever. He used to say that anyone arrested and set free by his orders was free for all time, but those favoured with the highest protection could not escape persecution against his will. He spoke the truth. The police were under the orders of RESHAD BEY for all purposes of political persecution. He himself gave and signed the instructions concerning the treatment of Armenians arrested and sent to the provinces under escort. And not ten per cent of those exiled remained alive beyond Ismid. The latest instance of this fact is the case of the Actor Ashod Madatiantz and his comrades. These eight persons arrested on suspicion and confined for ten months without trial, were finally set free by the Stambul Court Martial on January 3rd, 1917, but RESHAD BEY had them exiled to Brussa in chains and under police escort. On their way from Brussa to the interior, one of them succeeded in obtaining the written instructions given by RESHAD

BEY and they learnt that they were to be killed en route. (Three of these persons are now in Constantinople and can give evidence).

PERSONAL EXPERIENCES.

After the general arrests and the extermination of the principal Armenian intellectuals of Constantinople, I was one of those few spared by a miracle. Being on the list of RESHAD BEY, I was obliged to hide myself for one year (1915 April – 1916), RESHAD revenged himself by arresting and exiling (through his chief agent, Ali Riza Bey) my father who was cruelly beaten in his presence and sent to Konia and then on to Deir Zor. In my hiding place, I was in communication with our Committee at Sofia, sending them correspondence, reports etc. about the Armenian massacres, military operations, anti-Entente activity etc. (Many of my reports are published in Bryce's "The Treatment of the Armenians in Turkey" Blue Book). A Bulgarian named Vladimir Dimitreff, and agent of Tufenkdji Eff. and RESHAD BEY, formally attached to the Bulgarian Consulate, had abused the confidence of a friend, and, on the promise of assuring my escape to Bulgaria, had me delivered into the hands of RESHAD BEY on the 26th March 1916. (I was in prison and got my liberty after the Armistice, through the British Embassy, kind care of Commander Heathcote-Smith). Confined in the Police Direction for three months, I was always in chains by order of RESHAD; and Bedri Bey was the first Turkish official to beat me in the presence of RESHAD, on the second night of my arrest. RESHAD used every kind of Turkish torture to get my confessions as an Editor, Revolutionary leader and Ententist agent. Being driven to despair, I threw myself from the second storey of the Political Section meaning to kill myself, and had my leg broken. I was in bed for three months. Many Armenians were arrested and exiled after this event. Three girls and 16 men were sent to the Court Martial to be tried with me (June 12, 1916). The trial came to an end in January 1917 and I was sentenced to hard labour for five years, with two comrades, the other prisoners being set free. (RESHAD dissatisfied with this sentence, had those released again arrested and exiled, 9 of them to Brussa etc. with private instructions, as related above). One of the girls, my sweetheart, who had been in prison for 40 days, died after her acquittal, in consequence of the anguish she had been through.

Now I am the only one surviving from a generation of poets, political and social leaders, physicians and journalists exterminated according to the lists and orders of MUSTAFA RESHAD BEY. Perhaps he has been of some good to me, that is after my attempt at suicide and after my revelations of falsification of some documents used against me, but it would be a crime to forgive the wanton annihilation of more than 150 intellectuals – a generation of 50 years – of which RESHAD BEY was the leading spirit and the organisator. RESHAD's responsibility is not less than that of Talaat, Djemal, Bedri, Dr. Nazim etc.

Pera, July 25, 1920.

Victims of RESHAD BEY, now in Constantinople ready to furnish any evidence you desire:

1. Ashod Madatiantz, Actor Pera.
2. Dikran Boghos Vardanian, Pera.

3. Miss Siranoush Meguerditchian, Pera.
4. Mrs. Nazik Sabandjian, Pera.
5. Arshag Moosheghian, Pera.
6. Mrs. Vergine Khacherian, Pera.
7. Samo (A Syrian), Stamboul.
8. Meguerditch Hopiguian, Pera.
9. Vartouhi Hopiguian, Pera.

HADJI AHMED of Kildik or Kil Kidik (Sivas Vilayet)

Malta No. 2799

Interned 31.5.20

Appointments. C.U.P. Delegate at Sivas. Merchant and Government contractor.

Lists. On List VII. Supplementary. Name placed on list after arrest. This list was to Foreign Office under cover of High Commissioner's despatch No. 702/R.2718, dated 16.5.20.

Arrest. Appears to have first been arrested on 17.4.20 on an Italian ship bound for Black Sea ports. Released next morning he was again arrested on 21.4.20 by the Allied Police on the information of Sahag Kenarian.

W. 2178. The G.O.C. was requested by H. C. to maintain the arrest on 28.4.20.

N.B. A Hadji Ahmed Effendi was arrested by the Turkish Authorities on 21.8.19 and released by order of the C.M. towards the end of 1919.

Petitions. See below under head of 'Defence'.

N.B. In High Commissioner's despatch 1552/W.3667, dated 24.11.20 and covering report of special committee, it was recommended that HADJI AHMET be detained until brought up for trial.

ACCUSATIONS.

5029/A/34.

A. Signed statement of 21.4.20 by Sahag Kenarian of Sivas, now of Kara Deniz Appts., Galata. Describes HADJI AHMET's atrocities committed in the neighbourhood of Sivas 1916-1918, when a 'C.U.P.' member "Was the actual Governor of Sivas". Killed 120 Armenians in an hour, watch in hand etc.

B. Signed statement of 21.4.20 by Elmass Bosmadjian of Lloyd Triestino, Galata; late of Tuzasar. Eye witness of his Tuzasar atrocities. Killed four relatives before witness' eyes.

C. Signed statement of 21.4.20 by [Iskuhi Asadourian] of Davshanli; now of Lloyd Triestino, Galata. Atrocities at Gamiss; nailing horseshoes on to Armenians.

D. 21. Statement by Sahag Kenarian (vide supra).

a) Eyewitness of Ishkan Keui (near Sivas) massacres by HADJI AHMET as Tchete Bashi; acting under the orders of Muammer, the then Vali of Sivas.

b) Escaped from another massacre near Zara, 2 days [before] Bairam.

A Turk, Hadji Omar, informed witness of HADJI AHMET's intended departure from Constantinople on his return to Sivas. See Appendix A.

D. 21. Statement by a Turk, Hussein bin Mehmed who denounced HADJI AHMET. Witness was in Constantinople throughout the War.

D. 21. Further statement of above under his real name Omar Osman, (HADJI OMAR).

DEFENCE.

5029.A.34. 1st petition. Defence of Mustafa Said Effendi of 23.4.20 through General Officer Commanding-in-Chief on 4.5.20 says that HADJI AHMET has been denounced to the British by two adversaries in business, Talaat and Twefik. Adds names of Greek and Armenians as witnesses for the defence. Also says that HADJI AHMET has rendered various services to the Greek and Armenian Patriarchates and has received certificates from them for his charitable deeds.

21. 18/5/20. Statement by Kyrillos Kalaydjoglou, Greek Ottoman, late of Sivas, business friend.

Statement by Mustafa Said (vide supra), his uncle who saw him off to the ship.

21. 20/5/20. Statement by Christaki Kalaydjoglou, Greek Ottoman subject of the Ottoman Civil Service, cousin to Kyrillos Kalaydjoglou.

21. 20/5/20. Statement by M. Bostanjoglou of Sivas. He arrived in Constantinople from Sivas in December 1919. Known HADJI AHMET for the last nine years. During the war HADJI AHMET was a building stone contractor and later meat contractor to the Government. HADJI AHMET supplied meat (?) gratis to the Christian orphanage. Further statement describing the Armenian Passport syndicate in Galata.

5029.A.34. Petition (direct to High Commissioner), dated Malta 10.6.20 from HADJI AHMET.

His is an uncommon blackmail case, the British Authorities the dupes. Says that on 17.4.20 he was denounced by an Armenian of Kemis, in the district of Kotsh-Hissar, Sivas Vilayet, on board a steamer bound for Samsun. This Armenian was a member of the "Passport Syndicate". He was released by a British Officer. Another Armenian of Mris, on behalf of the Kemis one, then threatened him as a massacrer unless he paid up. He refused to be blackmailed with the result that he was rearrested.

Assistant High Commissioner 22.7.20: No action.

3rd Petition. 5029.A.34. Petition dated 8.9.20 through Governor of Malta on 10.9.20 again asserting his arrest due to professional blackmailers. Assistant High Commissioner on 23.9.20: No action.

APPENDIX A.

I am a native of Sivas. When the war broke out in November 1914 they took me as a soldier. I was attached to the Labour Battalion. One day a few Armenian soldiers and I were detached from the battalion to go to the village of Ishkhan Keui, half an hour's distance from Sivas, to fetch wood which came from the demolition of Armenian houses. We arrived at the village and found all the Armenian houses demolished so we took all the wood and loaded them on the carts to bring to Sivas. Ten minutes' distance from the village we met about 50 Armenians each 2 tied together. I saw with my own eyes HADJI AHMET directing his men – numbering 8 to 10 – to fire on these helpless Armenians. I also saw with my own eyes the fall of some of them; without stopping on the spot to see the final result, we hurried back to Sivas.

I knew this Ahmed before the war as a cattle collector. Then the deportations order came, the Vali of Sivas, Muammer Bey ordered this AHMET and some other C.U.P. leaders to visit Armenian villages and collect all the valuable and moveable properties.

After the deportation of the Armenian population of Sivas I was deported with the remaining Armenians to Zara, 15 hours' distance from Sivas. From there we were conducted to a dense forest where the Turkish gendarmes tied us 2 by 2 and began to shoot us. I managed to escape and came to Constantinople after several years of wandering about.

AHMED has acted as Tchete Bashi. I have never seen him in uniform but I have seen him with rifle and crossed cartridge belts.

It was AHMED who killed the above referred 50 Armenians just 2 days before the Turkish Bairam as a token of the sacrifice of their feast.

I could identify HADJI AHMED in any number of men. In April 1920, Hadji Eumer informed me of the intended flight of HADJI AHMED KELDIKLI; and while AHMED in company with Bostandji Oglou were engaged in loading their merchandise on board a ship for Samsun thence to Sivas, I applied to the British Police who gave me two policemen to help me. We went on board and I found this monster and pointed him out to the British Police. AHMED was accompanied by his nephew who had lately come from America, and was taking the goods with him to Sivas. Bostandji Oglou who had a very big share in the above mentioned goods tried to interfere through Kalayjoglou to get him rid of British custody. Bostandji Oglou who is thus losing his invested money, for the nephew of AHMED has taken the goods to Sivas and has sold it with big profits without paying a penny to the partner of HADJI AHMED viz. Bostandji Oglou. It is therefore well understood that the latter is trying hard to save AHMED in order he may be able to get his share from the goods sent to Sivas. Bostandji Oglou was great friend of AHMED and the latter has helped him in many ways during the war at Sivas.

(SD) SAHAG KNARIAN.

Address: Mirjan Charshi No. 71.

MUSTAFA ABDUL HALIK BEY

Malta No. 2800

Interned 7.6.20

Appointments. Vali in Bitlis, March 1914 to September 1915. Under Secretary of State, Ministry of Interior. Vali of Aleppo October 1915 to April 1917. A brother-in-law of Talaat.

Lists. His name appears on lists VI and VII (List VII is the Foreign Office List).

Arrests.

A. He was arrested by the Turkish Government on 9th March 1919, not at our suggestion. The charge was murder.

On the Turkish prison list of 7th February 1920, he is stated to have been released on bail; date not given, (probably some time between 20.9.19 and 7.2.20.)

B. He was again arrested by the British Military Authorities on or about the 14th May 1920.

Petitions. None to date, 25.2.21.

N.B. In High Commissioner's despatch No. 1552/W.3667 of 24.10.20 covering report of special committee, it was recommended that he be detained at Malta until brought up for trial.

ACCUSATIONS.

5027/A/20. Through Mr. Ryan on 19th September 1919. MOUSTAFA ABDUL HALIK, Vali of Bitlis, took part in the councils held at Erzerum to decide on the deportation and massacre of Armenians. These councils were presided over by Dr. Behaeddin Shakir, delegate of the central C.U.P. (one of the Principal Eight); other members were Tahsin Bey (a deportee), Vali of Erzerum; Muammer (a deportee), Vali of Sivas; Djevdet (a deportee), Vali of Van.

5030/B/10. On Sept. 26th 1919, Mrs. Sophie Varjabedian, a Bitlis refugee then at Haidar Pasha, c/o Rev. B. Bedrossian, Bible House, Constantinople, writes accusing MUSTAFA ABDUL HALIK, Vali of Bitlis of having had carried away under his personal superintendence the safe from the American Mission in Bitlis. The safe contained her money and jewellery. Miss Chane [Shane], now at Erivan, reported this to Mrs. Varjabedian. She asks for the restoration of her property and gives a list.

Assistant High Commissioner approved the suggestion of making enquiries at the United States Embassy but there is no record as to whether any action was taken.

5031/A/6. Name merely appears on a Bureau d'Information Armenian List of 30.12.18, as then Vali of Aleppo, in connection with Marash massacres.

5035/C/178. On June 7th 1919, Mrs. Ahisag Ahet Ahlahadian writes, through the A.C.R.N.E. (American Committee, Relief in the Near East), saying that she is a Protestant Syrian of Bitlis and that all her relatives have been massacred in 1915 in Bitlis in spite of the fact that she had paid the Vali, MUSTAFA ABDUL HALIK, to the extent of Lt. 541 gold.

5035/48.

A.   Account by Sympat Kerkoyan of crimes committed by MUSTAFA ABDUL HALIK at Bitlis in 1915. Starving prisoners; massacring 200 to 300 at a time outside the town; ravishing and massacring the women; extortion and looting of Armenian property. The stench from putrefying bodies was so bad that Buheddin, Director of Health, Bitlis, received orders to have the bodies incinerated. Buheddin was in Aleppo in 1918.

B.   Also murder of Djerdjis Kerkoyan, brother of Sympat after MUSTAFA ABDUL HALIK had extorted his fortune on promising to spare his life.

C.   MUSTAFA ABDUL HALIK replaced Bekir Sami Bey (the 'good' Vali, now a prominent Nationalist) at Aleppo on 4.10.15. There he gave orders for the deportation and killing of Sympat Kerkoyan. Thanks however to Hadji Yehia Galib Bey, the defterdar, (now defterdar of Kastambol) Sympat reached Mossul alive. The above per Mr. Rizzo on 16.10.19.

5030/A/21. Statement of Sympat Kerkoyan, merchant of Bitlis dated 19.5.20.

Bitlis May 1915 atrocities. Massacre of Kerkoyan's family; wife and three children; three brothers and their families.

Kerkoyan's deportation to Mossul by the Vali of Aleppo; MUSTAFA ABDUL HALIK, end of 1915.

N.B. Another statement by Kerkoyan appears above: 5035/48.

Renaissance 1.2.19. Account of Bitlis atrocities by an eye-witness, Mrs. Vartuhi Nahabedian. Deportations began in July 1915, commencing with the outlying Armenian villages. Formation of Tchetes recruited from Kurds and Turks. Tortures and burnings alive, hangings and crucifixions. The 'cleansing' of the town of Bitlis of Armenian males within a fortnight. Ravishing and massacre of the females Arapou-Tzorand at Tzag-Kar etc. Principals in these atrocities: The Vali Djevdet (deportee Vali of Van; Halil Pasha, the General and uncle of Enver (escaped from Seraskerat prison in August 1919); and Turkhan Bey, Commissioner of Police.

Renaissaince 25.6.19. M. Mihran Boyadjian's account of MUSTAFA ABDUL HALIK's complicity in the murder of the deputy Vramian on the road to Diarbekir from Bitlis, between Garzan and Bechiri-el-Modine, April 1915.

'Treatment of the Armenians'. Pages 80-97 give accounts of what took place in the Vilayet of Bitlis in 1915 during the tenure of office of MUSTAFA ABDUL HALIK.

Page 80. The chief Armenian centres were: the town of Bitlis; the town and villages of Mush; and the semi-independent highland community of Sassun.

"The extermination of the Armenians in these three places was an act of revenge for the successful resistance of the Armenians of Van and the advance of the Russian forces to their relief (April, May 1915). There was no pretence here of deportation and the Armenians were destroyed, without regard for appearances, by outright massacre, accompanied in many cases by torture." (Viscount Grey of Fallodon).

Page 83. Number of Armenians estimated to have been killed in Bitlis Vilayet is 150,000.

Page 89. Wounding of Dr. Knapp in Bitlis and death in Diarbekir.

Page 95. Massacres of Mush directed by Djevdet Vali of Van, General Halil Pasha, MUSTAFA ABDUL HALIK, Vali of Bitlis and Servet Bey, Mutessarif of Mush. (Servet now believed to be dead). Mush massacres began on 11th June 1915.

Les Massacres d'Arménie, Dr. J. Lepsius. Pages 128 et seq. refer to events in the Vilayet during MUSTAFA ABDUL HALIK's tenure of office. No specific crime mentioned.

B. 34. Report on MUSTAFA ABDUL HALIK's activities in the matter of the Sassun, Gardjgan, Seghere atrocities and murder of the Deputy Vramian, in conjunction with Nazim Nazmi, Commandant of Gendarmerie.

Also mentions the deportations from Aleppo to Der-Zor.

29.5. 20. Statement by Miss Ziazan Vartanian, now of Pera. Kaliondji Kuluk, Rue Enli Youkoush No. 5. Daughter of late Rev. Hatchik Vartanian of Bitlis; pastor of the Protestant Community, speaking in fluent English. Statement made at the British High Commission.

"I have been at the American College at Harput from 1912 to 1919. My father went to MUSTAFA ABDUL HALIK to protest against the method of deportation and to beg for the safety of those who had taken refuge in the American buildings at Bitlis. On June 22nd 1915 my father was arrested by the Police and sent by the Vali just after my father's interview with him. My father was the first Armenian to be imprisoned. Ten days later my mother, who carried his food for him, was told he was no longer in the prison; he has not since been heard of. The presumption is that my father was killed on the tenth day of his detention; many say he was burnt in the prison yard.

He never had any connection with political societies. My mother died two months later. I know Miss Shane of the American Mission at Bitlis. She was there all through the massacres; she left in November and came to Harput. She is today at Alexandropol, Caucasus. She is an eye witness of much that happened in Bitlis. Practically no men are left alive.

E. 2. Statement by Minasse Avedissian, Veterinary Colonel on retired pay, as to the murder of his son, Dr. Berdj Minasse Avedissian who was on the Medical Staff of the 36th Division. Dr. Avedissian was murdered in Bitlis by order of MUSTAFA ABDUL HALIK (apparently) and Colonel Yussuf Zia. Informant gives his address.

5018/24 18.8.20. Free translation of alleged copy of an official telegram from Talaat to MUSTAFA ABDUL HALIK.

"No. 830. 12.12.16. Collect and afford maintenance only to the orphans who are unable to recollect the terrors to which their parents were subjected. Send away the others in caravans." Telegram signed on receipt by MUSTAFA ABDUL HALIK, Vali of Aleppo.

Memoirs of Naim Bey. p. 11. "The Government . . . dismissed Bekir Sami Bey and sent in his place MUSTAFA ABDUL HALIK BEY (October 1915) who was already won over to their purpose. This man was an enemy of the Armenians and tried to crush out the whole Armenian race. The orders sent by him to the Deportation Committee

(Shukri Bey, deportee, and Djemal Bey (?) C.U.P. Secretary) are so ruthless that one can hardly explain them.

Minister of Interior's permits to remain were disregarded by MUSTAFA ABDUL HALIK, Vali of Aleppo, to Ali Suad Bey, Mutessarif of Der Zor. (Ali Suad held this appointment up to 1916), when he was dismissed.) No date is given to the following telegrams:

"It is contrary to the sacred purpose of the Government that thousands of Armenians should remain at Ras-ul-Ain. Drive them into the desert."

To which Suad Bey answered:

"There are no means of transport by which I can send the people away. If the purpose which you insist upon is slaughtering them, I can neither do it myself nor have it done."

MUSTAFA ABDUL HALIK BEY sent this telegram of Suad Bey's to the Ministry of the Interior (Talaat Pasha) and added the following report on Suad Bey:

"December 23rd 1915. We understand from the deputy of the general overseer of the Deportations Committee (i.e. Abdullahad Nuri Bey, whose surrender by the Turks the High Commissioner sought to obtain in November 1920) that the Armenians who have been sent to Ras-ul-Ain are still there and have built themselves good houses and established themselves comfortably, and that the person who is protecting them and allowing them to settle down is the Governor of Der Zor, Ali Suad Bey.

In spite of having written again and again that the crowding of Armenians in a small but locally important town like Ras-ul-Ain and the making of excuses such as the lack of the means of transport, and so forth, for keeping them there lays a great responsibility on us, yet we have seen no result. The partiality which Ali Suad Bey has shown for them and the protection he has extended to them have reached amazing proportions. According to what we hear he dresses and looks after some of the Armenian children himself, and he weeps and mourns with them over the sufferings of their parents. In this way the Armenians sent in that direction are enjoying a very happy existence and they are indebted for this to Ali Suad Bey.

But as the continuation of this state of things will cause needless delays in the transport of deportees from Aleppo, we are addressing Your Excellency on the matter, begging that you will make all necessary arrangements."

(SG) MUSTAFA ABDUL HALIK
Governor-General (Vali)

P. 27. Description of Ras-ul-Ain massacres. "The order for these criminal deeds at Ras-ul-Ain was given directly from Aleppo. The order was given to the Chiefs of the Guard. Some of them came to Aleppo and had interviews with MUSTAFA ABDUL HALIK" . . .

P. 52-64. "A cipher-telegram from the Ministry of the Interior addressed to the Government of Aleppo. From interventions which have recently been made by the American Ambassador of Constantinople on behalf of his Government, it appears that the American Consuls are obtaining information by secret means. In spite of our assurances that the (Armenian) deportations will be accomplished in safety and comfort, they remain unconvinced. Be careful that events attracting attention shall not take place in connection with those (Armenians) who are near the cities and other centres. From the point of view of the present policy it is most important that foreigners who are in those parts shall be persuaded that the expulsion of the Armenians is in truth only deportation. For this reason it is important that, to save appearances, a show of gentle dealing shall be made for a time and the usual measures be taken in suitable places. It is recommended as very important that the people who have given such information shall be arrested and handed over to the Military Authorities for trial by court-martial."

Minister of the Interior

TALAAT

"November 21st 1915, P.S. Without mentioning the cypher-telegram see the Director. Are there really such meddlesome people? In accordance with the order of the Committee, let the operations conducted there be a little moderate. To the Representative of the General Committee."

Governor General

MUSTAFA ABDUL HALIK

"A cypher-telegram from the Ministry of the Interior sent to the Government of Aleppo (No. 745)."

"Dec. 11th 1915. – We hear that the correspondents of Armenian newspapers travelling in those parts have faked some letters and a photograph showing certain criminal actions. which they have given to the American Consuls. Arrest and destroy such dangerous persons."

Minister of the Interior

TALAAT

The following cypher-telegram further demonstrates the anxiety of the Government:

"No. 809.

"To the Government of Aleppo.

"Dec. 29th 1915. – We hear that there are numbers of alien officers on the roads who have seen the corpses of the above mentioned people (the Armenians) and are photographing them. It is recommended as very important that those corpses should at once be buried and not left exposed."

Minister of the Interior

TALAAT

"No. 502.

"To the Government of Aleppo.

"Sept. 3rd 1915. – We recommend that the operations which we have ordered you to make shall be first carried out on the men of the said people (the Armenians) and that you shall subject the women and children to them also. Appoint reliable officials for this."

Minister of the Interior
TALAAT

"No. 537.

"To the Government of Aleppo.

"Sept. 29th 1915. – We hear that some of the people and officials are marrying Armenian women. We strictly prohibit this, and urgently recommend that these women be picked out and sent away (to the desert)."

Minister of the Interior
TALAAT

"No. 691.

"To the Government of Aleppo.

"Nov. 23rd 1915. – Destroy by secret means the Armenians of the Eastern Provinces who pass into your hands there."

Minister of the Interior
TALAAT

"No. 820.

"To the Government of Aleppo.

"Jan. 4th 1916. – It is decreed that all Armenians coming from the north shall be sent straight to their place of deportation, without passing through any town or village on the way."

Minister of the Interior
TALAAT

A cypher-telegram sent from the Government of Aleppo to the Government of Aintab.

"Jan. 11th 1916. – We hear that there are Armenians from Sivas and Kharput in your vicinity. Do not give them any opportunity of settling there, and by the methods you are acquainted with, which have already been communicated to you, do what is necessary and report the result."

Governor General
MUSTAFA ABDUL HALIK

"From the Government of Aintab.

"To the Government of Aleppo.

"An answer to the cypher-telegram of Jan 11th 1916.

"Jan. 18th 1916. – It has been ascertained that there are about 500 people from the said provinces in the vicinity of Roum Kalé, which is under our jurisdiction. The Kaimakam of Roum Kalé reports that most of them are women and children, and that, in accordance with the methods with which the Turkish officials are acquainted, communicated to them earlier, these women and children have been sent under Kurdish guards, with the understanding that they are never to return."

Governor AHMET

"No. 603.

"To the Government of Aleppo.

"Nov. 5th 1915. – We are informed that the little ones belonging to the Armenians from Sivas, Mamuret-ul-Aziz, Diarbekir and Erzerum are adopted by certain Moslem families and received as servants when they are left alone through the death of their parents. We inform you that you are to collect all such children in your Province and send them to the places of deportation and also to give the necessary orders regarding this to the people."

Minister of the Interior
TALAAT

P.S.   See the Chief of the Police about it.

"The Representatives of the General Deportations Committee,

"Governor General

MUSTAFA ABDUL AHLIK".

"To the Government of Aleppo.

"Sept. 21st 1915. – There is no need for an orphanage. It is not time to give way to sentiment and to feed the orphans, prolonging their lives. Send them away to the desert and inform us."

Minister of the Interior
TALAAT

"To the Government of Aleppo.

"Jan. 15th 1916. – We hear that certain orphanages that have been opened receive also the children of the Armenians. Whether this is done through ignorance of our real purpose, or through contempt of it, the Government will regard the feeding of such children or any attempt to prolong their lives as an act entirely opposed to its purpose, since it considers the survival of these children as detrimental. I recommend that such children shall not be received into the orphanages, and no attempts are to be made to establish special orphanages for them."

Minister of the Interior
TALAAT

"No. 830.

"A cypher-telegram from the Ministry of the Interior addressed to the Government of Aleppo.

"Collect and keep only those orphans who cannot remember the tortures to which their parents have been subjected. Send the rest away with the caravans."

Minister of the Interior
TALAAT

"No. 853.

"A cypher-telegram from the Ministry of the Interior addressed to the Government of Aleppo.

"Jan. 23rd 1916. – At a time when there are thousands of Moslem refugees and the widows of our martyrs[*] are in need of food and protection, it is not expedient to incur extra expenses by feeding the children left by Armenians, who will serve no purpose except that of giving trouble in the future. It is necessary that these children be turned out of your vilayet and sent with the caravans to the places of deportation. Those that have been kept till now are also to be sent away, in compliance with our previous orders, to Sivas."

Minister of the Interior
TALAAT

"To the Government of Aleppo.

"Collect the children of the Armenians who by order of the War Office, have been gathered together and cared for by the military authorities. Take them away on the pretext that they are to be looked after by the Deportations Committee, so as not to arouse suspicion. Destroy them and report."

Minister of the Interior
TALAAT

"No. 544.

"Cypher-telegram from the Ministry of the Interior to the Government of Aleppo.

"Oct. 3rd 1915. – The reason why the sanjak of Zor was chosen as a place of deportation is explained in a secret order dated Sept. 2nd 1915 No. 1843. As all the crimes to be committed by the population along the way against the Armenians will serve to effect the ultimate

---

[*] The Turks call their soldiers fallen in the War Shekid [sic, Shehid], or martyr.

purpose of the Government, there is no need for legal proceedings with regard to these. The necessary instructions have also been sent to the Governments of Zor and Ourfa."

Minister of the Interior
TALAAT

"To the Government of Aleppo.

"Sept. 16th 1915. – It was at first communicated to you that the Government by order of the Jemiet (the Ittihad Committee) had decided to destroy completely all the Armenians living in Turkey. Those who oppose this order and decision can not remain on the official staff of the Empire. An end must be put to their existence, however criminal the measures taken may be, and no regard must be paid to either age or sex nor to conscientious scruples."

Minister of the Interior
TALAAT

"No. 762.

"To the Government of Aleppo.

"Answer to the telegram of Dec. 2nd 1915.

"Dec. 17th 1915. – Communicate to those who wish to save themselves from the general deportations by becoming Moslems that they must become Moslems in their places of exile."

Minister of the Interior
TALAAT

H. 2. Statement made at the High Commission by Shefik Bey, ex-Kaimakam in the Eastern Vilayets: -

Extract. ". . . I have said above that the Kaza of Bulanik (Bitlis Vilayet) in 1918 was denuded of its agricultural population, which means there were no Christians left. It had been a wonderfully fertile and rich district with a population of about 20,000 Christians. The responsible agents for the massacres and deportations are: Essad Bey, Kaimakam of Bulanik; Vali ABDUL HALIK; Servert Bey, now dead, Mutessarif of Mush; . . ."

XIII & XIX. In Armenian Patriarchate's detailed list of September 1920 the name of MUSTAFA ABDUL HALIK is duly noted under the headings of "Vilayet of Bitlis" and "Vilayet of Aleppo".

K. 2. Extract from Patriarchate report of 26.2.21, on Suleiman Nazif, Vali of Mossul to December 1914: -

"Suleiman Nazif charged the worst Unionist of the town, a native of Bitlis named Ibrahim Fezi, to organise the bands of Teshkilati Mahsoussé. This Fezi with his bands of Brigands went through the sanjak of Hekkiari slaughtering the Armenians and Chaldeans and burning their villages. He was devastating the Christian settlements on one side, when Djevdet and MUSTAFA ABDUL HALIK were doing the same thing in the other part of Hekkiari."

BASRI BEY, Lieut. Colonel

Malta No. 2801

Interned 7.6.20

Appointments. Chief of Staff to Halil Pasha, XVIth Army Corps 1915-1918. Chief of the 1st Section (Milt. Movements) at the War Office 1919-1920.

Lists. On List VII, supplementary. List sent to F.O. under cover of High Commissioner's despatch No. 702/R.2178 of 16.5.20.

Arrest. By British Military Authorities on 24th May 1920.

Domicile. House of his father-in-law Djevad Pasha at Nishan Tash Doutlouk Sokak.

Petitions.

5040/272. 1st Petition of 31.5.20.

W. 2178. 2nd Petition of 12.6.20.

Do. 3rd Petition of 28.6.20. – from wife

Do. 4th Petition of 12.8.20. – from wife

5035.A.85. 5th Petition of 6.8.20. – direct from him

ACCUSATIONS.

5035.A.85. Report by Mihran Boyadjian of 3.4.20.

a) Responsible for outrages on Kut Prisoners.

b) Responsible for the famine in Mossul Vilayet, by which 60,000 persons perished.

c) Participated in secret councils held by Halil Pasha uncle of Enver; Vali Memduh; Nevzade, Commandant de la Place, Mossul and Nazim Nazmi, Commanding Gendarmerie 1918.

d) In league with Kemalists, Kadri Bey of the Intelligence and Mrizafer Bey, 1920.

N.B. (Mihran Boydjian is an ex Inspecteur Civil de 1ière Classe. He was in the Eastern Vilayets in 1917, 1918 and has a wide and accurate knowledge of events in Mossul, Bitlis and Van. Well known to the High Commission for his reliability and probity.)

C. 1. Report by Mihran Boyadjian of 23.1.20 being a copy of his evidence before Turkish Court Martial on 3.5.19. Mention only of BASRI BEY in Mossul. September 1917-1918.

E. 10. Patriarchate Report No. 1 of 8.9.20.

In Mossul Vilayet deportations and massacres were undertaken by the Military Forces and Gendarmes under the command of Halil Pasha. Halil Pasha's Chief of Staff at the time was Lieut. Col. BASRI BEY. Working under BASRI BEY were Capt. Nevzadé Bey (a deportee, see his dossier) and Hilmi Abdul Kadir (a deportee, see his dossier).

Hitherto BASRI BEY has been protected by his father-in-law Djevad Pasha, late Minister of War and an organiser of the Milli Forces. (Arrested by General Officer Commanding-in-Chief on 16.3.20). This efficient protection accounts for the fact that BASRI BEY was not brought before the Court Martial at that time that his two subordinates, Nevzade and Hilmi Abdul Kadir were sentenced to death in contumaciam. At the time of his arrest BASRI BEY was in close touch with Mustapha Kemal.

Original Letter in H. 2. Translation of letter from Tcherkez Bekir Sofi Bey, late Municipal Councillor of Mossul, in September 1920 at Ismidt. The letter is dated 26th Sept. 1920 and is addressed to the Armenian-Greek Section of the High Commission, by request.

"In reply to the questions asked concerning the atrocities committed on the Armenians by BASRI BEY, Chief of the General Staff of Halil Pasha, ex Commander of the 6th Army Corps, during his stay at Mossul I beg to inform you as follows:

The dispatching and treatment of Armenians who were at Mossul was done direct by Army Corps Intelligence as well as by the command. While I was at Mossul it was rumoured about and I heard that about 1,600 male Armenians, who were deported on the pretext that they were to be transferred from Mossul to Zahu were massacred in one day. Later on, two Armenians from Ismidt, named Hadji and the other Minas, who some how or other managed to escape the massacre and came back to Mossul, stated that the Armenians who were to be transferred to Zaho were attacked on the banks of the Tigris by surprise three times and thus exterminated by a Company under the Command of Abdullah Chaoush. The veracity of this was proved through the secret enquiries I had made from the Intelligence Bureau as well as at Army Headquarters. And as BASRI BEY was Chief of the General of Staff of the Army Corps, not a single Armenian or anybody else could be deported without his permission and his order. Since the order to deport emanated direct from BASRI BEY he had the entire confidence of Halil Pasha.

A baker named Sirub, about whom a decision had not been given was publicly hanged in the square of Government Konak. According to my enquiries it was BASRI BEY who gave this order also. Besides this one Seid-Taha, chief of a Kurdish tribe was hanged by Nevzat, Zekyai and Captain Hilmi, Director of the Mousafirhané, that is all three of them personally; this matter however was hushed up by BASRI BEY. The two above-mentioned Armenians Minas and Hadji, who brought the news of the massacre of the Armenians suddenly disappeared one night and nothing is known about them to this day.

Although he (BASRI BEY) had taken steps to murder Zaven Effendi, the Armenian Patriarch (then in exile), and Mihran Boyadjian Effendi, he suspected that I was informed of the matter and so the execution of the plan was put off. However, while he was completing the required arrangements for these murders, public opinion was excited against Halil, and so having felt that his life also was in danger, he, (BASRI BEY) fled to Constantinople with the General Staff.

For the completion of these half accomplished arrangements Memduh Bey, the ex-Vali did his best; but the arrival of Ali Ihsan Pasha left fruitless all the atrocities and wicked intentions of these (monsters).

This is all what I can state about BASRI BEY."

Original in H. 2. Statement by Shefik Bey, a Circassian, late Kaimakam of Ghevas, in Van Vilayet, now employed in the Municipality of Kadikeui, introduced by Mihran Boyadjian, ex 1st Class Inspecteur Civil in the Eastern Vilayets. Speaking Turkish interpreted into French by Mr. Boyadjian, at the High Commission on 16.9.20.

BASRI BEY was Chief of Staff to Halil Pasha, commanding the 1st Army Corps of the Expeditionary Force sent to Persia in 1915 under Halil Bey, later Pasha.

Diza is the Headquarters. I myself in April 1915 was kaimakam of Ghevaz (in Van vilayet) near Urmia; because I was known to Vali Djevdet as lenient to the Armenians, I was sent on 5.4.15 (O.S.) to Anatolia in Mosul Vilayet to settle a quarrel between two Kurd tribes. I returned to Ghevaz on 12.5.15 (O.S.) and found that nearly all the Armenians of the Kaza had been massacred by order of Halil Bey (later Pasha) who had remained some four days in the Kaza on his way back from his expedition to Urumia and Salamas. At this time BASRI BEY was Halil's Chief of Staff, Bekir Sami Bey (now prominent Kemalist) was in command of the Cavalry and Arslan Bey (now Kemalist) was in command of the Irregulars. Thus these four must of necessity be held responsible for this massacre. In my Kaza there were twenty Christian villages, in Diza there were between six hundred and seven hundred Christians. On my return after five weeks absence there were left not more than a total of two thousand five hundred Christian females with no men at all. They had been massacred on the spot and had not been deported. The population was wiped out by the Turkish regular Cavalry, the Turkish Irregulars and Kurds. Between Diza all the way to Mush the same thing happened.

It is well known that BASRI BEY, though very junior in rank, still as Chief of Staff of the 1st Army Corps of the Caucasian-Russian Expeditionary Force, was the most influential man in the Army and held the power; for it is a further fact known to everyone that Halil was a drunkard and womaniser, and reposed his friendship and confidence in BASRI. They always lived together. BASRI was the brains of Halil.

In my Kaza the Christian population were peaceable folk, they had supplied all the transport and provisions that I had ordered. To my knowledge they had not been engaged in any insurrectionary movement, they had not gone over to the Russians and I knew of no treason among them. In fact the most loyal part of the population in my Kaza were the Christians, for the Kurds would not obey my requisitions. I knew of no secret or revolutionary society among them.

There were no Christian intellectuals in my Kaza, there were not even any schools. The women lived secluded. Few spoke their own racial language. (The Christian population of the Kaza of Ghevaz as given by Cuinet in his 'Turquie d'Asie' was 11,200 the late Kaimakam says that the number in April 1915 was nearer 15,000. The large majority of the Christian population is Nestorian).

The reason for the massacre was merely the carrying out of the pan-Turanian policy of the C.U.P. as explained to me by Omar Nadji, now dead, the chief C.U.P. delegate to the Eastern Vilayets in September 1914, when he was in his cups. Nadji knew at that time that I was anti-C.U.P.

On the Russian advance I was appointed Kaimakam of Shemdinan (headquarters Nehri, the south-eastern kaza of the vilayet of Van, bordering on Persia to the east and the vilayet of Mosul to the south). This transfer took place in June 1915. I remained there about a year as Kaimakam and acting Mutessarif of Hakkiari. When I arrived at Shemdinan the Christian population had already been despoiled. The remaining refugees were in Urumia. The 200 families of Christians and Jews that I had saved in Ghevaz I took with me to Shendinan. These and about 200 other Christian families that I found in

Shendinan I took with me to Akra in the Vilayet of Mosul, to which I fled in May 1916 before the Russian advance. I left the 400 (approximate) families in this Kaza in the care of Kaimakam Fakhri Bey. Then I went to Mosul and returned shortly afterwards to Akra as acting Kaimakam.

In Akra I found the Christian families (my refugees) all well. I remained in Akra about three months and from there I was transferred as Kaimakam of Revandouz in the Sanjak of Shehrizor in the Vilayet of Mosul. In this Kaza Halil Bey had left no Christians, he had massacred them all on his passage through to Urumia. I was in Revandouz from January 1917 to December 1917. During this period I was much in Mosul. In December 1917 I was transferred to Ras-ul-Ain where I remained until October 1918. I was then transferred as Kaimakam of Bulanik, headquarters Gop, in the Vilayet of Bitlis, north north-west of Lake Van.

In Bulanik the town and villages were destroyed, there were no resident inhabitants left. Only brigands: there was no administration and even my own personal property and official books and papers were taken from me.

Under these circumstances I tendered my resignation and returned to Constantinople.

In Bulanik it had been Kiazim Bey, a relation of Halil Pasha, who had ordered the annihilation of the Chrisitan inhabitants. Kiazim Bey was later Colonel Commanding 36th Division. At the time of the massacres he was a major.

Halil Pasha, the principal massacrer in the far eastern Vilayets and in Persia, – principal because he was the commander of the special expeditionary force that carried out the massacres, – was a man of little education, originally a Corporal of Tchetes in the Balkans. BASRI BEY was the actual organiser and is known to have often acted without Halil's authority. It was BASRI who signed official documents 'for' Halil Pasha. I know one instance where one Avni Bey was instructed by Halil to proceed to Tekrit in Bagdad Vilayet and this order was cancelled by BASRI BEY.

N.B. The witness can give evidence against BASRI BEY in the matter of cruelties to our Prisoners of War on the road of Ras-ul-Ain.

G. XIX. In Patriarchate's detailed list of September 1920 BASRI BEY is duly noted as one of the Government's officers responsible for persecution in Mosul Vilayet.

MURAD BEY (of Smyrna)

Malta No. 2804

Interned 13.7.20

Copy in W/2886 of 11.12.20.

Appointments. Assistant Director-General of Police under Bedri and Azmi Beys.

Lists. On List VII, i.e. the Foreign Office List.

Arrest. Arrested by Turkish Government on 27.3.19 and subsequently released (previous to 23.7.19). Arrested by British Military Authorities on 25th May 1920.

Petitions.

W. 2178. Petition of 7.10.20.

W. 2886. Petition of 7.10.20, through Governor Malta of 11.12.20. In this he states that he ceased to act as Assistant Director-General of Police in 1916.

N.B. High Commissioner's report 1552/W.3667 of 24.11.20 recommended that MURAD BEY be brought to trial.

ACCUSATIONS.

'Renaissance' 29.5.19. Constantinople Hangings.

5035.A.28. Patriarchate Report of 19.7.19. Deportation of Armenian Intellectuals from Constantinople especially cases of Dr. Daghavarian, deputy of Sivas. The Russian subject Aghnouni and Dr. Zartarian deported to Diarbekir and murdered on the road.

Deportation of Diran Kelekian, editor of 'Sabah', Zohrab deputy for Constantinople and Vartkes deputy for Erzerum and murder at Chorum by the band of Yakub Djemil.

E. 14. Bureau d'Information Arménien report 8.9.20. As assistant to notorious Bedri Bey on April 25th 1915 he arrested 220 intellectuals in Constantinople. At his instance chiefly, they were deported to Tchangri and ultimately massacred. The responsibility for this he shares with Bedri Bey and Sezai Bey.

G. II. His name appears on the Patriarchate's list of September 1920, as one of the high Police Officials responsible for atrocities committed in Constantinople and, through their subordinates, in the Provinces.

H. 10. In Patriarchate's report of 22.12.20 on Mustafa Reshad Bey (see his dossier) MURAD BEY is mentioned as a member of the "Council of Terrorism" formed by Talaat Pasha at the beginning of the war. At that time MURAD BEY is described as "Assistant to Bedri Bey for administrative cases."

ALI DJENANI BEY

Malta No. 2805

Interned 13.7.20

Appointments. Deputy for Aintab. (Aleppo Vilayet).

Lists. On List VII, supplementary. This list was sent to the Foreign Office under cover of High Commissioner's despatch No. 702/R.2178, dated 16th May 1920. He had been noted in the High Commission for arrest since the spring of 1919.

Arrest. Arrested by British Military Authorities on 24th May 1920.

Petitions.

5033.A.12. 1. Petition of 9.6.20, from ALI DJENANI BEY.

5033.A.2. 2. Petition of 30.6.20 from ALI DJENANI BEY.

3. Petition of 8 [sic, 7].7.20, in which ALI DJENANI states that he left Constantinople for Aintab 20 days before the Armistice and left Aintab for Constantinople a week after the Armistice, and two days after Shevki Pasha left.

States also that at the beginning of 1919 he had been called before the Turkish Court Martial. He was called because of an information lodged by Mariam Ekerian, whose identity is not known.

4. Petition of Djelal Bey (the good Vali) on behalf of Vali DJENANI, dated 7.2.20 (Djelal was Vali of Aleppo 1.7.14 to June 1915, Vali of Konia, June 1915 to Sept. 1915; and appointed Vali of Adana on 1st November 1919).

In this petition Djelal Bey states that Shukri Bey was Mutessarif of Aintab when the deportations began. Shukri did his best to attenuate the effects of the deportation, following in this the example of Djelal Bey, the Vali. As a consequence of this both the Vali and the Mutessarif were removed and Ahmed Bey (a deportee) became Mutessarif of Aintab (in August 1915). Further ALI DJENANI was not in Aintab (apparently when the deportations began under Shukri Bey). See also petition No. 7.

W. 2910. 5. Petition by United States Commissioner.

2.11.20. On October 22nd 1920 the daughter of ALI DJENANI BEY, Sabina, a graduate of the Constantinople College, called at the British High Commission and handed in the name of an Armenian witness from Aintab: Khoren Bey Nazaretian, of Aintab, staying at Hotel Tokatlian, Pera, or at 40 Sirra Selvi Pera. This witness was written to the same day asking him to attend in the event of his being desirous of making a statement.

On 2nd November he attended, not in this matter, but in the matter of a claim. He stated that he had no statement to make. He had been in Egypt the whole time of the war.

5033.A.2. 6. Petition from wife, dated 27.11.20, with list of Turkish witnesses for the defence. No action. Assistant High Commissioner 3.12.20.

535/24. 7. Petition from Djelal Bey, ex Vali of Aleppo, dated 10.1.21.

Minute by Mr. Graves of 11.1.21. "I have discussed this with Mr. Ryan and we are agreed that there is nothing in Djelal Bey's letter to make us alter our opinion on ALI DJENANI's case."

N.B. In High Commissioner's despatch No. 1552/W.3667, dated 24.11.20. and covering report of special committee, it was recommended that ALI DJENANI BEY be detained and brought up for trial.

ACCUSATIONS.

R. 2910. Copy in 5033.A.12. Per Mr. Ryan on 20.3.20. "from what is said to be sober Armenian source, not known to me personally": - report

a. Active member of Ittihat.

b. He has been a member of former Medjlissi Meboussan as Me[b]ous of Aintab.

c. Lately again elected to Medjliss Mebousan,[member of parliament] to represent Aintab.

d. Intimate with Talaat, Enver, etc.

e. Predominant role in deportations from Aintab. He works in the shade and does not let his name appear.

f. "After the Armistice he acted more warily, but still actively. He is one of the founders and most active members of the Committee formed about a year ago for keeping Cilicia for the Turks. About six months ago he went personally to Aintab and distributed arms to Moslems there and especially to the villages round; he has declared himself personally." He is a great landowner (owning five or six villages) and very rich. His lands lie near the spot where lately two Americans were killed."

g. His men very probably are in the lands infesting the region between Kilis and Aintab.

h. "He is one of the chief supporters of the Milli movement in general, and main director of that movement in the Aintab region. He is always in communication with the Milli leaders there, (as lately as 10.3.20). Some of them are his relatives or subordinates.

i. "He is an exceedingly dangerous man though a little timid, very active and resourceful. He lives here in Nishantash in great style and his wife and daughter (the latter a graduate of the American Girls' College here) have often entertained American, French and Italian officers and civilians at tea and dinner parties during the last year."

W. 2910. Copy in 5033.A.12. Copy sent to French High Commissioner on 22.4.20.
Per Miss Burgese and Mr. Bond, from a reliable Armenian source – report:-

a. One of the leading men of the C.U.P. Took part in the Congresses held at Salonika and Constantinople, and installed their decisions.

b. After the Armistice he armed the Moslem population of Aintab. The British were about to arrest him when he took flight and left for Constantinople.

c. A principal in the deportations. He, together with the Mutessarif (Ahmed Bey, a deportee) kept secret the order from the Minister of the Interior concerning the non-deportation of Roman Catholics and Protestant Armenians.

d. He deported to Der-Zor many artisans who had been exempted and this eight months after the deportations had ceased. At Der-Zor they mostly died.

e. A founder of the Committee known as the Committee for the defence of the rights of Cilicia.

28. No. 2816 Mehmed Nouri Bey
29. No. 2817 Mehmed Ali Bey
30. No. 2818 Djemal Oghu Bey
31. No. 2819 Colonel Mehmed Adil Bey
32. No. 2777 Colonel Chevket Bey
33. No. 2768 Nouri Betlissi Effendi
34. No. 2806 Adavalli Oghlou
35. No. 2679 Lt. Colonel Ahmed Teufik Bey
36. No. 2680 Colonel Mehmed Teufik Bey
37. No. 2694 Captain Djemal Bey
38. No. 2700 Colonel Djevad Bey
39. No. 2707 Major Mauzlum Bey
40. No. 2710 Major Ibrahim Hakki Bey
41. No. 2745 Captain Tahir Bey
42. No. 2820 Captain Mehmet Roushti Bey

        Received.
        (Sgd.) G.L. Capley,
        Master,
        R.F.A. "Montenol"

25.10.21.

money. Sahakian was eventually murdered in Der-Zor by ALI DJENANI's men.

3. Extermination of the Karamanoukian family of Aintab and seizure of their goods, chiefly lace which he sold in Constantinople.

4. Just before the British entered Aintab in 1918, ALI DJENANI reorganised the Ittihads and incited them to defend the city. ALI DJENANI then left for Constantinople.

R. 2910. Verbal statement by Mrs. Libarian, now of Arnaoutkeui, Tramway Station 83, Telph. No. 2222; made at the High Commission on 2.6.20.

My husband was in Aintab at the time of the deportations in 1915. I was here in Constantinople with my children. My husband was a Protestant Armenian. The Gregorians had been deported and partially massacred in the summer but the turn of the Protestants came later when ALI DJENANI went expressly to Aintab for the purpose of getting rid of the Protestant Armenians who had so far been spared on the intervention of the United States' Ambassador. ALI DJENANI, then Deputy for Aintab, was particularly interested in getting the Protestant Armenians out of the way because many of them were rich. He in conjunction with a certain ? Haidar Bey, notable of Aintab, eventually usurped most of their property. ALI DJENANI is and was all powerful in Aintab. My husband together with many others was massacred at Der Zor. I hold ALI DJENANI to be absolutely responsible for the death of the Protestant Armenians of Aintab during the winter of 1915-16.

I know ALI DJENANI and his wife quite well here for I used to go to his house in Nishantash and see his wife to get news from Aintab. On one occasion his wife said to me that she would love to slaughter Armenians with her own hand. Three days ago she telephoned me to come and see her. I went and she threatened me, I had to give evidence on behalf of her husband. She said she knew it was two Armenian women who had caused the arrest of her husband and I would see what happened to them. Professor Riza Tevfik of Constantinople College was there, they were talking of all the strings that they were going to pull. Riza Tevfik said that if such a mother and daughters (latter young and pretty and American educated) were at work, the husband would surely be liberated. The wife talked of all her influential connections among Europeans, especially of Admiral Bristol [American High Commissioner, Mark L. Bristol]. I was there amongst them, sitting quietly and saying nothing. I have long had the entrée of the house.

ALI DJENANI is the son of a concubine of the brother of Kadri Pasha.

D.3. 9.9.20. Copy in W. 2910. Dr. and Mrs. Nakashian's answers to a reference made in a memo by the United States High Commissioner dated 24.8.20. (In W.2910, forwarded under cover of General Officer Commanding-in-Chief's 3211 'T' of 31.8.20).

ALI DJENANI is one of the most influential members of 'Union'; he was the M.P. of Aintab always, (even in this last Parliament) he did not save a single Armenian [not] even from his nearest neighbours.

If public opinion has any importance, if such a widespread rumour is to be believed, ALI DJENANI is one of the most dangerous men who work with their brain and not show it. There is not a single man among our countrymen who has any favourable thought of him. Some of his relatives who have stayed in his house (schooled in that house) have been most cruel, most terrible, in massacring. Hakki who went from here 1915 to Malatia is the celebrated man who nailed iron shods at the feet of Armenian priests, and he is called Hakki the shodder.

I think the public opinion made for DJENANI has its roots deeper. It begins from the massacres of 1895, when some Turks did not participate, and further protected the district where they lived, and they did not let any Turk touch their Armenian neighbours. For such Turks every Armenian will run for defence even now. But ALI DJENANI did not do so; I know it myself that he did not defend even his immediate neighbours; right under his eyes people were killed and houses were burnt, which he could prevent very easily. While the people believed that he encouraged and directed if not ordered.

(signed by Dr. Nakashian on 9.9.20.)

My husband Dr. Nakashian was arrested at the 24th April 1915 with 200 intellectuals in Constantinople; that same night they were taken away for 14 days we did not know where they were, or whether they were dead or alive. Not knowing what to do I went to DJENANI BEY, who was then a Parliament member, and also from the same city as my husband (Aintab) and even nearest neighbours. I appealed to him, beseeched him with tears, hoping to find out the trace of my husband through him, and mean time to try to do his best for his salvation.

Neither he nor his family did not show a bit of sympathy. One day when again I was asking for help, and trying to convince him that my husband was faultless and must be saved, his daughter Sabina said "Papa they will hang them all won't they?" You can imagine in what condition I threw myself into a carriage and came back home, deciding not to go again to their house.

(Signed by Mrs. Marie Nakashian on 8.9.20.)

N.B. It is thought that Mr. H. H. Khachadourian, Assoc. M.A. Soc. C. E. Formerly Member of the American Intelligence Mission to Trans-Caucasus and of the American Military Mission to Armenia might be able to throw light on further sources of information.

G. XVIII. In Patriarchate's detailed list of September 1920, ALI DJENANI is duly noted under the heading: Aintab Unionist Chiefs who were the organisers of the massacres in 1915.

No. W. 2910.
British High Commission,
Constantinople.
18th September 1920.

Sir,

With reference to Your Excellency's letter of the 24th August regarding the arrest of Ali Djenani Bey, which has been forwarded to me by the General Officer Commanding-in-Chief, Army of the Black Sea, I have the honour to inform Your Excellency that, according to the particulars in possession of this High Commission, Ali Djenani Bey, who as Deputy for Aintab was one of the most influential members of the Committee of Union and Progress, not only did nothing to protect Armenians from deportation and massacre but was himself one of the most active and cruel instigators of the horrors of 1915. In this connection I venture to refer Your Excellency to a letter dated 24th February 1919 which I received from the American Commissioner (Mr. Lewis Heck) denouncing Ali Djenani on the basis of information which had been received from a "conservative and reliable source".

2. I would also mention that the evidence of Dr. Nakashian of whom mention is made in Your Excellency's letter, has been taken and is far from being taken in Ali Djenani's favour.

3. The latter will be tried by the Tribunal to be indicated in due course under the Terms of the Treaty of Peace.

I have the honour to be,

Sir,

Your Excellency's obedient servant,

(SD.) J. M. de ROBECK.

HIGH COMMISSIONER.

His Excellency,
The United States High Commissioner.

---

* F.O. 371/5089

*

Arabian Han, Galata
June 9, 1920

To His Excellency The British High Commissioner,
British Embassy,
Constantinople.

Your Excellency,

One of the clauses of the peace treaty is that those who have taken any part in the deportations or massacres of Armenians shall be tried by a special court appointed by the Allies. To prevent these people from escaping, it has been decided to keep them under arrest. I now understand that I also am suspected of being one of those who have participated in the massacres.

In the peace treaties with Germany, Austria, and Bulgaria there was a special clause referring to war criminals and those who have committed atrocities during the war; and I knew that a similar clause would be applied to the Turks. My social position and politic knowledge enabled me to foresee this.

If I had ever taken part in the deportations, I should have the example of those who have run away. Being sure of my innocence and my guiltlessness, I did not follow their example nor will I ever stoop to such meanness. I have not stained the tradition of honour from my ancestors, whose record goes back for centuries nor will I ever stain the noble and honoured name of my forefathers. Until now no Armenian has ever risen up against me because I have never harmed any of them. On the contrary I have helped them as much as I could: the circumstances of the deportation in Aintab were as follows:

a) When Talaat Pasha's cabinet decided the deportation of the Armenians, the Parliament was not in session. Therefore a royal decree was issued; the "Irade" was taken and orders sent to all the Vilayets for the deportations. Strict measures were taken to carry out the order and the governor of Aleppo, Djelal Bey, refusing to accept the order, was transferred to Konia. The Vali who came after him ordered the governor of Aintab to deport the Armenians. How could I prevent the action of a law issued by the cabinet and approved by the Sultan?

b) During the deportation of Aintab not a single Armenian was killed or harmed.

c) When I went to Aintab I found out that Armenians were allowed to take their belongings with them, to sell them or to leave them in the charge of the Ottoman Bank. Most of the rich Armenians left their money and goods to the Ottoman Bank. Later on,

---

* F.O. 371/5089

the Ministry of the Interior, after having corresponded with the Ottoman Bank, gave an order that a commission should be formed with the right to sell these goods. The director of the Ottoman Bank was present at the auction and there was in consequence no complaint in Aintab.

d) When the British occupied Aintab after the Armistice there was no complaint neither against me nor against the population. Talaat Pasha's cabinet had appointed special officers to carry out the special order and we had nothing to do with it.

e) There was no personal complaint against me in Constantinople. There was only one petition signed by an unknown and nameless man that was given to the court martial last year against Ahmed Bey, the governor of Aintab. In the same paper there was an allusion to me but the witnesses that we called proved my innocence and since then not a single Armenian has said anything against me because I did not harm the Armenians. I did not take part in the deportations, but helped the Armenians a lot.

f) I suffered also from the deportations from Aintab. In Ballagi street in Aintab I owned a Raki factory which I rented to Kirkor an Armenian. Kirkor was deported and the factory left empty and he could not pay the rent for six months that he owed me.

Again in the same quarter my skin factory which I rent to Agba and company was taken over and used as a stable after the deportation of Armenians.

In Agyol, a paint factory is still empty because the Armenians who worked there were deported.

Six shops in Fatladji Bazar, twenty one in Aladjadji Bazar, and six in Amir Ali Han and two in Kazandji Bazar were left empty because their tenants were Armenians and deported. Most of the shops are still empty, besides these, two shops containing twenty work-benches for the manufacturing of belts are still empty because Gurtly Ogoullar were deported.

In Bostandjik, Guneisse, and Yeni-Yapan (my villages) three wet mills that I owned remained empty for a year because the millers were Armenians and had run away during the deportations.

My private secretary Hossep Porpossian and his brothers Kirkor and Ohaness were deported and sent to Aleppo. It took me five month to get permission from the Ministry of the Interior for their return to their work, and during that time there was no one to take care of my property and I lost thousands of pounds.

g) Not only did I save Porpossian's family but I gladly received thirty more Armenian families in my farms, gave them houses, land provision and capital. By doing so I saved the lives of more than two hundred Armenians on my farms, and my correspondence on this subject can be obtained from the Ministry of the Interior.

h) After a year the governor of Aintab issued an order for the Armenians on my farms to be deported. I applied to the Ministry of the Interior and succeeded in sending back to my farms those who were arrested. This communication also is in the Ministry of the Interior.

i) In the April of 1909 there was a massacre of Armenians in Adana and I was the only deputy in the Parliament who blamed the government and asked the ministers to stop the massacres. The details of my speech were published in the parliamentary papers for April and May 1909. But I could not oppose the government at this time because there was war and Martial-law. We had no freedom of speech during the war time. There was also an Armenian deputy of Aleppo in the Parliament who did not oppose the government.

Though there were many Syrians killed and several deported, the Syrian deputies could not stop it. One of the Syrian pashas was hung by the order of the government and his nephew Bediul-Mueyed Bey was a deputy. Yet Bediul-Mueyed Bey could not help his uncle.

Summary:

1) As the preceding statements show, there was deportation but no massacre of Armenians in Aintab.

2) The deportations were made by the order of the cabinet and a royal decree and was carried out by specially appointed officers.

3) No one's property was pillaged by the population.

4) In the whole Ottoman Empire there is no other city whose population has behaved as well as that of Aintab.

Why look for a criminal when no crime has been committed? I am not afraid of being tried and I am waiting for it. I accept English laws and English judges. Try me here but do not make me wait until the peace treaty is signed and a special court is appointed for the trial of the real war criminals. Either try me now or release me and let me wait at my home until the appointment of the court. I expect justice and only justice from the British government.

I beg to remain,
Your Excellency's obedient servant,
Ex-deputy of Aintab,
Ali Djenani.

*

Arabian Han, Galata

June 30, 1920

To His Excellency The British High Commissioner,
British Embassy,
Constantinople.

Your Excellency,

I cannot yet find out the reason of my imprisonment; also I do not know what is the charge against me. Had I been interrogated once I should have proved my innocence.

A rumour has been circulated that I have sold in Berlin carpets and jewels taken from the Armenians during the deportations in Aintab. As I have represented in my previous petition, the governor of Aintab, at the beginning of the deportations, was a good and honest man. He issued an order warning the Armenians and helped them to deposit their goods and belongings in the charge of the Ottoman Bank. For that purpose he rented Nazarian Han and deposited all the Armenian goods therein. Later on, Talaat Pasha's cabinet issued an order and these goods were sold by a special commission in the presence of the officials of the Ottoman Bank. I was not in Aintab when those goods were sold, consequently I did not buy anything. As everything was done in the presence of the director of the Ottoman Bank, M. Tahir and his Armenian secretary, they know the names of all those who bought any of these goods.

Both the registers of the commission charged to sell the goods of the deported Armenians, and those Armenians who remained in Aintab during the deportations, and the Turkish inhabitants of Aintab can prove my innocence.

The reason for my departure was to save my wife's life. She was to have an operation in Berlin, and the doctor who advised this course was Yenan Tewfik Bey. In Berlin they did not operate and advised us to go to Carlsbad; so after remaining a week in Berlin I went to Carlsbad.

When I went to Berlin I had nothing with me but some trunks containing my own clothes. The train registers can witness this. I did not make money either by commerce or profiteering during the war. I did not buy wagons. I love my honour better than anything else in the world and I did not stain it. I was contented with the revenue that came from my own property. If I had done like the rest I should have been the owner of a large fortune.

---

* F.O. 371/5089

But I did not deign to profit by the occasion and preferred to keep my honour unstained. English people know the value of honour and their conscience cannot let an honourable man be unjustly punished.

    Only ask me for the proofs, I am ready to prove my innocence.

                    I beg to remain,
                    Your Excellency's most obedient servant
                    Ex-deputy of Aintab,
                    Ali Djenany.

*

Arabian Han, Galata
July 7, 1920

To His Excellency The British High Commissioner,
British Embassy,
Constantinople.

Your Excellency,

1) I was never friends with Talaat and Enver Pashas. If I were friends with Enver I would have profited by the occasion and have a high position. When Enver became the Minister of War I absolutely broke relations with him, because our convictions were different. With Talaat it was the same. When he came to Constantinople Club in the evenings, I was never seen in the crowd encircling him. The club members can witness that.

2) In 1913 my relations with Talaat were broken because I advised the Unionists to make the C.U.P. a political party instead of keeping it a revolutionary committee. My point of view was that a revolutionary committee was harmful to the country. Consequently in the elections of 1914 the committee strongly opposed my election as a deputy. The government of Constantinople ordered the governor of Aleppo, Djelal Bey, to prevent the elections. Djelal Bey, made inquiries in Aintab and found out that the public insisted upon having me as their representative in the Parliament. He informed the ministry of the Interior of the public opinion in Aintab. As soon as I was elected I broke relations with the Unionists. The deputies of that time know all about it. After the Armistice, when the British came to Constantinople Club, they expelled all the unionists from the Club. After making inquiries about my relations with the unionists, they found out I was neutral and wrote me a letter informing me that I could keep my membership.

3) I left Constantinople twenty days before the Armistice and started back from Aintab a week after. During my sojourn in Aintab there was no order in the city and the Turkoman bandits were pillaging the villages, carrying the cattle away, and threatening the city. The governor of Aintab and the notables decided to ask the military commander to form a militia to act against the bandits. Shevki Pasha gave ninety rifles to the militia under the command of the gendarmery. This militia kept order until the British occupied Aintab. I left Aintab a week after the Armistice and Shevki Pasha left two days after me. The militia was organised by the permission of the governor and Shevki Pasha. I had no connection with it. Shevki Pasha is now residing in Constantinople, you can ask him about me.

---

* F.O. 371/5089

4) I strongly opposed the Armenian deportation in Aintab.

a) I was as much harmed as the Armenians themselves. As explained in my former petitions all my property was damaged because my tenants were deported.

b) Had I ordered the deportations, my first action would be to prevent my tenants from going.

c) It took me three months to succeed to save my Armenian secretary Hosseb Porpossian.

d) I gladly accepted thirty Armenian families to my farms and helped them to the end.

e) They accused me of being a nationalist. As I decided in 1914 to have no relation whatever with political parties, I certainly had no desire to mingle myself in their struggle. I preferred to be neutral until the fate of Aintab was decided by the Allies.

I did not join the nationalist party in the parliament, but opposed them openly. Most of the members of the parliament went to Asia Minor and joined Kemal Pasha but I stayed in Constantinople. The Kemalists pillaged all my villages and my relatives ran away to Aleppo fearing the nationalist attacks.

f) Some eighteen months ago I was called to the court martial. The president Chrisantos and his Armenian secretary, Missac Effendi, interrogated me. I answered all their questions. As they were satisfied with my answers I was set free and was never called there again.

g) There was no direct complaint against me at the court-martial. In a petition given to the court-martial against Ahmed Bey, the governor of Aintab, there was no allusion to my name. The petition was signed by a certain Mariam whose existence is unknown even to the Armenians of Aintab. It must be by someone who did not want to show his personality?

During four years of war I did not work with the Unionist I did not profit by any occasion, I did not trade and make profiteering. I did not approve the deportations and massacres and I saved the lives of more than three hundred Armenians. I can prove my innocence by hundreds of honest and good witnesses. Therefore I pray your Excellency to have a trial and not to let me suffer in the prison for a crime I have not committed.

I beg to remain,

Your Excellency's most obedient servant,

Ex-deputy of Aintab,

Ali Djenany.

Chichli Djadessi, Pera
July 7, 1920

To His Excellency The British High Commissioner,
British Embassy,
Constantinople.

Your Excellency,

The family of Ali Djenani Bey, ex-deputy of Aintab, who is now under arrest in the Arabian Han, has asked me to witness for him. On account of my position I know more than anybody else and I have accepted to prove his innocence for the sake of justice. The truth is as follows:

1) Before the war U.P.C. did not want to have Ali Djenany Bey elected as the deputy of Aintab. They wished to have Mouhtar Bey in his place and for this purpose sent Ali Bey, the delegate of the committee at Aleppo, to Aintab. But as the majority voted for Ali Djenany Bey, and I, finding no one more efficient, sided with the population, he was elected as a deputy against the will of the U.P.C. This is known all over Aleppo and Aintab.

2) I was the governor of Aleppo during the deportations as well as during the elections. I did never accept the idea of deportations and during my governorship not a single Armenian was deported. For this reason the Sublime Porte transferred me to Konia. As Shukri Bey, the governor of Aintab, was selected with me and had accepted all my political opinions he followed my example. I declared officially that I would not accept any responsibility for the deportations of Armenians and I did not give orders for the purpose. On account of this all the time that I was in Aleppo the Armenians in Aintab were at peace.

When orders were given to Shukri Bey for the deportations he tried to take more humane measures than any other governor. After corresponding with the governor of the Ottoman Bank, he rented a large Han to deposit the belongings of the deported Armenians. All the money and jewelry were deposited at the bank while the rest of their goods were put in the Han. This was proclaimed in the city for days and all those who wished left their goods in charge of the Ottoman Bank. Ali Djenany Bey was not in Aintab at this time. After more than half the Armenians were deported, colonel Ahmed Bey was made the governor of Aintab, and Shukri bey was transferred. As all the goods of the Armenians were deposited at the Bank until that time [and] Djenany Bey could not buy anything even if he wished to. According my belief he is exempt of all these faults. If he

---

* F.O. 371/5089

had committed even the smallest crime I would not say a word in his behalf and the man who witnesses for Ali Djenany Bey has saved the lives of eighty thousand Armenians in Adana and Konia. For this reason I hope that you believe all that I write.

> Yours most respectfully,
> Governor of Adana,
> Djelal.

AK DAGHLI OGLU MEHMET
otherwise known as ADVALLU MEHMET of Yozgad
or TSHIBISHIN OGLU MEHMET

Malta No. 2806

Interned 13.7.20.

Appointments. A leather merchant of Yozgad in the Vilayet of Angora. In 1915 he became a Tchete Bashi.

Lists. On List VII, supplementary. Placed on list subsequent to arrest. This list was forwarded to the Foreign Office under cover of the High Commissioner's despatch No. 702/R. 2178, dated 16.5.20.

Arrest. W. 2178. Arrested in Stambul on 8.4.20 by Captain Balley on Colonel Maxwell's instructions dated 8.4.20. Arrest duly maintained at High Commissioner's request to the President of Allied Police Committee, dated 26.4.20. A further letter on the same subject is dated 16.6.20.

Petition. For petitions received, see below under heading 'Defence'.

N.B. In High Commissioner's despatch No. 1552/W. 3667, dated 24.11.20, and covering report of special committee, it was recommended that AK DAGHLI OGLU MEHMET be brought up for trial.

ACCUSATIONS.

A. D. 4. 1.6.20. Signed statement by Eftik Danelian, of Yozgad, now of Kum Kapou, Kullik, Sakaghi No. 3.

Describes the deportation of 600 Armenians from Yozgad. At Keller-Dere, ADAVALLI OGLU MEHMET, Tchete Bashi [chief of irregular forces], murdered witness' father before her eyes, also her uncle, Hrek Agha, as well as all the other Armenian males of the convoy. Further, in order to terrorise the Armenians the witness saw MEHMET rip open a woman who was pregnant. As to the witness herself she received a cut from an axe on the head during this massacre. After having murdered her mother and three brothers MEHMET took the witness, bleeding and fainting as she was to his house in Yozgad and there criminally assaulted her. The witness is still suffering from the effects of the wound etc.

B. D. 4. 3.6.20. Signed statement by Vertaim (Vartouhi) Andonian of Yozgad, now living at Rue Koulbouk No.11. Maison de Bakal Yani, Kum Kapou Stambul.

"In June 1915 the father of the witness, Artaki, was a tanner and MEHMET was his Turkish partner. At the beginning of the deportations MEHMET became a Tchete Bashi. MEHMET then possessed himself of the tannery and all that it contained, he imprisoned Artaki and three days later the whole family was deported including Artaki. When the convoy arrived at Keller, MEHMET separated out Artaki and witness' uncle Krikor, he stripped them naked and murdered them in front of the witness. He then killed her mother. After the massacre of the men and the older women, the escort chose out the best of the remainder. MEHMET picked out for his own use Elmone, sister of Artaki, the witness herself, her two younger sisters and some others. They were taken to

MEHMET's house in Yozgad. After three or four months' use of Elmone, MEHMET sold her to his brother Osman. The witness, being then only about 10 years old, he 'betrothed' to his only son. Thus the witness, her two sisters and some other girls remained in MEHMET's house till after the Armistice when they were rescued by the Patriarchate. Besides killing the witness' relations, he murdered a number of others and was wont to rip up their bellies when he suspected jewels. The house in which he lived is full of carpets and stuffs stolen from the Christians."

C. D. 4. 3.6.20. Signed statement by Gulbenk Toumayian, of Yozgad, now of Selamsiz, Rue Kilisse Sokaki No.1. Scutari.[*]

"My name is Gulbenk Toumayian. On July, 1915, we were jailed by the leader of the Brigands, AK DAGHLI MEHMET. Three days later, we were split into three groups. The first group was deported, safe and sound, to Sivas; after Sivas, it was massacred. The second group reached Damascus unharmed. The Mutessarif Djemal having been replaced by Kemal (later hanged), the Kaimakam of Boghazlian ordered the massacre of the third group. My daughter Ovsanna, who was in this group, was taken away and raped by AK MEHMET who also murdered my brother Simbat at a place called Kurd Dere, four hours' distance from Yozgad."

D. D. 4. 3.6.20. Signed statement by Mme. Ovsanna Youssoufian of Yozgad, now living at Scutari, Rue Klisse No. 1.[†]

"My name is Ovsanna Djin Youssoufian. On July, 1915, AK AHMED came to us and bought from my husband hides worth 500 gold pounds, which he said he would pay the following day. When he came the following day, he asked for the keys of the tannery saying that he would look after the factory as we were going to be deported and our possession stolen. My husband gave him the keys. He came back after two hours and took my husband saying he wanted to register him in the lists of skilled workers. As my husband did not return that day, the following day I went to MEHMET to enquire about him. "I myself killed your husband, here are his clothes", he told me, "I will do the same thing to you.

Three days later, we were deported, together with other Armenians to Kurd Dere, four hours' distance from the town. There, upon orders from MEHMET all the men were killed, MEHMET himself taking part in the killing, after having separated all the young and pretty girls from the group, including myself. Later, they gave us away to the different villages of the region."

E. D. 4. 3.6.20. Signed statement by Ghazaross Toumayan, of Yozgad now of Scutari, Selamsiz, Rue Klisse No.1.[‡]

"On July, 1915, began the deportation of all the Armenian of Yozgad and its region, upon the orders of governor Djemal. This was later continued by Kemal Bey, his succes-

---

[*] The statement appears in French and has been translated into English –WCB.
[†] The statement appears in French and has been translated into English –WCB.
[‡] The statement appears in French and has been translated into English –WCB.

sor, who had been Kaimakam of Boghazlian. My partner, AK DAGHLI OGLOU MEHMET (called ANDAVAL) confiscated all my possessions and deported me to Damascus. He is one of the principal leaders of the Brigands."

F. D. 4. 3.6.20. Signed statement by Miss Ovsanna Toumayan, of Yozgad, now living at Scutari, Selamsiz, Rue Klisse No.1.[*]

"On July, 1915, AK DAGHLI MEHMET, leader of the brigands deported all the Armenians of Yozgad. We were taken to a place called Kurd Dere, four hours' distance from the town. Here, by order of MEHMET, all the men were put to death, after having separated all the young and pretty girls whom they dispersed in various villages of the region. I saw, with my own eyes, this MEHMET cut off the heads of men with a big knife. This monster MEHMET took me to Yozgad and raped me and kept me till the Armistice, although I resisted and tried to escape."

G. D. 4. 3.6.20. Signed statement by Miss Marian Tcherkezian, now living in Stambul, Gedik Pasha, Tulbendji Han No.17 Maison Mardiros Calfa.

"In 1915 in the month of June, MEHMET ANDAVAL OGLOU became chief of the Tchetes at Yozgad and when the deportations began, conducted all the Armenians to Keller Dere a distance of 8 to 10 hours [from] Yozgad. He ordered the separation of the males and killed my father and my two sisters with axes before my eyes.

The massacre lasted a whole day. I held my five year old brother in my arms. ANDAVAL OGLOU MEHMET ordered me to drop the child, having done so he trampled the child with his horse.

At night he took me into his house at Yozgad and dishonoured me. There were some other 15 girls whom he distributed amongst his friends.

He kept me 3 months in his house and then gave me to a friend of his, Safet Bey, Inspector of Telegraphs, who took me as his wife and brought me to Constantinople.

I left Safet at the Armistice, and came to live in the house of my cousin."

H. D. 4. 3.6.20. Signed statement by Miss Elmon Andonian of Yozgad, now living in Stambul, Kum Kapou, Rue Koullouk No.11. Maison Bakal Yani.

"In the month of June 1915, when the deportation order came to Yozgad, MEHMET ANDAVAL OGLOU who was a shoemaker in the town became the most notorious person.

Before the War he was the partner of my two brothers. When everybody was deported he came to our house and told my mother that no harm would befall her sons and that they ought to come out from their hiding place. My mother and myself entreated him to save these two young men. He then said: "send all your carpets and other furniture to my house and let these two young men walk freely in town."

Next day he came to our house with three gendarmes and forcibly took my two brothers and conducted them to the prison, from there they were sent under his supervision with others to the Keller Dere. We accompanied them and he stabbed my two brothers to death before my eyes, ordering us to go away and not interfere with his work. My mother

---

[*] The statement appears in French and has been translated into English –WCB.

was already dead from her emotion. When all was over and the dead bodies were lying before me, he came to me and said I had to accompany him home. I asked him why he murdered his partners (my brothers) he said: "I could not separate these two from the others and you can be quiet; I myself killed them." I remained in his house four months. He dishonoured me and I became his concubine. After this period he forcibly gave me to his brother Osman. There I remained two months when all Armenian girls were thrown out of Turkish houses. I then lived the most miserable life in Yozgad. I several times applied to MEHMET to have some money, he refused. At the time of my stay in MEHMET's house, he brought arms and fingers of women cut and having rings and bracelets and he hung them on the walls as mementos."

I. D. 4. 3.6.20. Signed statement by Mrs. Lucia Assadourian of Yozgat town, Bazar Yeri, Takhta Djami. Now living in Stambul, Arnaout Han, Bin Bir Derek. (An old woman. Statement made in Armenian, interpreted by Mr. Fenerdjian, taken down in the High Commission.)

"I know ADAVALLI by sight. I saw him last year in Yozgat. He himself came to my house in Yozgat town when the deportations were taking place. I had two sons and one daughter in the house. ADAVALLI himself and his men took us on the road to Maaden. Between Tash Punar and Sarimbey 3 days from Yozgat ADAVALLI took one of my boys, 16 years old, and had him killed before my eyes. The other boy, 13, I have not seen since; neither my daughter.

ADAVALLI is stout, white, a gray haired beard and moustache."

J. Statement by Mrs. Erani Kestakian of Kaussoglou village in Yozgat on the road to Sivas. Now living with her grand-daughter, Hosanna Tormayan in Scutari, Selamsiz, above an Armenian Pharmacy. (An old peasant woman, unintelligent. Speaking in Armenian, interpreted by Mr. Fenerdjian, taken down in the High Commission.)

"I know ADAVALLI well by sight. In 1915 he was a leading Tchete bashi in the Yozgad district; he did not wear uniform, he had a very large number of men, 40 to 50 under his orders. He was acting under government orders. He came to my village, smashed down our doors, took the girls away by force, ravished them, he and his men for three days, and then the girls disappeared; very few indeed have returned. The children he killed under our eyes and heaved their bodies into the river. The old men they also killed. The young men they mostly killed but some they took away, none at all have returned, except one, my son-in-law, who managed to escape to Damascus. Our village contained . . . (could not say)."

K. Signed statement dated 7.4.20 by Gulbenk Toumayan (see statement C.), informing against ADAVALLI OGLOU MEHMET for massacres at Kourd Dere on the 24th July 1915. Eye witnesses: his wife Ipek Toumayan and his daughter Ovsanna Toumayan (statement F.); also Ipek Kortian, Eranik Kestekian (statement J); Lucia Assadourian (statement I.). Besides these, the following can give the evidence of their eyes; Ardach Tcherkezian, Hoosep Assadourian, Nouritza Tcherkezian, Ovsanna Djin Youssoufian (statement D.), Krikor Kouyoumdjian and several others.

5029.A.22. A. MEHMET Director of Turkish Orphanages is mentioned in a Bureau d'Information Arménien List, dated 19.7.19. of Yozgad massacrers.

G. **IX.** In Patriarchate's detailed list of criminals of September 1920, ADAVALLU

OGLU MEHMET is duly listed as one of the notables of Yozgad and chief of tchetes, together with some other names. Noted against them: they executed the orders of the Kassab Kaimakam Ali Kemal and massacred the 30,000 Armenians of the district.

On 13.1.21 the Armenian Patriarchate forwarded an information against AK DAGHLI OGLU MEHMET. See Appendix C.

DEFENCE

D. 4. On 3.7.20 Mons. Jean Kenriot, Avocat of Agopian Han Galata, passed to British High Commission by Colonel Ballard, made an enquiry in this case. Since then he has made no sign.

W. 2178. 29.5.20. Petition, of 26.5.20. from Tahsin Bey, Director General of the Police to Colonel Ballard, praying for the prisoner's release as enquiries showed that he had not participated in the massacres. Also a petition from MEHMET (in Turkish) and two other documents (in Turkish) contained no facts.

Petition. Of 28.7.20 from MEHMET through Governor of Malta on 20.8.20 enclosing a photograph of himself. In this statement he alleges blackmail as the cause of his arrest. Assistant High Commissioner. 17.9.20: No action.

W. 2178. Recd. 7th Dec. 1920. Petition, dated Yozgad 3.11.20, signed by a number of Armenians and Greeks. Appendix A.

Do. This petition sent to Armenian Patriarchate on 11.12.20 for verification of signatures.

570/24. Patriarchate's answer of 13.1.21. Appendix B. enclosing biography (Appendix C.)

APPENDIX A.*

Copy: The original is in 570/24.

[translated from French]

TO HIS EXCELLENCY, THE AMBASSADOR OF GREAT BRITAIN IN CONSTANTINOPLE.

Excellency,

We have been informed that MEHMED OUSTA EDARALLI OGLOU, famed for his honesty and his kindness towards his countrymen has been removed to the island of Malta because of the deportation of the Armenians.

We present this petition because we believe in the justice and fairness of Great Britain. We bear witness to this fact and we expect you to do the same for us.

We beg to remain. Your Excellency, your most devoted and humble servants.

Yozgad, 3 November 1920.

Senekerim Keghonian	Senekerim Arslanian	Nazar Chebdjian
Ermeni Mektar Nazar (Seal)	Dr. Djessourian	Ardaches Sahagian

We have been informed that MEHMED OUSTA EDAVALLI OGLOU, the Yozgad merchant, has been removed to Malta because of the deportation of Armenians. We bear witness to his honesty and kindness in the name of our nation and request that you send him back to our country.

Your humble and obedient servants.

Yozgad, 4 November 1920.

Hadji Sava Anasstassidis	Jean Papazoglou	Aristidis Kehysoglou
Demetre Candiloglou	Jean Calfoglou	Jean Djavouchoglou
Roum Mektar (Seal)		

---

* The statement appears in French and has been translated into English –WCB.

APPENDIX B.

To His Excellency,

The British High Commissioner,

Constantinople.

Excellency,

We beg to submit to Your Excellency the results of our inquiries concerning the case of AKDAGHLI MEHMED. We were asked to make this enquiry by Your Excellency's letter No. W. 2178, in which was enclosed a petition on his behalf.

I. **Appendix C.** The particulars about the moral character of AKDAGHLI MEHMED and his participation to [sic] the Armenian atrocities, which the special services of our Patriarchate have been able to gather, are exposed at length into . . . 33 of the Dossiers on Turks responsible for the Armenian atrocities. We regret to state that they are far from being in his favour.

II. The petition signed by some Armenians and Greeks of Yozgad has been put up in Yozgad on the demand of AKDAGHLI MEHMED himself, who seems to have asked the forwarding of such a petition in a letter addressed from Malta to his wife, as it appears by the perusal of the copy of his wife's Turkish letter, which was attached to this petition. The textual translation of this letter is as follows:

Master.

We send you the affidavit (Mazrata) which you had asked us to send. We have no other preoccupation than your good health. All the children kiss the ends of your clothes. Do not be anxious, we are praying and your affairs are in a good state. In a short time we are sure you will come back. All the children kiss the ends of your clothes, master.

18.11.36 [1920]   From Your Harem.

III.   His relations, among whom his two "hooligan" brothers, Nedjib and Shukri, urged on by his wife, must have forced the Armenians and the Greeks, whose names appear under the petition to write and sign it, by terrorising them.

Our inquiries having proved that these signatories are all honourable men, the Armenian signatories, if they were here in security, would have had more than one heart-rending tales to tell against AKDAGHLI OGLOU MEHMED, for they are to be numbered among the few deportees from Yozgad, who having miraculously escaped death in the deportation time, did the great mistake to return to Yozgad after the Armistice. These unfortunates are living there since the beginning of the Kemalist movement, under a 'regime of terror' and they, as well as the Greeks who have signed the petition must have done it, through fear, knowing well that harm would happen to them and probably also to their community, if they refuse to do it.

IV.   The Armenian Union of Yozgad, fully aware of the culpability of AKDAGHLI OGLOU MEHMED, and the honourability of the persons who have signed the petition, is also conscious of the dangers by which the latter and the remainder of the Armenians would be threatened, if the causes of the refusal of the petition would reach the two brothers of AKDAGHLI MEHMED, Nedjib and Shukri. These two latter being prone then, to set the fanatical mob against them.

Consequently the Union of Yozgad relies humbly on Your Excellency's full knowledge of the "status" under which the Christians actually live in Anatolia, for protecting them while Your Excellency's High Righteousness decides of the necessity of calling this AKDAGHLI MEHMED to answer for his acts before the Tribunal ad hoc.

We remain Your Excellency's most gratefully,

The Armenian Patriarch.

APPENDIX C.

ADAVALLU MEHMED OF YOZGAD

(Alias: Tchibishin Oghlou Mehmed.

Alias: AKDAGHLI OGHLOU MEHMED.)

ADAVALLU MEHMED is the second member of a family of five brothers who live or have lived in Yozgad.

These five brothers were formally called the Tchibishin Oghlous from a nickname of their father.

AKDAGHLI, or by corruption ADAVALLU, is another family nickname. These five brothers were the following:

1. Ahmed. He was a courier carrying the mail to and from Yozgad and Kirshehir. He was killed in 1910 during one of his journeys by highway men trying to rob the mail.

2. Mehmed Custa. (He is the one who is imprisoned in Malta). He was born at Yozgad and is about 45 to 48 years old. He was a merchant in leather and shoes and he had a shop in the bazaar of Yozgad at the address of Bezesden Ounbazar. Before the war his wealth was estimated to 3,000 Ltq. Consequently he could be considered as fairly rich, according to Yozgad's standards.

3. Osman. Also a dealer in leather and shoes but less rich than his brother and having a separate shop in the bazaar in the neighbourhood of his brother's shop. This Osman died in 1917.

4. Medjib. A worthless character. Before the War he used to earn his living through gambling and tobacco smuggling. In his early youth he had been to Smyrna where he had killed somebody in a quarrel. He had served for this homicide a sentence of 15 years hard labour and had returned to Yozgad at his liberation.

5. Shukri. As bad as his brother, living in the same rough way and feared in the town.

The four brothers were living in a state of enmity. For instance the two merchants, Mehmed and Osman, who were not only dwelling in neighbouring shops in the Bazar, but also lived in neighbouring houses in the Arpalik part of Yozgad, had a family feud between them; the son of Osman having in 1913 carried away the daughter of Mehmed from his own house and forced her to marry him against the will of the father. Shukri and Medjib were also enemies. The two merchants Mehmed and Osman had been since the Constitution of 1908 fawning on the Central Committee of the C.U.P. of Yozgad, which was composed of Bakirdji Mahmud the President, and the members Ouzoun Ahmed, his brother Behdjet, Abdullah Nizamzade, Kambour Kalfa Nouri, Arab oglou

Abdurrahman, Tchapanlardan Dervish Bey, Feyaz Bey, Tevfik Zade Abdullah, Vehbi Bey, etc.

In this way they managed to avoid the payments of different sums of money gathered by the C.U.P. under the pretence of contributions to the Navy, Army etc. or the requisitions made during the Balkan War and after, at the time of the great war.

In 1915, when the propaganda began against the Armenians there was at Yozgad, an honest governor, Muhedine Pasha, who was refusing to set the Moslems against the Christians. He was for this reason discharged on May 16th 1915 by the C.U.P. and replaced by Djemal Bey.

Nedjati Bey[*] responsible delegate for the C.U.P. for Angora, and Ali Munif,[†] who was then Secretary for the Interior, came on a tour to Yozgad, to organise the deportation and the slaughter of Armenians. During their stay at Yozgad, they were the guests of Ouzoun Ahmed and Behdjet.

They wanted to impress on Djemal Bey, the necessity of not only deporting Armenians, but also of slaughtering the [convoys] on the way, but Djemal Bey did not agree with their views. He is said, by a Turkish witness to have uttered these words: "I will never allow the gendarmes to kill the deportees, you had better release all the convicts, and allow them for days to murder the Armenians, and after that allow me to catch with my gendarmes all the convicts and have them killed by my gendarmes."

And in fact, the search for arms among the Armenians and the sending away of the first [convoys] of deportees by Djemal Bey was done without atrocities being committed. This of course was not what was wanted by the C.U.P., so they had Djemal Bey discharged, and replaced him per-interim by Kemal Bey[‡] the Kaimakam of Boghazlian, and formed the Edjumen or secret council for exterminating Armenians and the Teshkilati Mahsousse or gangs of volunteer murderers. AKDAGHLI MEHMED OUSTA inscribed himself voluntary chief of Tchetes in that Teshkilati Mahsousse.

His brothers followed suit, Osman in an amateurish way, but Nedjib and Shukri as wilful tchetedjis.

From the day that Kemal came to govern Yozgad and the deportations of the Armenians began to be executed in the most bloodthirsty manner, ADAVALLU was seen to hang his gun in his shop and declare that he was trusted with the mission of hunting down the Armenians, and in fact he was everyday leaving his shop for one of the "Esnaf" (confraternity of shoemakers and leather merchants); he knew all the Armenians belonging to this trade, their whereabouts and the members of their families.

Taking with him other scoundrels of the Teshkilati Mahsousse he tracked down all the Armenians he knew and conveyed them to the prison where Vehbi the Mouhasbedji of the Vilayet, Tevfik the Gendarmeri commandant, and the other officials and gendarmes

---

[*] On F.O. List.
[†] Was under Secretary for the Interior from Sept. 1913 to Aug. 1915. Now deportee No. 2762.
[‡] Hanged by Turkish Court Martial on 10.4.19.

robbed them. These unfortunates were afterwards bound four by four and sent by groups of 100 or 150 to be slaughtered at Keler, Boghazlian, etc.

Each time that AKDAGHLI brought to the prison one of his Armenian fellow merchants trading in the same goods as his own, he obliged the Armenian to deliver a written statement that his goods had been sold to AKDAGHLI. AKDAGHLI promised that he would safeguard the goods and perhaps save the Armenians also. But afterwards he as a rule accompanied the convoys and murdered the Armenian merchants or had them murdered by others.

Among the bandits escorting these convoys his brothers Mehmed and Shukri were the most ferocious.

After the 10,000 Armenians of the town of Yozgad had been deported and 8,000 of this number had been slaughtered, AKDAGHLI MEHMED became a member of the Emlaki Matrouke and shared with the other C.U.P. members the spoils of the Armenians of his corporation. He is said to have had for his share more than 200,000 Ltq.

His brother Osman, who died in 1917, followed his example but on a minor scale. His two other brothers Shukri and Nedjib, who had been only common murderers and robbers of corpses, spent in a rowdy way all they had been able to rob during the slaughter of the convoys and are today as miserable as before living in the same rowdy manner.

AKDAGHLI MEHMED, after the Armistice, had come from Yozgad to Constantinople to sell some goods here, but he was recognised by Mr. Toumayan Gulbenk, one of the former chief dealers in leather and shoes at Yozgad, and whom he had robbed. Mr. Toumayan had succeeded in escaping from the dangers of the deportation and had come to Constantinople. AKDAGHLI was denounced by him to the British Military Authorities, who in their high sense of justice, had this murderer and plunderer arrested and imprisoned in Malta, pending his trial before the Allied High Tribunal, which is to deal with such cases, according to the article 230 of the Peace Treaty.

SULEIMAN FAIK PASHA

Malta No. 2807.

Interned 13.7.20.

Appointments. Commanding troops in Harput from May 1915 to February 1916. Also President of the Harput Conscription Commission.

Vali ad interim of Mamuret-ul-Aziz during absences of Vali Sabit Bey in 1915.

President of the Brussa Court Martial after the Armistice. In June 1920 he was commanding the 1st Army Corps at Haidar Pasha.

Lists. On List VII, supplementary. High Commissioner's despatch No. 702/R. 2178 of 16.5.20.

Arrest. In June 1920, he was under interrogation before the Turkish Court Martial. (5030/A/22)

W. 2178. Arrested by British Military Authorities on 30th June 1920, at High Commissioner's suggestion, dated 22nd June 1920.

Petitions.

1. **5030.A.25.** Petition of 28.8.20, through his daughter, Belkis Hanum.

2. **2099/24.** Wife's petition of 15.2.21.

ACCUSATIONS.

C. 17. S.S. Hachadourian, Prof. of Music, American College, Harput, states that SULEIMAN FAIK committed the worst atrocities, without authority, during the few weeks he was Vali ad Interim.

C. 18. Mrs. Assim Bey, wife of ex-Kaimakam of Harput city, denounces SULEIMAN FAIK PASHA as the organiser of the deportation of 3,500 persons all massacred. These deportations took place long after the general deportations.

Lepsius M.S. note p. 42. Mentioned in connection with Erzerum atrocities.

Partiarchate Report. E. 11. In Harput he acted under the authority of Mahmud Kiamil Pasha (deportee) who was commanding the IIIrd Army Corps. A report by Vehbi Pasha, successor of Mahmud Kiamil Pasha in the command of the IIIrd Army Corps, to the 1st Court Martial is said to exist. In this report Vehbi Pasha accuses Mahmud Kiamil and SULEIMAN FAIK of having organised the Harput and Diarbekir atrocities and explains how confiscated Armenian property was divided.

Patriarchate Report E. 18. A further Patriarchate report, dated 13.9.20, is as follows: In the month of May 1915, some days after he took possession of his post in Harput as Military Commandant, he issued orders and had the names of all Armenian soldiers of all grades in the different regiments and the military formations in the Vilayet of Harput, wiped off from the rolls. These Armenians were gathered in Harput. To their numbers were added all Armenians which were not of military age, and had not yet been called up to serve i.e. from 16 to 20 and from 45 to 50 years old; of these he ordered the mobilisation, which was executed in a most abusive way. From these Armenians, to the number of

7,000 among which were included school boys and men of good standing in life, as lawyers, professors, etc., he formed "Amele Tabouris" (military Labour Battalions).

He sent these "Amele Tabouris" to work on the road from Harput to Abussi, on the way to Malatia, where they suffered worse sufferings than convicts sentenced to hard labour, and died in great numbers.

After a month he had the remainder of these "Amele Tabouris" brought back to Mezré, the Headquarters of the Vilayet, and passed them in review before the "Kirmizi Konak" (his official residence). As was his wont every time he sent Armenians to death, he addressed them mockingly saying that he was the friend of Armenians and was sending them to a good place. Then he had them divided into battalions of reduced strength and sent all of these battalions, with a strong military escort, on the road to Diarbekir. These battalions were all slaughtered at the passes of Deve Boynu or Gughen Boghaz by the escorts and 'tchetes' waiting in ambush for them.

The following ciphered telegram No. 33 sent by SULEIMAN FAIK PASHA on the 16th April 1916 to the Commandant of the IIIrd Army at Tortum, referes to the slaughtering of a whole battalion of a thousand of these Armenians. This is the transcription of the telegram:-

"I have the honour to inform you, that according to the report of the officer supervising the convoying of the 'Amele Tabouri', put at the disposition of the Vilayet, this battalion had reached Maden without any incident. After Maden, at the place called Gughen Boghaz, Armenian brigands suddenly attacked the caravan and the Armenian Ameles began to desert, the escort opened fire and killed a great part of the battalion and the brigands. The officer seeing that there was no need to remain any longer on the spot, returned. In the affray one of our soldiers disappeared, three guns and a sword were rendered unserviceable."

This telegram produced before the first Court Martial [1919] induced Kurd Mustapha Pasha to submit SULEIMAN FAIK to a cross-examination.

Kurd Mustapha Pasha who is a righteous Moslem and on whose spirit of justice and impartiality it is possible, according to the experience of the Patriarchate, to rely entirely when the accused is not of Kurdish origin, interrogated SULEIMAN FAIK PASHA and asked him how and when a strong military escort is attacked in a narrow pass, such as Goghen Boghaz, by troops of numerous armed brigands on the heights, it is possible for that escort to kill the "convoi" [convoy] and the brigands, with the loss of only three rifles, a broken sword and one soldier missing. Mustapha Pasha could not be brought to believe that military nonsense, when his information was all to the effect that these "convois" had been slaughtered, and that telegram was SULEIMAN FAIK's only official report on the butchering, according to his own orders, of one of the convois of Amele Tabouri.

The result of the cross-examination, of which we can submit a translation, was so unsatisfactory for SULEIMAN FAIK PASHA that Mustapha Pasha decided to have him arrested, but he could not put that decision into execution owing to the great influence in the highest Turkish circles which protected SULEIMAN FAIK.

Apart from the above, referring as it does to his military duties, SULEIMAN FAIK is responsible for delivering up to Sabit Bey the Army doctors of the Hospital of Harput, namely the Head Physician, Ser Tabib Kaimakam Artin, Doctor Tchobanian and the Armenian chemists of the same Hospital.

II.

As to the charges against SULEIMAN FAIK PASHA, when he was Vali ad Interim, and against whom witnesses are ready to testify, we state the following: during the first fortnight of August 1915, Sabit Bey went on a tour of inspection in the Dersim region.

1. During this fortnight Sabit Bey was absent, SULEIMAN FAIK ordered the arrests of Doctors Hatchadour Manouekian, Sarkis Momdjian and his family, Artin Veznian and 150 other prominent Armenians, who had obtained from Sabit Bey through bribery the means of escaping deportation by conversion to Islamism. He sent them all on the road to Malatia and had them slaughtered on the way.

    The witness for this is Baghdassar Tashdjian, who escaped death in Malatia by converting himself to Islam and was serving as an assistant in the hospital under the name of Nedjati. He owes to the protection of the Turkish head physician his escape at that time and his imprisonment for two months instead of being sent to be murdered. He is now the director of the Armenian Refugee Depot at Ortakeuy.

2. During all the month of November 1915 Sabit Bey was absent from the Vilayet. He had been called to Erzerum by Mahmud Kiamil to take part in a council where were present, the Vali of Harput, Sabit; the Vali of Erzerum, Tahsin; the Vali of Sivas, Muammer; and the Vali of Trebizond, Djemal Azmi. At that time the Armenian persecution had slackened, and the few Armenians who had escaped through one means or other, were beginning to feel secure. As soon as Sabit Bey had left Harput, SULEIMAN FAIK PASHA had publicly announced in the streets that all Armenians who were in hiding could come out, as there would be no more persecution. In fact all those who began to appear, relying on this promise, were well treated for the first days, serving thus as a bait for others.

    After eight days, when there were some three hundred Armenians thus present in Harput, SULEIMAN FAIK had all of them arrested and sent as a "convoi" of deportees towards Malatia. All of these were slaughtered on the way. Among these deportees was a certain Ohannes Aghanikian formerly professor at the Turkish High School at Harput. Ohannes Aghanikian had in the first days of the deportations in June 1915 sought refuge in the American Consulate, where he remained in hiding until the month of November 1915. When he heard the promises of SULEIMAN FAIK announced publicly in the streets, he also made the mistake of relying upon SULEIMAN FAIK's word although he was advised not to do so by the Consul, Mr. Leslie A. Davis. When he was arrested, the American Consul intervened for his release but all his entreaties were in vain. The reports of the Consul in which these facts are related could not be sent to the American Embassy owing to the defiant attitude of the Turkish Authorities towards the American Consulate at that time. These reports were burnt when the Consul left Harput for Beirut via Aleppo. Mr A. Davis is now at Helsingfors, Finland, in the capacity of American Consul. The Patriarchate has written for his testimony. The evidence now in hand for this accusation is supplied by

Mr. Pekmezian, actually Director of the Armenian Orphans Trade School of Chichli, who was during all the year 1915 at Harput as interpreter of the American Consulate.

3. A third accusation against SULEIMAN FAIK, when he was acting Vali of Harput during the absence of Sabit Bey and for which Mr. Pekmezian is a witness, is the rounding up he made of the American Hospital of Harput. He had that Hospital surrounded by his soldiers and all the Armenian employees taken out and murdered.

4. At their deportation the Armenians of Erzerum knowing by the rumours that reached them of the fate of the previous convoys, that they would be sent via Malatia, and separated from their wives and children and killed on the way, had remitted to the Turkish Post Office at Erzerum sums of money and addressed the letters containing the postal orders "Poste restante" in their families' name at Malatia. In fact they were killed on the road and their wives robbed and misused on the way, arrived at Harput, where they were left in the most destitute condition. SULEIMAN FAIK prevented them from cashing their money, and sent the majority of them to continue their journey. In the month of October 1915 he obliged the Post Master to pay all that sum amounting to 8,000 Ltq. in gold to him. One of these women, who had remained in Mezre, is here and is a witness as to her share of this usurpation.

Under a refined appearance SULEIMAN FAIK is a most cruel character.

The educated witnesses who have been in contact with him and had all the opportunities of studying him, are:-

1. Mr. Artin Barsam, a notable Syrian of Harput, now living at Kadikeuy.

2. Dr. Deirmendjian in Harput during the year 1915, now at Ismid.

3. Mr. Kutchukian, Director of the Ottoman Bank of Harput in 1915, now the Director of the Ottoman Bank in Adana.

4. Mrs. Atkinson, an American Missionary lady, in Harput, in 1915 whose present address is 14 Beacon Street, Boston, Mass. This lady is expected to come back to Constantinople shortly.

5. The German Missionary Mr. Hayman in Harput during 1915, whose present address is: Mr. Hayman, c/o Mr. Leopold, Rue de la Grange, Geneva, Switzerland.

These two Missionaries, astonished by so much cruelty, used to say that they had never seen such a bloodthirsty man under such a polite and refined appearance.

We must add here some particulars that have transpired during our enquiry, which refer to the efforts made by the family of SULEIMAN FAIK to secure his release. Apart from the entreaties of his sister* Belkis Hanum, his brother has been persecuting the sisters of Mr. Dikranian, a shoe merchant at Abid Han, to secure from these a certificate of good character for SULEIMAN FAIK. One of the sisters of Mr.

---

* Under Petitions, Belkis is said to be his daughter.

Dikranian was kept in the house of SULEIMAN FAIK in Harput and converted to Islamism, with the intention of being given as a wife for one of his relations.

After the Armistice they freed themselves and came to Constantinople. The brother of SULEIMAN FAIK often tried by threats or entreaties to get a certificate from them, which they refused to give. Lately he had come and shown them some papers saying that he has no more need of their aid. He is supposed to have managed to get certificates from some Syrians, which must have been comparatively easy for him as the Syrians were not deported from Harput.

H. 4. Alleged copies of Turkish official telegrams, to or from SULEIMAN FAIK PASHA, communicates to the High Commission on 1.10.20. For translations see Appendix A.

Copy of an official telegram communicated through the Patriarchate.

J. 177 bis. From the Vali ad interim of Mamuret-ul-Aziz to the Vali of Mamuret-ul-Aziz at Erzinjan, (i.e. Sabit Bey).

October 21st 1915 (O.S)

In answer to your telegram of today's date. A Commission had been set up to ascertain what Armenians, either of this Province or from outside, are remaining in hiding. This Commission has lately despatched a convoy of such. In conformity with Your Excellency's instructions the Commission has still further accelerated its work and in a few days time an end will have been made of the situation (*bou guibilerine arkassi alnadjik*).

APPENDIX A

TRANSLATION OF COPIES OF TELEGRAMS FROM OR TO: SABIT BEY, VALI OF MAMURET-UL-AZIZ; SULEIMAN FAIK PASHA, VALI AD INTERIM OF MAMURET-UL-AZIZ; TAHSIN BEY, VALI OF ERZERUM.

(Originals in H. 4)

1. Telegram No. 33 dated 16th ? 1915 from SULEIMAN FAIK PASHA to the Commander of the 3rd Army Corps at Tortum. The application of the measures decided upon having been left (for execution) to the Vilayet, the Amele Tabouru [Labour Battalion] was to have been sent to Diarbekir [from Harput]. The Battalion reached Maden (Argeana Maden) without incident. After passing Maden and in the vicinity of Keban Bogaz, (i.e. in the Vilayet of Diarbekir) Armenian bands suddenly appeared on both sides and opened fire. This caused excitement among the men of the Labour Battalion mentioned above, all of whom broke from the column and ran to join the Armenian bands. (The escort) opened fire on those who were disobeying the order to stand. A great many of the men of the Labour Battalion, as well as men of the Armenian bands were killed. Both the Commandant and the Provincial Government sent out reinforcements, but in view of the inaccessibility of the ground, they were not able to take any prisoners. The rebels are being hunted down. During the fighting one soldier (of Turkish escort) was killed, three rifles and one bayonet were rendered unserviceable. The detachment (escort) considered it useless to remain any longer and they have now returned.

The above is from a report by the officer commanding the detachment (or escort).

2. Telegram No. . . . dated 25th July 1915, from Sabit Bey at Dersim (the sanjak north of Harput and in the same vilayet) to the Ministry of the Interior.

With the exception of the centre of Malatia, which will be cleared within the next few days, no Armenians are left in the Vilayet (of Mamuret-ul-Aziz) and its dependencies (i.e. ? the Sanjak of Erzingan in 1915).

With a view to prevent the many abuses taking place through the deportation of the Armenians and seeing that a thorough overhaul was necessary, SULEIMAN FAIK, Vali ad interim and Commander of the Army Corps, has today sent me the following copy of a telegram. I regret to say that I am convinced as to the truth of the whole question.

Nazim Bey, Delegate of the C.U.P. at Harput. On F.O. List for arrest. Mehmet Nuri Bey, deputy for Dersim (Vilayet of Mamuret-ul-Aziz). Now at Malta. I suggest that Inspector Nazim Bey should be recalled to Constantinople, that further measures against Nazim Bey and Deputy Mehmet Bey should be decided upon in Constantinople, and that the officials of the vilayet, whose complicity is proved, should be at once dismissed. I am ready to carry out whatever instructions are conveyed to me.

2. A. Copy (from SULEIMAN FAIK (? At Mezre) to Sabit Bey at Dersim.)

Nazim Bey, Inspector of the Union and Progress, considering the Armenian Deportations a great occasion to enrich himself has proceeded to several measures which later on became perfectly clear; and all this a little before your visiting Dersim. Great sums of money were stolen and everything, done in the name of the C.U.P. reached a point which can not be tolerated by anybody. Even the members of the Central C.U.P. have recently resigned and only the aforementioned Nazim Bey, together with the Secretary General Shevki Bey, are still connected with it. One of those who played the greatest role in these affairs is Mehmed Bey, deputy of Dersim. The Inspector, profiting by his position, has stolen much money and other things, and now begins to threaten the Sirianis (?) Under these circumstances I hope that in future you will continue to enjoy the unparalleled and perfect public confidence in view of your noble attitude, and that being connected with the honourable Committee, I particularly express to you my special satisfaction.

(SG) SULEIMAN FAIK.

2. B. Copy. To vali Sabit Bey at Dersim.

Nazim Bey, Inspector of the C.U.P., considering the Armenian deportations a great occasion for increasing his personal wealth has a little before your visit to Dersim, proceeded to several measures which became quite obvious, later on.

Thousands of pounds are being stolen. The evils done in the name of the C.U.P. have become intolerable. Six members of the Central Committee have recently resigned. He, together with the Secretary General and the Defterdar only remain. One of those who played the greatest role in these affairs is the Deputy Mehmed Bey. The Inspector, profiting by his position has looted much money, goods and girls, and now begins to threaten the Sirianis (?). Goods excepted, the amount of money collected up to now in the name of the Committee amounts to more than 10,000 pounds. Under these circumstances we hope that in the future you too will continue to enjoy the unparalleled and perfect general confidence because of your noble attitude, and, we consider it our patriotic duty to express to you our special satisfaction. Please take from the telegraphic office the copy of the telegram.

Signatures:

MEHMED ALI Central Commander	FERID Regiment Gendarmery Commander	FERID Maarif Mudiri
RUCHDI Police Mudiri		

N.B. Of the signatures, Mehmet Ali may be the Mehmet Ali Pasha who committed suicide on 11.3.19. Ferid Bey is the Provincial Director of Education who was arrested by the Turkish Authorities on 20.7.19 and released in January 1920. The other Ferid was a Major Commanding the Gendarmerie at Mezre, the headquarters for the Vilayet, noted as one of the principals in the Harput atrocities. Rushdi the Police Mudiri is not yet on index.

3. Telegram No. . . . dated the 16th July 1915, from Tahsin Bey, Vali of Erzerum to Sabit Bey, Vali of Mamuret-ul-Aziz.

The details given by your Excellency on the 13th July 1915 have made a great impression on me. The state of things described amounts to anarchy and it is contrary to the wishes of the Government and of our Party. I have communicated to the Minister, Talaat Bey, your statements as well as all that I have seen and heard. The welfare of the country requires that everyone at all responsible should be at once withdrawn. Everywhere I am saying that whatever we did, we have **not** done it in order to fill with money the pockets of some persons. It is because we are after the salvation of the Government that we are deporting Armenians to the south. This is the sole object. It is advisable that we too should write in this sense to the Ministry. Anyhow please, send the deported groups of Erzerum via Malatia. It may be that they will be attacked at Eghin. Please send trustworthy officials to the District between Kemakh and Eghin; it is necessary that officials should know the object and intentions of the Government.

The army advances with full success. I am going to inform you that 800 prisoners were taken.

N.B. Tahsin and Memduh both at Malta. The route taken by the majority of the Erzerum deportees was via Erzinjan (then a sanjak dependent of Erzerum), down the valley of Kara Su, past Kemakh and Eghin, to Arabkir, Malatia and the South. Very large numbers were duly massacred between Kemakh and Eghin (under instructions from Tahsin and his Mutessarif of Erzinjan Memduh Bey).

The boundary between Erzinjan and Mamuret-ul-Aziz is just north of Eghin.

ALI NAZMI BIN HUSSEIN

Malta No. 2808

Interned August 6. 1920.

Appointments. Prominent C.U.P. leader at Kir-Shehir in Angora Vilayet Public Prosecutor.

Lists. His arrest was suggested by Mr. Ryan to Grand Vizier in February 1919, and again suggested on 27th March 1919. Nothing however was done.

His name was included in the list sent to F.O. under cover of High Commissioner's despatch 217/R/2178 of 12 February 1920 (No. 10). This list was sent by F.O. to W.O., thence to General Officer Commanding-in-Chief, who, when arresting him acted on this Authority.

Arrest. Arrested by General Officer Commanding-in-Chief in Kedikeui on 3rd July 1920.

Italian High Commissioner's intervention, W. 2178. On 19.7.20 General Officer Commanding-in-Chief forwarded a letter from the Italian Section of the Allied Police claiming that ALI NAZMI was an Italian protected subject and asking for nature of charge against him.

W. 2178. High Commissioner wrote to General Officer Commanding-in-Chief on 27.7.20 informing him that ALI NAZMI was accused "of having participated in the massacres committed during the continuance of the state of war on territory which formed part of the Turkish Empire on 1st August 1914." (2) "ALI NAZMI will presumably be brought to trial before a Court, to be designated in due course, by the Allied Powers, under Article 230 of the Conditions of Peace with Turkey."

5035/A/94. From the Italian High Commissioner to High Commissioner dated 10.8.20 wishing to know High Commissioner's motives and intentions as regards this Italian protected subject.

5035/A/94. High Commissioner's of 15.9.20 in reply.

Do. Further letter of 7.12.20 from Italian High Commissioner

Do. Further letter of 21.12.20 to Italian High Commissioner

Petitions. W. 2178. Petition of 23.7.20 from mother through General Officer Commanding-in-Chief, letter 38740 (A) of 1.9.20, in which she says that ALI NAZMI was arrested at the instigation of an Armenian after attempting to blackmail him. ALI NAZMI was Procuror General at Kir-Shehir. He protected Armenians, punished the authors of deportations with the result that he risked his own position and life.

ALI NAZMI assisted:

Mr. James La Fontaine

Sheikh-el-Hazem (the Deputy for Syria) and Aram Bedrossian (of the British Censorship) see below under E 16.

ACCUSATIONS.

5032. see also 5031.A.7. below. Information as to Kir-Shehir massacres supplied to Canon Whitehouse in March 1919 by Aram Fosbikian, 18, grocer's assistant and Agop Terzie, 18, both of Kir-Shehir in Angora Vilayet.

On the 8th July 1915 arrests began and took place on five days. On July 8th, fourteen persons, including the Priest Der-Avedis; a lawyer, named Kirkor Der-Movsessian; Siragan Bairamian, the wealthiest trader in Kir-Shehir; and a student, named Garabed Keshishian were arrested. On July 9th, 65 persons were arrested; on July 10th, 135 persons; on July 13th, 41; about July 27th, 18 young boys. In each case, on the night following their arrest, they were marched with their hands bound a distance of 1½ hours to Geol Asar, accompanied by police and gendarmes under the command of the Commissioner of Police, Hami Bey and the Gendarmerie Tabur Commandant Burhan-ed-Din.[*] They were told to sit down and eat and soldiers came out of trenches and butchered them with swords, clubs and axes.

Eye witnesses to the above are: Mihran Calebji, who escaped wounded, returned to Kir-Shehir and recounted his experiences. He was after a few days taken away by Burhan-ed-Din in person and executed. Simeon Giobekjian, bootmaker, who escaped at the beginning of one of the massacres, served as a soldier, and is now at Kir-Shehir.

At the beginning of August 1915 the whole of the population was assembled in the barracks and the secondary school. They were kept three days, during which they systematically robbed and then allowed to return to their homes. About the middle of August they were sent off in batches of four families to villages in the neighbourhood, Dalakji, Caman, Mesekkeui Tensili, etc. Witness Agop Terzie was sent to Dalakji. Here they were lodged in one room and supported themselves by sewing etc. for the Moslem inhabitants. Those who embraced Islam were allowed to return; the others were kept there for nine months. Before the deportation the Mutessarif Hilmi Bey[†] offered to prevent their being sent off if they gave him all their valuables, but he did not keep his promise.

The following were the leaders in the massacres:

Hilmi Bey, Mutessarif of Kir-Shehir; now in prison here.

ALI NAZMI, Public Prosecutor (Muttei-Umuni), chief of the C.U.P. Committee. Now in Constantinople, where witnesses gave him in charge[‡] at Emun Eunu police station; he was released after a few moment's conversation with the Merkez Mudiri.

---

[*] Major Burhaneddin Hakki Bey, arrested by G.O.C. (on F.O. List) on 29.7.20.
[†] Hilmi Bey, deported to Malta, on 28.5.19.
[‡] There is no official record of this arrest. It must have occurred early in 1919.

Burhan-ed-Din, commanding Gendarmerie at Kir-Shehir.

Hami Bey, Commissioner of Police at Kir-Shehir

Kiazim Bey, Director of School, now Director of the Sultanié Secondary School at Smyrna.*

Omer Lutfi, Professor of School, still at Kir-Shehir.

Riza, Muhassibeji, now at Tokat.†

?   ?   Judge de Paix (Mastanjik) now in Kir-Shehir.

Bakirzade Zin Effendi, merchant who has made large fortune out of loot: still at Kir-Shehir.

Last six members of C.U.P. Committee and organised massacres and deportation.

5031/A/7. In another statement by Aram Fosbikian in French, forwarded to Military Attaché by G.S. '1' on 7.3.19, Aram describes himself as an eyewitness and amplifies the above quoted statement. He again mentions ALI NAZMI, Hilmi Bey and Major Burhaneddin as among the Chief organisers of the Kir-Shehir massacres.

5035/A/94. On 12.7.20. General Headquarters, A (Z) sent a list of nine witnesses prepared to testify: of these:

A. **E.9.** Mariane Kundurajian states that she knew ALI NAZMI personally in Kir-Shehir. Her address is Dolab Dere, Sinem-Keui, Rue Eshref Effendi, No. 194. In 1915 acting with the Mutessarif (now deported) Hilmi Bey, ALI NAZMI conducted the deportations of Kir-Shehir and their massacres, at 3 hours' distance from that town. ALI NAZMI detained the Armenian women in Turkish barracks and compelled them to give him all the gold they had. ALI NAZMI endeavoured to place the witness in his harem but she managed to escape. She and her children were deported, her house looted.

B. Elbis Dedeyan, of Feridié No. 79, states that she knew ALI NAZMI personally in Kir-Shehir. It was by his orders that the Armenian males were deported, the actual extecutant being Hami Bey (on index), the Commissioner of Police. The women and children were detained in the barracks and the houses looted. Her husband was deported and considered dead, when one day he re-appeared with wounds caused by an axe on his head and shoulders. He had bribed a Turk. But he was soon discovered by Hadji Etem (?), Nuri Eff. the Police Accountant (on index) and Major Burhaneddin Hakki Bey, the Commanding Officer of the local Militia (now under arrest). The witness' husband was taken away and has never returned.

ALI NAZMI was the C.U.P. leader in Kir-Shehir and actually responsible for the deportations and massacres.

C. **E.9.** Satenig Der-Movsessian of Kir-Shehir, now of Abbas Agha Mahalessi, Rue Yaldiz, No. 31, Beshiktash, states that she knew ALI NAZMI, he had lived in

---

* The arrest of Kiazim Bey was suggested by Mr. Ryan to Grand Vizier on 27.3.19. No action was taken.

† This may possibly be the same as Hamitli Riza Bey ex-Deputy for Kir-Shehir, who is on the F.O. List.

Kir-Shehir for some time before the war. When war broke out, he at once became known as an active C.U.P. leader. Even before the deportations en masse began, ALI NAZMI had deported her husband (the lawyer) Kirkor Der-Movsessian, and other Armenian males. ["]My husband never returned and ALI NAZMI used to boast that he had exterminated them all. The houses of Armenians were looted and their children taken away from them. Finally they were deported after paying away all the money they could raise.["] The witness considers the following Turks as the chief local officials responsible for the atrocities of 1915:

Hilmi Bey, the Mutessarif.

ALI NAZMI, Procureur-General and chief of local C.U.P.

Mehmet Riza, Muassebeji. (Not on index)

Major Burhaneddin Bey, Gendarmerie Commandant.

Hami Effendi, Police Commissioner (on index)

Kiazim, Mektab Mudiri (Mr. Ryan suggested his arrest to Grand Vizier on 27.3.19 but nothing was done).

Sayfeli Oglu Kara Mehmet (Identity uncertain).

D.   **E.9.** Takuhi Taslakjian of Kir-Shehir, now of Abbas Agha Mahallessi, Rue Yildiz, No. 31 Beshiktash, states that she knew ALI NAZMI when he was Kuddayi Umumi and Chief of the local C.U.P.

By his order all the women were detained 3 days in the barracks whilst the men were being massacred and the houses looted. On the first day of Bairam the women were permitted to return to their houses. As the witness belonged to the family of a soldier, she was permitted to remain some time longer in Kir-Shehir. She saw ALI NAZMI personally looting Armenian houses and shouting to the women still there that he had had their men massacred by order of the Government. She has seen Armenian girls forcibly detained for his use in his, ALI NAZMI's, house.

E.   **E.9.** Yeranuhi Yeremian of Kir-Shehir, now of Abbas Agha Mahallessi, Rue Yildiz No. 31, Bechiktash, states that she knew ALI NAZMI and knew him as the C.U.P. leader in Kir-Shehir. ["]The women were kept in the barracks whilst the men were deported; on their return to their homes the houses were bare. It was generally said that ALI NAZMI was the chief author of the disappearance of all our men."

F.   **E.9.** Haiganouche Kazandjian of Kir-Shehir, now of Rue Hari Bey No. 5. Misirli oglou Mahallessi Kadikeui, states that in 1915 she was in Kir-Shehir when the orders to deport the Armenians arrived. ALI NAZMI BEY the Mudayi Umumi and local C.U.P. leader; Hilmi Bey the Mutessarif, and Said Bey the school master, at once became prominent and influential in organising the deportations and what followed. The Armenian men were rounded up and slaughtered at Geul Hissar, some three hours distance from Kir-Shehir, the women were herded in barracks. ALI NAZMI made the women a speech declaring he was henceforth their God and that now their husbands had disappeared he would protect them.

ALI NAZMI and Said personally visited the Armenian houses to look for and extort all that he could find. He and Hilmi were the chief sharers in the proceeds. Later ALI NAZMI and Said personally conducted the massacre of 14 Armenian children at a spot half an hour distant from Kir-Shehir. These children had been left behind in the town when all the others had been deported. ALI NAZMI violated in his house a number of Armenian women; even Kemal Bey, the judge, was shocked though he had been benevolent as regards the massacre of the men.

E. 16. Letter from Mr. James La Fontaine, dated 9th September 1920, referring to the mention of his name in the petition of 23.7.20 from the mother of ALI NAZMI (in W. 2178): "I do not recollect the name of ALI NAZMI BIN HUSSEIN of Kir-Shehir although it is possible that if I saw this individual I may recognise him.

I understood that ALI NAZMI alleges to show kindness or assistance to me and three other Englishmen during our internment at Modjour (4½ hours from Kir-Shehir). I did not receive any marked assistance or kindness from any Turkish official with the exception of the Mutessarif of Kirshehir who at my request, and on his responsibility, altered our place of internment from Medjidie to Mojour. In any case, if assistance or kindness was granted (between August 1917 and January 1918) it is quite irrelevant to participation in the Massacre of the Armenians which occurred in 1915. I made numerous enquiries when I was at Kir-Shehir and the information I received convinces me that all Government officials without a single exception were implicated in the Massacres which took place in that town and the surrounding villages."

N.B. On 11.9.20 Mr. Bedrossian, now Chief Clerk; G.S. 'I'.

General Headquarters, had not answered a request for a statement. The whereabouts of Sheikh El-Nazem, also mentioned in petition of 23.7.20, are not known.

5035.A.94. Statement by Hovsep Haladjian, now of Rue Nemli Zade No. 42, Kadikeui, dated 8.9.20 giving a short account of the Kir-Shehir and Gul-Hissar atrocities in April and May 1915.

NAZIM BEY, Major

Malta No. 2809

Interned 29.8.20.

Appointments. President of the Samsun recruiting office and member of the Samsun Court Martial.

Lists. On List VII, i.e., on Foreign Office List.

Arrest. Arrested by British Military Authorities on 12.7.20.

Petitions.   W. 2178 of 29.7.20.   716/24.

1.   Through G.O.C. on 9.8.20.

2.   Petition of 17.12.20, through Malta of 7.1.21 asking for pay as an officer on the Active List.

ACCUSATIONS.

5029.A.20. Mention in statement by Geuvehenian.

M. 2245 (see also 5029.A.18). Hanging of the forty-eight. Captain Perring's telegram of 3.11.19.

G.X. Listed on Patriarchate's detailed list of September 1920.

E.3. Letter addressed to the High Commission, dated 22.7.20 from Constantin J. Filicos, c/o Sophianides Freres, Ismid.

Appendix A.

E.3.   5029.A.18. Statement made by Constantin Filicos at the High Commission on 26.7.20:-

I am an Ottoman Greek subject, tobacco expert of Kadikeui, a suburb of Samsun. In Nov. 1917, I was arrested by order of NAZIM BEY, chief of the Recruiting Department of Samsun. His rank was that of a Major in the Army. I was placed in a cellar for 25 days with water up well above the knee. It was clean spring water. All the Greeks had already been deported but I had been allowed to remain as a Turkish soldier, a tobacco expert. When NAZIM found me out, he arrested me.

On the 26th day I was called before NAZIM who informed me that he was about to hang me. I replied that I had committed no crime. Three days later through the intervention of an Army Lieutenant MILAZIM NIZZAMEDIN, I was released on paying NAZIM £T500. I was then incorporated in the Labour Batt. One month before my arrest I witnessed the hanging of 48 Christians; 3 Armenians, 2 Turks of very low degree and 43 Greeks. Their bodies were taken down but again hung up to please the wife of Behaeddin Bey, the Chief of the Police (police Mudiri) of Samsun. NAZIM was present at the execution. He was the favourite of Vehib Pasha, Commanding of VIth Army and what he ordered was carried out without appeal. These 48 men had never been tried by a Court, but had been brought before NAZIM and the decision to hang them was given by NAZIM alone.

The execution doubtless had the tacit approval of Vehib Pasha and the active approval of Refet Pasha. The burning of Greek villages was done by order of Vehib Pasha and actually carried out by NAZIM BEY and Refet Pasha, Commandant of Samsun.

NAZIM BEY and Refet Pasha were not on good terms for though Refet was Military Commandant of the Sandjak of Samsun still NAZIM was 'protected' by Vehib Pasha who was the supreme Military Commander.

Suleiman Nedjmi Bey, now in British custody, was Mutessarif when the Armenians were deported in July 1915.

I consider the men actually responsible for the deportation of the Greeks to be Refet Pasha and NAZIM BEY under the general authority of Vehib Pasha.

NAZIM BEY's son came to me 4 or 5 days ago begging me to make no statement. He is 15 years of age and has been twice to see me.

APPENDIX A.*

To the British High Commissioner
Constantinople

Your Excellency,

Having heard that Colonel NAZIM BEY, ex-chief of the Recruitment Office in Samsoun (Black Sea) has been arrested some days ago, I wish to profit from the occasion and submit to you my present report in order to acquaint you with the cruel conduct of the said Colonel during the World War and how I and so many of my dead compatriots became his victims.

I therefore accuse the Colonel NAZIM BEY of the following facts:

1. For reasons still unknown to me, I was arrested by him and imprisoned for 25 days in the underground cellar filled with one meter of water and which is located under the Recruitment Office.

On the 25th day, he had me brought before him and threatened me with hanging if I did not consent to pay him 500 Turkish Liras. I was obliged to pay him this sum, through his orderly, the Milazim Nizammedin, in order to save my life.

2. By his orders, all the houses of our village of Kadikeuy were demolished, so that of the 450 buildings before the War, only 80 to 90 remained of which only 15 are habitable.

He did this in order to carry off the contents of the houses to Shoube (Recruitment Office) so as to use them for the construction of various military installations.

3. After demolishing most of the houses he had a water canalisation four meters deep dug through the quarter for a so-called canalisation of the water of a well called St. Georges Well.

4. He himself judged and condemned to death by hanging 48 young men who were executed the following day in the square called Saat-Hane.

Hoping that my present accusation will receive your favourable consideration and certain that English Justice will punish those people who have wanted to endanger civilization.

I beg to remain, Your Excellency, your very humble servant.

CONSTANTIN J. FILICOS

Constantinople, 9/22 July 1920.
ADDRESS
Const. J. Filicos
c/o Sophianides Freres

IZMIDT: Now staying at
Hotel d'Europe
opp. British Embassy,
Pera.

---

* The statement appears in French and has been translated into English –WCB.

HODJA ILIAS SAMI BEY

Malta No. 2810

Interned 29.8.20.

Profession. Deputy for Marash. An Ulema.

Lists. Name appears on Lists III, and VII; that is: his name was suggested for arrest by Mr. Ryan to the Grand Vizier on 27.3.19 (III), his name also appears on Foreign Office List (VII).

Arrest.

A. By Turkish Government on our suggestion he was arrested in (?) April 1919 and apparently acquitted in March 1920. As during part of this time he was said to be insane, he may never have been in custody at all. His name appears on none of Capt. Wilson's prison lists. On 30.10.19 Minister of Foreign Affairs assured Mr. Ryan that he was really suffering from dementia.

B. Arrested by British Military Authorities in Beshiktash on 17.5.20. Since his arrest by the British there has been no question of his sanity.

Petitions.

1. To Mr. Ryan 4.6.20 (pack not numbered). Says he is the son of an Arab and Kurdish woman and therefore no connection with the C.U.P.

2. W. 2178. From wife dated 21.6.20. saying he had nothing to do with politics. No action.

3. W. 2178. From him through Governor of Malta of 25.9.20 saying he was twice arrested and released by the Turks.

4. 1289/24. From wife of 11.2.21.

ACCUSATIONS.

A. 5030.A.9. Account by Asniv Sayatian, a young Armenian woman; In the spring of 1915 [7.3.19] HODJA ELIAS was called to Mush by Servet Bey (VII, now thought to have died in 1915) the Mutessarif. Servet, HODJA ILIAS and Halil Pasha then prepared for the extermination of the Armenians in the Sanjak.

5035.A.5. **5030.A.4.** In conjunction with his friend Dr. Assaf (Mehmed Assaf; III, VI, VII) he massacred 465 of the wealthiest Armenians at Alizanan, sharing the booty with Assaf. The actual participants in the Mush atrocities, besides HODJA ILIAS and Assaf, were all relations of HODJA ILIAS:-

Hadji Mussa, uncle.

Hadji Falamoz, cousin (see also R. 14.12.18).

Reshid of Dido, a relation.

Address of Asniv Sayatian, ex inmate of HODJA ILIAS's harem, is Sarkis Pedeyan, Tchimen Street, 60 (or 26) Pancaldi.

B. 5030.A.9. British Intelligence report of 19.3.19: HODJA ILIAS one of the chief organisers of Mush atrocities. His religious propaganda, extortions and orgies.

N.B. A. and B. above are both probably from the same source. Names of a few local witnesses given.

"Treatment of the Armenians." Pages 84-95 describe Mush atrocities but only names of five Government officials are mentioned.

D. 22. Signed statement dated 21.6.20. by Stepan Messrikian of 59 Mahmud Pasha Street, Stamboul.

Writer describes HODJA ILIAS as the organiser of the Mush atrocities.

HODJA ILIAS had thirteen of the writer's relations put to death, after robbing them of all they possessed and promising them protection.

The writer himself, paid HODJA ILIAS Ltq. 500 (apparently in Constantinople) in order to avoid a similar fate.

Writer can produce witnesses. The Daron Salno Tzar association can also give full details of the massacres of the Armenians in Mush.

G. XIII. In a carefully compiled list of September 1920 of the principal massacrers in the Vilayet of Bitlis, HODJA ILIAS is thus described: All these chiefs of Kurdish clans who carried out the 1915 massacres (list of chiefs given) worked under the aegis of the deputy HODJA ILIAS SAMI. This man was an Ulema of great influence. He preached the Jehad against the Armenians and fanaticised the Kurds. He was the principal organiser in the Sanjak of Mush.

H. 2. Extract from a statement made on the 28.9.20 by Shefik Bey late Kaimakam of Bulanik in the Vilayet of Bitlis, now employed at Kadikeui: The two chief organisers in the sanjak of Mush were the Mutessarif Servet Bey (now dead) and the deputy HODJA ILIAS. They entrusted the execution of the plan of massacre to Colonel HADJI MUSSA BEY, chief of the Mutkam tribe of Kurds, and officer of the Hamidieh cavalry . . . I know HODJA ILIAS as addicted to the raping of Christian girls; it was so well known that it became a scandal among the Moslems, more especially as he wore a turban.

H. 12. Patriarchate's report on Fazil Berki, deputy for Changri (Kastamuni), dated 22.12.20.

"In March 1915 Fazil Berki passed through Konia on an anti-Christian propaganda mission. He was accompanied by HODJA ILIAS who was going on a mission of the same nature to Mush. They separated at Oulou Kishla, Fazli Berki taking the road to Sivas where he conferred with the Vali Muammer and Gani Bey, the responsible C.U.P. Secretary."

ATIF BEY (MEHMET ATIF BEY)

Malta No. 2811

Interned 29.8.20.

Appointments. Dentist at Makrikeui. C.U.P. Secretary at Makrikeui.

Lists. On List VI, i.e. on "Foreign Office List", sent in under cover of despatch 217/R.2178 of 12.2.20.

Arrest. Arrested by Allied Police on 23.5.20.

Petitions. 1st petition from wife of 26.5.20.

W. 2178. 2nd petition from wife of 5.8.20.

5035/A/18. 3rd petition from wife of 2.11.20.

W. 2178. 4th petition from wife 25.11.20.

N.B. High Commission's despatch 1552/W.3667 of 24.11.20 covering report of special commission, recommended that ATTIF BEY be brought to trial.

ACCUSATIONS.

A. 5035.A.18. Letter of 10.2.19 from Greek and Armenian councils of Makrikeui petitioning for the arrest of ATIF BEY who played a sinister role during the deportations.

B. Signed form by Dicran Tchiboukdjian, dated 22.3.19 accusing ATIF BEY of having superintended the destruction of the Russian Church at San Stefano; also of having 'collected' beds and money in favour of the "Défense Nationale".

C. Signed form by Petros Agopian, dated 22.3.19 regarding looting of his houses.

D. Extract from 'Djagadamart' of 24.6.20 regarding the signature to a [sic].

E. Statement by Dicran Tchiboudjian (B. Supra) dated 28.6.20, given at the H.C. Relates to the Turkish mob, led by ATIF, proceeding to and returning from the desecration of the Russian monastery and chapel at San Stefano. ATIF also caused 17 Armenians to be deported from Makrikeui, of whom 3 only are known to be alive.

F. Extract from 'Vertchine Lour' of 28.6.20 stating that the Armenian Patriarch had dismissed Maseh Olegian, President of the Armenian Ephorie of Makrikeuy, for having signed the petition mentioned under head Defence, paragraph A.

G. Signed statement by the priest of the Armenian Church at San Stefano dated 30.6.20.

See Appendix A.

H. Signed from by H. Vartian, dated 29.6.20, accusing ATIF, as an eye-witness, of the destruction of the Russian church at Galataria in 1914 and the deporting of 17 or 18 Armenians from Makrikeuy in 1916, of whom only 3 are now alive.

I. From Lt. Tucker, dated 3.8.20, "Nahid Bey's enquiries show that ATIF BEY, dentist, of Makrikeuy, was a famous active unionist during the War, to whom there is no doubt many unlawful acts are due.

G.11. In the Patriarchate's detailed list of criminals of September 1920, ATIF BEY is listed under the heading: Influential members of the propaganda committee who participated in the organisation of the massacre of Armenians. Against the name of ATIF BEY of Makrikeuy there appears the note: he was the cause of the destruction of the Russian Church of San Stefano.

DEFENCE.

A. 5035/A/18. Certificate of good conduct, undated, signed by Turks, three Armenians (two signatures illegible), also by E. M. Macnamara and Helen Papazoglou.

B. Letter from Miss Papagozlou, dated 19.6.20 saying that ATIF BEY had treated her well during the War.

APPENDIX A.
SIGNED INFORMATION AGAINST ATIF BEY

In the month of October 1914, on the day of the suppression of capitulations, I was going to San Stefano to my parish church. At Sirkedji, the train was overcrowded. When we arrived at Makrikeui, I saw ATIF BEDRI and other leading C.U.P. men take the train, there was music playing and Turkish flags flying. We arrived at San Stefano and the train proceeded no further in accordance with the time table. The mob, however, forced the engine driver to proceed to Kutchuk Tchekmedjé from where the Russian Church was nearer.

I got off the train at San Stefano and the train left. Three quarters of an hour later, a Turkish Officer came to me informing that "I was officially invited to the demolition of the Russian Church". I refused to go.

On the same day in the evening, the mob returned bearing trophies such as gospels, crosses, sacred vases, also the skulls and bones of the dead priests. I saw Bedri having in his hand a skull and two arm bones.

The church was demolished within 3 days with dynamite. In these three days there was a mob of 2 – 3,000 people who had come from the town with axes and other weapons in order to partake in the demolition of the church. On the first day of the demolition Imams had preached sermons and prayed for the welfare of the C.U.P. Government. ATIF was the chief of C.U.P. at Makrikeui and he exiled on the 16th August 1916, 18 Armenians from Makrikeui out of which there are left only 3 who have returned. He collected under the pretext of helping the Turkish soldiers all the valuable furniture of the Christians at Makrikeui. He is one of the worst scoundrels who did the greatest mischiefs to the Christian population of the village of Makrikeui. This ATIF is the same one whom I saw arrested a short time ago by the British Police.

(SG) FATHER HOUSIG KERESTDJIAN

The Priest of the Church of San Stefano

30.6.20

SULEIMAN MEDJMI BEY

Malta No. 2812

Interned 29.8.20.

Appointments. Mutessarif of Samsun, 1914 – 1916. Vali of Sivas January 1916 to March 1918.

Lists. On Lists VI (approved but not sent to Foreign Office and List VII, i.e. the Foreign Office List.)

On 23.7.19 Assistant High Commissioner minuted: "He should certainly be arrested. The method will be decided shortly."

Again on 16.8.19 Assistant High Commissioner minuted: "On list for arrest."

Arrest. By G.S. 'I' on 22.7.20.

Petitions. 1639. 24. Mother-in-law's of 16.2.21.

N.B. In High Commissioner's despatch 1552/W.3667 of 24.11.20 covering report of special committee, it was recommended that SULEIMAN NEDJMI be detained at Malta until brought up for trial.

ACCUSATIONS.

A. 5029.A.20. Signed statement of 1.7.19 murder of Hampar Zakarian in May 1915. Appendix A.

B. Krikor Nichanian's statement of 28.7.20. Torture and murder of Hampar Zakarian in Samsoun prison in April 1915.

Massacre of Tatarian family.

Death of the naked martyr at Tchakalli, Appendix B.

C. Hagop H. Gueuvchanian's statement of 5.8.20 on the general responsibility of SULEIMAN NEDJMI for the Armenian deportations and massacres. Appendix C.

APPENDIX A.[*]

Extract from a statement signed by a large number of Armenians of Samsoun; dated 1.7.19 and sent to the High Commission by the Armenian Committee of Samsoun.

N.B. Father Karekin Chinikdjian, the Armenian priest of Samsoun in May 1915 has since been massacred.

Hampar Zakarian was a poor Armenian (?) maker and without any cause like the other Armenians of the city has been taken into prison. In the prison he has been tried to make him confess the imaginary secretes of the Armenian Committees. He has refused to calumniate anyone. NEDJMI BEY (Mutessarif) has ordered to stripe and torture him by red hot irons. This could not be durated long, so on 7th May 1915 on Fridays midnight, at 3 o'clock a.m. an armed troop of Turkish gendarmeries have called the named Armenian priest Father Karekin Chinikdjian out of his house without telling him the cause and forced him to follow them. They have leaded him to the Armenian cemetery, there the Father has found a covered coffin near to a diged grave. They have ordered him to bury the unknown dead. The priest in the service when has opened the covering of the coffin, put a grasp of soil in it, (that is an ecclesiastical rule), with horror has seen that the unknown dead is Hampar Zakarian and his body is wholly tortured. Next morning every Armenian heard this sad news in detail tolled by the priest and Turkish gendarmeries. Forty days Turkish gendarmeries continually day and night have kept sentinel on the grave not to leave to anybody to approach to the grave and to hasten the putrifaction have put lime every day on the grave (they believe that lime does it):

b. SEILEYMAN NEDJMI BEY has declared to Armenians that whoever that turns Mohammedan will be safed. 300 Armenians have done it. He has send some of them to Baffra other to Phatza, after keeping them there about two weaks, has called them back and told that they will reside at Kavak but after sending them there has given order to the **meudir** of Kavak not to keep them there but send soon to Sivas into the hands of Moamber Bey (The Vali of Sivas) to be massacred by the organised troops of the later and in order that no Armenian whether has become Mohammedan or not to succeed to remain in Kavak has send Latif Bey the commander of gendarmery to pursue them and fulfil his desires:

c. There was an order from Constantinople that if there were Armenians who were taken into military service their families should be spared, but NEDJMI BEY in spite to this order has ordered to exile even this kind Armenian families.

d. During deportation of Armenians from Samsoun SEILEYMAN NEDJMI BEY has tried by every means not to spare even to pregnant women and sicks and ecclesiastics. Has hired heralds and told them to cry in the streets that if anybody whether Mohammedan or Greek that dares to keep safe an Armenian, should be judged and hanged. If today there are Armenians that in spite of such severe execution are saved that is by a miracle and every survived Armenian has its own history of horror, and to be true we must add that Greek prelate of Samsoun has done his best for the Armenians to help them in any way.

Sir, after leaving the case to Your Highness, we expect soon to see the judgement and the punishment of SEILEYMAN NEDJMI BEY.

---

[*] This statement was written in particularly poor English and has been left in the original –Ed.

APPENDIX B.[*]

Testimony of an Armenian from Samsoun Concerning the Criminal ex-Mutessarif of Samsoun, SULEYMAN-NEDJMI

I the undersigned, Krikor Nichanian from Trebizond, having lived in Samsoun during the period 1913 to 1915, hereby declare and testify in full conscience all that I know regarding the conduct of the above mentioned person:

1. Between 11th and 15th April, 1915, two months before the general deportation of the Armenians, SULEYMAN NEDJMI arrested and imprisoned in Samsoun 30 to 40 Armenian notabilities, among whom my friend Hampartzoum Zakarian.

I testify that Hampartzoum Zakarian having been brutally tortured, together with all the other prisoners, during the interrogation in the presence of the Mutessarif, was killed in his cell and buried in the following circumstances.

Towards the end of April, 1915, the vicar of the Armenian community, Father Karekin, was asked by the Mutessarif to undertake the burial of an Armenian who had died in his cell. The body was taken to the cemetery not by the main road of the Armenian quarter but through isolated cross roads, accompanied by the Vicar. In the cemetery, the Vicar raised the lid of the coffin and recognised the identity of the deceased who was no other than one of his parishioners, Hampartzoum Zakarian. The latter's head and face carried traces of horrible wounds and were covered with blood.

The following day, the Vicar informs the community and the family of the deceased of the facts of the case. The wife goes to the Mutessarif and asks for the body of her husband but this is rejected categorically.

Immediately, the Mutessarif sends some policemen with fixed bayonets to keep a close watch on the tomb. Some weeks later, the body is exhumed upon the orders of the Mutessarif and burned.

2. On the 21st of June, 1915, after the general deportation had taken place, my family and I were living in Samsoun, having been converted to Islam previously. On that day, one of my friends, Mr. Bedros Tatarian, who had been hiding at his home until then, came to me with all his family and asked me to intercede with the Mutessarif, who knows me, in order to allow them to become Moslems.

After accepting our demand, the Mutessarif ordered that my friend and his family be arrested and deported immediately. This order was carried out and since then I have no news about them.

I was deported to the town of Alatcham where I lived as a Moslem. But on July 16, 1915, I was brought back to Samsoun whence my family and I were deported to an unknown destination.

Half an hour later, we noticed that a man, naked and hands tied behind his back, was following our convoy. The policemen who accompanied us kept shouting at him **Hayde**

---

[*] The report appears in French and has been translated into English –WCB.

Ghiavour, Yétish and beat him with sticks all the time, to such an extent that the body of the man was covered with wounds. It was a fearful sight.

After a day's march and while we had hardly reached Tchakalli, we wanted to intercede with the policeman in favour of the man who was still following us. To our request that they should treat him more kindly, they answered that they had received firm order from the Mutessarif to do away with that man. Whereupon they gave the poor man such a beating with their whips that he gave up the soul, in front of our eyes. This order applied to the entire convoy but happily, we managed to bribe these ferocious men and escaped from the convoy. I reaffirm the truth of my testimony and declare that those of our convoy who miraculously escaped like me, can also give their testimony, should you want them to do so.

(S) KRIKOR NICHANIAN

ADDRESS
Krikor Nichanian
Achir Ef. Han 58, Stambul
Tel. Lt. 1404

APPENDIX C.

Statement Made At The High Commission On 5.8.20 by Hagop Gueuvchenian, Commission Agent of Samsoun; Now of Kutchuk Turkia Han, Chez Balukdjian Frers Stamboul.

I left Samsun 3 months ago.

I know SULEIMAN NEDJMI personally. He was Mutassarif from 1914 to 1916 when he became Vali of Sivas. He left Samsun just before the arrival of Refet Pasha and the beginning of the Greek deportations.

In June 1915 the deportation of Armenians began from Samsun. I myself was protected by the Persian Consul, but my family consisting of 10 people was deported into Sivas vilayet and massacred between Amassia and Tokat with the knowledge and consent of SULEIMAN NEDJMI at the end of June 1915.

Again in September 1915, I was deported together with 22 Armenian men, women and children, by direct order of NEDJMI. I myself escaped from the convoy but all the remainder were murdered just south of Amassia.

SULEIMAN NEDJMI knew as well as every other person in Samsun, what was to be the fate of all Armenian deportees.

Within a week of the first deportations every Armenian knew that deportation was a euphemism for massacre. The Mutessarif of course knew this better even than we did. He had placards put up about the town warning all Greeks against harbouring Armenians under pain of death by hanging. There were no wholesale massacres of Armenians within the boundaries of the sandjak. The massacres began just south of Kavak on the Sivas boundary.

Some 5 or 6 Armenian intellectuals of Samsun were arrested in May 1915 and thrown into prison. In 1916 NEDJMI ordered the then President of the Court Martial Osman Senayi Bey to condemn these men, but he refused saying there was no evidence against them. For this NEDJMI dismissed him and sent to Constantinople. Before leaving Osman Senayi came to say goodbye to the Persian Consul where I was hidden and told him the circumstances of his dismissal. Nazim, the President of the Recruiting Office was a member of the Court Martial. Though Nazim had full authority to do what he liked he was never President of the Court Martial Nazim was protected by Vehib Pasha. For the Greek atrocities I look upon Refet Pasha as undoubtedly chiefly responsible. Later Vehif Pasha dismissed Refet Pasha.

For practical purposes power passed into the hands of the Military after the occupation of Trebizond by the Russians.

Witness can corroborate in regard to murder of Hampar Zakarian by order of SULEIMAN NEDJMI; also in regard to the Tartarian family (502/A/20).

N.B. An intelligent witness.

BURHANEDDIN HAKKI BEY, Major

Malta No. 2814

Interned 20.9.20.

Appointments. Military Commandant at Kirshehir in Angora Vilayet in 1915. Major of Gendarmerie at Kirshehir.

Lists. On List III. i.e. his name suggested for arrest by Mr. Ryan to Grand Vizier. On List VI approved by High Commissioner but not sent to Foreign Office. On List VII Foreign Office List.

Arrest and Deportation. Arrested by British Military Police on or about 29.7.20. The arrest was reported to High Commissioner by G.O.C. in C. on 5.8.20, without mentioning date of arrest and proposed his transfer to Malta. On 19.8.20 High Commissioner suggested to G.O.C. his detention in Turkey.

W. 2178. On 26.8.20 G.O.C. objected to detention in Turkey. On 9.9.20 High Commissioner sent despatch 1263 to Foreign Office on the general subject of transfers to Malta. On 9.9.20 High Commissioner agreed to transfer to Malta.

Petitions.

1.   **W. 2178.** Petition of 29.9.20 through Governor of Malta of 6.10.20. In this petition he alleges his arrest was due to the information of a civilian who wanted his carpets etc. He alleges that after fifty-five days imprisonment he was released on payment of a fine of £tq 50 for having been in possession of a revolver and then he was re-arrested and sent to Malta the next day.

W. 2178. On November 6th 1920 the President, Allied Police Committee informed High Commissioner that carpets had been returned to their original owner, after careful investigation, by Lieut Mac Rae, Allied Police Control Officer at Kadikeui. Lt. Mac Rae's report attached. On November 12th 1920 High Commissioner informed Governor of Malta of the result of the enquiry and of the reason for his internment.

Further petition of 28.11.20, through Governor Malta of 2.12.20, in answer to above regarding carpets. He will claim damages. No action.

Petition of 12.12.20 asking that subsistence may be granted to his family; through Governor Malta of 15.12.20.

ACCUSATIONS.

5031.A.7. Statement by Aram Fosbiyikian, through G.S. 'I' of 7.3.19 describing the massacres of Gul-Hissar and the deportations from Kir-Shehir. His list of Turks responsible for the Kir-Shehir atrocities include:

HILMI BEY	Mutessarif (Deportee)
ALI NAZMI	Public Prosecutor (Deportee)
BURHANEDDIN	Military Commandant
KIAZIM	Professor
OMAR LUFTI	Professor

HAMI	Commissioner of Police
ALI RIZA	Assistant Commissioner of Police
NURI	Accountant of Police

5032.A.9. Further statement by Aram Fosbiyikian and Agop Terzie both of Kir-Shehir in which he denounces BURHANEDDIN and Hami Bey, Commissioner of Police as the executants of the Gul-Hissar massacres.

5035.A.94. Statement by Hoosep Haladjian, now of Rue Nemli Zade No. 42 Kadikeui, giving a short account of Kirshehir and Gul-Hissar atrocities in April and May (O.S.) 1915 mentioning BURHANEDDIN HAKKI BEY.

G. IV. In the Patriarchate's carefully compiled list of September 1920, BURHANEDDIN, of Rumeli, commanding the Kirshehir battalion is listed among the officers responsible for the Kirshehir atrocities.

Patriarchate report of March 1919.

Witnesses: Aram Fosbikian 18, grocer's assistant and Agop Terzie, 18, both of Kir-Shehir in Angora Vilayet.

On the 8th July 1915 arrests began and took place on five days. On July 8th, fourteen persons including the Priest Der Avedis; a lawyer, named Grigor Dermosisian; Siragan Bairamian, the wealthiest trader in Kir-Shehir; and a student named Garabed Kershishian. On July 9th 65 persons were arrested; on July 10th, 135 persons; on July 13th 41: about July 27th, 18 young boys. In each case on the night following their arrest, they were marched with their hands bound a distance of 1½ hours to Geol Asar [Gul Hissar], accompanied by police and gendarmes under the commands of the Commissioner of Police, Hami Bey and the Gendarmerie Tabur Commandant BURHANEDDIN. They were told to sit down and eat and soldiers came out of trenches and butchered them with swords, clubs and axes. Eye-witnesses to the above are: Mihran Calebji, who escaped wounded, returned to Kir-Shehir and recounted his experiences. He was after a few days taken away by BURHANEDDIN in person and executed. Simeon Giobekjian, bootmaker, who escaped at the beginning of one of the massacres, served as a soldier, and is now at Kir-Shehir.

RIFAAT BEY (MAHMED RIFAAT BEY) (RIFAAT SALIM BEY)

Malta No. 2815

Interned 20.9.20.

Appointments. Commissioner of Police, Sivas 1914-1915.

Member of Emvale Metrouke Commission.

Lists. On List VII, i.e. on Foreign Office List; despatch 217/R.2178 of 12.2.20.

Arrest. Arrested at Kadikeui by British Military Authorities on 31.7.20.

Petitions. 975/24. Petition from wife of 27.1.21.

N.B. High Commissioner's despatch 1552/W.3667 of 24.11.20. covering report of special committee, recommended that he should be detained at Malta and brought up for trial.

ACCUSATIONS.

5029/A/5. March 1919. Boghos Zeki Cantar, late of the Ottoman Diplomatic Service, exiled in Sivas, in 1919, of Pera, 11 Rue Anadol, Appartment Sarandi, No.1, now in Paris, states that RIFAAT BEY was the executive agent of the notorious Vali of Sivas, Muammer Bey, see his dossier, in the matter of atrocities then committed. Mentions Rushdi Bey, son of the ex Sheikh-ul-Islam Husni Effendi, who was in exile at Sivas.

5029/A/6. 19.1.19. Mr. Karageuzian's report on the Sivas atrocities mentioning RIFAAT BEY. Mr. Karageuzian was a member of the "Armenian Committee".

H.8. Patriarchate's accusation against Gani Bey, C.U.P. Secretary of Sivas; dated 3.11.20.

a) Mention of RIFAAT in connection with atrocities. Gani, RIFAAT and Halil, C.O. Gendarmerie did the actual killing of nightly batches at Tchel[e]biler Tzor, etc. [39.45N, 36.55E]

b) Before the Commission of Enquiry presided by Nazim Pasha, RIFAAT gave evidence for the Prosecution against Gani Bey and Dr. Fazil Berki (both deportees).

H. 12. In Patriarchate's report of 22.12.20 on Fazil Berki Bey, deputy for Changri and anti-Christian propagandist, it is mentioned that MEHMET RIFAAT made a declaration to the Commissioner of Enquiry set up by the Turkish Government after the Armistice, implicating Fazil Berki in the preparations made for the massacres in Sivas Vilayet.

G. XVI. In Patriarchate's detailed list of criminals of September 1920, RIFAAT's name is duly listed.

MEHMET NURI BEY (HADJI BALOSH ZADE MEHMET BEY)

Malta No. 2816

Interned 20.9.20.

Appointments. Deputy for Dersim in Harput Vilayet in 1915. Son of Hadji Balosh.

Lists. On List VII, No. 78 in list under cover of Despatch 217/R.2178 of 12.2.20; i.e. the F.O. List.

Arrest.

A. Arrested by Turkish Authorities on 4.6.19; the charge being given as "murder" and "Organising armed bands". He was tried by Turkish Court-Martial in connection with the massacre of Soldetek near his own estate in Harput Vilayet and was acquitted in common with most others dealt with by the Court Martial in 1919, on 13th January 1920, the Court Martial having failed to prove the charge (see Minister of War's letter of 16.2.21 in 2030/24)

B. Arrested by Allied Police in Stambul on 21.7.20.

Petitions.

A. **5030.A.23.** From wife of 23.7.20.

B. From MEHMET NURI of 31.7.20, per Sadik Wassif Bey on 12.8.20.

C. From wife of 14.8.20.

D. From wife of 1.9.20, through General Officer Commanding in Chief on 10.9.20.

E. **W. 2178.** From MEHMED NURI of 15.10.20, through Governor of Malta on 2.10 20, asking for original of Dr. Rigg's testimonial and other documents found by the Police.

2.12.20. President of Allied Police Commission forwards documents.

7.12.20. Passed to Governor Malta.

F. **869/24.** Petition of 8.1.21 through Governor Malta of 15.1.21 enclosing **copies** of two undated petitions to the Armenian Patriarch, signed by Armenians. (Copies sent are in English). No action.

G. **868/24.** Petition of 8.1.21 through Swedish Legation of 22.1.21 as above. No action.

H. **2030/24.** Petition from Minister of War of 16.2.21 through G.H.Q. 'I' of 25.2.21.

ACCUSATIONS.

B.30. 29.3.19. See also below. 5030.A.23. Dr. Marzbanian, native of Aghin in Harput Vilayet, now a dentist in Karakeui, Galata, accuses him of participation in Harput atrocities ("Organised, committed and commanded by this deputy") in May and June 1915. Accomplice of Sabit Bey, the Vali (Malta); Nazim Bey, Inspector of Ittihad

(No. 143 on F.O. List); Bulutli Halil, and Mektubji Shevket (perhaps the same as the Muhammad Shevki now (21.8.20) in custody).

Dr. Marzbanian gives the names and addresses of 4 eyewitnesses.

C. 2. 23.1.20 **(List by Dr. Barton).** MEHMET NURI's name appears on an American list, supplied by Dr. Barton, of "those who took an active part in the massacres in the city of Harput and villages in 1915 and after."

C. 17. 13.2.20. Statement, made verbally and taken down in High Commission, by S.S. Hachadourian, Professor of Music, late of Harput; a competent English speaking and educated witness.

"From personal knowledge and observation I consider the following to be the principals in the matter of the Harput atrocities: Sabit Bey (Malta) MEHMED NURI . . . and Hadji MEHMET (on F.O. List).

E. 4. Statement by an eye-witness, Haroutun Daghatelian, a blacksmith of Harput, now living in the Armenian school at Ortakeui, testifying as to his escape from the massacre of Han Punar in August 1915, superintended by the Deputy, MEHMET NURI.

E. 4. Statement by Asadoor Ghugassian of Harput testifying that the deputy, MEHMET NURI, was President of the C.U.P. at Harput, and as to his extortions under cover of fees to exempt Armenians from massacre.

E. 4. Statement by Donabed Bedrossian, baker of Harput, now of Ortakeui, corroborating the statement of Nishan Baghdassarian.

5035.A.50. 3.6.19. Dr. Chemoun Malke now of Moda accuses MEHMET NURI of having extorted Lt. 500 from his brother-in-law, Artin Barsam of Mezre, on the promise of his personal safety.

3.9.20. Speaking in English. 5030.A.23. Statement made in the High Commission by Dr. Michel Kechichian, Doctor of Medicine, Armenian Protestant, native and late practicing in Malatia (Harput Vilayet) now of 27 Rue Bilezik, Pancaldi.

"At the beginning of the War, I was called up for service with the Turkish Army Medical Corps in which I served till the Armistice with the XIXth Corps d'Armée under Tahsin Bey which was a reserve Army Corps stationed in Sivas. At the end of War I found myself in Batum and I was there when the British entered. For 5 months I was employed in the British Intelligence in Batum under Captain Lloyd.

In April 1916 I had leave to visit my family in Harput and remained with them some three weeks. In April 1916 I should say there were not more than 200 Armenians remaining in Harput city and Mezre exclusive of orphans and girls in harems, this out of a normal population of some 13,000. I was told on all sides that the chief organiser of the deportations and massacres under Vali Sabit Bey, was MEHMET NURI, deputy for Dersim. I can bring forward many witnesses to prove what I say, that is, that under the Vali he was the most influential person dealing with Armenians and that he received very large sums of money under promise of saving lives which promises he did not keep. But at the present time it will be most difficult to get anyone to come forward and openly state the facts as they are fearful of what may happen to themselves or to their relatives remaining in the vilayet.

I have heard of Dr. Riggs' letter to the Court-Martial. I know both Dr. Henry Riggs and Rev. Charles Riggs. So far as it goes I consider the letter to be true; like most other educated Turks MEHMET NURI was careful to cover himself; he helped the American Missionaries who were practically shut up in the college, he supplied them and their children with corn and saved a number of Armenians, his own farmers. At the same time he caused many thousands of others to be deported and massacred.

E. 13. Written statement by Dr. Kechichian in reply to MEHMET NURI's petition of 31.7.20. See Appendix A.

4.9.20 Speaking in Turkish interpreted by Mr. Stavrides. Statement made by in the High Commission by Mr. George Harpoutlian, merchant of Harput, established in Pancaldi during the past 25 years; address 102 Rue Konstantin.

"I have known MEHMET NURI during the past 40 years and his father before him. I know Assaf Bey and Assim Bey brothers-in-law of MEHMET NURI. The former I have seen lately, the latter not for a long time. I met Assaf Bey in the street two days ago. He asked me to arrange a meeting place as he had something important to communicate. I said I would meet him at a certain casino in Pancaldi. I went but Assaf never turned up. When Assaf meets me he usually asks for money on the plea of his being a compatriot and an old friend. It is absolutely and entirely false that I have ever approached Assaf or Assim Beys demanding money. Thirty members of my family have been massacred by MEHMET NURI or by his orders. There is not a grain of truth in the statement made by MEHMET NURI in his letter to His Excellency the British High Commissioner, dated 31.7.20 (in 5030.A.23). Never in my life have I been in the houses of MEHMET NURI or Assaf or Assim Beys.

4.9.20. Speaking in Armenian interpreted by Mr. Fenerdjian. 5030.A.23. Statement made in High Commission by Dr. Marzbanian, dentist, native of Aghin in Harput Vilayet, for the last 20 years practicing in Constantinople.

I am President of the Armenian Committee of Harput. My office and domicile is at Eyinli, Yere Batan Djamassi, Galata. Since the Armistice neither I nor my Committee have had any communication direct or indirect with MEHMET NURI; we helped to bring forward evidence for the prosecution during MEHMET NURI's trial before the Turkish Court Martial. The Court Martial refused to listen to all the Armenian witnesses except that of one woman. I had signed a petition to the Court Martial praying for the prosecution of MEHMET NURI, but I was not even called. The Court Martial acquitted MEHMET NURI (in January 1920). [January 13, 1920]

I know of Dr. Rigg's letter to the Court-Martial. Dr. Riggs is a friend of mine and he can not help but be sorry for the effect created by his letter. The writing of it may be explained by the fact that Dr. Riggs is a very good man; disinclined to believe evil of anyone; he was not allowed to communicate with the outside world, and as usual, NURI was careful to cover himself by doing good to Dr. Riggs and a few Armenians whom Dr. Riggs would know of.

Dr. Riggs, knowing nothing specific about MEHMET NURI and having just returned to Harput must have been anxious to secure the good will of MEHMET NURI; moreover, later it was being said that it was Dr. Riggs who had secured the arrest of MEHMET NURI by his intervention. It is most probably that MEHMET NURI, through his friends in Harput, and to cover himself in case he should be arrested, asked Dr. Riggs to write his letter "to all whom it may concern". At the trial there was also produced a petition on behalf of MEHMET NURI, signed by some 70 or 80 Armenians of Harput whom as I well know, had been compelled to sign.

The object of my Committee is the relief of the survivors of the massacres in Harput Vilayet and incidentally to help in the prosecution of the massacrers in accordance with the declarations made to us in 1915 by the Allied Government.

E. 18. 13.9.20. Mentioned in a statement by Mehmet Namik Bey, ex-Director of Police at Harput.

G. XV. In Armenian Patriarchate's detailed list of September 1920, MEHMET NURI Deputy, is duly listed.

H. 4. Translations of alleged official telegrams, dated 25.7.15 from Sabit Bey, Vali of Mamuret-ul-Aziz, then at Dersim (the sanjak north of Harput and in the same Vilayet) to the Ministry of the Interior (Talaat Pasha). Alleged translations communicated to the High Commission on 1.10.20.

"With the exception of the centre of Malatia, which will be cleared within the next few days, no Armenians are left in the Vilayet (of Mamuret-ul-Aziz) and its dependencies (i.e. ? the sanjak of Erzinjan in 1915).

Nazim Bey, Delegate of the C.U.P. at Harput, On F.O. List for arrest. MEHMET NURI BEY, Deputy for Dersim (Vilayet of Mamuret-ul-Aziz. Now at Malta.) With a view to prevent many abuses taking place through the deportation of the Armenians and seeing that a thorough overhaul was necessary, Suleiman Faik, Vali ad interim and a Commander of the Army Corps, has today sent me the following copy of a telegram. I regret to say that I am convinced as to the truth of the whole question. I suggest that Inspector Nazmi Bey should be recalled to Constantinople, that further measures against Nazim Bey and Deputy MEHMET BEY should be decided upon in Constantinople, and that the officials of the Vilayet, whose complicity is proved, should be at once dismissed. I am ready to carry out whatever instructions are conveyed to me."

A. Copy (from Suleiman Faik (? At Mezre) to Sabit Bey at Dersim)

Nazim Bey Inspector of the Union and Progress considering the Armenian deportations a great occasion to enrich himself has proceeded to several measures which later on became perfectly clear; and all this a little before your visiting Dersim. Great sums of money were stolen and everything done in the name of the C.U.P. reached a point which cannot be tolerated by anybody. Even the members of the Central Committee have recently resigned and only the aforementioned Nazim Bey, together with the Secretary General Shevki Bey, are still connected with it. One of those who played the greatest role in these affairs is MEHMED BEY, Deputy of Dersim. The Inspector, profiting by his position, has stolen much money and other things, and now begins to threaten the Sirianis (?) [Assyrians]. Under these circumstances I hope that in future you will continue to enjoy the unparalleled and perfect public confidence in view of your noble attitude and that being connected with the honourable Committee, I particularly express to you my special satisfaction. Signed Suleiman Faik.

B. Copy. To Vali Sabit Bey at Dersim.

Nazim Bey, Inspector of the C.U.P. considering the Armenian deportations a great occasion for increasing his personal wealth has a little before your visit to Dersim, proceeded to several measures which became quite obvious later on. Thousands of pounds are being stolen. The evils done in the name of the C.U.P. have become intolerable. Six members of the Central Committee have recently resigned. He, together with the Secretary-General and the Defterdar only remain. One of those who played the greatest role in these affairs is the Deputy MEHMED BEY. The Inspector, profiting by his position has looted much money, goods and girls, and now begins to threaten the Sirianis (?) [Assyrians]. Goods excepted, the amount of money collected up to now in the name of the Committee amounts to more than 10,000 pounds. Under these circumstances we hope that in the future too you will continue to enjoy the unparalleled and perfect general confidence because of your noble attitude, and, we consider it our patriotic duty to express to you our special satisfaction. Please take from the telegraph office the copy of the telegram.

(SIGNATURES):

MEHMED ALI Central Commander

FERID Regimental Gendarmerie Commander

FERID Maarif Mudiri

RUCHDI Police Mudiri

N.B. Of the signatures, MEHMET ALI may be the MEHMET ALI PASHA who committed suicide on 11.3.19. Ferid Bey is the Provincial Director of Education who was arrested by the Turkish Authorities on 20.7.19 and released in Jan. 1920. The other Ferid was a Major commanding the Gendarmerie at Mezre, the headquarters for the Vilayet, noted as one of the principals in the Harput atrocities. Rushdi, the Police Mudiri is not yet on Index.

DEFENCE.

5030/A/16. Letter from Rev. Charles Riggs, A.C.R.N.E. Headquarters dated 23.6.19 saying that he had received from his brother, Rev. Henry H. Riggs of Harput, an affidavit which he had handed over to the Turkish Court Martial engaged in the trial of MEHMET NURI, Deputy for Dersim. The affidavit was to the effect that MEHMET NURI not only had nothing to do with the said deportations but on the contrary saved in his own home and at considerable personal risk a goodly number of Armenians during the deportations.

5030/A/14. On 21.6.19, when MEHMET NURI was in Turkish custody a petition was received from him charging the Armenian Philanthropic Society with blackmail. (This

Society is said to be the Bureau Bazizmanian; Secretary, Dr. Bazizmanian dentist; Eyinli, Yéré Batan Djamissi, Galata). This petition was accompanied by a copy of a statement by Henry H. Riggs, dated Harput 24.4.19, as follows:

"To whom it may concern:

I have been informed that in the case of Hadji Balosh Zade MEHMET BEY the statement has appeared in the press that he was arrested on complaint of the American Missionaries.

I wish to state that so far as I know no such complaint has ever been made by the American Missionaries in Harput, and that we have had no cause for any such complaint. On the contrary MEHMET BEY cooperated in the rescue and care of the Armenians in 1915, saving a considerable number alive in his house when the owners were deported."

Harput, April 24th 1919.

Vu au Conulat Général des Etats Unis d'Amérique à Constantinople, pour la legalisation de la signature ci-dessus apposée de Mr. Henry H. Riggs, citoyen Américain, Directeur de la Section de Harpout, de la Commission de Secours Américaine, pour le Proche Orient.

Constantinople

Le 9 Juin 1919.

Le Vice Consul Des Etats Unis d'Amérique.

On the 10.7.20 the High Commissioner wrote to Dr. Peet asking whether Dr. Peet knew anything of the case.

On 12.7.20 Dr. Peet replied: "So far as I have been able to ascertain, the arrest of this man (by the Turkish Authorities) was not based upon any information given by any American Missionary. No steps have been taken by myself in this case and with the exception of a letter addressed by Rev. Charles T. Riggs to Commander Heathcote-Smith . . . none, so far as I have been able to learn, have been taken by any member of the A.C.R.N.E. to secure this man's release."

On 15.7.20 Dr. Peet qualified his former letter by saying: "I find this person's name in a list which I sent to Commander Heathcote-Smith on June 27th 1919 as (d) in paragraph 2 of a list of persons "who took an active part in the massacres in the city of Harput and villages in 1915 and after." **This list is the one referred to under C.2. sent on 23.1.20. It is a copy of the one sent to Com H-S on 27.6.19.** The list was furnished me by Dr. Barton on his return from the Interior. Dr. Barton is not at present in Constantinople but will be here in a few days. It was at his request that I furnished a copy of the said list. I will call his attention to the matter on his return". (No further action in this matter on record).

N.B. The petitions received contain further material for the defence.

APPENDIX A.

RE MEHMET NURI.

Deputy for Dersim

Written statement by Dr. Michel Keshishian

(Original in E. 13)

(Being a refutation of accusations in MEHMET NURI's Petition dated 31.7.20)

4.9.20.

Sir,

Enclosed you will find my answer and explanation for the letter of the Deputy of Dersim MEHMET, in which if you have the kindness to read it, you will notice:

1. in what circumstances and when I went to his house;
2. for what right my wife wished to demand money from him;
3. that it is false and untrue his saying that I have shown him the accusing paper prepared for him by the Armenian Union of Harput;
4. that still he lies in saying that I have given my thanks to him because he has saved my parents' lives during the massacres that took place 25 years ago.

I have explained that MEHMET has been a butcher and murderer.

Yours respectfully,

(S) Dr. M. KESHISHIAN

During the deportations of Mezre MEHMET NURI had taken LT 500 from my father and LT 500 from my brother-in-law. My wife being there and living in her father's house at Mezre, she is sure that her father and brother paid the money to MEHMET NURI in order that he might spare their lives. But after a few days they were deported and killed on the way to Malatia together with thousands of other Armenians. My wife's mother, her two sisters, her brother's wife and children were all robbed on the road; naked and hungry they arrived at Urfa. Some remained at Urfa, others were sent on to Der Zor, in the desert of Mesopotamia, where they lived as beggars, almost naked and living for several months on grass. After many difficulties we succeeded in finding their traces and learned where they were and began to help them as much as possible. My wife did her best for a long time; nearly four years she tried to send them clothing and money to make them live. At this time MEHMET NURI was living like a king as he had made for himself millions, he had caused thousands of houses and persons to be robbed and killed, so that he might be a rich man to enjoy it with his family, and he did so indeed, and for some time enjoyed like a king.

My wife was obliged to continue her help to those orphans but I am sorry to say that she had already spent all her money and every means, and there was no other way but to demand back the money which her father and brother had paid to MEHMET. So she desired and asked me to go with her to MEHMET's house to demand the return of the bribe in order to help the orphans. This we did.

Several weeks before the arrest of MEHMET in the early summer of 1919, I went to his house with her, but, we were told that MEHMET NURI was not in the house, he was out of doors; his servant Garabed, invited us to sit and wait for him, so we did and took chairs in the servant's room downstairs. After a few moments my wife was invited upstairs, to the ladies room; she went, and I remained along with the servant, but after ¼ hour MEHMET's son and his brother's son, both together came down and invited me upstairs to the parlour, where I introduced myself to them. After five minutes Asaf Bey, the husband of MEHMET's sister came in. This gentleman knew me before the war. We naturally began to speak about the friends and relatives we had lost. Asaf Bey expressed himself sympathetically and said that all that had happened was inhuman and brutal: so he comforted me gently. But I was obliged to tell them that MEHMET could have saved many lives, because he had great authority, because he had been the righthand man of the Vali, and because he had promised to save many lives and for that purpose he had taken a great deal of money, as he had taken from my father and brother-in-law. But they never answered to these words. MEHMET NURI did not come, so we said goodbye and departed from them, and never told them the purpose of our visit. We were told to call another time in order to see him but we did not. I advised my wife to have a little more patience, and wait a little more, when Interallied Courts of Justice should arrange all these things, and after this we never went again and have never seen MEHMET NURI.

1. His letter in which he says, that I have seen him and gave him my thanks because he has saved the lives of my parents twenty-five years ago during the Armenian massacres is false and untrue, on the contrary he and his brothers united with others have murdered hundreds of Armenians. During that time [1895] my father was living in Harput city, and neighbour to MEHMET's father's house; my mother during danger took the children and my father too, together to escape of the danger of massacre, ran towards this house hoping that there, they may be safe. On the way they saw MEHMET NURI and his companions with guns and swords in their hands, killing anyone they met. Whenever my parents approached their house, they took position and tried to shoot them, but my mother's high heart breaking crying was heard by MEHMET's mother sitting in the window. She noticed that my mother had raised her arms in cries; at the same time trying to protect her husband and son from danger, this sight affected MEHMET's mother's heart, she cried to her sons, "My sons do not touch them, do not kill them, if you will you are not my sons and the milk I have given you to nurse and nourish you let be poison to you all." Then MEHMET NURI's mother comes down and she saves the lives of my parents and MEHMET and companions go again to the Armenian streets to kill and rob.

History repeats itself again: this is the same MEHMET twenty-five years before and after, and the first time he had been young and killed and robbed, as others were doing. But in the last time he has grown big, in age, big in position, being the president of the Union Progress of Harput province, authorised to do anything he desired, to organise schemes, to make arrangements for deportations and by these means making for himself a great deal of money.

I can never accept that he saved the life of my parents. I have no reason to thank him.

2.   He was accused several weeks after I had gone to his house. At first, as I mentioned before I could not see him, second I have nothing to do with the Armenian Union of Harput. I cannot hand such a paper, and no reason to take such a paper to him. Who can pardon him for his deeds? While he has caused to perish and has ruined thousands of houses, killed thousands of people, robbed everything. I can never imagine a man, an Armenian so mean and low as to forget all these things to sell their rights for a few pounds and serve such a beast by taking the accused paper. Yes, I went to his house, but it was personal, I went to demand the orphans' right; nothing else and never promising to declare him innocent; but we could not meet him.

He says in his letter that my father-in-law has taken the accusing paper and given it to me. This is also quite untrue. My father-in-law being the chief and most honoured man at Mezré was made a prisoner by MEHMET, and to get my father out of the prison, MEHMET had taken five hundred pounds from him and his son, but after a few days MEHMET NURI deported and killed them with thousands of other Armenians; MEHMET cannot forget that he is a Turk. He belongs to the Union and Progress Committee and is President of it.

Today every man knows that the responsibilities for War and massacres rests with the men of the C.U.P. This is a proof. There are many witnesses to prove that he is guilty of massacre and deportation, and of robbing Armenians.

MEHMET ALI BEY (Hadji Bekir Zade Mehmed Ali Bey)

Malta No. 2817

Interned 5.10.20.

Profession. Director of Customs, Trebizonde.

Lists. List VII, i.e. on Foreign Office List, despatch No. 217/R.2178 of 12th February 1920.

Arrests.

A.   Arrested by Turkish Authorities on 6.1.19, and condemned to ten years imprisonment by Court Martial in May or early June 1919.

B.   **W. 2178.** In August 1920, the High Commissioner requested Minister for Foreign Affairs to arrange for his transfer to British Custody. On 9.8.20, General Officer Commanding-in-Chief reported that the transfer had been effected and on 30.9.20 that he had been sent to Malta.

Petitions. None to date, 12.3.21.

ACCUSATIONS.

5027.A.3. Unsigned diary of events in Trebizond (14.5.15 to 3.7.15), dated 27.12.18. In this MEHMET ALI is mentioned as one of the Principals in the atrocities.

5035.A.11.p. MEHMET ALI BEY listed as No. 20 in Part II of the first Patriarchate list of Criminals, dated 14.1.19. The following note is appended: "Director of the Custom House; member of the Ittihat at Trebizond. He threw into the Black Sea little children stuffed in sacks:"

G. X. In the Patriarchate list of September 1920 his name is given as a Principal among the Civil functionaries of Trebizond guilty of atrocities. He is described as President of the Red Crescent.

5027/a/22. Patriarchate report, dated 21.1.20: "MEHMET ALI is as notorious a criminal as Adjente Mustafa.* He retained at Trebizond young Armenian girls and, having robbed them of all the jewels and other precious objects which they had about them, he opened a department of the Red Crescent where he forced them to live. He kept a number of these girls at the Red Crescent Hospital while he distributed the rest among the important persons of the Ittihat at Trebizond. MEHMET ALI turned the lives of these poor creatures into a prolonged martyrdom of moral suffering."

---

* This notorious criminal escaped from Malta on 6.12.20.

STATEMENT MADE AT THE HIGH COMMISSION BY MRS. SOPHIE TAHMAZIAN, ALTOUN BACAL, RUE TCHAIR 87, PANCALDI, DAUGHTER OF LATE ONNIK MAHOKIAN, TRADER AND SHIPPING AGENT OF TREBIZOND

C. 22. Jan. 1920. I was living with my husband in Trebizond in 1915. The first incident occurred on 23rd June 1915 when about 25 Armenian-Russian subjects were put into boats and taken out to sea.

The next day one of these men, Vartan, turned up at Mr. Gorène, Italian Consul, now in Rome, and told him that all these Armenian Russian subjects had been shot in boats and bodies thrown into the sea; he had swum ashore wounded. Vartan disappeared a few hours after he arrived at the Italian Consulate which was then protecting Russian subjects. I recount this incident as it was the first and we began to fear for our safety.

On the 26th June 1915, a notice signed by Vali Djemal Azmi, appeared on the walls saying that all Armenian other than Roman Catholics must be ready to leave the town at the end of five days time. It was stated in this Government notice that anyone who allowed an Armenian to remain with him or took charge of his goods, would be hanged outside his front door and his house burnt. There were certain categories excepted from deportation but all these categories, e.g. sick, families without men, Roman Catholics, were deported with the rest. The deportations began on June 30th and continued for about one month until practically the whole Armenian population had left. A few hid themselves and these were killed as soon as found. A few girls remained who were converted or married to Turks.

On 30th June I had a vesika certifying that I was enceinte [pregnant]. On that day all my family to the number of about 27 were gathered in our home intending to leave together. Gendarmes came, though the notice had said we should not leave till July 1st. My mother was allowed to take her youngest child and two nephews to Mr. Crawford the American Missionary. Then my family went forth on foot. I remained in the house with an aunt suffering from heart disease and my aged grandmother. On the 3rd July we were taken to the Red Crescent Hospital established in the Convent of the Sisters of St. Joseph, presumably in order that our house might be pillaged in comfort. At this hospital there were many hundreds of women, the aged, the sick, and the pregnant. I was taken there on a Sunday and that evening Ali Sahib came and looked round the Hospital and apparently made a list. The next day more than half the women were taken away by gendarmes on the pretext that they were to be taken to another Hospital where there was more room. They were, however, deported inland and not one is now alive that I know of. I was allowed to remain because I was just about to give birth to my child, my name was on the list to go.

The following Sunday, Ali Sahib, the Vali Djemal Azmi, Adjente Mustafa, MEHMED ALI BEY, Nail, and Hadji Ali Hafuz Zade Hakke held a conference on the ground floor of the hospital. Then Ali Sahib went round the rooms making a list and on the next day the gendarmes took away nearly all the women that remained; ten or twelve remained; of this batch all, I believe, have disappeared.

After the first lot of women had left, the place was filled with children who were replaced by others as quickly as they died of hunger or by poison. As to myself, my father ONNIK MAHOKIAN, one of the largest traders and shipping agents in Trebizond, being well known to the Vali, I had implored the latter to allow me to remain in order to give piano and French lessons to his family. He gave me a promise although Ali Sahib and Adjente Mustafa were always threatening me. I remained 4 months in the hospital and left it in November. I, my aunt, and my aged grandmother were permitted by the Vali to remain in an empty Armenian house. I gave lessons to the Vali's children and to MEHMED ALI BEY's family. We were always in fear because a few other women like ourselves in Turkish employ had been murdered by the gendarmes. When the Russians took Erzerum and marched on Trebizond, the Turks ordered all converted Armenian women to be sent away. We begged the Vali and we accompanied his family to Samsun in March 1916.

C. 22. Further statement made at the High Commission by Mrs. Sophie Tahmarzian, widow, late of Trebizond, now residing at 87 Rue Tchair, Pancaldi; daughter or the late murdered Onnik Mahokian, trader and shipping agent of Trebizond.

"At the outbreak of War, Mehmed Ali was Assistant Director in the Customs at Trebizond. He then became Head of the Red Crescent Hospital established in the school of the sisters of St. Joseph.

I know him as whilst I was in this Hospital from July 1915 to November 1915, I continually saw him in company with Ali Sahib, Adjente Mustafa, Nail Bey, Talaat, Nuri and Hakki. He was a regular member at the conferences that took place at the Hospital.

MEHMED ALI was in full executive charge of the Hospital, Avni Bey was the Medical Officer in charge, Ali Sahib was the Principal Medical Officer of the Vilayet.

With the others mentioned above, MEHMED ALI is responsible, actually responsible, for all the cruelties, deportations and murders that I have described. It was he who first stripped the women entering the hospital of all that they possessed. In my own case he stole Ltq. 2,000 gold and jewels which I had hidden and whose hiding place he forced me by threats to disclose. In order further to facilitate stealing of my trousseau and my husband's property, he adopted me as his daughter. All my property and my deported husband's thus became his and the Vali could not claim it.

One day he took me and some 15 other girls to the Mosque and had us forcibly converted. Several girls he married forcibly to Moslems.

It was Ali Sahib's duty to order which of the children were to be sent away. I have constantly seen him packing large baskets full of infants' corpses that the hamals took away and threw into the sea.

One night in my first month in the hospital there was much noise outside. I looked out and saw and heard the Armenians of the Village of Fol being led up by Gendarmes. I heard MEHMED ALI ordering the taking away of the children and heard the cries of the parents and the infants. The latter were brought into the hospital. There were about 10 of them, one a girl of seven, another of about 4, the remaining were infants at the breast. Every one of these died or were made away with."

N.B. A reliable and intelligent witness, speaking French fluently.

D. 10. 7.6.20. Madame Koharig Sarian of Trebizond, now living at Rue Anderlich No. 19, Pancaldi, can give further direct evidence in the matter of MEHMED ALI's connection with the Red Crescent 'hospitals' in which and from which so much massacring was done.

C. 7.   27.1.20. Statement made at the High Commission by Mademoiselle Siranouch Moutafian, daughter of the late Nazareth Moutafian, carpet merchant of Trebizond, living at the Ecole Tebrotzesser, Fur Mmine Effendi, Zeki Pacha Konak, Nishan Tash, speaking in Armenian, translated into French by Madame Tahmazian.

"At the beginning of the deportations I was 13½ years old. I was taken to an Orphanage established in the house that before belonged to Dr. Hekimian. My mother was with me, she remained twenty days. Adjente Mustafa, Ali Sahib, MEHMET ALI, Nuri, and other Turks whose names I do not know came to the Orphanage and proceeded to separate out various groups of women and children, some were for deportation some to be "married" to Turks, etc. I clung to my mother and cried. My mother cried and begged MEHMET ALI. MEHMET ALI got angry with my mother, laid hands on her, gave her over to a Gendarme with the order to kill her along with the other women. I understand Turkish and heard all that was said. Two or three days later the same gendarmes told us all in the orphanage that my mother with the other women had been massacred by them near Deyermen Déré, just outside Trabizond. This was not an exceptional incident; the gendarmes continuously fetched away women from the Orphanage. When there were only a few, 20 or 30, they were massacred at Deyermen Déré; if there were many, they were taken further away. I have never heard of my mother from the time she was torn from me at the orphanage. On the same day some hundred children from 5 to 9 years old were taken away and have not since been heard of. They were drowned at sea. This again was not exceptional. Babies were constantly dying, there was no food or any sort of care. Ali Sahib seemed to be in charge of the babies."

The informant proceeds to detail the murder of Madame Aslanian and mentions that she saw MEHMET ALI with others at the waterside when the noyade [drowning] of Madame Aslanian, her two children and two other Armenian women took place.

'Renaissance' 22.4.19. Contains a poor report of Madame Vergine's evidence before the Turkish Court Martial.

DJEMAL OGHUZ BEY

Malta No. 2818

Interned 5th October 1920.

Profession. C.U.P. Secretary at Changri in Kastamuni Vilayet, from 1914.

A Commission Agent.

Lists. On List III, (i.e. his name suggested for arrest by Mr. Ryan to Grand Vizier on 27.3.19), VI, and VII, (i.e. the F.O. List).

Arrests.

A.   Arrested by the Turkish Authorities on 3.4.19 on charge of 'murder'.

'Renaissance' of 1.5.19 reports his name mentioned in the Public Prosecutor's opening statement as an organiser of the Changri atrocities.

'Djagadamart' of 23.12.19 reports his attempted suicide. In "Renaissance" of 9.1.20 it was reported that his trial had been remanded sine die. On 4th and 6th February it was reported that his trial for participation in Changri atrocities and massacre at Tunne was proceeding.

In the Turkish Prison List of 7.2.20 he is reported as being in Gumush Su Hospital.

On 17.2.20 "Renaissance" reported him to have been sentenced to five years imprisonment.

In "Bosphore" of 5.5.20 the sentence is reported to have been quashed by the Court of Cassation but re-affirmed by Kurd Mustafa Pasha's Court Martial.

On 1st July 1920, Captain Wilson reported him as undergoing sentence in Sultan Ahmed Prison.

B.   On 5.4.19 and again on 13.6.19 the "Renaissance" reported his arrest by the British Police for complicity in the murder of two deportees from Changri: the poet Daniel Varoujan and the author Roupen Tchilinguirian.

C.   **W. 2178.** On 2.8.20 the High Commissioner requested the Minister for Foreign Affairs to arrange for his surrender to the Minister for Foreign Affairs to arrange for his surrender to the British Military Authorities.

On 9.8.20 G.O.C. reported that the transfer had been effected.

On 30.9.20 G.O.C.: reported his transfer to Malta.

Petitions.

W. 2178. From a lawyer, undated, through G.O.C. on 7.10.20 alleging blackmail.

854/24. From his wife Anastasia of Rue Tepe-Ustu 76. Tchifte Bakal, Ferikeuy. (Maison Avramaki)

ACCUSATIONS.

"Renaissance" of 6.1.20 in 1358. In a very badly written summary of the Public Prosecutor's Shevket Bey's 'requisitoire' before the Court Martial, the opening words are the following:

"D'après les enquêtes et process effectués, à l'exception de DJEMAL OGHUZ, délégué responsible de Changri, convaincue de crime, de . . ."

"Renaissance" of 8.2.20, in C. 15. Summary of the evidence given by Mr Gaspard Tchéras before the Court Martial.

Mr Tchéras was avocat membre du Conseil Civil au Patriarcat Arménien in 1915. He was deported from Constantinople on 24th April 1915 to Changri. In Changri the witness knew DJEMAL OGHUZ as the Secretary of the C.U.P.; he was all powerful and all officials took their instructions from him. He organised the deportations. One convoy was massacred close to Changri, at Tunne, by one Ismail, an arabadji and notable of Changri. The Police Officer who chiefly collaborated with DJEMAL OGHUZ was Suleiman.

B. 10. Signed information, dated 12.3.19, by Hookan Vartabed Garabedian M.A., B.D., Secretary to the Armenian Patriarch Koumkapou, Stamboul.

The informant was exiled in Changri from June 1915 to February 1916.

He mentions as eye witness his fellow deportees: Artin Tcherkezian, Hotel Osmanieh, Yuksek Kalderim, Galata; Sarkis Srintz, 37 Rue Kabristan Pera.

Paladji Zade Hadji Shakir, Hotel Meshroutied, Sirkedji.

DJEMAL OGHUZ organised the murder of the poet Daniel Varoujian; the author and physician Dr. Roupen Tchilinguirian; the binder Onnik Maghazadjian; Vahan Kehyayan and Haroutian. These murders took place at Tunne on 13.8.15 by order of the C.U.P. Changri.

Through the deportations DJEMAL OGHUZ amassed much wealth. On his return to Constantinople he started business at Ralli Han, Sirkedji.

G. V. In Patriarchate's detailed list of September 1920 the name of DJEMAL OGHUZ occurs with the following note appended: "Délégué du C.U.P. coupable du massacre des Intellectuels deportés de Constantinople à Changri."

H. 12. In Patriarchate's report of 22.12.20 on Fazil Berki, deputy for Changri, DJEMAL OGHUZ is mentioned as the leading organiser in the formation of the Andjumen (secret committee organising the deportations) and the Emlak Metruke in the vilayet of Kastamuni. (pp. 3 and 5 of report).

ADIL HADJI AHMET, Lieut. Colonel

Malta No. 2819
Interned 20.11.20.
Appointments. Commanding Gendarmerie, Erzerum.

In 1920, Chairman of the War Office Committee on the revision of appointments.

Lists. On none.

Arrest. 5027.A.32. On 27th July 1920 he was arrested by British Police on the information of Missak Vartanian, late Kavass at the British Consulate, Erzerum. He was handed over to the Italian Section on duty, who released him. On 11th August 1920, High Commissioner requested his re-arrest.

Arrested by Allied Police on September 7th 1920. On 25th September 1920, High Commissioner requested his transfer to Malta.

On 19th September 1920, Hussein Hussni, Minister of War, wrote to General Shuttleworth saying that Lt. Col. MEHMET ADIL BEY, President of the Controlling Commission of Allowances, was in Arabian Han accused by Vartanian of having taken from him Lt. 250 and a horse at Mamahatum. ADIL BEY does not recognise the claimant and has never been to Mamahatum.

On 12.10.20, General Officer Commanding-in-Chief forwarded this petition to High Commissioner asking whether High Commissioner confirms his letter of 25.9.20.

On 27.10.20 High Commissioner wrote confirming.

On 13.11.20 he was deported to Malta.

Petitions.

5027.A. 32. From sister dated 2.11.20. No action.

5027.A. 32. From ADIL, in Arabian Han, of 7.11.20. In this petition he signs himself MOHAMMED ADIL, Lieutenant Colonel of the Turkish Ministry of Marine.

ACCUSATIONS.

Statement by Missak Vartanian dated 10.8.20, see Appendix A.

Statement by Garabed Deirmendjian, dated 11.8.20, see Appendix B.

Statement by Haig Tarpinian, dated 11.8.20, see Appendix C.

Further examination of Missak Vartanian and certificate of identification by six witnesses, see Appendix D.

APPENDIX A.

5027/A/32.

Statement by MISSAK VARTANIAN of 29 Rue Elmadaghi Djaddessi, Pancaldi, interpreted by Mr. Fenerdjian and taken down in the British High Commission, Pera, on 10.8.20.

I am an Armenian Gregorian of Erzerum, where I was cavass to the British Consulate from 1908 to 1912. After that I was in the employ of the British Inspector of Gendarmerie at Trebizond and elsewhere. In 1914, I was conscripted, but the Vice-Consul paid my exemption tax. When the Vice-Consul left Erzerum I was arrested and put into prison. In February 1915, after 2 months in prison, I was deported but escaped from the convoy and returned to Erzerum. In May 1915 the regular deportations began and I found myself in a convoy on the road to Erzingan. The escort was commanded by Major ADIL BEY, Commanding the Gendarmerie of the Erzerum district, whom I knew by sight. ADIL BEY joined us at Ilidje, 3 hours from Erzerum with 25 to 30 gendarmes to escort the convoy consisting of about (?) Armenians (some 6 hours to pass a given point). The massacres, conducted by ADIL BEY and his gendarmes, helped by some 250 tchetes from Mama-Hatum began at a point about 1 hour west of Mama-Hatum, a little more than half way on the direct road between Erzerum and Erzingan. Some 7,000 Armenians of all ages and sexes were killed here and I was left among the dead. Directing the massacre was ADIL BEY in command; the Kaimakam of Mama-Hatum (name not known); Muhurdar.

Muhurdar Oglu Assim,[*] a tchete bashi arrested last year by the British authorities and handed over to the Turkish Government; and Djaffer,[†] another tchete bashi now in Erzerum. This massacre took place without any selection of the victims. After this the survivors were despoiled of all that remained to them and at the bridge of Kutur-Kupru survivors were turned back and herded in the village of Firus. This was some 24 hours after the first massacre. I saw ADIL BEY on horseback at the bridge directing the convoy. Next morning the convoy was led to the banks of the Tuzla Su and there massacred by regular soldiers and tchetes under the direct orders of ADIL BEY, whom I again saw on horseback. I myself managed to escape to the mountains.

On 27th July 1920, I informed the Allied Police who arrested him and lodged him in the Pera Police Station. I pointed out ADIL BEY to a British Military Police who took ADIL to the Pera Police Station, Rue Abanoz. The prisoner was handed over to the Italians then on duty and the British Police then withdrew. The Italians then let ADIL go. I left, ran and caught ADIL intending to hand him over to the British Section. When the Italians saw this, they came out into the street and beat me. Finally the Italians consented to keep

---

[*] On List VII. Muhurdar Oglu Assim was arrested by the British Police in Constantinople on 5.2.19 on the information of Vartanian. He appears to have been handed over to the Turkish Police who soon afterwards released him. Present whereabouts not known (F.H.R.)

[†] This Djaffer is probably Djadder Abul Hindi, or Erzerumli Djaffer, known to this Section but not on list. (F.H.R.)

ADIL in custody on the intervention of an official Armenian interpreter in British service.

The next day I went to Rue Chichli Police Station and handed in a signed information. Then on the 9th August I saw ADIL BEY outside Tokatlian's hotel in the afternoon. He was walking with an Armenian lady and gentleman. ADIL smiled at me. I believe the British and Italian Sections of the Allied Police both know ADIL BEY's address.

APPENDIX B.

Original in E.6. 5027/A/32.

Statement in ADIL BEY, Commandant of the Gendarmerie of Erzerum.

I knew this man personally when he was Commandant of the Gendarmerie at Erzerum. The local Government gave us a vecika stating that my family consisting of 6 persons had to leave the military zone of Erzerum. (Vecika attached, Original in 5027/A/32).

ADIL BEY accompanied us on the 6/18 June 1915; the convoy consisted of rich Armenians of the city, numbering 1,200 persons of all ages.

ADIL BEY was in a carriage. In the same carriage there was the Defterdar and the Police Mudiri, both in tchete costumes. They accompanied us to Kara-Beyuk, 6 hours distant from Erzerum. ADIL BEY gave the necessary orders and instructions to the tchetes at that spot. We remained there two days, when ADIL BEY came back with another caravan, consisting of men, women and children from surrounding villages or Erzerum. Then we left Kara-Beyuk for Ashkala and from there to Maden and thence to Baiburt and from there to Erzinjan. We remained near Erzinjan 17 days. Tahsin Bey (Vali of Erzerum) came to Erzinjan and ordered us to go through Kemach where 180 young Armenians were thrown into the Murad Su. From there we were sent on to Malatia where our caravan was made over to two Arab Chiefs, Hadji Bedir and Zeinel, for 5,000 pounds.

These two Chiefs demanded a further ransom of 3,000 pounds for sending us safely through to Urfa. We handed the required sum and eventually reached Urfa. When Turks and Germans began to bombard the town, they shifted us to Selouj where we remained 6 months and thence went to Rakka where we stayed 2 years. As I was a coachman and before my deportation, I was going to a spot 3 hours distance from Erzerum to bring some military material to Erzerum. Half way on the road I saw: Stepanian, painter; Adrouni, Pilos, Hrant Keuseyan, Balasanian, lying there: all five persons shot to death and I saw on the same spot ADIL BEY with five Gendarmes just riding off.

I am ready to come forward and state that this is the principal organiser of the deportation of Erzerum and surroundings and that he personally took part in the massacres.

(S) GARABET DEIRMENDJIAN.

Address: Yeni Mahallé,
       Eglise Sourp Garabed,
       Scutari

TRANSLATION OF VESIKA.

No.68.

Name	Age	Quarter
Deirmendji Oglu Garabet	48 (exemption fee paid)	Ali Pasha
His wife Agapi	45	"
His son Barouir	6	"
His daughter Mariam	12	"
His niece Varsine	20	"
His servant Aganik	38	"

Six persons. They must be sent on Saturday 6 June 1915.

We certify that the above mentioned bearer Deirmendji Oglu Garabet, male and female in all six persons, must be sent with his family to Hinterland, from the zone of war, as the town of Erzerum is [sic]

5th June 1915.   (S) MEHMED DJEMIL

The seal: (Gendarmerie d'Erzeroum)

APPENDIX C.*
5027/A/32
Re. ADIL BEY

In May, 1915, ADIL BEY, commander of the police force in Erzeroum, came in person to our village Oumoudoum, and had all the villagers and the inhabitants of surrounding villages arrested, in all 30,000 men, women and children.

Then 40 gendarmes and 500 irregular troops took us to Kutur-Keupru, an hour's distance from Mama-Hatoum. There on his express orders they robbed us and then massacred half of us, including my two children, one three and the other four years old.

The remainder was led as far as Kemach all the while being massacred in Perouz, Ghargin, and Sansar Deressi. I was struck down and left for dead but during the night, I came to myself and fled through the mountains and disguising myself I reached Sivas.

The 30,000 villagers of the plain of Erzeroum were thus all massacred by the orders of the commander of the Police force in Erzeroum, ADIL BEY, after being robbed and tortured.

(S) HAIG TARPINIAN

Address: Waiter in the Restaurant of Union Française

---

*The statement appears in French and has been translated into English –WCB.

APPENDIX D.

Further examination of Missak Vartanian at the British High Commission on October 18th 1920.

Q. What was the name of the commander of the escort between Erzerum and Erzingan in May 1915?

A. ADIL BEY. I can not know his full name. He was known as ADIL BEY.

Q. What is the name of the man actually arrested?

A. ADIL BEY.

Q. What was the rank and Corps of the Commander of the escort?

A. Major. Commanding Gendarmerie of the town of Erzerum.

Q. What is the rank and Corps of the officer arrested?

A. He was a mufti [civilian clothes] when arrested. I know that it is now being said that he belongs to staff of the Ministry of War.

I can throw no light as to his name, only as to his identity as that of the officer who commanded the escort which massacred some 7,000 Armenians near Mama-Hatum.

IDENTIFICATION OF ADIL BEY.

On 19th October 1920 the following witnesses were taken down to Arabian Han, Galata where ADIL BEY is detained, viz:

Miguirditch Zarmanian, Tarakjilar 84, STAMBOUL.

Garabed Deyirmendjian, Orphelinat Armenien, de KULELI.

Paronnag Andonian, Scutari, Selamasiz, Centre des refugees Arméniens, Eglise de SOURP HATCH.

Aghanag Korkmazian, Kurkidji Han 7, STAMBOUL.

Missak Vartanian, Rue Elma Dagh 29, SOURP AGOP, PERA.

Puzant Pindjoyan, Koum Kapou, Eglise du Patriarcat.

Each one of the six above named witnesses severally and individually identified ADIL BEY under my superintendence. On being questioned the prisoner gave his name as ADIL BEY, then added MEHMED ADIL BEY.

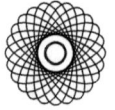

APPENDIX "J"*

List of prisoners submitted to the British Embassy in Washington in order to enquire about evidence that the U.S. Government might have regarding the prisoners.

NO DISTRIBUTION

Decypher. Sir A. Geddes (Washington)

June 1st 1921

D. June 1st, 1921
R. 11.20 a.m.   June 2nd 1921

No. 374

Your telegram No. 314

I have made several enquiries of State Department and today I am informed that while they are in possession of a large number of documents concerning Armenian deportations and massacres, these refer rather to events connected with perpetration of crimes than to persons implicated. Should His Majesty's Government so desire, these documents will be placed at the disposal of His Majesty's Embassy on the understanding that the source of the information will not be divulged.

From the description I am doubtful whether these documents are likely to prove useful as evidence in prosecuting Turks confined in Malta.

June 16, 1921

Sir,

In reply to your telegram No. 374 of the 1st instant I enclose, for your information, a list of names and brief particulars of the Turks who are being detained at Malta with a view to trial in connection with outrages perpetrated on Armenians and other native Christians. I shall be glad if you will ascertain as early as possible whether the United States Government can furnish evidence against any of these persons.

(signed)   LANCELOT OLIPHANT

---

* F.O. 371/6503/6311, pp. 261-271.

2667 Ali Ihsan Pasha
C-in-C in Mesopotamia from 1916 onwards, alleged to be responsible for massacres of Armenians, Assyrians, and other Christians e.g. at Van, Urmia, Nisibin, etc., and for murder of Mr. John Nooshy, an American patient in a hospital at ? Urmia.

2686 Sabit Bey
Mutesarrif of Dersim till 1914, deputy for Dersim, vali of Mamuret-ul-Aziz 1916, of Erzerum 1917, Sivas 1918, alleged to be responsible for massacres at Kharput. The American Consul, Mr. L. A. Davis, and the American Missionaries, Dr. H. H. Atkinson and Dr. H. Riggs, of Kharput, are stated to be able to supply evidence.

2687 Veli Nedjet Bey
Chief Clerk in the Secretariat of the Diarbekir Vilayet, Acting Chief of Police there May 1915, alleged to be guilty of promoting massacres at Diarbekir.

2690 Djevdet Bey

2696 Nevzade Bey
Commandant de Place at Mosul June 1917, alleged to be responsible for the deportation of 500 Armenians to Zaho.

2698 Fazil Berki
Deputy for Changri, alleged to be guilty of promoting massacres at Sivas and Erzerum.

2701 Ibrahim Bedreddin Bey
Mutesarrif of Mardin 1915, alleged to have been responsible for organisation of massacres there.

2704 Madjid Bey
Employed in the Audit Department in Erzinjan in 1915. Chief of Civil Transport and Delegate of C.U.P. there, alleged to have organised massacres there.

2706 Hodja Rifaat Effendi
C.U.P. Delegate at Ismid, alleged to have arranged massacres there in 1915.

2712 Hilmi Bey
Mutesarrif of Kirshehir (Angora vilayet) in 1915, alleged to have conducted massacres there.

2719 Ahmed Muammer Bey
Vali of Sivas 1915, alleged to have been responsible for massacres at Sivas, Samsun, Amasia, Tokat, etc. Evidence can perhaps be supplied by the Rev. G. White, President of Anatolia College, Merzifun, or by other members of that institution.

2723 Ghani Bey
Secretary of C.U.P. at Sivas 1915, alleged to have assisted in organization of massacres there.

2724 Ahmed Bey
Mutesarrif of Aintab 1915, alleged to have been responsible for massacres and deportations there. The American Commissioner at Constantinople appears to have had information about him in 1919.

2732 Suleiman Nouman Pasha
Director of the Army Medical Service alleged to have been responsible for the poisoning of Armenians in the districts of Erzerum, Sivas, and Erzinjan, and for the murder of Armenian surgeons in the Turkish Army.

2733 Memduh Bey
Mutesarrif of Erzinjan 1914, vali of Bitlis 1915, vali of Mosul 1917, alleged to have been responsible for the massacre or persecution of Armenians in each of these places.

2737 Faik Bey
Kaimmakam of Merzifun 1915, alleged to have been responsible for massacres there. Dr. White, an American Missionary of Merzifun, is understood to have evidence.

2738 Mufti-Zade Shukri Bey
A civil inspector, in charge of "emigration" in Aleppo and Adana vilayets 1914 and 1915, alleged to have been responsible for massacres in this area.

2743 Arif Feizi Bey
Deputy for Diarbekir, alleged to have played a prominent part in organising the massacres there.

2758 Mahmud Kiamil Pasha
C-in-C of 3rd Army at Erzerum 1915, alleged to have organised the massacres there.

2761 Mustafa Kemal Bey (Kara-Kemal)
Permanent member of the central C.U.P., Minister for Food Supplies at the time of the massacres and as such alleged to be partly responsible.

2768 Yussuf Shawish Ibn Nuri Bitlissi
Agent of Gendarmerie at Mardin 1915, alleged to have been implicated in the massacre of Armenians of Eksor, near Mardin, in June 1915.

2774 Tahsin Bey
Vali of Van 1914, vali of Erzerum 1916, vali of Syria 1918, and of Smyrna 1918, alleged, when at Erzerum, to have been a leading spirit in the council held there to decide on measures for carrying out deportations and massacres of Armenians. The Rev. Robert Stapleton and other American missionaries who were at Erzerum are understood to be in possession of evidence.

2789 Hilmi Abdul Kadir Lieutenant-Colonel
Civil Engineer, Kirkuk 1914, then in command of irregular bands, and later of a Labour Battalion attached to Turkish forces on Persian frontier, alleged to have carried out massacres in Kirkuk, Mosul, Tabriz, Urmia, etc.

2790 "Ejzaji" Mehmet Hassan
A noble of Erzinjan, leading member of local C.U.P. Committee in 1915, alleged to have been implicated in massacres in district of Erzinjan.

2792 Ali Refet Pasha Brigadier-General

Military Governor of Samsun during the winter of 1916-1917, alleged to have been responsible for persecution and deportation of Greeks and other Christians at that time.

2795 Mehmed Kiamil

Newspaper editor at Mosul, alleged to have been an informer responsible for the death of many Armenians there in 1917 and 1918, and to have been the cause of the imprisonment of Mr. Ackdjian, (Dragoman of the American Consulate at Alexandretta).

2796 Adjente Mustapha

Alleged to have been guilty of massacres at Trebizond.

2798 Mustafa Reshad

Director of the Political Section at the Prefecture of Police at Constantinople from May 1915 to the summer of 1917, alleged to have been responsible in this capacity for the persecution of Armenians.

2799 Hadji Ahmed of Kildik

C.U.P. Delegate at Sivas, merchant and government contractor, alleged to have carried out massacres at Sivas.

2800 Mustafa Abdul Halik

Vali of Bitlis 1914, Under-Secretary for the Interior 1915, vali of Aleppo 1915, brother-in-law of Talaat pasha, alleged to be guilty of massacres, particularly those perpetrated in the vilayets of Bitlis and Aleppo.

Miss Shane, of the American Mission at Bitlis, is stated to have evidence.

2801 Basri Bey Lieutenant-Colonel

Chief of Staff to Halil Pasha, (General Officer Commanding-in-Chief in Mesopotamia 1915 to 1918) alleged to have been responsible for massacres.

2804 Murad Bey

Assistant-Director-General of Police Constantinople 1915, alleged to have been responsible in organising massacres.

2806 Akdaghli-oglou Mehmet (otherwise known as Advallu Mehmet of Yozgad or Tshibishin-oghlu-Mehmet) Leather merchant and native of Yozgad, leader of a brigand band in 1915, alleged to have carried out massacres.

2807 Suleiman Faik Pasha

General commanding troops in Harput 1915-1916, acting vali of Mamuret-ul-Aziz (Harput) in 1915, alleged to have been guilty of massacres in vilayets of Mamuret-ul-Aziz and Erzerum.

Mr. A. Davis, formerly American Consul in Turkey, is stated to have evidence.

2808 Ali Nazmi

Public Prosecutor at Kir-Shehir, in the Angora vilayet, 1915, prominent C.U.P. leader, alleged to have been guilty of massacres perpetrated at Kir-Shehir.

2809 Nazim Bey, Major

President of the Samsun Recruiting Office and member of the Samsun Court Martial, alleged to have been responsible for persecution of Greeks and other Christians.

2810 Hodja Ilias Sami Bey

Deputy for Marash, alleged to have organised massacres in Sanjak of Mush, 1915.

2811 Mehmet Atif Bey

Dentist of Makrikeui, near Constantinople, local secretary of the C.U.P., alleged to have supervised the destruction of the Russian memorial church at San Stefano and the plundering and deportation of Armenians who lived there.

2812 Suleiman Nedjmi Bey

Mutesarrif of Samsun 1914-1916, alleged to have been guilty in that capacity of persecution, massacre, and torture of Armenians.

2814 Burhaneddin Hakki Bey

Gendarmerie Major, military Commandant of Kir-Shehir (Angora vilayet) 1915, alleged to be responsible for Armenian massacres there.

2815 Mehmet Rifaat (Salim) Bey

"Commissar" of police at Sivas and member of "Abandoned Properties" Commission 1914-1915, alleged to be responsible for the carrying out of massacres at Sivas.

2816 Mehmet Nuri Bey (Haji Balosh-Zade Mehmet Bey)

Deputy for Dersim 1915, alleged to have organised and carried out massacres at Harput. Dr. Barton, and perhaps other American Missionaries, are stated to have evidence.

2817 Mehmed Ali Bey (Haji Bekir Zade Kaptan Mehmed Ali Bey)
Director of Customs at Trebizond. ? President of local branch of Red Crescent 1915, alleged to have been guilty of the drowning of infants and other atrocities at Trebizond.

2818 Djemal Oghuz Bey
C.U.P. Secretary at Changri (Kastamuni vilayet) 1914-1915, alleged to have organised massacres there.

2819 Adil Haji Ahmet, Lieutenant-Colonel
Commandant of gendarmerie at Erzerum 1915, alleged to have carried out massacres there.

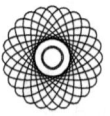

APPENDIX "K"[*]

Release of the last Turkish prisoners from Malta.
October 25, 1921
Release of Turkish Deportees

From: The Governor and Commander-in-Chief
        MALTA

To: The Secretary, War Office,
        London, S.W.1.

C.R. Malta No. 4133 (A)

Fortress Head Quarters,
Valletta, Malta.
29th October, 1921

Sir,

1. In reply to War Office Cablegram No. 89895 dated 30th September, 1921, and in amplification of my telegram No. C. 202 dated 25th October, 1921 – I have the honour to report that all Turkish deportees at Malta, to the number of 59 duly embarked on board H.M.S. "Chrysanthemum" and R.F.A. "Montenol" on afternoon of the 25th instant.

2. When intimation was first received that the deportees were to be repatriated at short notice there was only the R.F.A. "Montenol" available for this service and the Navy made all possible arrangements for the well being of the passengers.

3. When it became evident that some time must elapse before the deportees could be despatched, steps were taken to find better accommodation than could be provided by the "Montenol" and Admiral de Robeck who went into the question very thoroughly kindly placed H.M.S. "Chrysanthemum" at my disposal in addition. This relieved congestion on the "Montenol" and the deportees were divided into two batches, seventeen selected Turks being placed on "Chrysanthemum" and forty-two on "Montenol". Selection for the former, the better ship, being by status, or rank, and health of deportees. Accommodation on "Montenol" was improved as far as possible and 6 Maltese servants were detailed to look after comfort of Turks in "Montenol".

---

[*] F.O. 371/6505/12511

4. I am satisfied that everything possible was done by the Naval Authorities to ensure the reasonable comfort of the deportees and that the accommodation provided was adequate and the best available in the circumstances.

5. In addition to these arrangements, a selected Military Officer, used to dealing with these deportees, was detailed for each ship, to act as intermediary between deportees and Captain of the Ship.

6. All deportees were medically examined as regards their fitness to travel, and although Medical care on the journey will in all probability not be required, four Turkish doctors, divided among the deportees, are available in case of emergency.

7. The deportees refused to sign clearance certificates as they state that they intend to make indemnity claims in respect of their internment at Malta, but local accounts were squared up.

8. I hold a receipt from Captain of "Chrysanthemum" and Master of "Montenol" for each deportee embarked – Copy is attached.

9. Responsibility for safe custody and welfare of deportees passed to the Royal Navy with the embarkation of the deportees on His Majesty's ships.

I have the honour to be,

Sir,

Your obedient Servant,

(Sgd.) Plumer,

F. M.

Governor and Commander-in-Chief,

Malta

CLASS "A"

1. No. 2732   Brig.-General Suliman Nouman Pacha
2. No. 2756   Midhat Chukri Bey (Governor)
3. No. 2770   General Mursel Pacha
4. No. 2772   General Djemal Pacha
5. No. 2773   General Djevad Pacha
6. No. 2775   Essad Pacha
7. No. 2776   Admiral Raouf Bey
8. No. 2782   General Ali Said Pacha
9. No. 2784   Suliman Nazif Bey
10. No. 2792   General Refet Pacha
11. No. 2793   General Ali Pacha
12. No. 2794   Senator Seid Bey
13. No. 2797   General Abdulsalam Pacha
14. No. 2800   Mustafa Halek Bey

15. No. 2803   General Chevki Pacha
16. No. 2807   General Faik Pacha
17. No. 2786   Islam, Valet to No. 2782 Gen. Ali Said Pacha
                (Third Class accommodation).

Received.
(Sgd.) J. W. Scott,
H.M.S. "Chrysanthemum"

25.10.21

CLASS "B"

1. No. 2687   Veli Nedjet Bey
2. No. 2696   Dr. Berki Bey
3. No. 2705   Hussein Kadri Bey
4. No. 2706   Rifat Effendi
5. No. 2712   Hilmi Moussa Bey
6. No. 2742   Zulfi Bey
7. No. 2767   Major Arif Bey
8. No. 2781   Nouman Effendi
9. No. 2778   Colonel Uassif Bey
10. No. 2785 Djelal Nouri Bey
11. No. 2787 Ahmed Emin Bey
12. No. 2788 Moummar Bey
13. No. 2789 Hilmi Abdul Kadir Bey
14. No. 2790 Mehmed Hassan Bey
15. No. 2791 Enis Avni Bey
16. No. 2795 Mehmed Kiamil Bey
17. No. 2798 Rechad Bey
18. No. 2799 Hadji Ahmed Bey
19. No. 2801 Colonel Basri Bey
20. No. 2804 Mourad Bey
21. No. 2805 Ali Djenany Bey
22. No. 2808 Ali Nazmi Bey
23. No. 2809 Major Nazim Bey
24. No. 2810 Elias Sami Bey
25. No. 2811 Atif Bey
26. No. 2814 Major Burhaneddine Bey
27. No. 2815 Salim Rifat Bey

28. No. 2816 Mehmed Nouri Bey
29. No. 2817 Mehmed Ali Bey
30. No. 2818 Djemal Oghu Bey
31. No. 2819 Colonel Mehmed Adil Bey
32. No. 2777 Colonel Chevket Bey
33. No. 2768 Nouri Betlissi Effendi
34. No. 2806 Adavalli Oghlou
35. No. 2679 Lt. Colonel Ahmed Teufik Bey
36. No. 2680 Colonel Mehmed Teufik Bey
37. No. 2694 Captain Djemal Bey
38. No. 2700 Colonel Djevad Bey
39. No. 2707 Major Mauzlum Bey
40. No. 2710 Major Ibrahim Hakki Bey
41. No. 2745 Captain Tahir Bey
42. No. 2820 Captain Mehmet Roushti Bey

  Received.
  (Sgd.) G.L. Capley,
  Master,
  R.F.A. "Montenol"

25.10.21.

www.ingramcontent.com/pod-product-compliance
Lightning Source LLC
Chambersburg PA
CBHW080540230426
43663CB00015B/2657